What Ever Happened to
ORSON WELLES?

Other Books by Joseph McBride

Searching for John Ford

The Book of Movie Lists: An Offbeat, Provocative Collection of the Best and Worst of Everything in Movies

High and Inside: An A-to-Z Guide to the Language of Baseball

Steven Spielberg: A Biography

Orson Welles

Frank Capra: The Catastrophe of Success

Filmmakers on Filmmaking, Vols. I and II (editor)

Hawks on Hawks

Orson Welles: Actor and Director

Kirk Douglas

John Ford (with Michael Wilmington)

Focus on Howard Hawks (editor)

Persistence of Vision: A Collection of Film Criticism (editor)

What Ever Happened to ORSON WELLES?

A Portrait of an Independent Career

Joseph McBride

THE UNIVERSITY PRESS OF KENTUCKY

Publication of this volume was made possible in part by
a grant from the National Endowment for the Humanities.

The University Press of Kentucky
Scholarly publisher for the Commonwealth,
serving Bellarmine University, Berea College, Centre
College of Kentucky, Eastern Kentucky University,
The Filson Historical Society, Georgetown College,
Kentucky Historical Society, Kentucky State University,
Morehead State University, Murray State University,
Northern Kentucky University, Transylvania University,
University of Kentucky, University of Louisville,
and Western Kentucky University.

Editorial and Sales Offices: The University Press of Kentucky
663 South Limestone Street, Lexington, Kentucky 40508-4008
www.kentuckypress.com

10 09 08 07 06   5 4 3 2 1

Library of Congress Cataloging-in-Publication Data
McBride, Joseph, 1947-
What ever happened to Orson Welles? : a portrait of an independent career/
Joseph McBride.
p. cm.
Includes bibliographical references and index.
ISBN-13: 978-0-8131-2410-0 (hardcover : alk. paper)
ISBN-10: 0-8131-2410-7 (alk. paper)
1. Welles, Orson, 1915-1985—Criticism and interpretation. I. Title.
PN1998.3.W45M34 2006
791.43023'3092—dc22
[B]   31T   2006019970

This book is printed on acid-free recycled paper meeting
the requirements of the American National Standard
for Permanence in Paper for Printed Library Materials.

Manufactured in the United States of America.

Member of the Association of
American University Presses

For Ann Weiser Cornell,

sine qua non

It's the greatest railroad train a boy ever had.

—Orson Welles, after coming to Hollywood in 1939

May we be accursed if we ever forget for one second that he alone with Griffith—one in silent days, one sound—was able to start up that marvelous little electric train. All of us, always, will owe him everything.

—Jean-Luc Godard

CONTENTS

"The Film of Films": François Truffaut's description of *Citizen Kane* (1941). Despite the great acclaim the twenty-five-year-old Welles received for his first feature film, the backlash caused by its fictionalized portrait of the powerful publisher William Randolph Hearst caused permanent damage to Welles's Hollywood career. *(RKO Radio Pictures)*

INTRODUCTION

"THE HIGH PRIEST OF THE CINEMA"

When I was twenty-three and finishing my first book on Orson Welles, I had the good fortune not only of meeting the legendary and elusive filmmaker but also, even more improbably, becoming a character in an Orson Welles movie.

My fascination with Welles had begun four years earlier when I saw *Citizen Kane* in a film class at the University of Wisconsin, Madison. It was the afternoon of September 22, 1966, shortly after the beginning of my second year at college. The *coup de foudre* of seeing *Kane*—one of those rare experiences that can truly be called life-changing—made me put aside, at least temporarily, my ambition to become a novelist. I decided instead to write about movies and make movies myself. *Kane* excited me as a young man with its sense of unlimited possibility, its chutzpah in taking on the grandiose figure of William Randolph Hearst, and its breathtaking cinematic virtuosity. Most of all, *Kane* thrilled me because the 1941 film was the first feature of a twenty-five-year-old director, a prodigy who made Hollywood give him a virtual blank check and used it to revolutionize the movies. So I set myself the goal of writing and directing my first feature by the same age. I didn't realize how unrealistic that goal would prove to be.

My passion for *Kane* was shared by many other young film buffs of the post–World War II era. In 1959, the year the French critic-turned-filmmaker François Truffaut directed his first feature, *The Four Hundred Blows*, he observed that *Kane* "consecrated a great many of us to the vocation of cinéaste. . . . We loved this film because it was complete: psychological, social, poetic, dramatic, comic, baroque, strict, and demanding. It is a demonstration of the force of power and an attack on the force of power, it is a hymn to youth and a meditation on old age, an essay on the vanity of all material ambition and at the same time a poem on old age and the solitude of exceptional human beings, genius or monster or monstrous genius. It is at the same time a 'first' film by virtue of its quality of catch-all experimentation and a 'last' film by its comprehensive picture of the world. . . . To shoot *Citizen Kane* at twenty-five years of age, is this not the dream of all the young habitués of the cinémathèques?"

Like the brash young George Amberson Minafer in Welles's second feature, *The Magnificent Ambersons*, I believed that what I was studying in college was "a lot of useless guff," and I soon dropped out to concentrate on writing my critical study of Welles. Analyzing his work in depth—all his available film work, not just *Kane*—strengthened my emotional identification with the bearded wunderkind who, I was delighted to learn, had been born in Kenosha, Wisconsin. My feeling of sharing common ground with Orson Welles became literal when I discovered that he had spent a year in Madison at the age of ten, attending Washington School, just a couple of blocks from the student rooming house where I was writing my book.

The first published article about Welles, "Cartoonist, Actor, Poet and Only 10," appeared in the February 19, 1926, issue of the Madison newspaper the *Capital Times*. The article spotlighted the theme that would dominate all future writing on Welles: his "apparent genius." Reporting that Welles was "already attracting the attention of some of the greatest literary men and artists in the country," the paper noted,

> Orson has a fluent command of the language and a surprising number of large words equal to those of the average adult, which he uses in his every day speech. He reads constantly, . . . and in books far beyond his years, bringing, for home reading, books on the old masters in art and literature. . . . At times, when Orson is in the midst of a story and becomes particularly interested in one of the characters, he is seized with the inspiration to paint the character and forthwith takes up his box of oil paints, making a study that, though it is amateurish in technique, shows a keen insight and interpretation. . . . Orson has many ambitions. At the present time he cannot decide what he will be when he grows up. But Orson has not much time to think of the future, for he is kept busy these days wrestling with his arithmetic which he regards as a serious bugbear in his life.

I spent four years pounding out my *Orson Welles* on a 1940 Royal manual typewriter, surviving on as little as $10 a week and hot meals earned by washing dishes at fraternity and sorority houses. It wasn't *entirely* to emulate Welles that I grew a beard and started smoking cigars in that period; I did it mostly to seem older, since I was tired of receiving condescension for looking so young. Seen from my distant vantage point as a film buff stranded in Middle America, reports of Welles's doings in the late 1960s seemed wildly romantic and deeply mysterious, like the dossier on the shadowy title character in his 1955 film *Mr. Arkadin.* Occasionally I would find a cryptic item in *Variety* about some new Welles project that wouldn't be mentioned again for months, if ever, or a mention of his being hired to act in some terrible movie. I dutifully went to see them all, while yearning to see the Welles projects that for one reason or another were hidden from view. Every once in a while, to my excitement, an interview with Welles would appear in a European film magazine. Magisterially eloquent and self-analytical, if prone to spinning self-aggrandizing fables, he single-handedly provided the intellectual commentary on his career that otherwise was lacking in the media. But I was never quite sure where he was. An endlessly moving target, no doubt by self-protective design, he seldom seemed to stay long enough in one place to receive a letter. To borrow John Updike's famous observation about the aloof baseball legend Ted Williams, "Gods do not answer letters."

❖ ❖ ❖

My meeting with Welles in August 1970 came about in a strangely circuitous manner. By then I was working as a reporter for the *Wisconsin State Journal.* That summer I had been vainly sending letters to Welles along with sections of the book I had been publishing in magazines, as well as my 1968 book, *Persistence of Vision: A Collection of Film Criticism*, which also included parts of my work in progress. I sent the material in care of his New York attorney, the only address I had for the filmmaker, hoping to arrange to interview him for the book. I figured an interview would help explain some of the many mysteries about his career that I kept encountering in my research—unfinished films, unmade projects, studio butcheries, mysterious forays into television, political controversies, a long and vaguely explained exile from the United States.

On July 29, shortly after mailing the manuscript of *Orson Welles* to the British Film Institute, I wrote Welles another letter, feeling as if I were casting a bottle into the sea with a message that might never find its destination:

> Dear Mr. Welles:
>
> I've been meaning for quite a while to send you some of the articles I've been writing about you. I recently finished a book covering all of your films, and it's being considered for publication now. *Sight and Sound* is running my article on *The Immortal Story* in the next issue.

> On looking back at what I've written, I must admit that I sometimes fit your theory (as told to Dick Cavett)—"the younger the writer, the longer the words he uses." My only defense is that your movies are pretty complicated, too. I had to see *Kane* 60 times before I could write about it. And when you submerge yourself into something, you're lucky to come out with a short word left. I will follow your advice in the future, however.
>
> I understand that you will be in New York for a while acting in a film [Henry Jaglom's *A Safe Place*]. Would you have the time to grant me an interview? I have some vacation time coming up, and I could come to New York on short notice.

Again, no reply. My first trip to Hollywood the following month was for another purpose entirely: to interview another of my favorite filmmakers, John Ford, for a book Michael Wilmington and I had started writing about his work. The same day I interviewed Ford, I met the third great director in my personal pantheon, Jean Renoir, who was living in Beverly Hills. I naively assumed that glorious week would be typical of my future in Hollywood. Little did I know it would prove to be the pinnacle.

❖ ❖ ❖

I also contacted a young filmmaker and journalist whose work I admired, Peter Bogdanovich. His path to becoming a director pointed the way I intended to follow: creating my own "film school" by learning firsthand from the masters, while making contacts that somehow would lead to selling my scripts and directing them. I had been impressed by Bogdanovich's first feature, *Targets*, when I saw it during a break from being teargassed at the 1968 Chicago Democratic Convention. But I was most influenced by Bogdanovich's interviews with directors, especially his 1967 book-length discussion with the virtually-impossible-to-interview Ford; I was excited to read in *Variety* that Bogdanovich had undertaken a similar book with Welles. Milton Luboviski, the proprietor of Hollywood's Larry Edmunds Book Store, gave me Bogdanovich's telephone number. Peter was still living in a $145-a-month rented bungalow in Van Nuys with his wife and collaborator, Polly Platt. When I called Peter, I did not know that he was in preproduction on his film of Larry McMurtry's novel *The Last Picture Show*, which was to begin shooting that fall in Texas. Welles had encouraged Bogdanovich to take the daring step of filming the 1951-set *Last Picture Show* in black-and-white, which would help give it a bittersweet nostalgia reminiscent of Welles's *Magnificent Ambersons*.

The first words Peter said to me on the phone were: "I'm on the other line with Orson."

I could hardly believe I was connected (however tenuously) to the mythic figure I'd been so fruitlessly pursuing. While I held on in a state of suspended animation, Bogdanovich came back to say that Welles wanted me to call him at 5:30 that afternoon.

I made the call from a phone booth at one of the Schwab's drugstores on the Sunset Strip. Welles invited me to lunch that Saturday and then came quickly to the point: He was about to start shooting a new film called *The Other Side of the Wind*. Would I like to be in it?

Not knowing quite what to say, I blurted out, "Is this going to be a *feature-length* movie?"

With the full humorous effect of his rumbling, sonorous voice, he chuckled, "We certainly hope so." Without quite meaning to, I'd already raised the question that would bedevil *The Other Side of the Wind* and so many other film projects of Welles's later years: whether it would ever be finished.

Welles described what he was about to shoot as "test scenes" to help him raise money to complete the film. *The Other Side of the Wind* centers around a disastrous Hollywood birthday party for the legendary Jake Hannaford (John Huston), part of the Hemingwayesque old director's desperate attempt at a comeback in the "New Hollywood" during what we now call the *Easy Rider* era. Hannaford is surrounded by members of the media, younger filmmakers, and old cronies as he tries to raise completion money for his "with-it" film filled with arcane symbolism, nudity, and radical-chic violence, also titled *The Other Side of the Wind*. "The joke is that the media are feeding off him," Welles told me, "but they end up feeding off themselves. It's sort of his last summer. That's what it's all about."

It transpired that, just before I called, Welles had asked Bogdanovich to recruit some film-buff types for the movie. Before even meeting me, Peter sensed I would be perfect casting for the role of a wide-eyed young film scholar. On August 22, 1970, the day before shooting began, I went to Welles's rented house high in the Hollywood hills to meet him for lunch. He immediately flattered—and floored—me. I found *Persistence of Vision* prominently displayed on the mantelpiece in his living room. As we shook hands, Welles announced, "I finally meet my favorite critic." I asked him why he considered me that.

Welles replied, "You're the only critic who understands what I try to do."

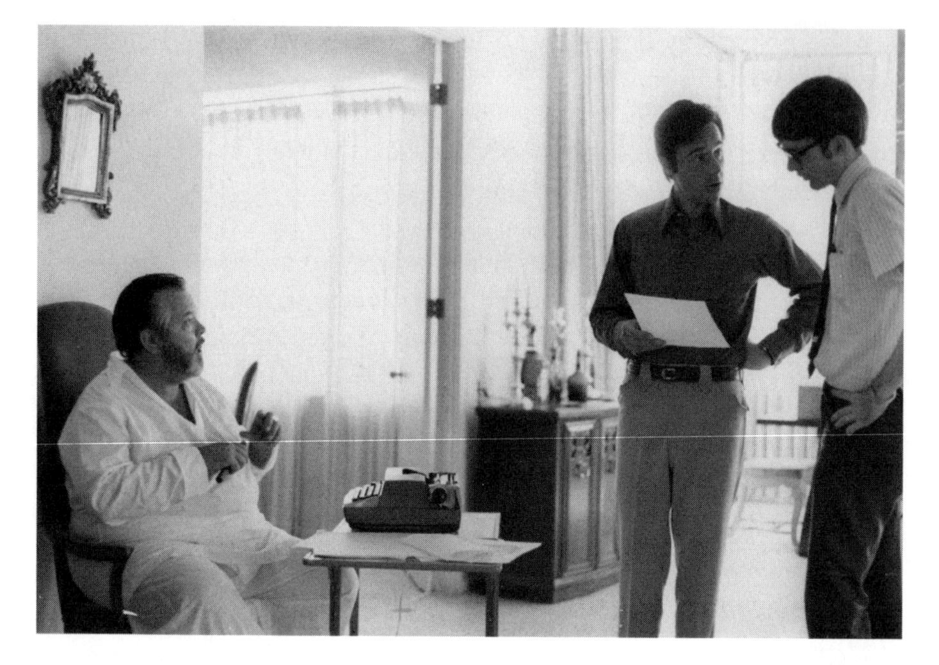

A film buff's fantasy comes to life: Joseph McBride (right) with Peter Bogdanovich (center), being directed by Orson Welles. On the first day of shooting *The Other Side of the Wind* in Los Angeles, August 23, 1970, Welles rehearses the two young film critics as satirical versions of themselves; Bogdanovich later switched parts to play a hot young director, but McBride continued playing his character, Mister Pister, for six years. *(Felipe Herba)*

❖ ❖ ❖

Even though *The Other Side of the Wind* takes place on the last day and night in the life of Jake Hannaford, the improbable adventure of making the film continued off and on for six years. Just as Welles had engaged Bogdanovich to interview him for a book intended to "set the record straight"—finally published in 1993 as *This Is Orson Welles*—I believe I was put on the set of *The Other Side of the Wind* partly to ensure that the shooting was documented accurately. But because of a Byzantine tangle of legal and financial problems, the film is still unfinished, like so much of Welles's later work.

I play a comically exaggerated version of myself, Mister Pister, who follows Hannaford around asking pretentious film-buff questions; Welles and I had a great time writing them together. Mister Pister, who is writing a scholarly book about Hannaford, is earnest and ultrasquare, hopelessly out of place among all the Hollywood sophisticates, hipsters, and dope freaks ("*Drugs!*" I exclaim to myself in one scene, my horrified face distorted by a wide-angle lens). If Welles's attitude toward Pister seemed mostly mocking, I went along with the gag because there's painful truth in this satire of maniacal film buffs and a blinkered intensity to my character that makes him more than a mere comic grotesque. Watching the rushes one night and seeing me advance toward the camera through a cloud of colored mist, holding a large black tape recorder to my chest as I stare dreamily up at a drive-in movie screen, Welles facetiously described my character as "the high priest of the cinema."

Playing Mister Pister and collaborating with Welles on my dialogue was a Walter Mitty–ish fantasy come true for a film buff and the beginning of my own checkered career in the movie business as a screenwriter, producer, sometime actor, and "talking head" in documentaries. For someone who had never acted before Welles gave me the opportunity, appearing in front of the camera for the cinema's greatest director of actors felt like one of George Plimpton's prankish forays as an amateur into the world of professional sports. But working for Welles, I thought, offered more than that. *The Other Side of the Wind* surely would become a major cinematic event: Welles's artistic summation, perhaps, and certainly his grand final statement on the corrupted promise of Hollywood and the wonderful but ultimately disappointing medium of which he was the master in exile.

While knowing Welles for the last fifteen years of his life, I also worked with him on three television specials and asked him a question in his documentary *Filming "The Trial."* During the forty years I have been studying his films, I have met and worked with many other people who knew Welles in various stages of his life and have given me the benefit of their perspectives on his kaleidoscopic talent and personality. Observing Welles at close range from both sides of the camera has given me a perspective few film critics and historians have been fortunate enough to have on their subjects. It enables me to present an unvarnished and multifaceted view of his working methods and personality.

This vastly influential filmmaker has become so encrusted with myth (partly created by Welles himself) that the man behind the myth is in danger of seeming illusory or smaller than the image, like the Wizard of Oz. The conventional wisdom on Welles in the United States today is largely negative: The trajectory of his career is usually seen as a path spiraling steadily downward from the heights of his early theater and radio successes and the pinnacle of his astonishing debut feature. If it's true, as F. Scott Fitzgerald once contended, that there are "no second acts in

American lives," it would seem no one exemplifies that truism more than Orson Welles. Or is the truism really true in his case? Did he simply succumb to what he described, late in life, as "the devil of self-destruction that lives in every genius"?

To believe it, one must ignore, first of all, the evidence of the masterpieces he made after *Citizen Kane*—*Ambersons*, *Touch of Evil*, *Chimes at Midnight*, and *F for Fake*—and his dazzling achievements in such films as *The Lady from Shanghai*, *Macbeth*, *Othello*, *The Trial*, and *The Immortal Story*. Such a brilliant and innovative record of creative work would be enough to bring glory to any artist's career, were it not for the widespread tendency to look at the glass of Welles's career as half empty rather than half full. The perception that he "squandered his promise" stems from his well-publicized difficulties with Hollywood studios, his endless scrambling for funds, and the false perception that he did nothing in his last fifteen years except eat, drink, and make television commercials. We can choose to lament what Welles didn't do, just as we could speculate on what his career would have been like if only Hollywood had been a little less venal, a little less crass, a little less . . . Hollywood. Or we can choose to celebrate all that he did do in Hollywood and elsewhere throughout his long and astonishingly fertile career. But to do so we must also examine why, as the radio dramatist Norman Corwin put it, "The world was cheated of his creativity in the later years of his life because of the difficulties strewn in his way."

I had many opportunities to talk casually with Welles, in wide-ranging conversations about his life and work. He often called me aside during the shooting of *The Other Side of the Wind* to make a point he wanted remembered. He seemed to enjoy the process of disclosure, even if he often teased me about my role as omnipresent observer and chronicler. Once you write a book, keeping up with the subject becomes a lifelong occupation. Following my *Orson Welles* in 1972 (revised and expanded in 1996), I wrote a study of his acting career, *Orson Welles: Actor and Director*, in 1977. During a break in the taping of Welles's unsold television talk show pilot *The Orson Welles Show* on a Hollywood soundstage in 1978, he spotted me jotting something on a pad of paper and asked with a humorously raised eyebrow, "Mister Pister . . . taking notes for his *third volume?*" I witnessed Welles's endlessly resourceful, brilliantly unorthodox creativity as he came up with solutions to time, money, and logistical problems that would have daunted other directors. I saw at first hand his ability to transform his movie on the spot when some providential accident occurred; Welles memorably defined a director as "a man who presides over accidents—but doesn't make them." And I saw Welles in many unguarded moments that revealed unexpected facets of his personality. I saw and heard the protean sense of humor and gargantuan laugh, the outbursts of bullying anger (much of it directed at me), and the surprising emotional vulnerability that combined to make him such a complex and endlessly intriguing man.

But even after knowing him and writing about him for all those years, I felt I needed to understand more about the struggle he faced to make movies in his later years and why he still found himself in such difficulties three decades after making *Citizen Kane*. This book is my investigation into the troubling question often heard from casual filmgoers and Welles aficionados alike: "What ever happened to Orson Welles?" To answer that question, we need to understand both what Welles was doing in the little-known final years of his life and what happened before then to set the pattern of his career. Much of the answer lies in his still largely misunderstood early years as a film, theater, and radio director and progressive political activist, when he antagonized powerful adversaries in New York, Hollywood, and Washington and became a pawn in a studio power struggle that, he said later, forever "branded" him as "Crazy Welles."

During the course of my research into Welles's life and work for this book, I discovered unmistakable evidence, hidden in plain sight, that Welles's political and cultural activities had caused him to be blacklisted during the postwar era. His decision to leave the country in late 1947, just as the Hollywood blacklist was being imposed, and his reinvention of himself as a wandering European filmmaker, largely out of necessity, hastened his already strong bent toward independence from the commercial system. Although Welles later returned to his native country to live in Los Angeles for long stretches, he was never fully accepted back into the American cultural mainstream and ultimately turned his back on it to become a fully independent filmmaker. As screenwriter and film critic F. X. Feeney observes, Welles suffered through an "ironically Soviet-style 'internal' exile—harsher, subtler, meaner and longer than what even [blacklisted screenwriter-director] Abraham Polonsky suffered, because it could be disguised under the 'Crazy Welles' rubric. Look how fat he is now, ha ha."

In this "portrait of an independent career," I hope to stimulate a deeper public understanding of the complex circumstances that caused one of the twentieth century's major artists to become a pariah in Hollywood while still in his twenties, an exile from the United States for many years, and an artist laboring largely in obscurity during his final years.

Despite all the difficulties Welles faced, his old age was far from being a tragic wasteland. It was a period of great artistic fecundity and daring, even if it was largely hidden from public view. What does that say about the nature of his artistic personality, and what does that say about our culture? How much of the fault for Welles's difficulties in completing films and reaching an audience lies with Welles himself, and how much with us? In exploring why one of our greatest filmmakers gradually turned into an almost private artist, and in shedding light on the adventurous body of work he continued to create in his later years, I hope to provide answers to these troubling questions.

What Ever Happened to
ORSON WELLES?

"I work very freely with the actors. I try to make their life pleasant": On the set of *The Other Side of the Wind* in Arizona in the early 1970s, Welles enjoys the company of cast members John Huston (left) and Peter Bogdanovich (right). *(Gary Graver)*

Chapter One

"GOD, HOW THEY'LL LOVE ME WHEN I'M DEAD!"

The enemy of society is the middle class, and the enemy of life is middle age. Youth and old age are great times—and we must treasure old age and give genius the capacity to function in old age—and not send them away.

—Welles in conversation with Peter Bogdanovich, 1970

"God, how they'll love me when I'm dead!" Welles was fond of saying in his later years, with a mixture of bitterness and ironic detachment. But that's a half-truth at best. More than two decades after Welles's death, his career is, in a very real sense, still flourishing. But it is a disturbing irony that Welles is more "bankable" now than when he was living.

Of course, this is nothing new in the arts. When the pesky presence of the living artist is out of the way, it's easier to appreciate and market his work. Vincent van Gogh may have sold only one painting in his lifetime and died in poverty, but for the price of one Van Gogh painting now, you could run your own international corporation. Jane Austen didn't make much money writing her six novels, but she flourished as the film industry's most popular (and still underpaid) writer in the 1990s, and her small body of work continues to be recycled. Show business cynics have quipped that Elvis Presley's death at age forty-two was "a good career move." Elvis was revitalized in death, his bloated, middle-aged silhouette magically slimmed and his raspy voice restored to its youthful luster.

As Welles expected, his death in 1985 opened the floodgates for the release of some of his films, and fragments of films, that had been languishing unseen, as well as for revivals and restorations of classic Welles films. Scripts he was not able to film have been redone for shooting by others or published in book form. Documentaries and docudramas about his life and work have proliferated. Welles predicted this gold rush to his friend and fellow director Henry Jaglom, saying, "Just wait till I die. Everything will happen. They'll be coming out of the woodwork. They'll dig up old scripts that I had something to do with, or they'll create stories about my life. These things will suddenly become saleable."

❖ ❖ ❖

Although I didn't fully recognize it when I met Welles in August 1970, his return to Hollywood earlier that year to live more or less permanently in the United States was a crucial turning point in his career. He came back to town thinking it might be an ideal time for him to find backing for his highly personal, iconoclastic film projects. The "New Hollywood" of the late 1960s and early 1970s produced such landmark movies as *Bonnie and Clyde*, *Easy Rider*, *M*A*S*H*, the first two *Godfather* films, *The Conversation*, and *Chinatown*. That brief flowering of personal filmmaking within the commercial system was born not only out of the cultural upheavals of the late 1960s but also from the economic collapse of the studio system in that period. Hollywood was hit with rampant unemployment as studios divested themselves of valuable real estate and were taken over by faceless conglomerates for whom individual artists were nothing but commodities. But the financial crisis at first led to a desperate and uncharacteristic willingness to experiment. The studios briefly turned over creative control from square and clueless older executives to a new generation of iconoclastic filmmakers including Francis Ford Coppola, Martin Scorsese, George Lucas, and Steven Spielberg. Some of the more irreverent middle-aged filmmakers, such as Robert Altman and Arthur Penn, also came into their own during that period. But a youth movement whose mottoes included "Never trust anyone over thirty" had relatively little room for older directors. Nor was the vaunted "independence" of the younger filmmakers easily transferable to someone with such heavy historical baggage as Welles was dragging around, chained to his troubled past like Marley's ghost. He would find even less support from the new, decentralized, supposedly "freer" Hollywood system than he had when he worked within the old studio system.

Partly by necessity and partly by design, Welles pursued his own maverick brand of filmmaking in his later years, largely financing his own works and scrambling to get them finished and distributed. Though astonishingly prolific and artistically rich, the final period of his life remains little known to the public because of Welles's marginalization by the film industry and the media as a tragic failure. To understand why this happened, we need to take a snapshot of how the American public regarded Orson Welles when he came back to his native land in 1970.

Even though Richard Nixon was president, the unsettled political climate in the United States and the breakdown of the old Hollywood system were seen by Welles as propitious signs for his return. Still, he retained a certain protective skepticism, derived from long and bitter experience of Hollywood's values. The cultural and political climate seemed to be freeing up, although, characteristically, he remained only cautiously optimistic. In a November 1970 article for *Look* magazine, "But Where Are We Going?" he observed: "Box-office hopes are riding, rather desperately, on the very youngest generation of directors. And they've all been given just that freedom, just that total control over their own work that was uniquely, and briefly, mine all those years ago. . . . This is a sign of panic, of course, but it's also the best hope for the future. For American films, I mean. Disadvantaged as I am by experience (not all of it good), my own future may well take me back to the old country. Europe for me is more necessity than choice. I'd rather be here with the kids. Who wouldn't?"

Insisting that the job of director is "often grossly overrated" and that a totally incompetent director can make a long and successful career for himself by relying on his collaborators, Welles deliberately flouted fashion by warning, "We need, at last, to take the mickey out of the myth of the Director as The Great Man of Our Times." And he took a swipe at the Hollywood producers "now frantically pandering to youth . . . these ugly, greedy little hustlers [who] are opening up old hernias by hopping on the bandwagon." But he cast his lot with the largely inexperienced new directors who shared a "bright sense of discovery [that] is bringing to the screen, if not a new language, at least a new and most attractive style."

That new style is both adopted and parodied in *The Other Side of the Wind*, which uses a deliberately haphazard-looking, handheld, cinema verité approach for the framing scenes of director Jake Hannaford's birthday party. Welles's skepticism toward the "New Hollywood" was reflected in Hannaford's ambivalent position. Jake's attempted comeback, pandering to the youth movement in a pretentious and incoherent fashion that renders his film unsalable, proves the end of him. But what are his alternatives? Either reinventing himself as a pseudo "hippie" filmmaker or allowing his work to go unfinished. Both options are unbearable. For Welles, who presents Hannaford's tragedy as a cautionary tale for an older filmmaker, it's clear what the more honorable and less self-destructive option must be.

Welles's film performances ranged from the sublime to the ridiculous. Examples of both: his sardonic Cardinal Wolsey in Fred Zinnemann's 1966 film of Robert Bolt's play *A Man for All Seasons*, and his barbarian Burundai, clumsily wielding a sword in the 1962 Italian peplum saga *The Tartars*, while signaling his amusement over the role. *(Columbia Pictures/MGM)*

By 1970, the American public barely knew Welles as a director. With a myopic perspective fostered by the largely hostile American media, they knew him mostly as a buffoonish has-been, a cameo player in bad movies and a guest on Dean Martin's television variety show. Occasionally Welles was allowed a serious turn on the show, such as his electrifying single-take recitation in 1967 of Shylock's "Hath not a Jew eyes?" speech from *The Merchant of Venice*, performed as an outburst of righteous anger.* But the more pervasive impression of Welles left by *The Dean Martin Show* was of him trying to look like a good sport as he mugged his way through comedy skits and even sweated through soft-shoe musical routines with Martin and other guests. Welles also became a frequent guest on *The Tonight Show*, sometimes substituting for host Johnny Carson, a gig that brought such indignities as holding up a can of cat food for a commercial, chatting with singer Engelbert Humperdinck, and earnestly questioning comedian Flip Wilson about his golf cart. Carson once asked Welles about his hobbies, and he admitted later, "Questions like that absolutely defeat me."

Welles appeared much more relaxed in his many appearances on *The Merv Griffin Show* with the indulgent, adulatory host in the late 1970s and early 1980s, including an especially mellow session of reminiscences with biographer Barbara Leaming on the last night of his life. Welles seemed to welcome the opportunity of letting his hair down on such shows, however trivial the subject matter placed before him. He sought to play the game to his own advantage, since it enabled him to avoid dealing with difficult or unpleasant topics, such as his own past. Even when the host or other guests tried prodding him in those directions, he preferred to spend his time on *Merv* indulging his fondness for performing elaborately tedious magic tricks, often involving members of the studio audience, among whom Welles liked to plant shills, such as his young cameraman Gary Graver.

Welles's celebrity became a double-edged sword in later years, keeping him financially afloat by bringing him work as an actor, TV personality, and pitchman and affording him whatever tenuous "bankability" he still had in the film industry. But at the same time, it dominated his pro-

---

* Such transitory glimpses into Welles's artistry were granted by the show's producer, Greg Garrison, who was responsible for bringing Welles back to Hollywood for brief periods in the 1960s. A longtime friend since he had worked, as a youth, on Welles's 1946 musical stage production *Around the World*, Garrison was put through college by Welles and later was named the executor of his will.

"We will sell no wine . . . before its time": This is how most of the American public knew Welles in his later years, as a TV pitchman for Paul Masson wine. In this 1979 commercial, he compares the ripening of wine to the slow gestation of Margaret Mitchell's novel *Gone With the Wind. (Paul Masson/Doyle Dane Bernbach)*

fessional reputation to the point of almost entirely eclipsing, in his native land, awareness of his career as a director. Unlike John Huston, who didn't balk at directing mediocre movies for hire in order to remain bankable, Welles was heroically unwilling to compromise as a director. But he was willing to do almost anything as an actor/personality. When asked why he consented to appear in Jim Beam whiskey ads, he shrugged, "It's the most innocent form of whoring I know." Unfortunately, since the American public rarely saw the films such whoring allowed him to direct, whoring was all most people thought he was doing.

His reputation abroad did not suffer from his commercial shilling or his sillier TV appearances. Talking with French film students in 1982, Welles pointed out, "In America, I'm an entertainer. I do magic, I tell jokes. I have another career." Welles became notorious in America for making a series of commercials for Paul Masson wine, a modestly priced brand that hired him to provide an aura of up-market savoir faire. Dressed in a black suit with a flowing tie or a white suit and brightly colored shirt with flaring collar, seated alone or at a spartan table while others around him were making merry, Welles would intone variations on the company's advertising line "We will sell no wine . . . [pregnant pause] before its time."

In one of those commercials, Welles holds an open copy of a best-selling novel and tells the audience, "Margaret Mitchell began writing *Gone With the Wind* in 1926 and she finished it ten years later. [Closes book] The writing of a great book or the [pause] making of a fine wine takes time. . . . Paul Masson will sell no wine . . . before its time." The subtext comparing wine's slow ripening to the lengthy gestation of Welles's own work fell on deaf ears. The commercial catchphrase became a joke, and a signature line for Welles himself, helping to define his personality in the media as that of a hedonist who preferred to dawdle over his vineyard interminably, releasing the fruits of his labor only rarely, if ever.

❖ ❖ ❖

The barbs directed at Welles in the American media took on a progressively nastier tone as he became more vulnerable to age and ill health. It seemed he was getting his final "comeuppance" for presuming to think himself so special. The Anglo-Irish actor Micheál MacLiammóir, who plays Iago in Welles's 1952 film *Othello*, witnessed the effect of the celebrity syndrome on Welles more than three decades before the great man's death, noting "that jocular interest he can so easily inspire in the ignorant and impressionable public, always more attracted by the glittering bauble in the crown than by the gold of the crown itself."

With fat jokes rudely added to the mix by Carson and others, the caricature was complete: Welles, the dissipated has-been who couldn't finish a movie and had betrayed the youthful promise of *Citizen Kane*. His weight, which reached more than 350 pounds, became an irrational fixation of public interest, eclipsing everything else about him in the American consciousness. In a society of mostly overweight people obsessed with thinness, Welles's unapologetic girth—which to a more sympathetic observer can be seen as stemming from glandular problems—is widely viewed as a deliberate effrontery, an act of moral turpitude, a metaphor for an out-of-control, undisciplined, and ultimately immobilized personality. In short, a puritanical metaphor for a self-indulgent radical artist. For people who knew or cared little about Welles's art, making fun of his weight served as shorthand to disparage his unconventional career choices. Does anyone care that Alfred Hitchcock and Jean

Renoir were fat? Hardly. But Hitchcock was a commercial success, so his weight was an enjoyable eccentricity. Renoir was foreign and wasn't held to the same standards of commercial success as Welles, who began his career in America before going into European exile and then into his "internal exile" at home. Welles's weight was an obsessive theme in his American obituaries but was mentioned in few of the obituaries outside the United States, which tended to concentrate more on his artistic achievement.

Uninterested in the actual circumstances of his later years, many writers of articles and even some books on Welles have clucked their tongues so puritanically at Welles's gourmandizing that it has come to assume the status, in the popular imagination, of his primal sin. The implicit suggestion, irrational and shallow as it may seem, is that Welles took the money he earned from humiliating himself as a commercial pitchman and squandered it on piggish gluttony. That caricaturish image was distilled by novelist Mordechai Richler in a premature obituary that appeared in *GQ* just days before Welles's death: "Had he been blessed with the artistic acumen to die at the age of twenty-four, after completing *Citizen Kane*, he would undoubtedly still be mourned today as the ultimate American filmmaker, a man who would certainly have gone on to create a body of classics if only . . . [But] Welles has lingered on, Hollywood's ancient mariner, telling and retelling his sad tales at [Patrick Terrail's West Hollywood bistro] Ma Maison, almost all his other projects incomplete for one convoluted crybaby reason or another, his outsize life reduced to self-serving anecdotes. For all that, on the spurious Hollywood standard, many still grieve for him as an unfulfilled genius. Some genius. Imagine, if you will, the 26-year-old Chekhov, unable to finance his next play, sitting still for a vodka commercial. Or Bach, his fridge running low on caviar or Dom Pérignon, phoning his agent to see what he could set on the table for him."

Making commercials was nothing new for Welles, however, but part of the price he always had to pay for whatever commercial viability he possessed. He was the "Voice of Cornstarch" on radio during the 1930s, and when Campbell's Soup became the sponsor of his acclaimed CBS radio series *The Mercury Theatre on the Air*, enabling it to reach a much wider audience, the title of the series was changed to *The Campbell Playhouse*. In 1945, Welles had a short-lived radio series for Cresta Blanca Wines, *This Is My Best*. He would describe the sponsor's product as "a wine to serve proudly, saying, 'This is my best, this is Cresta Blanca.'"

No one in those days thought such commercial tie-ins were a scandal; by working in a medium financed by product selling, Welles was able to use the system for his own ends, as he later would do by financing his own films as an actor and commercial pitchman. But it's a sign of the changing attitudes toward Welles that Tim Robbins's 1999 film, *Cradle Will Rock*—which deals in part with the controversial and triumphant Welles–John Houseman production of Marc Blitzstein's labor opera, *The Cradle Will Rock*, for the Works Progress Administration's Federal Theatre Project in 1937—retroactively turns Welles's commercial huckstering into a scandal.

Robbins offers a surprisingly vitriolic portrait of the young Welles, played as a drunken lout by Angus MacFadyen. Looking at Welles through the distorted lens of hindsight, Robbins buys into the conventional wisdom that Welles was a tragic failure and trivializes Welles's youthful radicalism by portraying him as a dilettantish playboy rather than a man of commitment. By showing the freshly minted theatrical prodigy as a prematurely dissipated, self-destructive sellout, Robbins finds himself in the strange position of denouncing a radical avant-garde director for putting commercialism ahead of art (and of bringing that charge in a film made for the Walt Disney Company!). Even Welles's willingness to help finance his shoestring Federal Theatre projects with the money he earned from his radio appearances—he liked to boast, "I'm the only man who ever dishonestly put money into a government project!"—is treated contemptuously, as evidence of guilty expiation for personal indulgence. Hank Azaria's Blitzstein pompously warns Welles about his radio "prostitution," asking, "Where do you draw the line? *Do* you draw the line? How long before you're doing soap commercials?"

The harm such attacks did to Welles's reputation in the United States stems partly from the rigid distinction Americans make between art and commerce, in theory if not always in practice. Other distinguished actors of Welles's generation did not draw such vehement criticism for doing commercials. Laurence Olivier's shilling for Polaroid didn't do much, if any, damage to his reputation (even if John Travolta's character in *Saturday Night Fever* knows him only as that guy in the Polaroid commercials). American stars who have escaped unscathed include Henry Fonda with his commercials for Life Savers, Bette Davis for General Electric washing machines, and Paul Newman for American Express. Robbins's condemnation of Welles for supporting his artistic endeavors by making commercials makes no sense except in light of critic Jonathan Rosenbaum's observation that the "scandal" of Welles's film career was that he was willing to violate the American film industry's "taboo against financing one's own work." That subversive practice threatens the Hollywood economic system, throws its values and hierarchies into question, and spurs envy in those who can't afford to invest their own money in their own work or are unwilling to do so.

In a 1974 interview for British television, Welles recalled that when he first went to Hollywood in 1939, he was already seen as

> this terrible maverick. . . . I was sort of forty or thirty years ahead of my time. . . . a sort of ghost of Christmas future. There was the one beatnik, you know, there was this guy with a beard who was going to do it all by himself. I represented the terrible future of what was going to happen to that town. So I was hated and despised, theoretically, but I had all kinds of friends among the real dinosaurs, who were awfully nice to me. And I had a very good time.
>
> But I believe that I have looked back too optimistically on Hollywood. Because my daughter has a group of books about Hollywood that she bought, I don't know why, probably vainly looking for references of her father in them. And I took to reading them lately. And I realized how many great people that town has destroyed since its earliest beginnings—how almost everybody of merit was destroyed or diminished, and how the few people who were good who survived, what a great minority they were. . . . And when I take my own life out of it and see what they did to other people, I see that the story of that town is a dirty one, and its record is bad.

From his early days in radio to his later years as a guest on TV talk shows, Welles tried to head off the resentment of his double-edged, media-promoted image as a "genius" by defensively poking fun at that image and at other parts of his personality that some people found offensive: his eating habits, his egotism, and his theatricality. Welles insisted that he never *seriously* referred to himself as a genius. As early as 1937, at age twenty-two, he was being ironic about the word: "I'm either the genius they say I am or the world's godawfulest ham. It's a fifty-fifty split." And even in *Citizen Kane* there's a wink to the audience about Welles's fabled love of food. "Are you still eating?" Joseph Cotten's Jed Leland asks Kane as dawn breaks outside the *Inquirer* office. Kane replies impatiently, "I'm still *hungry.*" The older Welles's roles as the grotesquely fat police detective Hank Quinlan in *Touch of Evil* and as Shakespeare's buoyantly fat Sir John Falstaff in *Chimes at Midnight* were designed to play off and mock his own public image.

But all this good-natured raillery failed to disarm Welles's later detractors. They ignore (or, more likely, have never heard) the splendid Shakespearean self-defense he offered as Falstaff:

> If sack and sugar be a fault, then God help the wicked! If to be old and merry be a sin, then many an old host that I know is damned. And if to be fat is to be hated, then Pharaoh's lean kine are to be loved. No, my good lord: banish Peto, banish Bardolph, banish Poins. But for sweet Jack Falstaff, kind Jack Falstaff, true Jack Falstaff, valiant Jack Falstaff, and therefore more valiant being, as he is, old Jack Falstaff, banish not him thy Harry's company, banish not him thy Harry's company, banish plump Jack, and banish all the world!

❖ ❖ ❖

At the same time Welles's reputation had seemingly bottomed out in the United States, he enjoyed an exalted reputation with film aficionados around the world. At the 1966 Cannes Film Festival, the ambitious, richly textured, deeply moving *Chimes at Midnight* brought him both the Prix de la Commission Supérieure Technique and a special prize, the festival's twentieth-anniversary award. "Jeers and whistles greeted many of the other prizes," Kenneth Tynan reported, "but for this one, everybody rose—avant-garde critics and commercial producers alike—and clapped with their hands held over their heads. The ovation lasted for minutes. Welles beamed and sweated on the stage of the Festival Palace, looking like a melting iceberg and occasionally tilting forward in something that approximated a bow."

Chimes at Midnight is one of Welles's greatest films, in some ways his greatest. It certainly contains his finest performance, as the bounteous rogue he described as "the character in whom I believe the most, the most entirely good man in all drama. His faults are trivial and he makes the most enormous jokes from them. His goodness is like bread, like wine." Yet the film hardly played in the United States after being released here in March 1967, prosaically retitled *Falstaff*, and very few people have seen it since. What makes the ignominy of the film's mistreatment particularly painful is that *Chimes* is so accessible and entertaining.

Welles's marginalized status in the film industry was evident in the picture's erratically synchronized dialogue and the doubling of absent actors in many scenes. Those technical imperfections did not unduly bother European audiences. But in her sympathetic review of the film in the *New Republic*, Pauline Kael lamented that its rough edges contributed to its difficulty in finding an American audience:

> So many people—and with such complacent satisfaction, almost, one would say, delight—talk of how Welles has disappointed them, as if he had willfully thrown away his talent through that "lack of discipline" which is always brought in to explain failure. There is a widespread notion that a man who accomplishes a great deal is thus a "genius" who should be able to cut through all obstacles; and if he can't (and who can?), what he does is too far beneath what he should have done to be worth consideration. On the contrary, I think that the more gifted and imaginative a director, the greater the obstacles. . . .
>
> Welles—the one great creative force in American films in our time, the man who might have redeemed our movies from the general contempt in which they are (and for the most part, rightly) held—is, ironically, an expatriate director whose work thus reaches only the art-house audience. And he has been so crippled by the problems of working as he does, he's lucky to reach that. . . . *Falstaff* came and went so fast there was hardly time to tell people about it, but it should be back (it should be around forever).

❖ ❖ ❖

So by the late 1960s Welles was truly a prophet without honor in his native land. His films were far outside the commercial mainstream with their eccentric subject matter and deliberately unfashionable visual style, whether operatic, as in *Chimes*, or resembling chamber music, such as his 1968 adaptation of an Isak Dinesen novella, *The Immortal Story*. Welles's films not only didn't do much business, they seemed hardly to *exist* in the mass American consciousness. People still find it easy to condemn Welles as a failure while being blithely ignorant of his adventurous later work. Invariably, when I ask a Welles detractor if he or she has seen *Chimes at Midnight* or Welles's audaciously freewheeling 1974 documentary, *F for Fake*, the answer is no. Almost as invariably, Welles's detractor hasn't even *heard* of those films—and seems to feel no shame in attacking him from a position of such ignorance.

Welles was perpetually short on funding for his projects in his old age and had many heartbreaking misadventures. Sustaining himself on "hope and enthusiasm," he poured his own money from acting work into the independent films he directed, a radical departure from conventional practice that confirmed Hollywood's wariness of him and all he represented. When asked at a University of Southern California gathering in 1981 how much money he had made from *The Trial*, Welles replied that by putting his own funds into the production he had *lost* $80,000.* "Sev-

* The event was recorded by Welles as part of a documentary called *Filming "The Trial,"* a companion piece to his *Filming "Othello"* (1978) that was not publicly exhibited, in its unfinished form, until 1999.

Welles left behind a complex cinematic legacy of unfinished work, hundreds of cans and boxes of film, videotape, and audiotape for others to catalog, assemble, and restore, keeping his career alive long after his death. *(Orson Welles: The One-Man Band; Medias Res/The Criterion Collection)*

eral of my movies as a director have not only been made for nothing but they cost me money," he said on another occasion. He added, "So in a sense I'm an amateur director . . . amateur in the sense that 'amateur' derives from love." However commendable in artistic terms, this practice made his films seem to many people more like hobby or vanity productions than commercial ventures. And the idea of *willingly* losing your own money on a film was simply beyond the ken of most people in what Rosenbaum calls "the media-industrial complex."

Welles's methods had a less admirable side that often proved self-defeating. He was a terrible businessman with a flexible sense of contractual obligations and an unfortunate tendency to deal with dubious patrons. Partly for those reasons, many of his later projects fell into legal and financial limbo. To his credit, Welles was willing to accept some of the responsibility for that recurring problem. He told biographer Barbara Leaming that a "character failing" could be involved: "It's like somebody who every time he goes out gets struck by lightning."

❖ ❖ ❖

The Promethean daring of Welles's first feature has become his glory *and* his curse, the standard against which all his subsequent work is compared and found wanting. "If there was a downfall, then it was entirely of his own doing," Welles's former partner John Houseman insisted. "I mean, nobody stopped him from producing more *Citizen Kane*s." *Kane* has been named the greatest film from any country by polls of international critics surveyed by the British Film Institute every ten years since 1962 and by the BFI's polls of international directors in 1992 and 2002. Welles's influence on other directors has always been profound, and the stylistic ground he broke in *Kane*, with its flamboyant camera movements, intricate flashback structure, and self-consciously foregrounded editing style, has had a revolutionary effect on world cinema ever since. But the general line on Welles's later years in the media is summed up in the sensationalistic title of a 1992 television documentary: *Orson Welles: What Went Wrong?*

The truth is that his later years were anything but solitary or creatively arid. They were a rich and intense period of filmmaking activity in several countries, characterized by daring artistic experimentation. That adventurous period involved a heightened preoccupation with eroticism (thanks to the influence of his much younger companion, Oja Kodar, a Croatian sculptress, writer, and actress), a deepened concentration on death and dissolution, mordantly satirical reflections on Welles's own media image, and ambivalent observations by the master on the cinema itself. Why he couldn't get the work before the public is a different question, although not unrelated to the nature of the work he was doing. Welles never stopped working on film projects. He told the French film students in 1982, "I feel young, happy, and ready to make movies."

❖ ❖ ❖

Welles's fatal heart attack at age seventy in the bedroom of his Hollywood home on October 10, 1985, came while he was typing script material for a new project he was planning to launch that morning at UCLA. The anonymously written *New York Times* obituary the following day defined the conventional wisdom about his life and work, "the feeling of many that his career . . . was one of largely unfulfilled promise. . . . By age 24, he was already being described by the press as a has-been—a cliché that would dog him all his life. But at that very moment Welles was creating *Citizen Kane*, generally considered one of the best motion pictures ever made. . . . For his failure to realize his dreams, Welles blamed his critics and the financiers of Hollywood. Others blamed what they described as his erratic, egotistical, self-indulgent, and self-destructive temperament. But in the end, few denied his genius."

The veteran film critic Stanley Kauffmann commented in the *New Republic:* "He was a man for whom everything was possible, absolutely *everything*, in the worlds of theater, radio, film, television. He could have been a major changer and shaper of our performing arts. But in the middle 1940s the spoiled child took over. He had overcome plenty of difficulties before then, but about that time he seemed to assume that the world now owed him a smooth path and that he would pay the world back for its refusal to pamper him by giving it only virtuosic arrogance."

After the obituaries appeared, *New York Times* film critic Vincent Canby countered with a column eloquently honoring Welles's legacy. Turning a favorite lament of Welles's detractors on its head, Canby wrote:

> I can't think of a more futile question to ask at this point than "What ever happened to Orson Welles?" Nothing "happened." He directed several of the greatest movies ever made—a feat not equaled by many other film makers. Why blame the man for being himself? . . . He didn't wind up—like some—broke, or forgotten, or as a hopeless drunk, or as a mean-spirited has-been. One shouldn't worry about "the rise and fall of an American genius," which is the subtitle of Charles Higham's new book on Welles. That sort of speculation is cheap. Instead, one should celebrate the accomplishments. . . . His great films are as alive and as influential today as they've always been. The rest of the world is still trying to catch up.

❖ ❖ ❖

Unfortunately, anyone who genuinely admires Welles must continue to worry about the cheap sort of speculation offered by such biographers as Higham and David Thomson, for their work is taken seriously by people who share their preconceptions. One of the final passages in Thomson's indiscriminately praised 1996 biography *Rosebud: The Story of Orson Welles* brings together all the negative clichés about Welles while shamelessly admitting the author's failure to inquire into the filmmaking activities of Welles's later years:

> There are twenty-five years left to go in this life we are assisting [*sic*], and I suspect that it would be neither reasonable nor kind—to Welles or to ourselves—to track them closely, as I have tried to do in the book so far. That might prove too grim and relentless; it would make too much of the lost chances, the wild hopes, the disappointment, the solitude and the humiliation of being Orson Welles and having to hear the question, What ever

> *happened* to him? Not that those sadnesses can be omitted. But it was tough enough to live that life day by day while putting on the resilient air of appetite still—and him such a fake actor. Why could he never really lose weight? people ask. Because that would have begun to concede the regret, the melancholy and the horror. So he ate grandly, and often made a show of being seen at his food.

Scorning Welles as a tragic failure of gargantuan proportions seems to satisfy a public need (at least in America) to point a finger at an archetypal "spoiled artist," to bring genius down to the level of everyday mediocrity. If the truth about what Welles was doing in his later years were widely known, it would be harder to use him as the symbol for everything uncomfortably self-indulgent (i.e., individualistic) that had to be expelled from Hollywood so that the industry could concentrate its entire resources on the quest for the latest impersonal blockbuster. Welles serves as a perfect whipping boy for those in the film industry and in the media who uncritically worship the imperatives and products of the commercial system.

Why doesn't the American public know about Welles's indefatigable creative work in his later years? Primarily because during that period he functioned outside the Hollywood studio system and the media apparatus that supports it so symbiotically. For a brief time in the early 1940s, his youthful success in the radio and theater enabled him to work under studio sponsorship to make *Kane* and *The Magnificent Ambersons* for RKO, but the Hollywood system proved unable to accommodate his radical talent, and he was fired by the studio in 1942. "What is surprising is that I lasted as long as I did," Welles reflected. Jonathan Rosenbaum, who has written some of the best scholarly work on Welles in recent years, points out that because Welles's first two features were studio-financed films,

> this has led many recent commentators to regard Welles as an unsuccessful studio employee throughout his career rather than as an independent filmmaker, successful or otherwise. Insofar as most film histories are written by industry apologists of one sort or another, this is an unexceptional conclusion, but not necessarily a correct one. To my mind, Welles always remained an independent who financed his own pictures whenever and however he could, and perhaps the only movie in his entire canon that qualifies as a Hollywood picture pure and simple, for better and for worse, is *The Stranger.*
>
> In many cases, one can easily separate his features between Hollywood productions (e.g., *The Lady from Shanghai, Macbeth)* and independent productions (e.g., *Othello, F for Fake)*, but the divisions aren't always so clear-

> cut: the unfinished *It's All True* started out as a studio project and ended up as an independent project; according to Welles, *[Mr.] Arkadin* in its release form was even more seriously mangled by its producer than any of his Hollywood films; [and] *The Trial* was largely financed by Alexander and Michael Salkind, some of whose productions (including *Superman* and *The Three Musketeers)* can be loosely labeled as "Hollywood" or "studio" releases.

Welles turned his habitual way of working into a direct challenge to the system. In later years, he made a few halfhearted attempts to pursue studio funding for one project or another, but he spent most of his time on the fringes of the industry directing what crew members of *The Other Side of the Wind* called "the greatest home movie ever made." He said at the time, only partly in jest, "The answers to a great many questions having to do with my 'oeuvre' [laughs] end up having to do with the fact that I didn't have any money." Out of both inclination and necessity, Welles blazed a path for all the independent filmmakers who have followed, from John Cassavetes and Jean-Luc Godard, whose work defined the word "independent" in the late 1950s and early 1960s, to Spike Lee, Oliver Stone, Martin Scorsese, and John Sayles, who have shrewdly used the studio system to pursue their stubbornly independent visions. Accepting his American Film Institute Life Achievement Award in 1975, Welles diplomatically explained to the well-heeled Hollywood audience how he used their money to indirectly finance his work:

> This honor I can only accept in the name of all the mavericks. And also as a tribute to the generosity of all the rest of you—to the givers—to the ones with fixed addresses. A maverick may go his own way but he doesn't think that it's the only way or ever claim that it's the best one—except maybe for himself. And don't imagine that this raggle-taggle gypsy-o is claiming to be free. It's just that some of the necessities to which I am a slave are different from yours.
>
> As a director, for instance, I pay myself out of my acting jobs. I use my own work to subsidize my work. In other words, I'm crazy. But not crazy enough to pretend to be free. But it's a fact that many of the films you've seen tonight could never have been made otherwise. Or if otherwise—well, they might have been better. But certainly they wouldn't have been mine.

Welles signed off by saying that he remained "not only your obedient servant, but also, in this age of supermarkets, your friendly neighborhood grocery store."

❖ ❖ ❖

Where does that leave Welles's idiosyncratic body of work, which he found so difficult to place before audiences? To paraphrase Jean Renoir's Octave in *The Rules of the Game*, there is one terrible thing about Welles's career, and it is that every unfinished film has its reasons. Each of the many projects that remained uncompleted at the time of his death has a different story behind its state of collapse, suspension, or disappearance. That's why it's dangerous to offer a general theory, such as Higham's claim that Welles had a "fear of completion," to simplistically explain a far more complex history.

But even some of Welles's friends share that view. Fellow director Curtis Harrington, who appears in *The Other Side of the Wind*, told Welles scholar Peter Tonguette, "I wouldn't presume to do an amateur psychological analysis of his fear of completion, but I think that it did exist. In some ways, I suspect that it was because of that overwhelming success and brilliance of his beginning work. My theory—and it's only a theory—is that weighed on him as time went by. And he wanted to create, he wanted to keep working, but at the same time, I think he realized—in fact, I know he realized—that a great deal of what he was doing was not up to his own standards. And what better way to cut that off than to be unable to complete it?"

The Other Side of the Wind was the most prominent of the many "lost films" that litter the Wellesian canon, the project of his later years for which Welles harbored the greatest hopes. He never abandoned it, as he more or less did *The Deep*. Even though the filming of *The Other Side of the Wind* essentially was completed, the ten hours of negative footage remains locked in a Paris vault; Welles managed to edit only forty-two minutes of it. He showed two scenes when he received his AFI tribute. The crowd laughed when Welles explained archly that one of the scenes involves a Hannaford stooge screening part of the old director's unfinished *Other Side of the Wind* in hopes of raising "end money." Other parts of the film—notably a bravura seven-minute sex scene in a moving car during a rainstorm, one of Welles's most dazzling stylistic achievements, unlike anything he had done before—have been seen in documentaries and other public venues. But more than thirty-five years after Welles began shooting his last word on the Hollywood system that he regarded with such ambivalence, it continues to be anyone's guess when, or if, the film will ever be completed.

When I encountered John Huston for the first time on location in early 1974 in an isolated desert house in Carefree, Arizona, I opened a bedroom door and found the legendary filmmaker pulling on his pants over his bony white legs. I retreated with a muttered apology. I introduced myself when Huston emerged, telling him how happy I was that he was playing the role of Jake Hannaford and saying that I'd been waiting for him to show up for the last three years. With sudden alarm, Huston said, "You've been in this picture for *three years*?" Perhaps that was the moment he realized just what a surreal escapade he was getting himself into.

With its prolonged shooting history, secretive production methods, and bizarrely assembled cast, *The Other Side of the Wind* acquired the status of a legendary lost film even before it finished shooting. One reason the completion has been continually stalled is the daunting artistic challenge of reconstructing Welles's unorthodox vision and editing style in his absence. Attempts by others (including myself) to find backing for its completion have so far been unsuccessful. Even more disastrous than its consequences for the film itself was the effect of its production history on the rest of Welles's career. This ambitious labor of love unfortunately crystallized the conventional wisdom about Welles: that he was unable or unwilling to finish projects.

"Orson is not a man who can bow down to idiots. And Hollywood is full of them," Huston observed in a 1981 interview. "Orson is a big ego. But I've always found him to be completely logical. And I think he's a joy. I also look on Orson as an amateur. I mean that in the very best sense of the word. He loves pictures and plays and all things theatrical. But there is something else that needs accounting for. So many of his things go unfinished. I don't know why. That is one I can't answer. Even one that we did together, *The Other Side of the Wind.* I haven't seen a foot of it myself, and I don't know why it hasn't been released. Now, there's always a reason. But it's happened too often with Orson for it to be entirely accidental."

That tendency to leave projects strewn in his wake—even ones he financed himself and had no obligation to finish, except perhaps to his audience—brought severe criticism from journalists and biographers who accused Welles of wastefulness and irresponsibility. "Why should I have to answer all of these questions?" Welles told the *New York Times* in 1976. "I haven't committed a crime. I'm just a poor slob who's trying to make pictures." But the questions are worth asking, for we need more enlightened and nuanced ways of accounting for all the Sturm und Drang of his career.

Welles may have been in some ways his own worst enemy, yet the implication by many critics that he failed to complete projects because he was lazy or dilatory is simply false; he was an indefatigable worker. An inventory of Welles's work fills an astonishing 131 pages in the appendix Rosenbaum and Peter Bogdanovich compiled for the Bogdanovich-Welles interview book. Has any other artist of his generation had anything close to such an industrious career? While some was hackwork and some was highly uneven, much was groundbreaking and influential.

Further evidence of that industriousness can be seen in the treasurehouse of film, videotapes, and audiotapes deposited by Oja Kodar in 1995 with the Filmmuseum im Münchner Stadtmuseum, also known as the Filmmuseum München (the Munich Film Museum). Shipped from Los Angeles in about a hundred crates weighing a total of 1.8 tons, the collection comprises the bulk of Welles's unfinished work. Some of these films—such as *The Deep*, *The Dreamers*, *The Merchant of Venice*, *Moby-Dick*, and *Orson Welles' Magic Show*—can be glimpsed in a 1995 documentary directed for German television by Kodar and Vassili Silovic, *Orson Welles: The One-Man Band*, which is included with the 2005 Criterion Collection DVD release of *F for Fake*. The Munich Film Museum, headed by Stefan Drössler, has assembled and shown much of its Welles holdings at retrospectives in Munich and elsewhere in Europe and the United States. It brought *Filming "The Trial"* to the screen in 1999, helped put together a "comprehensive version" of *Mr. Arkadin* released on DVD in 2006, and has been working on a restoration of *The Deep*, a feature Welles filmed between 1963 and 1969. Another major unfinished Welles film, *Don Quixote*, which he began shooting in 1955 and was reediting when he died, was poorly presented in a 1992 version by the Spanish director Jesús Franco and still needs to be fully assembled from materials held at the Filmoteca Española in Madrid and elsewhere.

Welles's unfinished work has received little other exposure in the United States, and scant explanation has been offered the public for its near invisibility. Even America's "paper of record" made the common error of believing that Welles "had been inactive as a director for some years before his death," as Canby claimed in a *Times* article accompanying Welles's obituary. With much of the unfinished work finally surfacing, something approaching a complete picture of Welles's film career is only now becoming possible. Every previously "lost" or missing work and every variant version or fragment sheds new light on unexpected facets of Welles's kaleidoscopic artistic personality and should cause us to reevaluate our assumptions about his career. The quality that made

Welles such a fascinatingly adventurous artist—the fact that he was impossible to categorize, never making a film like any he had made before, always setting out in new directions—was the same characteristic that confounded reviewers and potential backers in the United States, who prefer that an artist remain in his assigned niche.

Walter Murch, the editor and sound designer who reconstructed *Touch of Evil* according to Welles's specifications in 1998, said of him in 2006, "He was a guy who was twenty to twenty-five years ahead of his time. That was his glory and why he had such problems. Hollywood doesn't like people who are that far ahead of their time. They like people who are just ahead of their time, like *six seconds* ahead of their times, because those persons make the most money."

In his later years, Welles thumbed his nose at the industrial system of making movies by shooting with small nonunion crews on erratic schedules whenever he could get the money for more shooting or simply whenever he felt like it. He made movies on subjects that interested him without worrying about whether they were "commercial" or not. Nowhere were his radical differences from the norms of what he called "this conglomerated world of ours" more apparent than in his later work. As Stefan Drössler put it, "After *Othello* (1952), which he produced entirely on his own, Welles freed himself from the constraints of traditional production methods to work for as long as he wished on projects, rather like a writer or a painter. Welles did not consider films to be finite works. He believed his work as an artist was always work in progress. In that respect he was a precursor for someone like George Lucas, who reworks his *Star Wars* films for DVD release."

But Lucas works in a different universe commercially from the niche inhabited by Orson Welles. The reductio ad absurdum of the animus expressed by many writers against Welles and his later work is David Thomson's comment on *The Other Side of the Wind:* "One day, it may be freed. I hope not. *The Other Side of the Wind* should stay beyond reach." Though admitting that he had seen little of the footage and mistakenly claiming that there was never a script written for the film,* Thomson

---

* The 1971 screenplay by Welles and Oja Kodar was published in a combined English and French edition in 2005 by *Cahiers du Cinéma* and the Festival International du Film de Locarno (Switzerland), in conjunction with that year's Locarno Welles conference and retrospective.

describes *The Other Side of the Wind* as "essentially a terrible but superb fantasy inflicted on reality, an outrage, an imposition on friends and followers, a test of his authority. It was a Xanadu—a place no one can go to but which no one should forget. *The Other Side of the Wind* was always, in Welles's mind, a monstrous, ruined film, an impossibility such as only greatness could command. . . . There are creations, works and wonders that are more significant in their nonexistence, their disappearance and their shadow than in being there."

It's worth noting that only in the film world, and more specifically in the American film industry, where such large sums of money are at stake, does an "unfinished" work provoke such opprobrium. Painters and writers and composers typically have drawers or trunks or closets full of half-finished projects; seldom are they chastised for not completing those works unless the lack of completion becomes a dominant theme in their careers. And sometimes not even then: Kafka is celebrated, not reviled, for the novels he left unfinished and wanted destroyed after his death. Schubert is honored for his *Unfinished Symphony* and Mozart for his *Requiem*, which a pupil completed; and part of the appeal of Fitzgerald's posthumously published novel *The Last Tycoon* is that it was left tantalizingly unfinished, like *The Castle* by Kafka, which Welles wanted to film, settling on *The Trial* instead.

Other artists have had creative blocks in later life. Hemingway had trouble finishing his novels; Dashiell Hammett had trouble starting his. Welles's later years were a cornucopia by comparison. But recurring incompletion became the dominant theme in his career, a mystery to his admirers and a standard complaint of his detractors. He was handicapped by working in an expensive, collaborative, highly commercialized medium. Welles could shoot his handmade movies largely at his own pace, but getting them to market was another issue. Nor was he granted the luxury afforded to artists in other media of choosing to keep some of his work private.

Somewhat disingenuously, Welles publicly tried to oversimplify the problem to his own advantage, claiming in 1981, "I have two main projects which are unfinished. One is *The Other Side of the Wind* and when I tell you that my partner in that project is the brother-in-law of the late Shah of Iran, you will understand why we are having a little legal difficulty. The other unfinished film is *Don Quixote*, which was a private exercise of mine, and it will be finished as an author would finish it—in my own good time, when I feel like it. It is not unfinished because of financial reasons. And when it is released, its title is going to be *When Are You Going To Finish* Don Quixote*?*"

It's seldom considered that there may have been a part of Welles that positively *reveled* in his tendency toward incompletion. After being burned so many times by the commercial system, he may have felt, perhaps subconsciously, that it was a gesture of defiance against the accepted way of doing things in an overcommercialized culture. Ironically, even *Citizen Kane* almost went unreleased (because of its controversial similarities to the life of the powerful publisher William Randolph Hearst) and has a leitmotif of incompletion. The Samuel Coleridge poem "Kubla Khan," perhaps the most famously unfinished work of art, is quoted in the newsreel sequence as the source for the name of Kane's estate, Xanadu ("In Xanadu did Kubla Khan / A stately pleasure dome decree"). The allusion offers a gloss on Kane's obsession with accumulating money and objects and his inability to find any kind of satisfying resolution for his public and private lives. As Joseph Cotten's Jed Leland tells the newsreel reporter, "He never finished it. He never finished anything, except my notice [his bad review of Susan Alexander Kane's opera singing]." The film's bleak images of the elderly Kane in his cavernously lonely Xanadu were seen by some as prophetic of Welles's later years, however tenuous the other connections between Welles and Kane were, and those scenes certainly helped mold the public image of the older Welles.

Leaving films unfinished or keeping them in a perpetual work-in-progress state may have been a declaration of independence, Welles's protest against the shackles of the commercial system that had failed and rejected him. Here again he resembled Kane in his grandeur and isolation: "He was disappointed in the world," says Leland, "so he built one of his own." Defiantly declaring that it was none of anyone's business but his own when *Don Quixote* would be finished was Welles's way of cocking a snook at the commodification of art, which he attacks in *F for Fake*. An unfinished work can be seen as a postmodernist statement foregrounding the external circumstances surrounding the work and inviting the audience to join in the process of completion, real or imaginary, as Welles does in *F for Fake* by literally inviting the audience to join him in the editing room. He wanted the public to pay attention to the central importance of the artistic process rather than fetishizing the result.

"I never go to see my movies once they're finished," Welles explained, "because they're on film, in a tin can and can never be changed. If you direct a play, it's opened, and if you see it again after it's been running awhile, and you don't like it too well, you can take the cast and say, 'Well, we'll have a rehearsal tomorrow, we'll rewrite that scene, we'll play that a little differently,' but a movie is locked up forever."

But if Welles occasionally abandoned film projects, he did so less frequently than supposed. On the contrary, his life is replete with evidence of his dogged tenacity in sticking with favorite subjects and projects in various media. Welles had a proclivity for continually reworking not only his unfinished films but even those that had already been released. He spent years trying to raise completion money for *It's All True;* revised his *Macbeth* and *Othello* for reissues; reedited parts of *Othello* many years later for his documentary *Filming "Othello";* and in the 1960s announced plans to reshoot the lost ending of *The Magnificent Ambersons* with the same actors, by then realistically aged into their roles (the project had to be abandoned after Agnes Moorehead died in 1974).

"Why, one may ask, did Welles, do this?" Rosenbaum asks about Welles's constant tinkering. "Because he loved to work, one might surmise, and because for him all work was work-in-progress—both reasons helping to explain why he often wound up having to finance much of the work himself. To love the process of work to this degree evidently offends certain aspects of the Protestant work ethic."

Consciously or not, Welles left his body of work in a largely unfinished state in order to keep it alive, to keep his admirers wondering about his intentions, and to invite them to collaborate on his films after his death. It was a clever way to assure the legendary status of such films as *Don Quixote* and *The Other Side of the Wind* and keep people puzzling over and writing about his work. Maintaining his oeuvre as a perpetual work in progress assured that Welles's career would never be finished, that his legacy, like the work of the child prodigy he was, would forever be seen as "promising."

The story of the last fifteen years of his life is a saga of untiring work, dedication, creativity, and indomitable courage in the face of overwhelming obstacles placed before him by a society that tragically undervalues its great artists. My investigation of that part of Welles's story will, I hope, not only bring to light his bold departures in old age from what was expected of the former "boy wonder" but will also prompt a reconsideration of the shallow and clichéd views of his entire life and artistic legacy. And to fully answer the question "What ever happened to Orson Welles?" we need to look back to the beginnings of his film career, to uncover the still largely unknown story of what caused him to be ostracized as a director by the major studios. By closely examining those events, we can finally understand what led Welles on the circuitous journey from *Citizen Kane* to *The Other Side of the Wind.* Perhaps the young man who made a masterpiece with his first feature and the old man who was unable to finish his last major work were not so far apart in their audacity.

“Rosebud”: The themes of death and lost Eden preoccupied Welles throughout his career. His first feature, *Citizen Kane*, begins with his character’s death, conveyed in the slow-motion dropping of the glass ball representing Charles Foster Kane’s memories of childhood (frame enlargement). *(RKO Radio Pictures)*

Chapter Two

"COMMITTING MASTERPIECES"

Showmanship in Place of Genius: A New Deal at RKO.

—RKO trade advertisement after Welles's firing, 1942

In *F for Fake*, Welles wryly tells the story of a fictitious painter of fake Picassos. Challenged by Picasso about his transgression, the painter asks what is his crime, "Committing masterpieces?" It's hard not to regard this mot as a commentary by Welles on his own checkered career in the Hollywood marketplace. During the early 1940s, he gave RKO two of the greatest films ever made, only to have the first almost burned by the other Hollywood studios to appease the Hearst empire (in a sad irony, the negative of *Citizen Kane* was destroyed in a studio vault fire in 1970) and his second feature, *The Magnificent Ambersons*, hacked to pieces by RKO. And while directing his third film for the studio, his South American documentary, *It's All True*, he was fired and the film itself was aborted. Some of the footage was actually dumped years later into the Pacific Ocean.

Such a nightmarish denouement could stand as an allegory for the shameful way artists too often are treated in America. What happened to Welles in his early years in Hollywood was at the root of all his later troubles. Yet to many film industry apologists, Welles's crime was not "committing masterpieces" but not playing the Hollywood game with sufficient enthusiasm and guile, or being insufficiently willing to prostitute his art. He was stigmatized as a negative example of what an American artist should be: uncommercial and unconventional, a bad businessman, and a maker of "difficult" works for marginal audiences. Hence the contemptuous blend of indifference, mockery, and outright vilification that became the party line on Welles in Hollywood and the press, fed by the RKO publicity department to justify the firing of a man who just sixteen months earlier had inspired novelist John O'Hara to write in *Newsweek:*

> It is with exceeding regret that your faithful bystander reports that he has just seen a picture which he thinks must be the best picture he ever saw.
>
> With no less regret he reports that he has just seen the best actor in the history of acting.
>
> Name of picture: *Citizen Kane.*
>
> Name of actor: Orson Welles.
>
> Reason for regret: you, my dear, may never see the picture. . . . Do yourself a favor. Go to your neighborhood exhibitor and ask him why he isn't showing *Citizen Kane.*

❖ ❖ ❖

When Welles came to Hollywood at age twenty-four, he had already conquered the theater and radio. The surest barometer of celebrity in those days was the cover of *Time* magazine, and Welles had his face on the cover of *Time* in May 1938, when he had just turned twenty-three. Befitting his precocious preoccupation with old age, he made his appearance engulfed in makeup and whiskers as George Bernard Shaw's octogenarian Captain Shotover in *Heartbreak House*, a Mercury Theatre production in which Welles was then starring on the New York stage. Describing him as a "marvelous boy" who had shaken up both radio and the theater with his innovative talent and creative energy, *Time* accurately observed that "the sky is the only limit his ambitions recognize."

Five months later, Welles caused a panic throughout the country with his CBS Radio version of H. G. Wells's novel about interplanetary war, *The War of the Worlds.* Satirizing the American public's susceptibility to radio fearmongers, Welles did the show as a faux newscast, interrupting a phony dance program with breathless bulletins about Martians landing in New Jersey. The fakery was surprisingly convincing to many members of the public, who took to the streets and hills in terror. Angry voices were raised, demanding that Welles be held accountable for his prank. The country's anxiety over the Munich crisis was seen as the underlying cause for the panic Welles triggered; Adolf Hitler described the incident as an example of how easy it was to terrorize the American public, and Welles later claimed that his prank had the serious intent of demonstrating the country's susceptibility to demagoguery.

The notoriety from the event proved beneficial to Welles's career. His *Mercury Theatre on the Air* found sponsorship as *The Campbell Play-*

house, and he was now a household name. The offers to make movies became more enticing, particularly when the calamitous failure of his grandiose 1939 Shakespearean stage production, *Five Kings*, left him short of money, impelling him to seek a lucrative deal in a new medium. He intended to resume the production of *Five Kings* with some of his movie proceeds. According to his oldest daughter, Christopher Welles Feder, Welles disregarded the urging of his first wife, Virginia Nicolson, that he stay in the New York theater, although he came to believe, much later, that Virginia had been right.

I asked Welles in 1971 if he regretted anything about the *War of the Worlds* broadcast. "*Regret?*" he snapped. "What's there to regret?" I was thinking of how that incident eclipsed so many more substantial achievements of his career. But I was too intimidated to say so. Today, however, the broadcast can be viewed with a more nuanced perspective. Welles offered a wry observation on how it affected him. In his 1974 documentary *F for Fake*, he re-creates the *War of the Worlds* broadcast (fittingly, by faking it) and relates what happened in its aftermath: "I didn't go to jail—I went to Hollywood."

❖ ❖ ❖

François Truffaut observed in 1959 that what makes *Citizen Kane* so special is that "it is the only 'first' film directed by a famous man." As a result, Welles "was forced to make not a film which permitted him to get started in the industry, but THE film, the one which sums up and prefigures all the others. And, my God, this mad gamble was very nearly won." But schadenfreude has always been one of the favorite pastimes of Hollywood, and the burden of expectations placed upon Welles at the beginning was so great that it made his fall from grace virtually inevitable.

From childhood, he was expected to be a great man, as if he had little choice in the matter. Perhaps that legacy was what led to his deep affinity with Shakespeare's tragedies, and to his characteristic sense of fatalism. Even Welles's earliest films are shadowed by that precocious obsession with tragedy and mortality. In *The Hearts of Age* (1934), a short amateur film he made when he was nineteen, Welles plays Death, playfully taunting an old lady with portents of hanging, bells tolling, and burial. His first feature begins with his own character's death, then circles back fatalistically to chronicle Kane's tragic downfall from blighted childhood to lonely old age. "Mr. Kane was a man who lost almost everything he had," one character observes, and another says, "That's Charlie's story—how he lost it."

But at the time of his astonishing debut as a Hollywood director, even that precociously tragic perspective could not have enabled Welles to imagine his own fate in the movie business. Even taking into account his status as a boy genius and the resultant hostility he provoked from the outset in Hollywood, how could he have envisioned his future in the film capital, which would bring such final ignominies as narrating the trailer for *Revenge of the Nerds* or playing the voice of Planet Unicron in an animated film, *The Transformers*? Part of him, though, realized that *Kane* would remain his moment of greatest triumph—and that it held the seeds of destruction for his Hollywood career.

"I started at the top," he said, "and have been going downhill ever since."

❖ ❖ ❖

Hollywood studios at first wanted Welles only as an actor, not as a director. He resisted the offers until he could dictate his own terms. In the summer of 1939, he chose one from RKO Radio Pictures, a second-tier studio that needed the prestige that accompanied him. RKO's fortunes, along with those of much of the film industry, had plummeted during the early years of the Depression. In 1933, the studio went into equity receivership under the provisions of the federal Bankruptcy Act allowing the reorganization of companies under court supervision. RKO did not emerge from receivership until 1940. By offering relative creative freedom to several major directors, RKO had lured them to make some notable films in the 1930s, including John Ford's film of the Liam O'Flaherty novel *The Informer*, Howard Hawks's screwball comedy *Bringing Up Baby*, and George Stevens's Fred Astaire–Ginger Rogers musical *Swing Time*. But by 1939, the Astaire-Rogers cycle was winding down, and the studio coffers were strained by Stevens's production of *Gunga Din*, whose cost overruns made it the most expensive film RKO had ever made. RKO needed another infusion of creative power to keep it from returning to receivership.

Welles's two-picture contract, signed on July 21, 1939, guaranteed a degree of creative freedom that, while not unprecedented, was highly unusual within the studio system. He benefited from the enlightened patronage of studio president George J. Schaefer. Schaefer, who came from the East Coast distribution side of the business, had been recruited from Paramount by Nelson Rockefeller, a major RKO stockholder, shortly before the *War of the Worlds* broadcast and had been encouraged to find fresh talent in New York. But hiring the daring and controversial Welles, who was sure to take an unorthodox approach to Hollywood filmmaking, was a major gamble for a new studio president.

Welles's first official project at RKO, an adaptation of Joseph Conrad's 1899 novella, *Heart of Darkness*, was canceled in preproduction after Welles shot a day of test footage. The budget exceeded the studio's parameters, particularly with the loss of the European market due to the outbreak of World War II. Welles conceived of the film as an antifascist allegory: "The picture is, frankly, an attack on the Nazi system." He had many fresh ideas about employing a first-person approach to the story, inspired by his *First Person Singular* radio style. He wanted to use a subjective camera with only his offscreen voice playing Marlow, the story's narrator (Welles was also planning to play the evil embodiment of colonialism, Kurtz).

Continuing to pursue antifascist themes, Welles then proposed a comedy-thriller, *The Smiler with the Knife*, based on the novel by Nicholas Blake (British poet C. Day Lewis) about a couple who discover a secret fascist plot to seize power in England. Welles's adaptation transposed the story to the United States, reshaped the leader of the plot in the image of aviator-industrialist Howard Hughes, and included a Hearst-like character described in Welles's notes as "W. N. Howells, the great newspaper publisher, also to be avoided in dark alleys." Welles wrote a screenplay from another British novel, *The Way to Santiago* by Arthur Calder-Marshall, which would have been filmed in Mexico. Welles was to have played an amnesiac mistaken for a fascist radio commentator (resembling the Nazi propagandist William Joyce, known as "Lord Haw-Haw"), whose jungle radio station he seizes to broadcast a warning to the world. But RKO agreed to none of these projects.

Welles's perceived inactivity for his first several months in Hollywood—despite his efforts in preparing those three unmade pictures—provoked a new spate of negative remarks. "Do you remember way back when a chap from the Mercury Theatre named Orson Welles was going to make a picture?" joked the *Hollywood Reporter*, and radio gossip Jimmy Fidler gloated, "Ha! They're saying Orson Welles has increased his production schedule. Instead of *not* making three pics for RKO, he'll *not* make five!" A sympathetic three-part profile of Welles in the *Saturday Evening Post* by Alva Johnston and Fred Smith in January-February 1940 satirized the already apparent, bizarrely precipitous tendency to regard Welles as a failure: "Some of the oldest acquaintances of Welles have been disappointed in his career. They see the twenty-four-year-old boy of today as a mere shadow of the two-year-old man they used to know."

Welles's inability to get a picture off the ground even sparked interest at the Federal Bureau of Investigation. A 1943 FBI report summarizing information received earlier by the bureau states, "During the years 1939 and 1940 when Welles was first associated with the RKO pictures [*sic*], it is reported he was extremely intimate with [deleted]. This same source states that RKO pictures did not produce any of the scripts written by Welles [deleted] during that period because the subject matter of the same was considered to be too far 'leftist' to be used by the studio." This claim is unverified, but no doubt there was some political timidity behind the studio's repeated rejections of his antifascist projects, since Hollywood was hesitant to deal with the European situation before the United States entered the war in 1941.

More than thematic daring was at the root of Welles's early troubles in Hollywood, however. "Welles was hated in Hollywood long before he'd made a movie; he was hated almost upon his arrival," Pauline Kael pointed out. "From time to time, Hollywood used to work up considerable puerile resentment against 'outsiders' who dared to make movies. The scope of Welles' reputation seems to have infuriated Hollywood; it was a cultural reproach from the East, and the Hollywood people tried to protect themselves by closing ranks and making Welles a butt of their humor." Welles's difficulties getting RKO to agree on a project added fuel to this hostility.

A particular object of scorn in Hollywood was Welles's beard. The beard even inspired an F. Scott Fitzgerald short story published in the May 1940 issue of *Esquire*, "Pat Hobby and Orson Welles." Using the forlorn figure of Hobby, a hack screenwriter, to reflect his own bitter struggles in Hollywood, Fitzgerald satirizes the fear and hostility Hollywood displayed toward Welles. Hobby has paranoid delusions that his problems finding work are the result of Welles coming to town. When Hobby begs a pass to a studio lot, a veteran studio executive named Marcus tries to fob him off by saying, "Just now I've got things on my mind. I'm going to a luncheon. They want I should meet this new Orson Welles that's in Hollywood." The story continues:

> Pat's heart winced. There it was again—that name, sinister and remorseless, spreading like a dark cloud over all his skies.
>
> "Mr. Marcus," he said so sincerely that his voice trembled, "I wouldn't be surprised if Orson Welles is the biggest menace that's come to Hollywood

> for years. He gets a hundred and fifty grand a picture, and I wouldn't be surprised if he were so radical that you had to have all new equipment and start all over again like you did with sound in 1928."
>
> "Oh my God!" groaned Mr. Marcus.
>
> "And me," said Pat, "All I want is a pass and no money—to leave things as they are."

Film critic and screenwriter F. X. Feeney observes, "*To leave things as they are.* The dark heart of our industry is in that line." Fitzgerald captures the absurd hysteria provoked among the fearful slaves to the studio system by the brash young "radical" in their midst. The notorious beard was a potent, all-purpose symbol of intellectualism, bohemianism, eccentricity, effeminacy, and, more subtly, of un-American, "Red" tendencies. Welles, for his part, cultivated Hollywood enemies with reckless insouciance, tweaking their prejudices with mischievous glee. He arrived in Hollywood wearing the beard he had grown for his 1939 vaudeville show *The Green Goddess,* planning to wear it on-screen as Kurtz, and once he realized the facial hair irritated people, he kept it. What really rankled Hollywood, far more than the beard, was the twenty-four-year-old's rampant creative potency and his relative freedom from traditional studio constraints.

It's often said, erroneously, that Welles was the first person in Hollywood ever to have full artistic control over his own films. That ignores Charles Chaplin, who had complete autonomy because he was rich enough to pay for his own films and co-owned his distribution company, United Artists. And though Welles won the rare concession of final cut on *Citizen Kane,* he still had to bow to censorship demands, and he needed story, budget, and cast approval for all his projects at RKO. Because of the difficulties with getting the studio to agree on his first project, Welles had to renegotiate his contract repeatedly, agreeing to make a third film without salary and surrendering final cut on his second feature, *The Magnificent Ambersons,* a concession that proved disastrous. But the widespread perception of his initial contract was close enough to the truth to have antagonized many envious people when Welles swept into town, attended by squads of reporters buffing his larger-than-life media image. "I would have hated myself too," he joked in retrospect.

❖ ❖ ❖

Once *Kane* was under way in the summer of 1940, it was supported fully by George Schaefer, who lived up to his promise to allow Welles creative freedom and then bravely defied the forces that wanted the film suppressed. But the trouble between Welles and RKO began well before *Kane*. In fact, according to Reginald Armour, Schaefer's right-hand man in Hollywood, Welles's position at the studio was always tenuous. Armour's revelation to longtime Welles assistant Richard Wilson in an early 1980s interview throws a strikingly different light on Welles's eventual downfall at RKO: "From the very beginning on *Citizen Kane*, Orson was a marked man. I don't think that the board really approved the original Orson deal. I never saw the actual contract for Orson, but I'm pretty certain that the board were not too enthusiastic about it, because they kept on, question after question, after Orson arrived from Hollywood." Years after Welles's firing, Armour met up with him again in Italy: "I found him mellowed and not too bitter about the RKO experience, and speaking very highly of George Schaefer. But he said that it had 'ruined him' because even then, *Citizen Kane* had not been played in London and a number of other places."

Welles was an instinctive, inveterate troublemaker, a lifelong challenge to establishments of any kind. From New York to Hollywood, South America to Europe, wherever he worked he came crashing up against the powers that be. His progressive, antifascist, and pro-black political stands and his refusal to be confined within conventional boundaries of either "art" or "entertainment" made him seem dangerous to political and cultural czars and to supporters of the status quo from both ends of the political and cultural spectrum. Whether it was Welles's particular glory to be such a maverick or whether it was a case of "self-destructive genius" depends upon one's point of view toward artists and their relationship to society.

Not content with challenging the Hollywood establishment at its own game, Welles went out of his way to defy one of the lions of the American media. He took on the aging yet still mighty media magnate William Randolph Hearst, whose papers had immense power to flatter, promote, and intimidate Hollywood. Welles's Hollywood career never recovered from the battle over releasing *Citizen Kane*.* And its ramifications helped account for the unusual shape of his post-Hollywood career. John Huston noted that Welles's problems with the film industry stemmed from the fact that he "offended the establishment in two ways" with *Kane*.

---

* The 1995 documentary *The Battle over "Citizen Kane"* speciously tries to draw political and personality parallels between Hearst, the fascist media baron, and Welles, the progressive artist.

Because the film angered Hearst and his minions, Hollywood "went about detracting Orson" even before it was completed, in order to placate the publishing and movie magnate. "And then Orson had the arrogance and downright insolence to have made the movie a great success." Welles, said Huston, "violated two cardinal rules. First, you're not supposed to go against the establishment. And if you *do* go against the establishment, you're supposed to suffer."

Welles did, in fact, suffer. His daring—or hubris—in mounting such a bold attack on entrenched economic and cultural power with *Citizen Kane* caused lasting damage to his career. In what he called "my hot youth," how much did he conceive of *Kane* as a calculated effrontery? How much naïveté was in his attitude, how much defiance of the gods, how much self-destructiveness? Was he a young man whose political zeal exceeded his sense of self-preservation? Where does the line between courage and self-destruction blur?

❖ ❖ ❖

Welles and veteran screenwriter Herman J. Mankiewicz, a former journalist, jointly came up with the story idea and basic structure for *Citizen Kane* in early 1941. They share screenplay credit on *Kane*, with Mankiewicz in first position, but that joint credit became a major issue in 1971 when Pauline Kael published her two-part *New Yorker* essay "Raising Kane." She claimed that Welles had little to do with writing the film and had tried to usurp credit from Mankiewicz; Welles responded in a letter to the *Times* of London that Mankiewicz had unjustly sought sole credit. Bogdanovich came to Welles's defense in a 1972 *Esquire* article, "The *Kane* Mutiny," which, according to Jonathan Rosenbaum and Oja Kodar, actually was written by Welles himself (Bogdanovich has admitted that Welles took "a strong hand in revising and rewriting" the article). During the shooting of *The Other Side of the Wind* and soon after Kael's essay appeared, Welles told me that while Mankiewicz was in Victorville working on his draft, he had been writing a separate version in Los Angeles, and that he subsequently combined both versions into the shooting script. This version of events is somewhat at variance with Robert L. Carringer's authoritative research into the various drafts. In his 1985 book *The Making of "Citizen Kane,"* Carringer reports that Welles's extensive rewriting took place only after Mankiewicz had written the first two drafts. Nevertheless, the two men had substantial story conferences before any script was written, and Carringer's research makes clear that each man amply deserved his joint screenplay credit.

In my 1968 book *Persistence of Vision,* I discuss the differences between the screenplay of *Kane* and the film itself, as well as the similarities and differences between the film and the life of Hearst. I note that Welles played down Mankiewicz's contributions to the script by claiming that Mankiewicz was responsible only for "several important scenes" and for Rosebud.* Andrew Sarris has pointed out that I gave Mankiewicz the first sustained critical attention he ever received for his work on the film. That seems ironic since Kael's "Raising Kane" singled out for ridicule my writing on *Kane* by indirectly quoting a couple of my phrases as examples of ludicrous highbrow commentary. Kael wrote:

> It is difficult to explain what makes any great work great, and particularly difficult with movies, and maybe more so with *Citizen Kane* than with other great movies, because it isn't a work of special depth or a work of subtle beauty. It is a shallow work, a *shallow* masterpiece. Those who try to account for its stature as a film by claiming it to be profound are simply dodging the problem—or maybe they don't recognize that there is one. . . . Apparently, the easiest thing for people to do when they recognize that something is a work of art is to trot out the proper schoolbook terms for works of art, and there are articles on *Citizen Kane* that call it a tragedy in fugal form and articles that explain that the hero of *Citizen Kane* is time—time being a proper sort of modern hero for an important picture. But to use the conventional schoolbook explanations for greatness, and pretend that it's profound, is to miss what makes it such an American triumph—that it manages to create something aesthetically exciting and durable out of the playfulness of American muckraking satire.

As the sole author of all those offending "articles" (actually just one modest piece in *Film Heritage,* which I rewrote for my 1972 book on Welles), I plead guilty to what Woody Allen once labeled "jejunosity." Yet I still prefer my earnest and impassioned attempt to come to grips with *Kane*'s intricately structured network of themes and imagery to Kael's philistine condescension toward a great film. Kael's underlying motive in attacking Welles seemed to be to undermine the auteur theory, which she had been ridiculing for years, particularly in its American im-

* In *This Is Orson Welles,* Welles was more generous to his collaborator, stating, "Mankiewicz's contribution? It was enormous. . . . The actual writing came only after lots of talk, naturally . . . just the two of us, yelling at each other—not too angrily." Bogdanovich places this conversation during the filming of *Catch-22* in Mexico in the summer of 1969, more than a year and a half before Kael's piece was published.

portation by Sarris. If the film usually considered the greatest ever made were to be seen as more the product of a writer than of its director—and if that writer could be shown to have been cheated of credit by the director—the case for auteurism would be largely demolished. Kael did her polemical work smoothly enough that even today people who know better continue to swallow her unscholarly claims.

The day the first installment of her essay appeared in the *New Yorker*, I received a call out of the blue from Pauline Kael. She said she hoped I wasn't offended that she made fun of me and hadn't cited me by name. She explained that her editor, William Shawn, had curbed her previous fondness for quoting other critics mockingly; Shawn allowed her to do so, she said, only sparingly and without using names. I assured her I wasn't bothered by her ridicule but wondered why her argument against Welles was so one-sided. She explained that she had deliberately avoided speaking with Welles or with his partisans because she knew from Welles's past statements what he would say, and because his partisans were "emotionally involved" in the dispute. She admitted she had written "a brief for Mankiewicz."

I brooded over the motive behind Kael's phone call for several weeks, finally concluding that she had hoped to placate me in order to head off a public response to her essay. When "Raising Kane" was reprinted as a companion to the screenplay in her 1971 volume *The "Citizen Kane" Book*,* I wrote a response, "Rough Sledding with Pauline Kael," for that fall's issue of *Film Heritage.* Pointing out that she had even scanted the importance of Welles's *direction* of the screenplay, I also called attention to evidence that contradicted her conclusions about his supposed usurpation of credit for the screenplay. One of the pieces of evidence, ironically, was a quote from Welles's former producing partner in the New York theater, John Houseman, who later admitted that he was a major source for Kael's attack. Houseman served as Mankiewicz's editor during the writing of *Kane* and, as Welles acknowledged, made important contributions of his own to the script. Houseman recalled in 1969 that after he and Mankiewicz finished their work, "Orson took over and visualized the script. He added a great deal of material himself, and later he and Herman had a

* It's a lamentable irony that the screenplays of Welles's first two features have been published with introductions attacking the man principally responsible for these two great films. Carringer's 1993 book on *The Magnificent Ambersons* perversely allots more blame for the film's mutilation to Welles than to RKO.

dreadful row over the screen credit. As far as I could judge, the co-billing was correct. The *Citizen Kane* script was the product of both of them."

❖ ❖ ❖

While RKO and Welles were still arguing over the final budget for *Citizen Kane*, Welles cannily started shooting three days of "test scenes" on June 29, 1940. Unlike the test scenes he had shot for *Heart of Darkness*, which were intended to work out the first-person shooting style, those for *Kane* comprised three entire sequences of the picture: the projection room, Susan's nightclub, and Susan's suicide attempt. Presented with such an impressive fait accompli, Schaefer officially greenlighted the film. Though Welles quickly showed his mastery of the film medium, he still had a few things to learn. For the first few days, following his practice in the theater, he arranged the lights, until a crew member told him that that was the job of the cinematographer, Gregg Toland. Toland, who had offered his services to Welles by saying "I want to work with somebody who never made a movie," had been following Welles around the set, silently signaling adjustments to the crew.

Most of the cast members were new to motion pictures. Paul Stewart, a Mercury radio veteran who played Raymond the butler, told me how nervous he was the first time he appeared before a movie camera. It was for his introductory close-up as he lights a cigarette in the gloomy Great Hall of Xanadu and says to the newsreel reporter, "Rosebud? I tell you about Rosebud—how much is it worth to you?" Just before Welles rolled the camera, he leaned in close and said, "Remember, Paul, when this movie comes out, your face will be forty feet high on the screen of the Radio City Music Hall." That piece of direction, intended to keep Stewart's expression restrained, was the worst possible advice Welles could have given, the actor said, because it caused him to freeze up entirely. When the camera rolled, Stewart forgot what he was supposed to say and blurted out, "*Goldberg?* I tell you about Goldberg."

Too bad that moment of hilarity wasn't depicted in the 1999 cable-TV docudrama about the making of *Kane*, *RKO 281*. With its grim portrait of Welles as a megalomaniac, it fails to capture the general atmosphere—a mingling of intense labor with prankish fun—that surrounded the making of any Welles film. But such a distorted portrait fits the conventional view of Welles's life as a Greek tragedy rather than the Shakespearean tragicomedy it more closely resembles.

❖ ❖ ❖

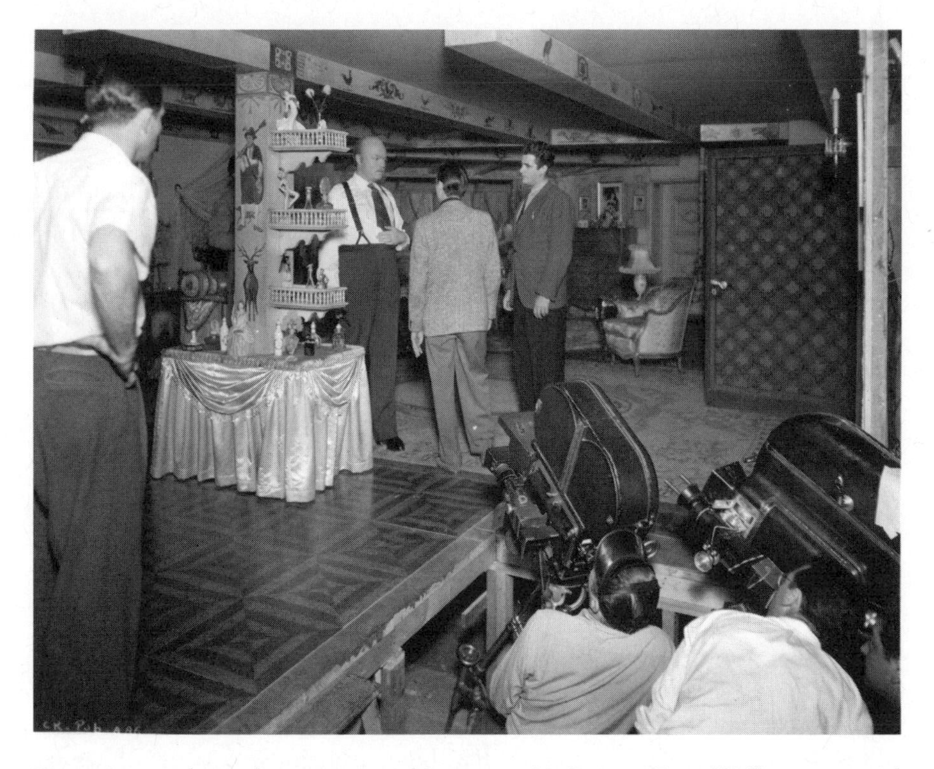

Preparing to shoot the room-smashing scene in *Citizen Kane,* Welles, costumed as Kane, confers with his great cinematographer Gregg Toland. The camera operators are positioned below floor level, at Wellesian low angles. *(RKO Radio Pictures)*

"Movies should be rough," Welles told me when we first met in 1970. That was the film credo of his later years, but it surprised me because it came from the man who began his feature-directing career with perhaps the most fanatically *perfect* film ever made.

Kane is a dazzling tour de force devoted to demonstrating, as if in a conjurer's trick, that there was nothing behind the curtain of the spectacular life of Charles Foster Kane, the quintessential twentieth-century "hollow man." Much of *Kane* is artifice: miniatures and matte paintings combined on the optical printer with live action, composite shots (including some of the most famous instances of "deep focus" photography) created by optically combining images. Welles resorted to those devices partly because of the challenge of making a large-scale movie about American politics and media, spanning a seventy-eight-year period, on a relatively modest budget. But he also fell in love with the creative possibilities offered by the optical printer, according to RKO special effects creator Linwood G. Dunn, who carried out Welles's elaborate demands. The film's labyrinthine structure and intricate visual stylization reinforce its corrosive satire of media-fabricated imagery, political deception, and the illusion of worldly grandeur.

In his subsequent work, however, Welles departed radically from the *Kane* model of film as objet d'art and spent the rest of his career as a director celebrating the importance of inspired accident, spontaneity, and emotion.

❖ ❖ ❖

The premiere of *Citizen Kane* on May 1, 1941, at the Palace Theater in New York City was not only an artistic triumph for the twenty-five-year-old wunderkind but also a victory over the Hearst empire's attempt to stop the film's release. The impresario Billy Rose told Welles, "Quit, kid. You'll never top it. Quit while you're ahead." Telling Bogdanovich that story, Welles said, "You know, maybe he was right." The battle with Hearst over *Citizen Kane* proved a Pyrrhic victory in which lay the source of all Welles's subsequent career problems.

In trying to suppress the film, Hearst dealt primarily with MGM studio chief Louis B. Mayer. Hearst had been a business partner of Mayer when the publisher's Cosmopolitan Studios, which often featured his mistress, Marion Davies, made films in conjunction with MGM. Under pressure of blackmail from Hearst and acting on behalf of all the major studios, Mayer offered to pay RKO $800,000, a little less than the production cost of *Citizen Kane*, if it would allow the negative of Welles's film to be burned.

Hearst subscribed to the canard that the words "Communist" and "Jew" were virtually synonymous, and his threats of blackmail against Hollywood executives if *Kane* were released included raising the specter of anti-Semitic publicity. Herman Mankiewicz recalled, "Mr. Hearst casually gave them [the studio chiefs] a hundred examples of unfavorable news—rape by executives, drunkenness, miscegenation and allied sports—which on direct appeal from Hollywood he had kept out of his papers in the last fifteen years. General observations were made—not by Mr. Hearst but by high-placed Hearst subordinates—that the portion of Jews in the industry was a bit high and it might not always be possible to conceal this fact from the American public." Hollywood's sheltering of refugees from Nazism was a particular target of the nativist, isolationist publisher. The *New York Times* reported in January 1941 that Hearst representatives "began an investigation of the alien situation in Hollywood, something about which the industry is most sensitive. In making their inquiries, they explained that the information was being gathered for Mr. Hearst's private use." The Hollywood establishment was terrified by Hearst's threats and angered at Welles for provoking them. With such double-barreled opposition, only the staunch support of Schaefer and Welles's own persuasive powers, including the threat of a lawsuit against RKO, saved *Kane* from destruction.*

Robert Wise told me about listening to Welles giving what Wise considered his "greatest performance" during the battle to get *Kane* released. In a projection room at New York's Radio City Music Hall, Welles convinced the heads of RKO and the other major studios, as well as their lawyers, to allow *Kane* to be released. Welles did so by urging them not to give in to the enemies of free speech and democracy at a time when fascism was threatening the future of the world. The scene is dramatized in *RKO 281*, with John Logan's script and Liev Schreiber's performance capturing the passion Welles radiated on that occasion. But *RKO 281* undercuts Welles by inventing a scene of Schaefer asking Welles if he really meant what he said about freedom of speech and Welles giving an equivocal reply. Doubting Welles's sincerity on this point flies in the face of all the evidence of his antifascist political beliefs and his unbending commitment to seeing *Kane* released.

Nevertheless, Hearst instituted an edict against RKO advertising in his papers, which were forbidden to review the studio's pictures or mention RKO in their news columns. RKO had difficulty finding theaters willing to play *Kane*, so the film did not earn back its cost until many years later. Welles was forever stigmatized as a loose cannon in the eyes of both the studios and the press, and thanks to Hearst he fell under the baleful watch of J. Edgar Hoover's FBI.

❖ ❖ ❖

---

* Theatrical prints struck after the negative was destroyed in the 1970 vault fire, including those made by Paramount for the fiftieth-anniversary theatrical reissue in 1991 (with timing supervised by the film's editor, Robert Wise), lack much of the luster of the original. But for the 2001 DVD release, Warner Home Video went back to 1940s nitrate materials—principally a 1941 fine-grain interpositive—and utilized digital restoration techniques, with remarkably good results. Details of Toland's cinematography I had never seen before are visible in this DVD edition.

British film critic Laura Mulvey's 1992 monograph on *Kane* focuses attention on its antifascist themes, which have received far less attention than its formal aspects or the controversy over its roman à clef exposure of Hearst's private life. Welles scathingly satirizes Kane's hobnobbing with Hitler and other dictators while the publisher smugly assures the public that "there'll be no war." Mulvey notes that the film reflects "the battle between intervention and isolationism [that] was bitterly engaged in America, with President Roosevelt unable to swing the nation into support for his interventionist policy. . . . Not only was the war in Europe the burning public issue of the time, it was of passionate personal importance to Orson Welles, with his deep involvement with European culture and his long-standing political commitment to Roosevelt's New Deal and the anti-fascist struggle. . . . In the rhetoric of *Citizen Kane*, the destiny of isolationism is realised in metaphor: in Kane's own fate, dying wealthy and lonely, surrounded by the detritus of European culture and history."

Such a frontal and radical attack on Hearst and all he represented both personally and politically could hardly have failed to produce an equally intense response. The anger of Hearst and his organization was kindled partly by the caricature of the publisher's mistress, Marion Davies, as Kane's "Wife Two, one-time opera-singing" Susan Alexander (Dorothy Comingore), a drunken, no-talent harridan who walks out on her tyrannical husband. It's alleged that "Rosebud" was Hearst's pet name for Davies's pudenda and that it was used as Kane's dying word by Mankiewicz and Welles as a malicious joke on the Old Man's sex life.* The one element of the film Welles regretted was what he called its "libel" of Davies. "I always felt [Hearst] had the right to be upset about that," Welles said. He tried to make amends in 1975 by writing the foreword to Davies's posthumously published autobiography, *The Times We Had: Life with William Randolph Hearst.* Welles called Davies "one of the

---

* Kael speculates that Mankiewicz, as a child, "may or may not" have had a sled bearing the "Rosebud" label and that because he always mourned the loss of a stolen bicycle, he "simply put the emotion of the one onto the other." There's another possible derivation for Kane's last word. In Sinclair Lewis's 1920 novel *Main Street,* the movie theater in Gopher Prairie, Minnesota, is the Rosebud Movie Palace. On the jacket of the first hardcover edition, the theater marquee ("ROSEBUD MOVIE") is displayed behind the silhouetted figure of the heroine, Carol Kennicott. Lewis writes, "In the sensitive art of the Rosebud Movie Palace there is a Message, and humor strictly moral." Stripped of their withering irony toward small-town America, those words could apply to the films of Lewis's fellow midwesterner Orson Welles.

most delightfully accomplished comediennes in the whole history of the screen. She would have been a star if Hearst had never happened. She was also a delightful and very considerable person."

In his youthful zeal and hubris, Welles admittedly failed to anticipate the possibility that his film might be shelved or even destroyed in retaliation for his egregious insult of Hearst and Davies. And he probably did not realize until it was too late that attacking Hearst would bring down the wrath of a whole powerful network of right-wing red-baiters, including the FBI, the Dies committee, and the American Legion, all of which were allied with and supported by the vociferously anti-Communist publisher. The grounds for the battle were clearly drawn in an FBI report: "The evidence before us leads inevitably to the conclusion that the film *Citizen Kane* is nothing more than an extension of the Communist Party's campaign to smear one of its most effective and consistent opponents in the United States."

Citizen Kane satirizes the tendency in American politics to engage in such broad-brush pejoratives. In quick succession, the film shows Kane's wealthy guardian, Walter Parks Thatcher, telling a congressional committee that Kane "is, in fact, nothing more or less than a Communist"; a leftist speaker in New York's Union Square proclaiming that Kane "is today what he has always been and always will be—a fascist"; and Kane himself pompously declaring in a silent newsreel, his words filling the screen in a title card: "I am, have been, and will be only one thing—an American." The reporter for *News on the March*, Thompson, speaks for Welles when he says at the end, "I don't think any word can explain a man's life."

❖ ❖ ❖

Welles had been a bête noire of the Hearst papers long before the controversy over *Citizen Kane*. His progressive political views, expressed in speeches and print, and his politically radical work in the New York theater made him an increasingly prominent and inviting target in the late 1930s. Hearst's *New York American*, which in 1935 hailed the nineteen-year-old Welles as "one of the most promising artists of our day," turned on him after he began mounting plays for the Federal Theatre Project. The New Deal's Works Progress Administration and its Federal Theatre were among the primary targets of Franklin D. Roosevelt's enemies; right-wingers saw both programs as dangerously radical and infested with Communists.

Somewhat defensive in later years about his political views, no doubt from an excess of caution developed during the blacklist period, Welles downplayed the radicalism of his 1937 staging of the Brechtian labor opera *The Cradle Will Rock* and attributed it largely to its composer, Marc Blitzstein. The unproduced (but published) screenplay that Welles wrote in the 1980s about the events surrounding the show's controversial opening deals more with personal than political issues, tending to portray his younger self as dilettantish rather than radical.* "I was only radical because I was showing off," he claimed to biographer Barbara Leaming. "I've never been anything more than a progressive. I allowed myself to be thought of as farther to the left than I was because I didn't want to lose [Blitzstein's] friendship."

In fact, Welles gave every evidence of genuine commitment to progressive ideals during the Popular Front era. He made public appearances for left-wing causes, spoke out on behalf of the New Deal, and championed social equality for African Americans. His and Houseman's Federal Theatre Project 891 and subsequent Mercury Theatre drew much of their support from radicals and progressives and received generally favorable coverage in the Communist newspaper the *Daily Worker*. Welles said at the time that he had been "waiting for a good worker's play; *The Cradle Will Rock* is just that, offering a tale that is ideologically sound and a perfect fusion of music and drama." But political persuasion was not Welles's overriding concern as a director. The manifesto for the Mercury Theatre (written by Houseman but issued in both their names) declared, "While a socially unconscious theater would be intolerable, there will be no substitution of social consciousness for drama."

Welles never abandoned his progressive principles, but his social outlook became more inflected as he matured, and his work as a film director always approached political themes through paradox, examining what Truffaut described as "the angel within the beast, the heart in the monster, the secret of the tyrant. . . . The weakness of the strong, this is the subject that all of Orson Welles' films have in common." Welles also learned to weigh his public statements more cautiously as the American political climate became less hospitable and he fell into the suspect category of "premature antifascist." But despite Welles's later defensiveness about his political evolution and his general aversion to polemics on stage or screen, his artistic career—from such early succès de scandale as the

---

* Tim Robbins claimed he had not read Welles's script before writing and directing his 1999 film *Cradle Will Rock*. See chapter 6 for further discussion of Robbins's and Welles's divergent viewpoints on that pivotal event in the young director's life.

Federal Theatre's "Negro *Macbeth*" and *Citizen Kane* to his adventurous European period of the 1950s and his satire of the dying Hollywood studio system in *The Other Side of the Wind*—was always profoundly radical.

There was no mistaking the radicalism of *The Cradle Will Rock* in 1937, which set the pattern for Welles's career as an artistic and political provocateur whose work mingled controversy, high achievement, and equally spectacular ruination. When the WPA, acting under pressure from reactionaries in Congress, canceled the show and padlocked the theater, Welles led his company and members of the public uptown to the old Venice Theatre. Because Actors Equity forbade the actors to appear onstage, the first public preview was performed with only Blitzstein and his piano on stage and cast members brave enough to perform rising from the audience. In effect, Welles and company made the Federal Theatre live up to its principles, despite the cost. "I was very ambiguous in my feeling, and I wasn't sure that we weren't wrecking the Federal Theatre by what we were doing," he said in retrospect. "But I thought if you padlock a theater, then the argument is closed."

The Federal Theatre was investigated in 1938 by the temporary House Special Committee on Un-American Activities, also known as the Dies committee after its chairman, the reactionary Texas Democrat Martin Dies Jr. (when the committee was made permanent in 1945, its name was changed to the House Committee on Un-American Activities, commonly known as HUAC). The committee charged that the Federal Theatre and another branch of the WPA, the Federal Writers' Project, were "doing more to spread Communist propaganda than the Communist Party itself." Hearst editorialized against the Federal Theatre, contending that "nobody can any longer seriously deny that the stage is prostituted to Communism." The damage done to the Federal Theatre by both the Dies committee and *The Cradle Will Rock* helped hasten the innovative project's demise in June 1939. Welles, however, escaped with his reputation not only intact but enhanced.

❖ ❖ ❖

Hearst was a longtime ally of Dies in opposing Communism and the New Deal. "In many ways Hearst and the [Dies] committee were indeed one and the same," Louis Pizzitola writes in his 2002 book *Hearst over Hollywood: Power, Passion, and Propaganda in the Movies*. "Hearst used the [Motion Picture] Alliance [for the Preservation of American Ideals], his widely read columnists and editorialists, and other operatives such as J. B. Matthews to support the committee, and the committee in turn used its channels to Hearst as sources of information and as a machinery of publicity. A symbiotic relationship was created between Hearst and the committee that advanced Hearst's decades-long crusade against Communism." Hearst pressured the committee to investigate Hollywood, writing of the film industry in a 1940 editorial, "It is not only fashionable to be pink, but profitable too. The screen is almost wholly Technicolor these days, and the favorite Technicolor is rosy red. . . . But still, there is lacking ACTION. Every healthy American movement to expose Communism and to preserve the essential character of the American Government dies when it reaches Washington."

Hearst had been close to J. Edgar Hoover since the early 1930s and energetically promoted the FBI in his publications and newsreels. Hearst also helped supply information to Hoover about suspected Communists and fellow travelers. The American Legion provided crucial support in their anti-Red crusade. The veterans' organization went on to become an integral part of the postwar blacklisting network. The legion supplied names for the Hollywood blacklist, ran a "clearance" program for those willing to capitulate, and promoted boycotts against theaters playing films involving people it deemed subversive. The threat of boycotts was seldom carried out but proved a potent tool against studios fearful of public backlash.

Spurred by the enmity of the Hearst press and the legion, the FBI opened a file on Welles in April 1941 and kept it open until 1956 (the contents of the file were first reported on by Welles scholar James Naremore in his 1991 *Film Comment* article "The Trial: The FBI vs. Orson Welles"). Welles's file—222 pages of which, some partly or wholly redacted, have been released through the Freedom of Information Act—makes clear that the Dies committee and its successor, HUAC, also maintained files on him for many years. The 1948 report of the California senate's Tenney committee—the state legislature's red-baiting "little HUAC," chaired by Jack B. Tenney—listed Welles in connection with eighteen alleged Communist front organizations, dating back as early as 1935. When Hearst died in 1951, Tenney declared, "Much of the success attained by the California Legislative [Senate Fact-Finding] Committee on Un-American Activities was due to his efforts to place the facts before the public."

The FBI investigation of Welles began shortly before the much-delayed release of *Citizen Kane*, which the FBI noted was "violently attacked by the Hearst Syndicate." On April 24, Hoover wrote a memo for Matthew F. McGuire, assistant to the attorney general, stating:

> Information has been received confidentially to the effect that the Dies Committee has collected and correlated information concerning the alleged Communist activities and connections of Orson Welles and [name deleted]. It is reported that Mr. Dies intends to give publicity to the alleged Communist connections of these individuals in the near future.
>
> For your information the Dies Committee has collected data indicating that Orson Welles is associated with the following organizations, which are said to be Communist in character:
>
> Negro Cultural Committee
> Foster Parents' Plan for War Children
> Medical Bureau and North American Committee to Aid Spanish Democracy
> Theatre Arts Committee
> Motion Picture Artists Committee
> The Coordinating Committee to Lift the Embargo
> Workers Bookshop
> American Youth Congress
> New Masses
> People's Forum
> Workers Bookshop Mural Fund
> League of American Writers
> American Student Union. . . .
>
> The Bureau also has information relative to the alleged subversive activities of Orson Welles. . . .

Such a laundry list of alleged Communist "front" organizations was typical of the FBI's files on Hollywood liberals and leftists. Welles was also identified by the FBI as being a supporter of such organizations as the United Nations, the Free World Society, the National Federation for Constitutional Liberties, the American Committee for Protection of the Foreign Born, the Joint Anti-Fascist Refugee Committee, the Artists' Front to Win the War, the Hollywood Democratic Committee, and the Congress of American Soviet Friendship. Though the USSR was an American ally in the war, the FBI found it suspicious that Welles "[had] always been identified with programs designed to praise Russia."*

---

* Other alleged Communist front groups with which Welles was affiliated, according to the 1948 report of California's Tenney committee, included ARTEF, the United Spanish Aid Committee, the Friends of the Abraham Lincoln Brigade, Russian War Relief, and the American Committee for Yugoslav Relief. The Tenney report claims Welles was responsible for the Hollywood Demo-

From today's perspective, most if not all of the causes with which Welles was involved seem innocuous or unexceptionable. The FBI's suspicion of their motives stemmed partly from informers' claims of Communist infiltration and partly from Hoover's virulent paranoia and racism. Guilt by association, hearsay, and innuendo were enough to cast career-threatening doubt over a celebrity, particularly one such as Welles, with his genuine affinity for progressive causes. His outspoken, eloquent voice tirelessly promoted such causes at mass rallies and on the national airwaves, making him an inviting target for the forces of reaction. His willingness to associate with Communists and other leftists both in his work and in progressive causes also made him vulnerable, even though he was never in agreement with the doctrinaire aspects of Communism and was not a defender of Stalinism.

An FBI informant examined the records of the northwest section of the Los Angeles County Communist Political Association on June 30, 1944, and "was unable to find any record of WELLES' membership." The bureau's Los Angeles office admitted in 1944, "[I]t should be pointed out that this office has never been able to establish that WELLES is an actual member of the former Communist Party or the present Communist Political Association." That report nevertheless went on to allege that "an examination of WELLES' activities and his membership in various organizations reflects that he has consistently followed the Communist Party line and has been active in numerous 'front' organizations."

Despite the FBI's admission that Welles was not a party member, Los Angeles special agent in charge R. B. Wood took the drastic step of recommending to Hoover in November 1944 that Welles be listed as a Communist on the FBI's Security Index. That little-known roster gathered the names of people who supposedly represented threats to national security. Originally the Custodial Detention Index, it was designed by Hoover to facilitate the rounding up and detention of alleged subversives during a national emergency. Welles's name was on the Security Index from 1945 to 1949.

One activity that especially outraged the American Legion and the FBI was Welles's role in protests over the threatened deportation of the West Coast labor leader Harry Bridges, a native of Australia who was

---

cratic Committee changing its name to the Hollywood Independent Citizens Committee of the Arts, Sciences and Professions [HICCASP] in 1945. "Thus an old Communist front was given new life under a new name," the report states.

accused of being a Communist. The Citizens' Committee for Harry Bridges was cofounded in April 1941 by Welles, record producer and critic John Hammond Jr., and literary critic F. O. Matthiessen. The committee stated, "Mr. Bridges is now on trial in a second deportation hearing, the only man in the United States ever to be tried twice in this manner. . . . We join in an attempt to inform public opinion as to the realities behind Mr. Bridges' second trial, which we consider an attack on all organized labor, on the rights of minorities and a focal point of the entire current attack on civil liberties." The U.S. Supreme Court in 1945 overturned Bridges's deportation order, but the government continued its unsuccessful efforts to deport him until the late 1950s.

The Sleepy Lagoon murder case was another cause that brought Welles into the FBI's sights. The Hearst press in Los Angeles stirred up bigotry toward Mexican Americans and stereotyped zoot-suited youths as delinquents. In August 1942 the murder of a twenty-two-year-old farmworker named José Diaz at the Sleepy Lagoon reservoir in southeast Los Angeles, a crime the police alleged was gang related, led to a roundup of hundreds of Chicano youths. Those arrests, and the murder and assault charges filed against seventeen young Mexican Americans, led to the formation of the Citizens' Committee for the Defense of Mexican American Youth, later renamed the Sleepy Lagoon Defense Committee. Welles and his second wife, actress Rita Hayworth, who was Mexican American, were actively involved in the committee. Welles served as a spokesman for the defense and wrote the foreword to a 1943 pamphlet, *The Sleepy Lagoon Murder Case.*

An FBI report on a Hollywood fundraising forum for the Sleepy Lagoon defendants sponsored by the Pan-American Security Council at the Beverly Hills Hotel on November 30, 1942, spotlighted Welles's role: "Welles, as chairman, opened the forum by stating that the most important minority question in the country today is the Negro question but that almost of equal importance is the question of the Mexican minorities, which is of particular interest in Los Angeles and Southern California." The FBI reported that many members of the Pan-American Security Council were on the defense committee, which the bureau claimed was "controlled by the Communist Party." The ethnic tensions exacerbated in Los Angeles by the Sleepy Lagoon roundup and trial led to the "Zoot Suit Riots" of June 1943. But through the committee's efforts, the convictions of the seventeen young men in the Sleepy Lagoon case were overturned in 1944 by the state district court of appeals.

❖ ❖ ❖

Rather than backing down politically before Hearst and other reactionary forces while fighting to get *Kane* released, Welles boldly courted further controversy with his and Houseman's New York stage production of *Native Son*, which opened in March 1941. The play was adapted by Richard Wright and Paul Green from Wright's best-selling novel about a Chicago black man named Bigger Thomas (Canada Lee), who, in a state of panic, kills a young white woman for whom he works as a chauffeur. The African American novelist had worked as a publicist for the Chicago Negro Theatre division of the Federal Theatre and had been a member of the Communist Party. But he broke with the party in 1940, later explaining that he was angered by Communists' criticism of "my conception of Negro experience in my writing" and felt that the party had regressed in its positions toward the American Negro, showing a "narrow-minded, bigoted, intolerant" nature.

Rawly exposing the pathology of American race relations, *Native Son* avoids taking the safe liberal path of simply evoking pity for Bigger as a victim of racism and instead depicts him as a victim who is also guilty of hatred and violence, a man maddened by his desperate social circumstances. Welles maintained Wright's radical focus on the unjust system that drives Bigger to kill. *Native Son* also broke ground for the Broadway stage with its frank portrayal of interracial sexuality, with Welles showing Bigger and the white woman, Mary Dalton (Anne Burr), kissing onstage. Hearst's *New York Journal-American* attacked the production as "propaganda that seems nearer to Moscow than Harlem." Ironically, the final preview, Houseman recalled, was picketed by a "small, rigid faction of the American Communist Party, which could not forgive Richard Wright for defying Party orders and refusing to rewrite certain sections of his book at their behest." Because Hoover's FBI was notorious for its racism, Welles's efforts on behalf of civil rights are frequently noted in his FBI files as evidence of his "subversive" nature. A summary of the Welles files provided to the State Department at its request in April 1943 said of *Native Son:* "This production reportedly dramatizes certain alleged discriminations against the Negro. It has been reported that certain lines in the show are extremely inflammatory in effect and border on being subversive in intent. It is known that members of the cast of this production during its road tour were in contact with known Communist Party members."

Another opportunity for Hearstian forces to attack Welles in the spring of 1941 came when he wrote, directed, and narrated a Free Company radio play about civil liberties, *His Honor, the Mayor.* The Free Company arose from a Justice Department request for a radio series to counter fascist propaganda with dramatizations of the Bill of Rights. The series aired on CBS Radio, but the group of American writers, actors, and directors who worked on it were "unpaid, unsponsored, and uncontrolled," in the words of Free Company chairman James Boyd. Such leading playwrights as Maxwell Anderson, Robert Sherwood, William Saroyan, Archibald MacLeish, and Marc Connelly were among the contributors.

Defending free speech and free assembly for people espousing unpopular causes, Welles's play *His Honor, the Mayor* centers on a small U.S. town on the Mexican border whose mayor, Knaggs (Mercury regular Ray Collins), defends the right of an extreme right-wing group, the White Crusaders, to express its views. The play includes a Hearst-like character, a publisher named Colonel Engelhorn, who "built that big ranch," financially backs the White Crusaders, and uses his publications to spread "anti-Semitic garbage" throughout the United States. Rather than simply engaging in rhetoric, Welles characteristically uses irony to show how both extremes of the political spectrum need their rights protected for speech to remain truly free. While the irony may have been lost on Welles's right-wing critics, his defense of civil liberties for Communists as well as fascists was another red flag in their eyes. (Mayor Knaggs says "there's nothin' illegal about bein' a Communist. . . . There's no law in this country against havin' opinions.")

For defending American constitutional liberties in a time of war, Welles and the Free Company found themselves denounced by the Hearst press the day after the April 6 broadcast of *His Honor, the Mayor* as communistic "attackers of the American way of life." In a coordinated onslaught against the radio play that transparently reflected Hearst's wrath at Welles over *Kane*, the *New York Journal-American* enlisted the support of the California Sons of the Revolution and the American Legion, which declared, "The Welles broadcast was one of the most offensive of all in the series because it was an outright appeal for the right of a subversive fifth-column group to hold anti-American meetings in the public hall of an American city." Hearst's campaign against Welles was coordinated by Kent Hunter, who did double duty as a reporter for the *Journal-American* and as a publicity director for the American Legion. Hearst Hollywood columnist Louella Parsons, who maligned Welles regularly in her column and personally lobbied studio executives to ban *Citizen Kane*, also participated in the smear campaign against *His Honor, the Mayor* and the Free Company.

On May 3, 1941, FBI agent P. E. Foxworth filed a fifteen-page report on the Free Company and several writers and actors involved in the series, starting with Welles. The report stated: "The Legion bitterly objected to Orson Welle's [*sic*] recent radio script entitled 'His Honor, the Mayor' which one Legion post in California termed as 'encouraging radicalism.' Spokesmen for the American Legion charged that the [Free Company] broadcasts were subversive in nature and definitely Communistic . . . although camouflaged by constant reference to democracy and free speech."

❖ ❖ ❖

In the spring of 1941, Welles felt compelled to issue a public denial that he was a Communist:

> William Randolph Hearst is conducting a series of brutal attacks on me in his newspapers. It seems he doesn't like my picture *Citizen Kane.* I understand he hasn't seen it. I am sure he hasn't. If he had, I think he would agree with me that those who have advised him that "Kane" is Hearst have done us both an injustice.
>
> I have stood by silently in the hope that this vicious attack against me would be spent in the passing of a few weeks. I had hoped that I would not continue to be the target of patriotic organizations who are accepting false statements and condemning me without knowing the facts.
>
> But I can't remain silent any longer.
>
> The Hearst papers have repeatedly described me as a Communist. I am not a Communist. I am grateful for our constitutional form of government, and I rejoice in our great American tradition of democracy. Needless to say, it is not necessarily unpatriotic to disagree with Mr. Hearst. On the contrary, it is a privilege guaranteed me as an American citizen by the Bill of Rights.
>
> Hearst papers and others whose actions have been suggested by those papers have had much to say about my having signed a protest at the second trial of Harry Bridges. Many others signed that protest, but my name was singled out. Why? Because Mr. Hearst doesn't like *Citizen Kane.* In signing a protest against Harry Bridges' second trial, I believed that the Federal Government was trying him a second time for the same offense. I would just as quickly sign a similar protest if Mr. Hearst were the subject of such double jeopardy. The Hearst smear campaign has chiefly concerned itself with my part in the Free Company broadcasts. . . .

Welles concluded his statement by declaring: "I'm proud of my American citizenship. As a citizen I cherish my rights, and I'm not fearful of uncertainty. I only ask that I am judged by what I am and what I do."

Interviewing Welles on British television in 1974, at the time of the Watergate scandal, Michael Parkinson wondered what might happen if Welles became president and was subjected to an investigation. Welles replied, "I've *been* investigated over and over again by the Americans, by all kinds of American committees, the FBI and everybody. Sure. Sure. . . . You know my trouble during the investigation period, when I was being investigated a lot was during the anti-American, McCarthy period, you see. And I never got to testify because I kept begging to be allowed to. . . . [T]his was a line of argument that nobody else took. And it absolutely shocked them. I said, 'Oh, please let me go and explain why I am not a Communist.' 'Well, we'll let you know.'"

Welles also recalled his interrogation at RKO in the early 1940s by Dies committee investigators. Dies, he told Parkinson,

> had an anti-American, or whatever it was called, affairs committee long before McCarthy started. And he sent a few louts over to see me in my office in Hollywood. . . . [T]hey were particularly uneducated and dumb, and they fell into a marvelous trap. Because they said to me, "Are you a card-carrying Communist?" Of course I've never been even faintly pro-Communist, but I am on the progressive side, as I imagine you've guessed. But I said, "Will you define what a Communist is?" And this is when they fell in the trap, you know. They said, "What do you mean?" I said, "I want to answer your question honestly. How can I answer your question if you don't tell me what you mean?" "Well, what's Communist? Well, I guess it's where whatever you make goes to the government." I said, "Well, I'm eighty-six percent Communist. The rest is capitalist." That's the income tax that one pays in America.

Alas, irony and wit were no defense in what blacklisted screenwriter Dalton Trumbo called "the time of the toad."

❖ ❖ ❖

Welles may have felt that his fame and his friendship with President Roosevelt would insulate him from such political attacks. But even his activities on behalf of the president seemed suspicious to the FBI. The fact that Welles was "prominently featured as a speaker on behalf of President Roosevelt during the recent election campaign" was noted by the FBI in November 1944. The FBI also cited Welles's introduction of Vice President Henry Wallace at a Madison Square Garden campaign rally for Roosevelt that September. Welles appeared with Roosevelt at rallies, wrote speeches and gave frequent radio talks on the president's behalf, and even stood in for FDR in a New York debate with Republican candidate Thomas E. Dewey. In one campaign speech, Welles declared, "The Red bogey must be strongly rejected by the majority of the people. The words 'communism' and 'communist' can no longer be used to smear every liberal and progressive measure."

What was most ironic about the FBI scrutiny of Welles was that he spent much of World War II working on behalf of the U.S. government and its allies. Far from being "subversive," Welles's activities during the war, in addition to his politicking for FDR, included his goodwill diplomacy and the making of the documentary *It's All True* in Brazil for the U.S. Office of the Coordinator of Inter-American Affairs (CIAA) and RKO, entertainment of troops in Hollywood and elsewhere, and frequent radio and lecture appearances discussing the war and American values.

Welles also was asked by the U.S. government to make a short film of Albert Einstein explaining his theory of relativity. While waiting to enter a lecture hall at the University of Southern California in 1981 to conduct a discussion with the audience for his documentary *Filming "The Trial,"* Welles told me the following previously unrevealed story. To film the great physicist, he took a small crew and spent a day with Einstein at Princeton University. Intrigued by the 35mm camera Welles brought along, Einstein asked him to explain how it worked. He was particularly curious to know how the sound and picture were synchronized. Welles showed how the camera mechanism recorded the image a few frames ahead of the soundtrack so that the two would be in synch. Einstein pondered a while, shook his head, and declared, "It won't work." Welles laughed uproariously when he told me the story. Perhaps he was reflecting on the notorious problems he had with synchronization in his European pictures. The film Welles shot at Princeton has never surfaced. Since the war's most closely guarded secret was the building of the atomic bomb, a weapon originally proposed to Roosevelt by Einstein, filming him may have been the brief secret assignment that Welles was asked to perform by FDR in August 1944.

The FBI learned of the assignment from reading Hedda Hopper's Hollywood gossip column. The right-wing columnist reported that Roosevelt had called Rita Hayworth to explain that her husband would have to be away from home doing special work for him. An agent subsequently interviewed Hopper, who "stated she did not know exactly what the President was having WELLES do but she did know that he was on some kind of mission for the President."

❖ ❖ ❖

"The end of the communication between people": In the lost ending of *The Magnificent Ambersons* (1942), Eugene Morgan (Joseph Cotten, right) visits Fanny Minafer (Agnes Moorehead) in her bleak boardinghouse. This is a publicity still from part of the approximately fifty minutes cut by RKO from what may have been Welles's greatest film. *(RKO Radio Pictures/Lilly Library)*

If ever a film appeared at the wrong time and in the wrong place, *The Magnificent Ambersons* was that film. Welles's second feature, a bleak portrait of an overly materialistic, naively insular America collapsing into the twentieth century, was adapted by the director from Booth Tarkington's 1918 Pulitzer Prize–winning novel. It opened in the summer of 1942 and was starkly in opposition to the kind of cheery, uplifting Hollywood fare that prevailed in U.S. movie theaters during the war years. The film's indictment of industrialization seemed almost subversive to a nation exerting all its industrial might for victory over the Axis powers. But Welles, who had begun shooting *Ambersons* on October 28, 1941, thought he had made "a movie so good . . . I had absolutely no doubt that it would win through in spite of that industry fear of the dark movie. . . . It was a much better picture than *Kane*—if they'd just left it as it was."

The first part of *Ambersons*, especially, is exhilarating in its freshness and audacity, introducing us to the characters and vividly filling in their social context in a witty, elliptical manner that owes much to Welles's work in radio (for which he first adapted the novel in 1939). The ballroom sequence with its flowing choreography of actors and camera is breathtakingly beautiful, conveying the evanescent, illusory grandeur of the Amberson family and their overwrought midwestern mansion. Welles's mellifluous narration, caressing the images with gentle tristesse and equally delicate irony, tells us that "this pageant of the tenantry was the last of the great, long-remembered dances that 'everybody talked about.'"

Welles considered that sequence "the greatest tour de force of my career," with astonishing tracking shots that were fragmented when RKO hacked up, reshuffled, and reshot the picture in the director's absence. RKO panicked because its costly film was denounced by preview-goers as "the worst picture I ever saw" and "a horrible distorted dream . . . as bad if not worse than *Citizen Kane*," even though others in the same audience wrote on their preview cards, "I think it was the best picture I have ever seen" and "This picture is magnificent. The direction, acting, photography, and special effects are the best the cinema has yet offered. It is unfortunate that the American public, as represented at this theater, are unable to appreciate fine art." RKO released the film in an eighty-eight-minute version missing about fifty minutes of Welles's footage, including his somber ending in a boardinghouse with the middle-aged automobile inventor Eugene Morgan (Joseph Cotten) visiting the spinster Fanny Minafer (Agnes Moorehead), who has wasted much of her life hopelessly pursuing him.

The evisceration of *Ambersons* has been described by Bogdanovich as "the greatest artistic tragedy in the movies." But we can still relish and celebrate what remains of this somberly ambitious meditation on the decline of American life in the industrial age. Reaching back into his own midwestern boyhood for nostalgic evocations of an earthly paradise before the fall, Welles proceeds to demolish that sense of nostalgia with a tragic portrayal of a wealthy family collapsing along with the genteel values it precariously maintains. The film becomes a midwestern equivalent of Chekhov's play *The Cherry Orchard.* Welles was attempting a picture of American life narrower in focus than that of *Citizen Kane* but broader in its implications: a devastating critique of the shortsighted embrace of the machine age. Welles said that his basic intention with *Ambersons* "was to portray a golden world—almost one of memory—and then show what it turns into. Having set up this dream town of the 'good old days,' the whole point was to show the automobile wrecking it—not only the family but the town."

The political implications of *The Magnificent Ambersons* were not lost on RKO, particularly in the studio's gun-shy mood following the battle with Hearst. The recutting, carried out at RKO's orders by editor Robert Wise in a misguided attempt to "save" the film, concentrated largely on minimizing the "downbeat" aspects that accounted for the restlessness and rude laughter of some members of a preview audience at the Fox Theatre in Pomona, California, on March 17, 1942. When I asked Wise, fifty-eight years later, how he felt about the recutting, he said:

> I have to admit that *Ambersons* was a better film in its full length, but it was a victim of its time. We were shooting in the automobile factory when war was declared, when December 7 happened. So by the time we got out for our previews in March 1942, the whole country was geared up for the war effort, guys were going off to training camps, women were working in the aircraft factories. They just didn't have any understanding or care about the Amberson family in turn-of-the-century Indianapolis. Had the film come out a year before, there might have been a whole different reception.
>
> We took *Ambersons* out to sneak previews. We took it first to Pomona, and it was a disaster. They laughed and laughed at the Aggie Moorehead character. In the first reel they walked out in droves. During the course of the film, a lot of people left. It was long and they didn't find it interesting. We had three more previews, cutting more and more. Finally we had cut so much that we had a continuity problem and we needed a new sequence between George, played by Tim Holt, and his mother, played by Dolores Costello, in her bedroom when he comes to see her about a letter the Joseph Cotten character wrote. Since Orson was away, I was asked to direct it. [Actually, this was a reshooting of a scene earlier directed by Welles, part of which can be glimpsed in the film's trailer; it was reshot to make George's treatment of his mother seem less cruel.] Then there was a new ending put on. Freddie Fleck, who was the production manager, directed that.

I told Wise that some of the people who attended the Pomona preview loved the film, and that one person considered it "the best picture I have ever seen."

"Oh, really? A lot of people just couldn't stand the film," Wise said. "We took this one out thinking we had a smash hit, and to have people just laugh at it and walk out, boy, it's tough. Then at the fourth preview, which was down in Long Beach, everybody sat for it, they didn't laugh at it, and nobody walked out. It played and that was the picture. It's too bad, because it was a marvelous film at its full length, but they couldn't stand it."

RKO's dismal ending shows Eugene and Fanny in a hospital corridor mindlessly glossing over the ruination of all the characters' lives. Its phony, dispirited sentimentality utterly reverses the mood Welles intended for the conclusion. Welles described *his* final sequence to Bogdanovich:

> If only you'd seen how [Moorehead's Fanny Minafer] wrapped up the whole story at the end. . . . Jo Cotten goes to see her after all those years in a cheap boarding house and there's just nothing left between them at all. Everything is over—her feelings and her world and his world; everything is buried under the parking lots and the cars. That's what it was all about—the deterioration of personality, the way people diminish with age, and particularly with impecunious old age. The end of the communication between people, as well as the end of an era. Sure, it was pretty rough going for an audience—particularly in those days. But without question it was much the best scene in the movie.

When I met Bogdanovich in 1970, he showed me several dozen frame enlargements Welles had saved of the missing scenes, including the stunning final shot, a long shot of Eugene's automobile turning into what has become the hellish urban landscape of the once Edenic city: a tiny machine disappearing into a densely baroque composition of skyscrapers, smokestacks, elevated train tracks, and smog. The automobile, the symbol of destructive "progress," vanishes from view around a corner as Welles says, "That's the end of the story." Welles was too direct and explicit in his social criticism for a Hollywood studio to support his vision, particularly when the times called for jingoistic celebration of American know-how and industrial might. Bogdanovich told me in the 1990s that he had sent those frame enlargements of the missing scenes to Oja Kodar. Only a few frame enlargements (not including the final shot) are now in the Welles and Bogdanovich collections at the Lilly Library of Indiana University in Bloomington. As for the missing footage, all that has turned up are several brief shots in RKO's trailer for the film, which resurfaced on Turner Classic Movies in the 1990s. The remainder of the cut footage was reported to have been burned by RKO in December 1942, but Welles scholars have been holding out hope that the work print sent to Welles in Rio de Janeiro when he was filming his next feature, *It's All True*, or a dupe of the work print, may still exist somewhere in Brazil—a hope that has achieved the status of an urban legend. In 2004 Laurence Klavan published a mystery novel called *The Cutting Room*, whose story begins with the murder of a film buff who claims to have found the uncut *Ambersons.**

A Welles fan from Michigan, Roger Ryan, has taken the bold step of assembling his own "reconstruction" of *Ambersons.* Using publicity stills to replace some of the missing scenes, Ryan had some of his friends perform with him the dialogue from the cutting continuity, and he undersored the new scenes with music by Bernard Herrmann that had been dropped by RKO. Ryan's unauthorized 1993 reconstruction, which runs 111 minutes, was shown at the 2005 Locarno conference on Welles. The result is somewhat amateurish, but endearingly so, and it works surprisingly well in giving a sense of Welles's overall vision for the film. The very lack of slickness in Ryan's presentation makes it clear that this is not a substitute for Welles's version but a suggestion of how it might have felt to see and hear it; Ryan's lingering on a limited number of stills throws more of the weight of this reconstruction on the dialogue, bringing out with greater clarity Welles's thematic concentration on the ruination of an earlier American way of life. Ryan's imaginative labor of love, which remains a work in progress, gives us a window onto the richer sociopolitical fabric Welles was weaving with *Ambersons* and allows us a fuller sense of its extraordinary emotional complexity.

It's rarely noted that the reason Welles couldn't do anything to stop the butchery of *Ambersons* was that he had surrendered his precious right of final cut. At the suggestion of studio lawyers, RKO had ordered some small cuts in *Kane* to diminish Kane's resemblance to Hearst, notably in a section of the newsreel that linked Kane to the McKinley assassination, as Hearst had been linked because of inflammatory editorials in his newspapers. But those changes, implemented by Wise over a five-week period, fell within any studio's legal right to protect itself from lawsuits. Otherwise, Welles had final say on *Kane* once the project was approved by Schaefer. But after the imbroglio over the release of *Kane*, Welles's position at the studio was somewhat precarious. He had little or no support

* After buying the RKO library, Ted Turner colorized *Ambersons.* After that, there was little more that could be done to the film short of running a lawnmower through the negative. In another egregious insult to Welles's memory, his screenplay for *Ambersons* was anonymously rewritten, but still credited to him, for a 2002 cable TV remake poorly directed by Alfonso Arau. Advance publicity for that movie falsely claimed that it was based closely on Welles's screenplay for his longer, uncut version of *Ambersons.*

among the executive ranks other than from Schaefer himself. RKO was having trouble finding enough playdates for *Kane* to earn back its production cost, and Schaefer's position was further weakened by the poor performance of other RKO films. The studio was running in red ink again, causing anxiety among the major stockholders and potentially putting Schaefer's job in jeopardy. Welles felt it necessary to renegotiate his contract, surrendering the right to final cut in exchange for being allowed by Schaefer to proceed with *Ambersons.*

Welles tended to avoid mentioning that unpleasant fact in later years when excoriating the studio and Robert Wise for what they did to *Ambersons.* When I asked Welles if he thought I had hit Wise a little too hard in my first published essay on *Ambersons* in assigning him the principal blame for mutilating the film, Welles replied, "You can't hit him too hard. You can *never* be too hard on Robert Wise. Wise was the real villain." Welles thought Wise had catered to RKO's wishes in order to advance his own directing ambitions. Wise contended that in light of the fact that *Ambersons* has achieved the status of a classic, "I think it's apparent we didn't completely vitiate everything Orson did." Certainly there was some responsibility to be attached to Welles, not only for surrendering his right of final cut but also for absenting himself from the postproduction process, however pressing his reasons were for both decisions and however little leeway he had left with Schaefer and the studio. Nevertheless, blaming Welles for abandoning his film, as biographers such as Charles Higham and David Thomson have done, is simplistic and misleading. RKO had promised Welles that Wise would go to Brazil to complete the editing of *Ambersons* with him while Welles was shooting *It's All True*; Wise was also supposed to edit *It's All True.* But the studio reneged on its promise to send Wise to Rio, blaming wartime travel restrictions.

After the ruination of a great work of art, any artist would have had difficulty in putting the pieces of his shattered career back together. "They destroyed *Ambersons,* and the picture itself destroyed me," Welles said. "I didn't get a job as a director for years afterwards."

Writing Welles in Rio on March 21, 1942, Schaefer shared his unhappiness over the box-office prospects of *Kane* and *Ambersons,* telling him that upon his return to the States, "we must have a 'heart to heart' talk. Orson Welles has got to do something commercial. We have got to get away from 'arty' pictures and get back to earth. Educating the people is expensive, and your next picture must be made for the box office. God knows you have all the talent and the ability for writing, producing, directing—everything in *Citizen Kane* and *Ambersons* confirms that. We should apply all that talent and effort in the right direction and make a picture on which we can get well."

Welles always regarded Schaefer as his champion, "an absolute hero. He was marvelous with me." Welles maintained this view despite Schaefer's involvement in the mutilation of *Ambersons,* which was part of the executive's desperate attempt to hold on to his job. Welles became a pawn in the power struggle between major studio stockholders Nelson Rockefeller and Floyd Odlum, a prominent aviation financier and head of the Atlas Corporation. A Hearst associate who had been increasing his holdings in RKO since Welles's hiring, Odlum was concerned about the studio's losses under Schaefer and about the worsening situation between the studio and Welles, who had been supported by both Schaefer and Rockefeller. Ousted by Odlum and his allies in June 1942, Schaefer was replaced as the company's chief executive by N. Peter Rathvon, with Ned Depinet taking over as head of the studio. Charles Koerner, a more hardheaded businessman who had been in charge of RKO theaters, continued as production chief, a post he had assumed a few months earlier. Koerner's new slogan for the company that summer was a flagrant dig at the departed Welles: "Showmanship in Place of Genius: A New Deal at RKO."

Not all film historians have shared Welles's positive view of Schaefer, who also ordered the termination of *It's All True,* the documentary Welles made in Brazil after shooting *Ambersons.* In his 1999 monograph on *Ambersons,* V. F. Perkins calls Schaefer's managerial record at RKO "disastrous" and argues that he "was unwilling to do what other moguls had done when faced with expensive movies that turned out to have dubious box-office appeal: accept the gamble in a robust spirit and try to give the picture effective support as it went to the theatres to meet its fate. Schaefer had invested in Welles as an innovator, yet now he complained that the boy wonder had not supplied a commercial, by implication conventional, product." Welles may have argued with Schaefer and been disappointed by him, but he never forgot that Schaefer was the man who stood up to the rest of Hollywood to release *Kane* and tried to defend *Ambersons* in his absence until the pressures exerted by RKO's money interests and the impending regime change became too great for him to withstand. Schaefer's support for Welles, who never had the full backing of the RKO board, was one of the major factors that cost the executive his job. Welles could hardly overlook the fact that Schaefer sacrificed his own presidency largely by championing an unpopular, iconoclastic young filmmaker.

It's a wasteful Hollywood tradition for a new studio regime to abandon the projects of its predecessors; supporting films someone else launched is seen as a no-win proposition. But in Welles's case the new regime went beyond the norm in its flagrantly public and highly personal hostility toward its former wunderkind. *Ambersons* was contemptuously dumped onto the market in July 1942 on a double bill with, of all movies, the Lupe Velez comedy *Mexican Spitfire Sees a Ghost.* But contrary to its reputation as an unmitigated box-office disaster, *Ambersons* opened well in some cities, even without studio support. *Variety*'s box-office reports on the early weeks of release indicated that it was doing "sensationally" in San Francisco and "holding up beyond expectations" in Los Angeles; business was "nice" in New York and Baltimore, "good" in Denver and Omaha, "not bad" in Boston and Philadelphia, etc. In some cities, such as Chicago and Cincinnati, it was playing "below expectations," but overall, according to *Variety*, *Ambersons* had a "spotty" rather than a disastrous start. Nevertheless, the film was pulled suspiciously quickly in most places, even where it was doing well. So the evidence indicates that RKO deliberately dumped *Ambersons* to help justify its firing of Welles shortly before the opening.

But *Ambersons* has always been a difficult film for some audiences with its downbeat picture of American "progress" and prescient warnings of environmental disaster, mixed with a devastating family tragedy caused by a largely unsympathetic protagonist. For many years, audiences focused their derision on Agnes Moorehead's harrowing performance as Aunt Fanny. But when the women's liberation movement began gathering force in the late 1960s, there was no more laughter at Aunt Fanny. Suddenly it was no longer acceptable to mock the sexual frustrations of "spinsters." "Poor old Fanny Minafer" may still be subjected to ridicule from her loutish nephew and other characters in the film, but the bleakness of her existence now moves audiences to pity rather than mirth.*

---

*It came as a shock when I read in *This Is Orson Welles* that one of the people who advised RKO on the cutting was a relative of mine, producer Bryan (Brynie) Foy. Known as "the King of the B's," Foy told studio executives that *Ambersons* was "too fuckin' long." He advised them to "just throw all the footage up in the air and grab everything but forty minutes—it don't matter what the fuck you cut. Just lose forty minutes." I didn't realize I was related to Foy until after I wrote his obituary for *Daily Variety* in 1977, and my mother informed me that he was my great-uncle. Perhaps the bad karma from Foy's role in helping eviscerate *Ambersons* somehow led his grandnephew many years later to make amends by championing the film and lamenting its mutilation.

❖ ❖ ❖

Welles's departure for Brazil to make *It's All True* meant that the completion of postproduction work on *Ambersons* was left in the hands of RKO, for which he has been severely, and to some degree rightly, criticized. Undoubtedly, Welles should have been more protective of the film, more concerned that something disastrous could happen in his absence and that the studio might renege on its commitments. But it's important to recognize the compelling sense of obligation Welles felt as a draft-exempt celebrity to aid the war effort in that anxious period just after Pearl Harbor. He told Kenneth Tynan in 1961, "I'm still suffering from the traumatic effect of being forbidden to do what all my friends were doing." Even at that late date, Welles felt compelled to spin a fanciful tale of secret missions he allegedly performed for the U.S. government during the war, such as a time when he "was flown into Lisbon as Harrison Carstairs, the ball-bearings manufacturer, and there were twenty people waiting at the airport for my autograph."

Explaining how *It's All True* came about, Welles said in a 1982 interview, "I was in terrible trouble then because I was sent to South America by Nelson Rockefeller and Jock Whitney." Rockefeller was not only a major RKO stockholder but was also charged with combating Axis influence in South America in his capacity as the U.S. government's coordinator of inter-American affairs. John Hay Whitney, the wealthy socialite and Hollywood financier who had been David O. Selznick's principal investor in *Gone With the Wind*, was head of the CIAA's Motion Picture Division. In a December 20, 1941, telegram to Welles, Whitney wrote, "PERSONALLY BELIEVE YOU WOULD MAKE GREAT CONTRIBUTION TO HEMISPHERE SOLIDARITY WITH THIS PROJECT." Welles recalled, "I was told that it was my patriotic duty to go and spend a million dollars shooting the carnival in Rio. Now, I don't like things like carnivals and Mardi Gras and all that, but they put it to me that it would be a real contribution to inter-American affairs in the Latin American world and so on. So without a salary but with a budget of a million dollars, I was sent to Rio to make up a movie about the carnival." The reason he had to leave Hollywood shortly after shooting was completed on *Ambersons* was that Carnival (or, in Portuguese, *Carnaval)* was about to start. Under the circumstances, he would have found it hard to respond, "Sorry, I have to stay in Hollywood looking after the movie I'm finishing." If he had done so, it's even possible that he would have been drafted and ordered to make the documentary in uniform.

Despite his fervent antifascist sympathies, Welles was not eager to join the military service. While he was fighting to get *Kane* released, *Variety* reported "persistent inquiries at the draft board as to why Welles hadn't been drafted." This campaign was another outgrowth of the attacks by Hearst, his columnist Louella Parsons, and the American Legion. Parsons biographer Samantha Barbas reports, "In an attempt to expose Welles as 'unpatriotic,' Louella had placed calls to the local draft board demanding to know why Welles had not been called into the service." The FBI's Los Angeles field office in October 1941 informed the agency's Washington headquarters that Welles's activities on behalf of Harry Bridges and his Free Company broadcast had caused the national committee of the American Legion as well as California executives of the organization to investigate "the military service of ORSON WELLES or his exemption from military service."

Drawing its information from a May 27, 1941, article in Hearst's *Los Angeles Herald-Express*, the FBI reported:

> The article states that ORSON WELLES, age 25 [actually twenty-six], was due for classification before Selective Service Board 245 in Westwood, where his order number was 1027. It appeared that a questionnaire had been mailed ORSON WELLES on April 1, 1941, and WELLES did not return the questionnaire until April 30, 1941 as he had been given extended time. The article states when ORSON WELLES appeared before the classification board, he had informed the board that he was willing to serve if passed, but declared that he suffered from "inverted flat feet" and that his "spine was not in good shape either." The article states that after his appearance before the board, ORSON WELLES visited several bone specialists and that the report of these specialists would be made known to the Selective Service Board. This article states that ORSON WELLES sought and obtained permission from the Draft Authorities to make a trip to Mexico.

Welles initially received a 1-B classification, meaning that he was unfit for active military service but available for limited duties. But that exemption was due to bronchial asthma, not his problems with his feet and spine. After visiting the bone specialist to whom he was referred by the draft board, he denied trying to escape the draft and was quoted as saying, "I will be glad to go if I can—or if they can give me some kind of light work." The *Hollywood Citizen-News* claimed that Welles "confessed that he had difficulty walking more than a block" but volunteered that he might be able to drive a tank. However, Welles said in 1946 that he had turned down a U.S. Army commission because he felt he wasn't worthy of it. That "inverted snobbery" was a decision he came to regret, adding, "I spent five months pounding on doors in Washington, trying to give my services to someone. I got nowhere. The incompetent ones were afraid I would show them up; the good men were afraid I'd be too irresponsible." Welles was reclassified 1-A in February 1943 but finally classified 4-F, ineligible for military service because of "chronic myoditis [possibly myositis: muscular discomfort or pain] and original syndrome arthritis, bronchial asthma, high fever and inverted flat feet."

Dr. Russell W. Starr, chairman of the American Legion public relations committee, made no bones about the organization's motive for putting public pressure on Welles over the draft issue in 1941, telling the Hearst press: "We are looking into his case regarding possible military service the same as we would look into that of any other person who has come out openly and vigorously in favor of Bridges and against the deportation of an alien." Welles's executive assistant on the RKO films, Richard Wilson, said that a major reason Welles accepted the assignment to go to Brazil on behalf of the U.S. government was the enormous pressure he was feeling about his draft status. "I didn't want to do it, really," Welles said to Bogdanovich of *It's All True*. "I just didn't know how to refuse."

❖ ❖ ❖

The making of *It's All True* was "the one key disaster in my story," Welles said. His firing by RKO in the midst of shooting and the malicious stories the studio spread about his conduct in Rio to justify aborting the project prevented Welles from getting another directing job for the next three years. But the effects on his career were never-ending. In 1970, a financing deal Welles thought he had for *The Other Side of the Wind* fell through because of a *Newsweek* article recycling the old allegations about *It's All True*. But in another sense, the filming of the documentary on location in Brazil was a liberating experience for Welles, setting him on a creative path that he would follow in much of his later work.

The conventional account of what happened in South America was that Welles drank and wenched his way through Rio nightclubs and hotel rooms while working only sporadically on his documentary, recklessly overspending as he continually embroidered on a sketchy, ever-changing script. In this account, it was Welles's irresponsibility and the incoherence, mounting expense, and uncommerciality of his evolving project that led RKO to pull the plug before he was able to finish shooting. This

"The one key disaster in my story": Welles in Rio de Janeiro working on *It's All True* (1942), his unfinished documentary about South American culture, made for the U.S. government in an attempt to promote hemispheric solidarity against fascism. RKO terminated the production and fired Welles, but parts of the remaining footage were restored for the 1993 documentary *It's All True: Based on an Unfinished Film by Orson Welles. (RKO Radio Pictures/Bill Krohn)*

is the cornerstone of what Welles later referred to as the "Crazy Welles" myth that dogged him for the rest of his life.

Welles was sent to Brazil not only as a filmmaker but also as a goodwill ambassador (both roles in which he served without pay). Rockefeller convinced Welles that he was needed to encourage friendly ties between North and South America as part of the U.S. propaganda effort to discourage the spread of fascism. In addition to filming *It's All True*, Welles's mission was to make personal appearances and radio shows promoting hemispheric solidarity. Rockefeller arranged for RKO to distribute the documentary, with the studio putting up the production cost for the Technicolor and black-and-white film, in exchange for being entitled to all the potential profit. Welles was later criticized by the studio for going to Brazil without a script, even though it had been agreed that he would create a storyline based on what he discovered on location.* He also ran afoul of RKO for taking time for his other duties, which the U.S. government considered equally important.

Welles alarmed the government of Brazil's dictator, Getúlio Vargas, by going beyond the expectedly picturesque Technicolor filming of Carnaval to trace the proletarian roots of the samba in the *favelas*, the hillside slums where many of Rio's black citizens live. Rather than shooting a frivolous tourist travelogue, as both governments expected, Welles was turning the film into a sympathetic celebration of minority cultures and a protest against their economic and political mistreatment. His radical political and artistic agenda included a re-creation of the previous year's epic journey of four raftsmen, or *jangadeiros*, from Fortaleza to Rio to demand better living conditions for fishermen. It didn't take long for the Brazilian government and RKO to form a common purpose of thwarting Welles's goals, if necessary by shutting down the production.

Stories were spread in both countries to impugn Welles's conduct, painting the director as wasteful and reckless and claiming that he was dragging out the Rio filming to avoid being drafted. The studio exploited racist and puritanical bias with gossip about Welles drunkenly carousing with black women in Rio nightclubs. While Welles was still shooting in Rio, *Life* magazine ran a photo spread of him shooting scenes for *The Story of Samba (Carnaval)* segment with such captions as "Welles (foreground) feels good at one of the low-class 'people's dances,'" "Welles

---

* *It's All True* evolved from an earlier Welles project at RKO for an omnibus film of that title about the Americas. A story by Robert Flaherty about a boy and his pet bull, *My Friend Bonito*, was carried over from the first blueprint for *It's All True*. Norman Foster, who directed the Eric Ambler thriller *Journey into Fear* for Mercury and RKO, shot some lushly beautiful footage in Mexico for *My Friend Bonito* in 1941 with cinematographers Alfred Gilks and Floyd Crosby, but the segment was left uncompleted.

squirts ethyl chloride from vial at guest at Copacabana Palace," and "Poor whites and blacks are too dazed to respond to Welles's direction." The slander campaign was surprisingly effective, for its poison has persisted until the present day, tainting even some biographies of Welles, such as those by Frank Brady and David Thomson, as well as Charles Higham's two vitriolically anti-Welles books.* The effects of the "Crazy Welles" image from Rio can also be seen in Angus MacFadyen's portrayal of the young Welles as a drunken, irresponsible tyrant in Tim Robbins's *Cradle Will Rock*.

It's no accident that the stories spread by RKO to demonstrate Welles's extravagance and irresponsibility contained elements of racism. The racist arguments made against the film in both Brazil and the United States, in 1942 and beyond, are a symptom of a deeper underlying discomfort with Welles's conception of *It's All True* as a radical critique of Brazilian socioeconomic injustice, contrasted with a celebration of the democratic vitality of that country's black culture.

The film's unit production manager, Lynn Shores, constantly feuded with Welles on location about what Shores considered wasteful production costs, the time Welles spent away from the film on his government duties, and, as Shores saw it, the unstructured nature of the story and most of the footage being shot. Shores sent weekly reports, largely negative, back to the home office and told RKO as early as March 9, "I do not believe that the material is here for a successful picture. . . . As for the continual of the carnaval [shooting], the more you see, the more hopeless it becomes." Shores complained to Brazil's Department of Press and Propaganda about Welles's "continued exploitation of the negro [*sic*] and the low class element in and around Rio," which he considered "in very bad taste." To RKO, Shores reported that Welles had been filming in "some very dirty and disreputable nigger neighborhoods throughout the

* It was a review of Higham's 1970 critical study *The Films of Orson Welles* by Raymond Sokolov in *Newsweek* that Welles blamed for scaring off a potential investor. Richard Wilson, Catherine Benamou, and Robert Stam have corrected the record in thoroughly researched articles. Wilson, with Myron Meisel and Bill Krohn, also codirected the 1993 feature *It's All True: Based on an Unfinished Film by Orson Welles*, with research by Benamou. Their stirring and lovingly crafted documentary includes *The Story of Samba (Carnaval)* and *Bonito* footage and a forty-eight-minute restoration of the jangadeiros segment, *Four Men on a Raft*, building on Wilson's 1986 twenty-two-minute short *It's All True: Four Men on a Raft*.

city," and described one week's worth of samba footage as "just carnival nigger singing and dancing, of which we already have piles." Welles recalled what happened back at the studio when the new RKO regime took over in June 1942: "They ask to see the rushes of what I'm doing in South America. And they see a lot of people, black people, and the reaction is, 'He's just shootin' a lot of jigaboos jumpin' up and down,' you know."

Thomson's biography *Rosebud* expresses a similar distaste in marginally more polite language, blaming Welles's supposed distraction from his filmmaking duties on his cavorting with black women in Brazil, "especially those who embraced the libertarian attitudes of carnival." Claiming that Brazilian women "felt honored to have American attention," Thomson compares Welles's roistering to the sexual adventures of the HMS *Bounty* crew on Tahiti. In such lubricious hostility, with its neocolonialist overtones, we see a resistance to what Rosenbaum has called Welles's "radical pro-black stance, including the fact that he enjoyed the company and collaboration of blacks, as well as his insistence on featuring nonwhites as the pivotal characters in both the film's Brazilian episodes."

❖ ❖ ❖

It's impossible to read the anguished six-page letter George Schaefer wrote Welles on April 29, 1942, without feeling sympathy for the studio executive. Detailing "the crisis which has arisen in my relationship with my company and my relationship with you," he reminded Welles that he had supported and defended *Kane* at great cost to the studio as well as at great personal cost. Schaefer complained that Welles's initial assurances that he could make films for between $400,000 and $500,000 apiece had been forgotten as the budgets for *Kane* and *Ambersons* increased substantially. But Schaefer downplayed the fact that he approved those budget increases, if not the two films' relatively modest cost overruns.

The fact that Welles produced *Citizen Kane*, a film that gives the impression of enormous grandeur and scope, for only $839,727—below the norm for a major Hollywood production in that era—is evidence of his economical shooting methods. He did take enormous pains over the detail work that helps make *Kane* such a great film, frequently sending visual effects back for redoing, but the result demonstrates Michelangelo's dictum "Trifles make perfection, and perfection is no trifle." Welles went over budget on *Kane* by $101,987, or 14 percent. *Ambersons* was budgeted at $853,950, about the same as the final production cost of *Kane*, but had a larger cost overrun, $159,810, or 19 percent. Welles's uncut version cost $1,013,760, and RKO spent an additional $104,164 in revising the film. Again, this was a matter of concern to RKO, but not enough to indict Welles for reckless inefficiency.

In a cablegram to Schaefer from Rio in April 1942, Welles blamed his *Ambersons* overrun on cast illnesses and on his "criminally slow cameraman" Stanley Cortez. Gregg Toland was unavailable to shoot the film because of a contractual obligation to Samuel Goldwyn, so Welles hired Cortez partly because of his record of speedy work on B pictures. A brilliant craftsman whose later work included Charles Laughton's 1955 classic, *The Night of the Hunter*, Cortez unfortunately took the opportunity of his first major assignment to become painstakingly deliberate, and he proved incapable of executing some of Welles's visual demands. He further exasperated Welles with his habit of describing lighting in terms of painting or music, making such comments as "Orson, I see Major Amberson as Rembrandt's *An Old Man Seated*" and "Orson, doesn't this scene remind you of Respighi's *Fountains of Rome*?" No doubt Cortez was referring, with some justification, to two of the most beautiful and chilling scenes in the film, Major Amberson's soliloquy about the end of human existence and Isabel's deathbed scene, with its rippling shadows from an off-camera lace curtain. But Cortez's pretentious, overbearing manner clashed with Welles's own grandiosity, which, unlike the cameraman's, was leavened with self-mocking humor. In the 1970s, Welles told me with astonishment that he had just been invited to participate in a tribute to Cortez, "the only cameraman I've ever fired." Welles said that Cortez had begged him in tears to let him remain on the film. So the director relented, and while Cortez would take his time setting up scenes on one set, faster cameramen, Harry J. Wild, Russell Metty, and Jack McKenzie Sr., were busy on other sets shooting most of the remaining scenes.

Despite these mitigating factors, George Schaefer can hardly be blamed for placing some of the responsibility on Welles for the difficulties he was experiencing in trying to hold on to his job as studio chief. If Schaefer was no longer concerned about the quality of *Ambersons*, only about its cost and the audience discomfort with the film, and no longer supported Welles's need to explore the creative imperatives of *It's All True* on location without a completed script, that was a function of Schaefer's desperate position at the studio.

Criticizing Welles for shooting the Brazilian footage in a "haphazard" manner and "wasting time and money," Schaefer commended his work on behalf of the U.S. government but inaccurately recast the terms of Welles's dual assignment:

> Let me remind you, you are making a picture for our company and are not down in South America as a representative of the Government or an Ambassador of Goodwill. That, while secondary, is something you naturally were supposed to do and is expected from any good American. . . . I am now again put in the painful position where I have to write you a letter which I never, in God's world, thought I would have to write wherein I am begging you to fulfill in an honorable way your obligations and not put such a terrific load on my shoulders. . . . I made my decision to stand by you [on *Kane*] and I saw it through. I have never asked anything in return but in common decency I should expect that I would at least have your loyalty and gratitude. To the extent I have received it with respect to the Brazilian enterprise up to the present time, I would say it has been merely lip service.

Schaefer concluded that while the final decision had not been made about the fate of *It's All True*, "It would be painful to share with you the closing of the show and your instructions to return."

As Richard Wilson put it, "the two saddest casualties" of the power struggle at RKO were Schaefer and Welles. "Both lost. It had a Greek classicism to it. . . . the Odlum-Koerner forces made Orson the rock on which they broke Schaefer. Schaefer in turn broke Welles." That Welles fully understood the tragedy involved was reflected in his refusal to blame Schaefer for what happened to him.

On April 24, 1942, five days before writing his letter to Welles, Schaefer called his Hollywood factotum, Reg Armour, from New York to say he had decided to send Phil Reisman, RKO's foreign manager, to Rio to confront Welles personally about the problems with *It's All True.* Reisman was to hand-deliver Schaefer's letter to Welles and was delegated the authority to decide whether to shut down the production. Armour called Reisman in New York on April 27 to pass along Schaefer's orders. The transcript of that telephone conversation, preserved by RKO, is the smoking gun in the studio's mistreatment of Welles. It proves that the RKO management was deliberately deceiving and undermining him in Rio in order to use him as a scapegoat to prevent Schaefer from being deposed. The transcript reveals that Welles was not being told the truth about the budget, while at the same time being blamed for illusory overruns.

And it demonstrates that RKO was not (at least officially) the source of Welles's understanding that the budget was $1 million. The actual budget of *It's All True*, Armour tells Reisman, was $1.2 million. This is verified by the studio's summary of its April 1, 1942, production agreement with the CIAA, which states that the negative cost was "deemed to be actual production cost or the sum of $1,200,000 (unless a higher figure is subsequently agreed to by Coordinator)[,] whichever is the lesser." RKO was to put up the $1.2 million and receive all profits; the agreement further states that if the film lost money at the box office, the government would reimburse RKO for up to $300,000 of its total negative cost. RKO's summary of the production cost of *It's All True* as of June 22, 1942, when Welles was doing the last shooting for the jangadeiros segment in the fishing village of Fortaleza, lists $590,235 in direct costs, plus studio overhead of $162,313, for a total of $752,548; the film's cost as of August 1943 (more than a year after shooting was terminated) was carried at $832,347, including $620,630 in direct costs and $211,717 in overhead. These figures prove that Welles was correct in asserting in later years that he did not go over budget and that the studio publicly lied about the situation to blame him unfairly.

The studio also misled Welles when it told him the $150,000 he was requesting to complete the "Pan-American Night" pageant at Urca Casino, the grand climax of the picture, would put him over budget. That was one of the reasons the film was terminated, even though he had agreed to reduce the cost of the Technicolor sequence to only $18,000 and managed to finish it before RKO took away the cameras. According to Wilson, that "fabulous" eight-minute musical number was "the only sequence of the film ever totally printed in color, edited and considered complete" in Welles's partial work print of *It's All True* that was later assembled in Hollywood.

Notes prepared by Wilson in Rio for the CIAA and/or Schaefer while the film was in jeopardy state: "We must remind them that we arrived in Rio with no knowledge of what Carnaval was like, without equipment, no stars, no story. We had to shoot film from which we could make an acceptable picture. We must explain the reasons for the large amount of footage. Looking back on it now, I see how we could have shot only half as much film. . . . Welles told all concerned it would cost from $850,000 to $1,000,000 to make this picture. He is now being heckled unmercifully about the cost—this must stop." Welles evidently never realized how far *under* budget he actually was at the time of his firing ($447,452). The charge about wanton overspending that has been made ever since by hostile journalists and biographers to tar his reputation is based on false information stemming from RKO's deceptive tactics against him.

The April 27 telephone conversation between Armour and Reisman even reveals that the studio was considering seeking a reversal of Welles's draft exemption from the U.S. government in order to rid itself of him:

Armour: You're elected for Rio, brother.

Reisman: . . . I want to find out from the legal department about Welles's contract—what rights he has. . . . Do you have the breakdown of [the] actual cost to date—what the Mexican part [of the] picture *[My Friend Bonito]* cost to date? Has there been any budget set?

Armour: No—it will be about a million two altogether—but we don't want to talk to him about that—we don't want him to know.

Reisman: Someone must have told him—because when I was down there he was telling everyone the picture would cost a million dollars. It's going to be a documentary film—and we'll never get it back. George is sending me down there with the right to shut the God damn thing off if I want to—and bring him home and take the loss right now.

Armour: I saw *Magnificent Ambersons* and *Journey Into Fear*—they are both bad.

Reisman: I would like you to send me a consensus on both pictures—and put *Citizen Kane* in too—showing how much money we will lose.

Armour: We may break even on *Kane*—but that will be all—we will be lucky if we do.

Reisman: Have you talked to [Jack] Moss at all? [Moss, Welles's associate producer, was supervising *Ambersons* and other Mercury business in Hollywood.]

Armour: They [Moss and other Mercury personnel] are beginning to rat on Welles.

Reisman: In what way?

Armour: They say, "We told Welles to [do?] so-and-so—and now we're being disloyal to him—but we'll do it."

Reisman: Any information you can send me I will appreciate—please mark the information you don't [want] Welles to know "confidential"—it will help me to know all about everything. . . . He's a tough baby—he has done a magnificent job of selling himself to Nelson Rockefeller.

Armour: From what we have seen from here [i.e., the information received in letters from unit production manager Lynn Shores], the best thing you can do is to send him back—the crew do not feel any loyalty to him. We have received 60,000 feet [of film] here and there is no picture in it. If we can get 800 or 1,000 feet out of it, we will be doing well. We have roughly $60,000 in film stock in Technicolor.

Reisman: Maybe we could make a couple of shorts out of it.

Armour: I don't think so. George will lose his job out of this.

Reisman: George wrote Orson a strong letter which I am to deliver. After he has read the letter, he will either come back, as George says—or quit.

Armour: I think Orson wants to stay out of the country. He wants to duck military service.

Reisman: I think I could get the authorities to take him off our hands.

Armour: This picture will put us back in 77B [bankruptcy receivership].

Reisman: Do you really think so?

Armour: Yes, I do, Phil.

Reisman: . . . Reg, give me a complete picture—what we have spent and what we will have to spend [to finish the film]—and make it as tough as you can.

Remarkably, after Reisman went to Rio in May, Welles used his powers of persuasion to convince the previously skeptical executive that he was indeed trying to finish the film and make something special of it. Reisman did not immediately exercise his authority from Schaefer to pull the plug on *It's All True*, and Welles did not quit after reading Schaefer's letter. Instead, Reisman worked with Welles and Shores to come up with an accelerated schedule to finish the Rio shooting by June 8, when the equipment and most of the crew would be returned to Hollywood. After that, a smaller crew would accompany Welles to Fortaleza to film the *Four Men on a Raft* segment. Reisman wrote Schaefer that Welles was "working like a dog . . . he realizes his whole future is at stake in the results of this picture."

But on May 19, when the jangadeiros' raft was being towed into Guanabara Bay for a reenactment of its triumphant arrival in Rio, an unimaginable nightmare occurred. A wave capsized the raft, and the leader of the four raftsmen, Manuel Olimpio Meira, known as Jacaré ("Alligator"), was lost at sea. The death of Jacaré effectively killed *It's All True*. He and the other jangadeiros were to figure prominently in the Technicolor footage Welles was shooting in a Rio studio, tying their story in with that of Carnaval. Furthermore, the Brazilian public's grief over the loss of Jacaré for a film caused considerable hostility toward Welles and the rest of the company. After conferring with Schaefer by

Even after RKO pulled the plug on *It's All True*, Welles remained in Brazil to shoot his tribute to the jangadeiros, four Brazilian fishermen who made an epic journey by raft to protest their working conditions. In this frame enlargement from the *Four Men on a Raft* segment, the director is shown at work in the fishing village of Fortaleza in June 1942. The segment was restored for the 1993 Paramount documentary *It's All True: Based on an Unfinished Film by Orson Welles. (RKO Radio Pictures/Paramount Pictures)*

long distance, Reisman reluctantly closed down the picture. Welles made an impassioned plea to be allowed to shoot *Four Men on a Raft*, arguing that it would be a tribute to the memory of Jacaré and would help calm the public's outrage. Reisman agreed, giving Welles $10,000, a crew of five, 45,000 feet of black-and-white film, and an old soundless 35mm Mitchell camera for a few weeks' shooting in Fortaleza.

If Welles did not fully convince Reisman he would find a way to patch together *It's All True* back in Hollywood, he at least bought himself a last chance to persuade RKO that the project could be salvaged with creative restructuring and narration. But upon his return, Welles found that in the hostile climate that existed at RKO toward everything he touched, the studio had no more interest in *It's All True*. Welles's Mercury Productions unit had been ordered off the studio lot on July 1 to make room for a unit producing a Tarzan picture. "So I was fired from RKO," Welles said in retrospect, "and they made a great publicity point of the fact that I had gone to South America without a script and thrown all this money away. I never recovered from that attack."

RKO let him shop around *It's All True* to other companies and try to persuade the CIAA to keep backing him, but the studio refused to pay Welles to complete a script that he began writing for a scaled-down version. RKO's concern was entirely to recoup some of its costs from another film company and/or the government. Welles kept trying to find a way to finish the film until 1946, eventually striking a deal to buy back the footage on the installment plan, telling RKO that he had a backer. But the funding failed to materialize, Welles defaulted on the agreement in December 1946, and the footage had to be returned to the RKO vaults.*

That *Four Men on a Raft* survived to be reconstructed in *It's All True: Based on an Unfinished Film by Orson Welles* is one of the miracles of film history. Welles's tribute to the community of Fortaleza is filmed with cameraman George Fanto in the romantic documentary style pioneered by the author of *My Friend Bonito*, Robert Flaherty, in such films as *Nanook of the North* and *Man of Aran*. Welles's poetic evocation of the quiet strength of the Brazilian fishing community and the raftsmen's epic journey has a looser, more improvisatory feel than his first two RKO films. Wilson recalled that in Fortaleza, despite all the catastrophes that had been happening, "Orson was happy then, because he was creating." Exemplifying what Welles later told me became his filmmaking credo ("Movies should be rough"), the segment relies, by necessity, more on montage than on long takes. Its semidocumentary style uses a mixture of

---

* Ownership of the footage eventually passed from RKO to Desilu to Paramount. In 1982, 309 cans of nitrate negative from *It's All True* were rediscovered in the Paramount vaults by studio postproduction executive Fred Chandler. The 1993 documentary on the film drew from that footage, housed at the UCLA Film and Television Archive and at Paramount. Much of the footage shot for the film still has not been transferred from perishable nitrate film to acetate, including most of *My Friend Bonito*. At my suggestion, the Los Angeles Film Critics Association gave UCLA $9,000 in 2000 to begin preserving this material, but much more is needed to complete the job. Catherine Benamou, who inaugurated the *It's All True* Preservation Project and is the author of the forthcoming book *It's All True: Orson Welles in Pan-America*, reported in 2005 that at least 143,345 feet of the film needs to be preserved, and that 48,370 feet of that material, 3,000 of it in Technicolor, is at risk for nitrate deterioration.

actors and nonactors, filmed on real locations rather than on studio sets. For a love story involving a fisherman lost at sea, Welles cast a fifteen-year-old village girl, Francisca Moreira da Silva, as his leading lady and gently cajoled from her a naturally affecting performance that enables the film to symbolically mourn the loss of Jacaré. The range and flexibility of this new style appealed to Welles's eclectic creativity and was carried over into his later films, which largely escape studio confines while expressionistically transforming actual locations. Welles's adaptability to changing circumstances was characteristic of what Truffaut called "his position as an avant-garde director."

Reviewing Simon Callow's biography *Orson Welles: The Road to Xanadu* for the *Nation* in 1996, Stuart Klawans complained that Callow's account of Welles's early years largely ignores the political aspects of his career while depicting his attitude toward money as that of an indulgent child.

> But you might say more generously that he was a kind of utopian socialist who struggled against a world in which all of life is dominated by economic relationships. . . . Welles's lifelong push-and-pull with systems of power becomes nothing more than evidence of a character flaw; it's drained of political meaning, as we might expect in most accounts written today, when harmony with faceless "market forces" is thought to be the highest good (the unthinkable alternative being a return to that old bogeyman, faceless communism). Too bad. I'd prefer to imagine that an individual might at least try to act autonomously, and that he or she might at the same time take the part of working people. That's what Orson Welles did.

When the "coup" against Welles's unit at RKO occurred as he was shooting the Fortaleza segment of *It's All True*, Klawans points out, "He could have hurried back to Hollywood and tried to rescue his career, but he stayed put . . . , living out his commitment to a bunch of peasants. That, and not the commercial fizzle of *Kane*, was the real turning point in Welles's professional life."

Welles's first fully independent feature, *Othello* was made in Europe from 1948 through 1952 and marked an adventurous new phase of his filmmaking career. Costumed as Shakespeare's tragic title character, the Moor of Venice, "one that loved not wisely but too well," Welles directs Suzanne Cloutier as Othello's wife, Desdemona. *(Castle Hill)*

Chapter Three

ORSON WELLES AT LARGE

Hollywood is a gold-plated suburb suitable for golfers, gardeners, assorted middlemen and contented movie stars. I am none of these things.

—Welles in 1947

With his directing career in ruins, Welles, still only twenty-seven in 1942, probably thought more seriously about the possibility of quitting moviemaking than at any other time in his life. It seemed the decision was being made for him. He was (temporarily) blackballed in Hollywood as a director, but he was still in demand as an actor. *Jane Eyre*, opposite Joan Fontaine in 1944, was his first starring venture for another film director (British emigré Robert Stevenson); Welles claimed he also served as an uncredited producer on that intelligently mounted adaptation of the Charlotte Brontë novel by Aldous Huxley, Stevenson, and John Houseman (William Goetz is billed as "in charge of production"). Welles's grand, gaudy, operatic performance as the "proud, sardonic, and harsh" Mr. Rochester showed that he could have a lucrative career as a face and voice for rent in popular moviemaking. But he wasn't content to pursue a career as a movie star for its own sake, only as a way to support his personal projects. Like the bullfighter in the Hemingway story who was destroyed but undefeated, Welles began to turn increasingly to his many other options outside the film business.

Part of his stature as a filmmaker has always come from the fact that he was more than just a filmmaker. One of the most truly cosmopolitan directors ever to emerge from America, he did notable work in several other media as well as films, including radio, theater, vaudeville, television, recordings, magic, oratory, and journalism. "I've never been excited by movies *as movies* the way I've been excited by magic or bullfighting or painting," Welles told me in 1970. "After all, the world existed for a long time without people going to movies." For several years after his firing by RKO, before he left the United States for more than eight years of exile in Europe, Welles seriously pursued his interests in magic, theater, politics, and journalism. He even considered turning his talents to teaching and making educational films. But he never stopped developing his own projects for feature films.

❖ ❖ ❖

The years he spent vainly attempting to raise the funding to complete *It's All True* belied the widespread belief that he habitually abandoned projects. "I tried everything," he lamented. "I was near it, near it, near it. And I wasted many years of my life. If I'd just forgotten it—turned my back on it the way the studio did—I would have been way ahead. But I kept trying to be loyal to it, trying to finish it. And I began a pattern of trying to finish pictures which has plagued me ever since."

In 1943 he wrote a screenplay based on Antoine de Saint-Exupéry's fantasy novel *Le Petit Prince (The Little Prince)*, planning to play both himself (as narrator) and the aviator. He would have used animation for the space-travel sequences.* But he couldn't get backing. He adapted Tolstoy's *War and Peace* for a film version he hoped to shoot in the USSR for producer Alexander Korda, one of several projects with Korda in the 1940s that fell through because of the producer's inability to raise funding. Welles even tried to sell Hollywood on a romantic comedy called *Don't Catch Me*, based on a novel by Richard Powell about an overweight man who tries to shape up to win an athletic woman.

In the 1940s, the theater seemed Welles's likeliest American venue. It's usually harder to raise money for plays than for movies, but the Mercury Theatre productions of the late 1930s had been mounted for surprisingly frugal sums. The acclaimed bare-stage *Caesar* cost only about $12,000. Between film-directing jobs, Welles continued to pour money from his radio work into his theatrical ventures, including *The Mercury Wonder Show* (1942) and *Around the World* (1946), his adaptation of Jules Verne's *Around the World in Eighty Days*. The *Wonder Show*, a whimsical potpourri of magic and comedy skits, was performed for the troops in a tent on Hollywood's Cahuenga Boulevard as well as at army bases and in Universal's 1944 troop-entertaining film *Follow the Boys* (Welles directed his own segment). *Around the World* was a virtuoso attempt to transform

* In 1995 his screenplay was published in Italian translation as *Il piccolo principe*.

Verne's globe-spanning adventure into a spectacle of theatrical magic, using silent-movie sequences to bridge scenes. Despite its music and lyrics by Cole Porter, the lavish production was a commercial debacle, eating up $320,000 of Welles's own money. Welles took solace from Bertolt Brecht's praise of *Around the World* as "the greatest thing I have seen in American theater. . . . This is what theater should be."

"My real interest in life lies in education," Welles told columnist Hedda Hopper in 1945. "I want to be a teacher. All this experience I've been piling up is equipping me for that future. I shall know how to dramatize the art of imparting knowledge. I shall have the equipment of the theater, the radio, motion pictures." When Hopper asked if he planned to "lead the people to a way of thinking," Welles replied, "No. The people can be trusted to do their own thinking. . . . I shall try only to help people to the knowledge that will aid them in forming correct conclusions." Welles became wistful as he mentioned his alma mater, the Todd School in Woodstock, Illinois, in which he had a "personal and financial interest. One day I shall leave all this behind me, go back there, and give full rein to my ideas. That's when life will really begin for me." His daughter Christopher attended the school in the late 1940s, living with her father's surrogate father, headmaster Roger Hill, and his wife, Hortense. In his poignant and hilarious 1978 filmed interview with the Hills,* Welles describes the school as his "Camelot." Welles tells Roger Hill that he took up dramatics to avoid acrobatics "and in an attempt to get your attention." Hill retorts, "Mainly I was always trying to get something to keep you busy and keep you out of my hair."

Welles announced in October 1944 that he and his Mercury staff had been preparing educational film projects on "some sample subjects, like the Bill of Rights, China, and other subjects to be shown in schools everywhere. I think the emphasis in pictures will be on education rather than entertainment." He sketched out a grand vision for his role as a

* Sixty-one minutes of documentary footage shot at the Hills' home in Sedona, Arizona, was first shown publicly on August 10, 2005, at the Locarno conference in Switzerland as a restoration in progress, *Orson Welles Talks with Roger Hill;* the Munich Film Museum has five more hours of Welles's interview footage with the couple. Welles had various plans for the material, as part of a documentary series to be called *Orson Welles Solo* or as a segment of *The Orson Welles Show,* his talk series that never went beyond the pilot stage. He told the studio audience for the pilot that the series "won't just be show business. But if you're going to sell it, you have to do the pilot on Burt Reynolds, not your headmaster."

multimedia educator: "If I really had my way, I would be working in a foundation financed by three or four Marshall Fields on adult education and political science for the purpose of selling the dignity and solemn obligations of democracy. I would have with me a group of people—educators, show folk, Washington people—and we would make movies, recordings, hold public forums, show slides. It would be strictly a non-partisan project. Pericles once said, 'We hold that the man who takes no interest in the affairs of the State is less than nothing.' I think I'm equipped for that job."

The FBI noted with alarm in December 1944 that Welles was "planning to make several motion picture shorts on minority problems . . . for showing in schools throughout the country." FBI informants said the shorts would be about "race relations and 'The American Negroes' [*sic*] Contribution to Music and Letters.'" But those intriguing plans never came to pass. "I went to all the big foundations," Welles recalled, "and said that I would give up all acting and so on and use my skills for popular education to try to rejuvenate the idea of a civilized generation of students, and nobody was remotely interested." Nevertheless, Welles would continue to pursue his interest in documentary filmmaking in future years, with his 1950s TV series *Around the World with Orson Welles* and *Orson Welles' Sketch Book* and his 1970s essay films *F for Fake* and *Filming "Othello."*

"Certainly, I love the stage and screen," Welles told an interviewer in January 1945. "But things are happening in the world today that are more important than the theater." Welles wrote a column for the *New York Post* from January through November 1945. Originally titled "Orson Welles' Almanac" and later "Orson Welles Today," it contained whimsical comments on a wide range of subjects but dealt largely and passionately with politics. Welles campaigned for continuance of New Deal policies after the war and for a more internationalist approach to world affairs. Of Latin America, he wrote, "Our attitude towards the policy of the good neighbor matches the rest of our foreign policy. But it doesn't match at all the high principles by which we would justify our leadership in the Americas. We have armed dictators, strengthened unnecessarily the political hand of high churchmen, and everywhere underrated the Democratic aspirations of the people." Welles's passionate concern with civil rights broadened his accusation about the "glaring" inconsistencies between U.S. policy at home and abroad: "An Atlantic charter is perused by foreigners with one eye on a lynching in Arkansas. A Crimea communique is studied in reference to a Detroit race riot. A declaration at Mexico city stirs memories of a place called Sleepy Lagoon. . . . That's the connection between the hand of American friendship extended to Haile Selassie, to Farouk of Egypt, to the leader of Saudi Arabia—and the noose around a Negro's neck in Alabama." Referring to the jingoistic proclamation of Time Inc. chief Henry Luce that an "American Century" was at hand, Welles presciently cautioned that it might come true, "and God help us all. We'll make Germany's bid for world supremacy look like amateur night, and the inevitable retribution will be on a comparable scale." An FBI informant claimed that Welles's *Post* column was "ghost written by [a] Communist" who had previously written some of Welles's radio programs.

Welles took a keen interest in helping to promote the establishment of the United Nations. At the UN World Security Conference in San Francisco in April 1945, he gave radio talks, edited a daily newsletter published in three languages, and wrote editorials for the newspaper *Free World* supporting what he called "World Citizenship." The FBI had an unidentified female informant who worked for Welles and reported extensively on his activities before and during the conference, including his arrangements for regular phone calls from Hollywood to a contact in San Francisco and affairs he allegedly was conducting with a film actress and a stripper. The informant further claimed that Welles had eight employees at his home but "no money at all."

Around that time, Welles explored the idea of running for the U.S. Senate from California (as a Democrat). He said in 1982 that he demurred partly because of opposition from the Communist Party in southern California, which regarded him as a "dangerous revisionist," and that he was further dissuaded by northern California journalist and liberal activist Alan Cranston, who eventually became a four-term senator himself, "so I don't think he was totally disinterested." When the state's longtime Republican senator Hiram Johnson died in August 1945, an informant told the FBI that Welles had declined overtures earlier that year to run for a senatorial seat. Roosevelt, who told Welles he would make a great politician, urged him to run instead from his home state of Wisconsin in the upcoming 1946 election. Veteran U.S. senator Robert M. La Follette Jr. was planning to retire, before he changed his mind and switched his party affiliation from Progressive to Republican. Welles gave careful consideration to running for La Follette's seat, even entertaining fantasies of using it as a stepping-stone to the presidency. He finally decided against entering the Wisconsin race because he "didn't think anybody could get elected President who had been divorced and who had been an actor. I made a helluva mistake."

Perhaps most crucially, in studying the political scene in his home state, Welles discovered that "the dairy interests, who I felt I had to fight, were so powerful that I would almost certainly be beaten unless I was the greatest campaigner ever known. But now, supposing I *was* the greatest campaigner ever known . . . there never would have been Joe McCarthy." A reactionary circuit judge who grossly exaggerated his war record in the Marines, Joseph R. McCarthy eked out an upset victory over La Follette in the Republican primary and so would have been Welles's opponent in the general election if Welles had won the Democratic primary. McCarthy went on to easily win the Senate seat in the fall over the lackluster Democratic candidate, a political science professor and former congressman named Howard McMurray. "So I have that on my conscience," Welles said. Given the volatility of the postwar political picture in Wisconsin, Welles might have prevailed over McCarthy. He would indeed have made a spectacular campaigner, for as *Citizen Kane* demonstrates, one of his greatest talents was oratory. But even though McCarthy had yet to make anti-Communism the centerpiece of his rhetoric, perhaps the specter of red-baiting was an unspoken factor that discouraged Welles from running for political office.

❖ ❖ ❖

None of Welles's other pursuits held enough appeal, in the end, to lure him away from his love for making movies. His film career after the RKO debacle and his wartime blackballing as a director was a continual struggle, with many setbacks and, inevitably, an uneven record of achievement. But that is the price an artist pays for independence, and it enabled him to make daring and groundbreaking films that would not have been possible if he had remained in Hollywood throughout his career.

Most of the time Welles was able to regard his Hollywood misfortunes with a certain sardonic philosophical detachment. "I had luck as no one had," he reflected in a 1965 interview with *Cahiers du Cinéma*. "Afterwards, I had the worst bad luck in the history of the cinema, but that is in the order of things: I had to pay for having had the best luck in the history of the cinema." But he could not help expressing an occasional bitterness over his career struggles. He reflected toward the end of his life, "I would have been more successful if I'd left movies immediately, stayed in the theater, gone into politics, written, anything. I've wasted the greater part of my life looking for money and trying to get along, trying to make my work from this terribly expensive paintbox which is a movie. And I've spent too much energy on things that have nothing to do with making a movie. It's about two percent moviemaking and ninety-eight percent hustling. It's no way to spend a life."

Relating "a long, wistful meditation on his career" by Welles in a 1979 interview, film historian Robert Carringer reported that Welles "started out wanting to be an American Charles Dickens." When Welles received a career achievement award from the Los Angeles Film Critics Association in 1978, he paid tribute to predecessors in attendance, pioneering directors King Vidor and Allan Dwan, regretting that he didn't have their popular touch. Again Welles invoked Dickens as the kind of artist he would have liked to be, one with "that final gift to make a blockbuster." Welles added, "I'm awfully tired of old men saying they have no regrets. We're loaded with, burdened with, *staggering* under regrets."

Why, then, did Welles keep making films long after coming to the realization that he was not, by nature, a truly popular artist? Was it a masochistic urge, a stubborn refusal to face facts, a thumb in the face of Hollywood, a defiance of fate, or simply a passion for the medium that he couldn't shake? Despite feeling that he "made essentially a mistake in staying in movies," Welles said he was prepared to keep doing so for the rest of his life: "Oh, I'm gonna go on being faithful to my girl. I love her. I fell so much in love with making movies that the theater lost everything for me, you know. I'm just in love with making movies."

❖ ❖ ❖

In the immediate postwar years, Welles tried three different approaches to working within the studio system on single-picture contracts, with varying degrees of creative freedom. The three films he made between 1945 and 1947—*The Stranger*, *The Lady from Shanghai*, and *Macbeth*—are experiments in pushing the boundaries of popular filmmaking while still trying to satisfy genre expectations. Only the first was a box-office success, and *Shanghai* and *Macbeth* were mercilessly derided by reviewers. "I'm really not interested in anything but experimentation," Welles said in 1947, shortly before he began shooting *Macbeth*. He declared, "It doesn't matter to me whether I'm popular in Hollywood, or whether I'll be written up in the history of the theater. I'm only interested in opening up new fields or leaving the old ones better than they were when I entered them."

The Stranger was an anomaly in his career, an attempt to demonstrate to Hollywood, as Welles put it, "that I didn't glow in the dark . . . that I could direct a standard Hollywood picture, on time and on budget, just like anyone else." This relatively straightforward thriller centers on an escaped Nazi named Franz Kindler (Welles) hiding out as a teacher in a Connecticut boys' boarding school much like Welles's alma mater, the Todd School. Although it's the only Welles film that was a sizable commercial success, he always considered it the least of his work. Parts of the film, indeed, could just as well have been directed by any journeyman director (Welles later admitted, "I can't be a competent hack. If I try, I do a lousy job"), and Welles's own performance is so over the top that its only reasonable defense has been advanced by critic Michael Anderegg, who suggests that Welles had a Brechtian intent: "Welles's Kindler is so transparent a villain, so clearly not what the all-American inhabitants of Harper, Connecticut, think him to be, that America's complacency and naïveté becomes a dominant issue in the film. . . . Almost as if afraid of allowing the evil of Nazism to appear even momentarily attractive, Welles refuses to act out the charm and plausibility that other characters presumably see in Franz Kindler. . . . Throughout *The Stranger*, Welles delivers even the most innocent-sounding lines with the guilty subtext clearly indicated, continually providing commentary in tandem with representation."

The Stranger has the distinction of being the first Hollywood postwar feature to deal with the Nazi death camps, giving a brief glimpse of documentary footage of the camps and presenting Kindler as the architect of the Final Solution. Welles thought of Kindler as being Martin Bormann, Hitler's right-hand man, rumored to have escaped to South America after the war. *The Stranger* furthered Welles's antifascist concerns by warning about a possible resurgence of Nazism if war criminals were not punished and Germany truly reformed. Another remarkable feature of *The Stranger* is a virtuoso long take in which Kindler kills a fellow Nazi (Konstantin Shayne). The sinuous and tense four-minute tracking shot through the woods was executed by the two men later responsible for the famous opening crane shot in *Touch of Evil*, cinematographer Russell Metty and his assistant John Russell.

The Lady from Shanghai was regarded at the time, even by Welles's friends, as a disgraceful comedown for the maker of *Citizen Kane* into lurid B-movie melodrama. But with its offbeat and incandescent imagery, its deliciously perverse take on sexual intrigue, its sheer weirdness, *Shanghai* has rightly come to be regarded as a classic of film noir. The film's misogynistic tone is a staple of the genre but also reflects more personal emotions, Welles's ambivalence toward his estranged wife. Rita Hayworth plays a murderess luring Welles's Irish-seaman character into a nearly fatal trap. Despite his naïveté about women, Michael O'Hara is something of a radical, admitting that he killed a Franco spy while fighting for the Loyalists in Spain. Columbia Pictures president Harry Cohn, on seeing Welles's rough cut, told his staff, "I'll give a thousand dollars to anyone who can explain the story to me!" Cohn compounded the problem by ordering that the film be extensively recut and larded with a dreadful musical score. Though shot in 1946, it was not released until 1948, the same year as *Macbeth*.

Welles's low-budget *Macbeth* was made for Republic Pictures, the B-movie studio best known for churning out pulp Westerns. But Republic's tobacco-spitting president, Herbert J. Yates, liked to take an occasional flier into culture, and he was the only Hollywood executive Welles could persuade to let him film a Shakespearean tragedy. Ingeniously shot in twenty-three days on a handful of rudimentary sets, *Macbeth* was slammed by the American press for supposedly roughing up the text (*Life* magazine's spread on *Macbeth* was headlined "MURDER! Orson Welles doth foully slaughter Shakespeare in dialect version of his *Tragedy of Macbeth*"), an odd complaint about a faithful-in-spirit rendition of a horrific tragedy that revolves around witches' prophecies and primitive bloodletting. Of Welles himself, *Life* sneered that "a few sad years ago [he] was the Boy Wonder of Hollywood." Welles's compellingly rough-hewn, theatrically stylized, yet intensely cinematic visualization of Shakespeare also suffered from its proximity to the more acceptably genteel style of Laurence Olivier's 1947 *Hamlet*, which won that year's Academy Award for best picture.

As if living out the traditional curse of the "Scottish play"—or Welles's jocular claim, taken seriously by some of his admirers, that a "curse" has hung over his career since his entanglement with voodoo practitioners during the ill-fated making of *It's All True*—Welles's *Macbeth* was soon pulled from release and butchered. Republic ordered it shortened by twenty-one minutes and the soundtrack redubbed into less accented English, but this crudening, condensation, and Americanization, released in 1950, also died at the box office. Surprisingly, Welles sanctioned the overhauling, even though he correctly considered the original soundtrack not only more authentic but also more intelligible. He has been roundly criticized for remaining abroad while his loyal assistant Richard Wilson was doing most of the reworking. Even the usually admiring Barbara Leaming writes, "It was almost as if, in some subliminal way, Orson had felt compelled to repeat the grave mistake he had made in leaving *Ambersons* unfinished [to go abroad]." But Welles's absence may have stemmed more from necessity than from desire. He did make one brief trip back to Hollywood, at the studio's urging, to finish the dubbing. And he vociferously criticized some of the vocal overhaul, particularly that of Jeanette Nolan's Lady Macbeth, which, as he pointed out in a memo to the studio from London, ruined her incisive performance by substituting for her Scottish accent an "unfortunate Montana whine, wheeze, and scrape."

The 1980 full restoration of *Macbeth* by Robert Gitt of the UCLA Film and Television Archive with Wilson's assistance drastically changed my view of the film, which I had considered an ambitious failure. The Scottish accents give a rugged texture to the performances that brings them disturbingly alive, and the added footage, particularly the restoration of the full ten-minute take of King Duncan's murder, a tour de force that brilliantly sustains an almost unbearable suspense, helps make *Macbeth* one of Welles's major achievements. Welles was both accurate and overly modest when he called his *Macbeth* an "experiment," for it is one of the most fully realized translations of Shakespeare into cinematic language, an expressionistically stylized nightmare of sound and imagery, as audacious in its own way as his "Negro *Macbeth*."*

Welles's strenuous attempts to bend the studio system to his own purposes in the 1940s can now be viewed in a different light from the record of failure they seemed to most observers at the time. Film historian Douglas Gomery notes that Welles, an essentially independent and uncommercial filmmaker, was hired as a director only by the "Weaker Four" majors (RKO, Columbia, Universal, and United Artists) and not by the "Stronger Four" (Paramount, Twentieth Century–Fox, MGM, and Warner Bros.):

> Furthermore, he was only able to work for these less important companies in very specific situations. That is, he slipped through the cracks of the existing system and operated as best he could. Welles was never part of the

* In a fascinating rediscovery around the same time Welles's film of *Macbeth* was restored, four minutes of documentary footage of his "Negro *Macbeth*" came to light at the National Archives. The play's climactic scene, with Jack Carter as Macbeth and Maurice Ellis as Macduff, was included in a 1937 WPA documentary short on federal job programs for African Americans, *We Work Again* (available on *Treasures from American Film Archives*, a 2000 DVD set from the National Film Preservation Foundation). The *Macbeth* footage is historically valuable but shot in an unimaginative manner by, ironically, a Hearst Metrotone Newsreel crew, clearly without Welles's involvement.

> dominant Hollywood power structure, but rather an outsider sought by less powerful companies in their efforts to boost themselves—always unsuccessfully—in the industry hierarchy. He exploited these weaker companies, convincing them to permit him to make the type of non-traditional film he sought. Thus, he always worked on the margin of the industry—only the degree of which changed over the years.

Mainstream Hollywood liked to believe that Welles was habitually and wildly profligate as an excuse to stigmatize him for his real crimes, his lack of orthodoxy and malleability. The real "curse" hanging over his career is capitalism. He did go over budget on his first two films, but by sums that can hardly be considered outrageous. Furthermore, his ability to make much from small resources throughout his career has fooled people into thinking his films must have cost more than they did, an impression heightened by media exaggeration. "I'm not an overspender, though I've sometimes been a delayed earner," Welles insisted in a 1967 interview, pointing to *Kane* as an example. Of Welles's four postwar Hollywood films—*The Stranger*, *The Lady from Shanghai*, *Macbeth*, and *Touch of Evil*—two, *The Stranger* and *Macbeth*, came in under budget, and only one, *Shanghai*, went seriously over budget (the film reportedly was budgeted at $2.3 million and went almost half a million dollars over).

In an undated memo written to Welles several months after the completion of shooting on *Shanghai* to help "refute charges of wastefulness or extravagance" leveled against the director by Columbia president Harry Cohn, Welles associate Richard Wilson tried to blame much of the cost overruns on alleged illness and fatigue suffered by its female star, Rita Hayworth, who at the time of the shooting was still married to the director. However, Adrienne L. McLean's *Being Rita Hayworth: Labor, Identity, and Hollywood Stardom* (2004) produces evidence that those were false excuses made to cover Welles's own responsibility for the overruns (Welles also blames Hayworth's illness when prompted by Bogdanovich in *This Is Orson Welles*). McLean reports that "often Hayworth was scheduled for shooting but never called to the set because of Welles's demands and delays, his decisions to rebuild sets, recostume or remakeup minor characters, rewrite scenes, and so forth—all possibly admirable artistically but none the result of Hayworth's intransigence or temperament." Hayworth did walk off the set once, but according to accounts McLean received from crew members, "it likely had to do with her being 'fed up' with Welles's actions as director, his public indiscretions with other women, and his erratic production methods."

When asked by Hedda Hopper why *Shanghai* had gone over budget, Welles replied, "Who doesn't overrun his budget in this town?" That somewhat glib comeback contradicts his later claims never to have gone over budget, but as an argument it was not without justification. The amounts Welles was given to make films, and the extent of his occasional budget overruns, were modest compared to the huge sums routinely spent and often wasted by directors today, even after inflation is considered. There's a lot of selective hypocrisy surrounding the subject of budgets in Hollywood, where going over budget is tolerated if a film turns out to do well at the box office or if the director's track record is generally successful. Welles was vulnerable on both points, and Columbia showed no faith in *Shanghai*'s commercial potential, virtually ensuring its failure by dumping it on the market belatedly. That action further stigmatized Welles as financially irresponsible.

In the overall scheme of Welles's career, *Shanghai* was an anomaly. As I saw at first hand during the making of *The Other Side of the Wind*, Welles was able to shoot quickly and take advantage of unforeseen circumstances rather than being fazed by having to change his script. One night while shooting a party scene at Bogdanovich's home in Bel-Air, Welles decided on the spur of the moment that he wanted to track the camera along with Paul Stewart and Tonio Selwart as they walked through a roomful of guests. But there was no dolly. So Welles used what he told me was a trick he learned from Jean Renoir, "the poor man's dolly"—having the cameraman lie on his back on a rug that was pulled along the floor. It worked beautifully, and I could see how delighted Welles was to come up with such an economical way of shooting.

The impression that "[Welles] is an extravagant director is a big canard," said his *Touch of Evil* costar Charlton Heston. "It is simply not true. I mean, Warren Beatty can spend sixty million dollars making *Reds* half an hour too long and it crosses nobody's lips that that's too much money to spend. But there's *no* reason to say it about Welles. You can say *other* things about him, but not that."

❖ ❖ ❖

Welles's problems with studios, audiences, and critics in the postwar years helped convince him that it was time to leave Hollywood. By 1947 he felt that his career as a studio director was, if not entirely finished, barely sustainable. He planned to try his fortune in Europe with Alexander Korda, with whom he was discussing a long-cherished plan to film Ros-

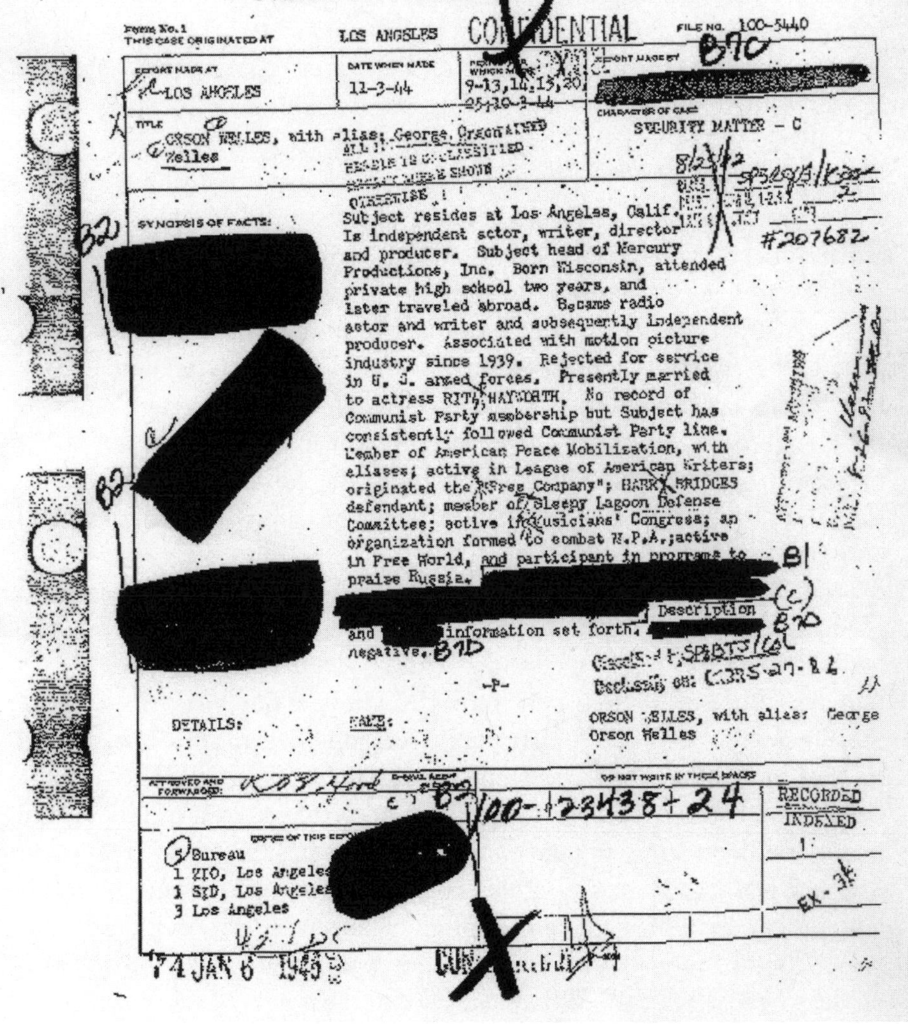

CONFIDENTIAL

FEDERAL BUREAU OF INVESTIGATION

Form No. 1
THIS CASE ORIGINATED AT LOS ANGELES CONFIDENTIAL FILE NO. 100-5440

REPORT MADE AT	DATE WHEN MADE	PERIOD FOR WHICH MADE	REPORT MADE BY
LOS ANGELES	11-3-44	9-13,14,15,20,25;10-3-44	

TITLE: ORSON WELLES, with alias; George Orson Welles

CHARACTER OF CASE: SECURITY MATTER – C

SYNOPSIS OF FACTS:

Subject resides at Los Angeles, Calif. Is independent actor, writer, director and producer. Subject head of Mercury Productions, Inc. Born Wisconsin, attended private high school two years, and later traveled abroad. Became radio actor and writer and subsequently independent producer. Associated with motion picture industry since 1939. Rejected for service in U. S. armed forces. Presently married to actress RITA HAYWORTH. No record of Communist Party membership but Subject has consistently followed Communist Party line. Member of American Peace Mobilization, with aliases; active in League of American Writers; originated the "Free Company"; HARRY BRIDGES defendant; member of Sleepy Lagoon Defense Committee; active in Musicians' Congress; an organization formed to combat N.P.A.; active in Free World, and participant in programs to praise Russia.

Description and information set forth, negative.

-P-

DETAILS: NAME: ORSON WELLES, with alias: George Orson Welles

APPROVED AND FORWARDED:

100-23438-24

RECORDED
INDEXED

COPIES OF THIS REPORT
5 Bureau
1 ZIO, Los Angeles
1 SID, Los Angeles
3 Los Angeles

74 JAN 6 1945

A page from Orson Welles's FBI file, maintained from 1941 through 1956. This 1944 document summarizes the bureau's attitude toward Welles, a lifelong progressive: "No record of Communist Party membership but Subject has consistently followed Communist Party line." The FBI flatly labeled Welles a "COMMUNIST" when it put him on the Security Index, a list of people who supposedly represented threats to national security, in 1945. This hostile U.S. government scrutiny caused Welles to be blacklisted by the film industry and to exile himself from the United States in 1947. He worked mostly in Europe until returning to live in Hollywood in 1970. *(Federal Bureau of Investigation)* tand's *Cyrano de Bergerac.* But there was another, equally compelling but still little-known motive for Welles's decision to exile himself to Europe.

Although it's usually reported that he left Hollywood in 1948, he actually left in late November 1947. It's not coincidental that he did so shortly after the House Committee on Un-American Activities began its hearings that month on alleged Communist influence in Hollywood. Welles lent his name to public protest of the hearings as a member of the Committee for the First Amendment, a short-lived coalition of Hollywood liberals and leftists formed to defend constitutional rights and fight political repression. The hearings, which led to the imposition of the Hollywood blacklist, stemmed from information that had been supplied to HUAC that May by members of the film industry in closed-door Los Angeles hearings. "Hundreds of very prominent film capital people have been named as Communists to us," HUAC chairman J. Parnell Thomas (R–New Jersey) told the press during those hearings. Most, if not all, of those who supplied the names belonged to the Motion Picture Alliance for the Preservation of American Ideals, founded in 1944 by Hollywood anti-Communists.

The alliance was backed wholeheartedly by the American Legion and William Randolph Hearst. Several of the leading members of the alliance had longtime ties to Hearst, and Pizzitola's *Hearst over Hollywood* notes that one of them, screenwriter James Kevin McGuinness, helped form the alliance "to serve as a 'better public relations' organization established for motion pictures than the one represented by people like Charlie Chaplin and Orson Welles." When an emergency council of Hollywood guilds and unions met to condemn the alliance in June 1944, Welles and Rita Hayworth "sent a congratulatory telegram to this meeting congratulating them upon their magnificent fight against the Motion Picture Alliance," the FBI reported, adding that they were commended for doing so by the *People's World*, the West Coast Communist newspaper.

Welles kept up his political activity after the war in spite of the growing resistance from the right. He made a strong statement about racial injustice in 1946 in the case of Isaac Woodard Jr. An African American World War II veteran, Woodard, upon his return to South Carolina, talked back to an abusive white bus driver who called him "boy," and as a result was beaten and blinded by the white police chief of Batesburg, Lynwood Shull. The NAACP asked Welles to become involved in the case, and he did several impassioned radio shows about Woodard for his ABC series *Orson Welles Commentaries.* "God judge me if it is not the most pressing business I have," Welles told his audience. "The black soldier fought for me in this war. The least I can do is fight for him."

Threatened with libel suits because of Welles's radio crusade, ABC dropped the series in October 1946. The controversy put a virtual end to Welles's career as a political commentator on radio. "I had the satisfaction of being instrumental in bringing that particular policeman to justice," Welles later reflected. "The case was brought to my attention, and I brought it to the attention of the radio public and we did finally manage to locate this man and bring him into a court of law." Those remarks, delivered on a segment of his 1955 British TV series *Orson Welles' Sketch Book*, omitted the fact that Shull was acquitted by an all-white jury. And Welles's televised remarks were marred, ironically, by his repeated references to Woodard as a "boy."

But the Woodard case had a far-reaching effect by raising President Harry S. Truman's consciousness about the unjust treatment of black soldiers and helping convince him to integrate the U.S. Army in 1948. Welles's involvement in the case is reflected in his portrayal of Captain Hank Quinlan in his 1958 film *Touch of Evil.* What Welles says of Chief Shull in the *Sketch Book* can also be applied to Quinlan: "That sort of policeman is a criminal in uniform." *Citizen of America: Orson Welles and the Ballad of Isaac Woodard*, a 2005 documentary film by Robert Fischer and Richard France about Welles's radio crusade, reveals that Rep. John E. Rankin (D-Mississippi), a notoriously racist member of HUAC, wrote FBI director J. Edgar Hoover that the committee was concerned about Welles's advocacy for Woodard. The progressive radio writer Norman Corwin, whose works Welles performed in the 1940s, expresses surprise in *Citizen of America* that "it's been little-known up to now, [Welles's] problems with the FBI."

Welles took a combative approach in the postwar years to the growing chorus of innuendos that he was a dangerous subversive. In October 1946, he filed a million-dollar libel suit against the vice president of the American Federation of Labor, Matthew Woll, for accusing him of "communistic leanings." The charge came in an article Woll wrote for a trade paper, *American Photo Engraver*, criticizing "leftist influence in Hollywood." Welles said what "bothered him most" was that the article was reprinted in a film industry trade paper, the *Hollywood Reporter.* After the *Reporter* printed a retraction, Welles dropped his suit against Woll. Actress Myrna Loy, also accused in the article of communistic tendencies, sued the *Reporter* and won retractions from both the paper and Woll.

Articles clipped from the *New York World-Telegram* about the Welles and Loy lawsuits were placed in Welles's file by the New York field office of the FBI.

Short of testifying before HUAC, the most prominent public clearance ritual for a Hollywood figure was to give an interview to Hedda Hopper, one of the ringleaders of the blacklist. Hopper was an aggressive member of the Motion Picture Alliance and used her column to stigmatize or clear people suspected of Communist ties. In a July 1947 interview with Hopper, Welles described Hollywood as "enemy territory." He behaved as if he were on trial in a star chamber, forced to prove his innocence of something that wasn't even a crime. But Welles clearly felt the need to do some groveling to save what was left of his Hollywood career, and his extreme agitation during their two-hour interview was noted by Hopper. As he talked, he paced restlessly around the room, "flinging himself into chair after chair," lighting and relighting his cigar at least twenty times.

"Now, Orson," she said, "you know we haven't seen eye to eye on many things in the past."

Welles "bellowed with laughter," responding, "That is the understatement of the year."

"Tell me," she said, "just what is your political philosophy?"

"Well, for one thing," he replied, "I'm sick of being called a Communist. It's true that I've worked for some of the things the Communist party has advocated. But that was merely coincidental. I'm opposed to political dictatorship. And organized ignorance I dislike more than anything in the world. I'm particularly interested in civil liberties for all people, regardless of race or creed.

"Last year I put up a fight for a Negro who had been brutally beaten and blinded by a policeman in the South. I'd have fought just as hard for a Wall St. broker had he been in the spot that the Negro boy was. It's my idea that the best way to lick communism in this country is [to] compete with it and beat it at its own game. I've been accused of reading editorials from communist papers over the air. That I have never done, as a check of my records will prove. In fact, I've been repeatedly attacked by Communists.

"My appearance at that meeting in [New York's] Carnegie Hall [in 1942, for the Artists' Front to Win the War], arranged by Charlie Chaplin, calling for a second front during the war [to aid the Soviet Union in its battle against Nazi Germany] was grossly misinterpreted. I'd been given to understand that it was an anti-fascist affair and a benefit for Spanish war veterans. When I learned at the last minute what the meeting was all about, I did what I think was the bravest act of my life. I was supposed to speak for an hour. But I talked for only 10 minutes, and used that time telling the audience what I thought of being deliberately misled as to the purpose of a meeting to which I'd agreed to lend my support."

(An April 16, 1943, FBI summary of its file on Welles, furnished to the State Department at its request, claims of the Carnegie Hall event: "Information has been received reflecting that this rally was at the instigation of the Communist Party and that it was a 100% Communist affair." Other speakers included playwright and screenwriter Lillian Hellman, journalist I. F. Stone, and Dutch documentary filmmaker Joris Ivens.)

"As far as a cure for the ills of the world," Welles told Hopper, "I have no blueprint for salvation. The problem is vast and long-ranged. If it's ever solved, we've got to teach each man to think for himself."

❖ ❖ ❖

That limited but humiliating mea culpa was a preview of what Welles probably would have said if he had been called to testify before HUAC. Despite Welles's claim that he begged to testify in order to deny on the record that he was a Communist, he was not among the "Hollywood Nineteen," the group subpoenaed by the committee in October 1947 for its November hearings. The group included two writers who had been involved with Welles: screenwriter Howard Koch, the radio dramatist of *The War of the Worlds;* and Bertolt Brecht, whose play *Galileo* Welles had discussed directing on stage in Los Angeles earlier in 1947 (Welles considered it "a perfect anticommunist work" because he thought it portrays the Catholic Church as Stalinist, an interpretation with which Brecht did not agree). Koch was never called to testify, and Brecht left the country for East Germany. The hearings prompted the studios to instigate the blacklist, beginning with the "Hollywood Ten" who refused to cooperate with HUAC.

No doubt if Welles had stayed in Hollywood he would have been called in HUAC's far more extensive second round of Hollywood hearings in 1951, when the blacklist was greatly expanded. But he could see the handwriting on the wall in 1947 and decided to leave town in late November, feeling, like Falstaff in *Chimes at Midnight,* that "The better part of valour is discretion, in the which part I have saved me life!" (Another factor in the timing of Welles's departure may have been the fact that his divorce proceedings with Hayworth had occurred earlier that month.)

The mystery that has long surrounded Welles's departure from the United States in 1947 left a gap in understanding through which has emerged a fantastic piece of calumny. Incredibly, a writer has advanced the theory that Welles left the country to avoid being investigated in the Black Dahlia case, the still-unsolved murder of Elizabeth Short, a would-be movie actress whose grotesquely mutilated body was found on a Los Angeles vacant lot in January 1947. Mary Pacios, who claims to have been a childhood friend of the "Dahlia," fingered Welles as the prime suspect in her self-published 2000 book, *Childhood Shadows: The Hidden Story of the Black Dahlia Murder.* Without offering any actual evidence linking Welles to the heinous crime, Pacios engaged in her wild speculation after learning that Welles sawed women in half in his *Mercury Wonder Show* and seeing a production still of his Crazy House set for *The Lady from Shanghai.* Welles painted the figures on that set, including a grinning blonde woman whose mouth is slashed from ear to ear, not unlike the Dahlia's. Pacios sees that as a sign that Welles was subconsciously confessing his murderous impulses toward women and takes the fact that the figure does not appear in the film as an indication that Columbia excised incriminating evidence from *Shanghai* to protect itself and Welles. Pacios also suggests that Welles had dated Short, who was known to have been involved with men in the film industry.

The Pacios book would not be worth mentioning were it not the most bizarre manifestation of the hostility toward Welles that has metastasized throughout the American mass media in recent years. Perhaps to some fevered imaginations Welles has become the successor to Roscoe (Fatty) Arbuckle, the silent comic whose obesity seemed to inspire sick fantasies about his sexuality, leading to his railroading in a notorious 1921 murder case; two acquittals were not enough to remove the suspicion from Arbuckle in the popular imagination. Welles is safely dead and unable to sue for libel, so the notion that he might have been the Black Dahlia killer shows signs of becoming an urban legend. It found its way into a 2001 novel about the case, *Angel in Black*, by Max Allan Collins, who portrays Welles as worried that he might have killed the Dahlia in a fit of insanity. In an afterword to the novel, Collins admits that "liberties have been taken with the facts" and that "Pacios is the source for the theory that Orson Welles is a Black Dahlia suspect—a notion I frankly find absurd, though Pacios makes a good enough case for me to justify the inclusion of the great filmmaker as a character, here."

Welles's activity immediately after leaving Hollywood has also been the subject of a novel. This one involves him in political intrigue. Italian writer and filmmaker Davide Ferrario's 1994 novel *Dissolvenza al nero* (*Fade to Black)* begins with Welles's arrival in Rome in November 1947 to star as the eighteenth-century occult magician Cagliostro in *Black Magic*, which he unofficially codirected with Gregory Ratoff. In the novel, when a man dies at Welles's feet on the first day of shooting, the police call the death a drug overdose. Welles sets out to investigate what he believes to be a murder, uncovering a conspiracy to counteract the rising Communist influence on Italian politics. The conspirators include the Vatican, the Italian film industry, gangster Lucky Luciano, and the U.S. government. Ferrario's storyline is indebted to Welles's films *Mr. Arkadin* and *The Stranger* and to reports of his political activities in the 1940s, including his dinner with the Italian Communist Party leader Palmiro Togliatti. A photograph of the two men at dinner found its way into Welles's FBI file, along with a note from a French informant stating (in the FBI's translation) that "if this photograph should come to the attention of a member of the State Department, WELLES will undoubtedly be brought before a court in charge of prosecuting actors suspected of Un-American activities and perhaps even excluded from Hollywood definitely." Danny Huston (John Huston's son) plays Welles in the 2006 film version of *Fade to Black*, directed in Europe by Oliver Parker, who adapted the novel with John Sayles.

From Hollywood's and the public's point of view, Welles might just as well have quit directing movies after he departed for Europe, since his subsequent career as a filmmaker seemed so obscure. He was an "uncommercial, art-house director" whose films took years to arrive in the United States and then were scarcely seen in his native country. In 1949 an informant told the FBI that Welles, who was living in Italy, "is badly off financially at the present time, and stated facetiously that WELLES had been making pictures over in Italy these past two years in order to finance a trip home to the United States." That kind of insularity and xenophobia, abetted by the rampant anti-intellectualism of America in the 1950s, ensured that Welles's European works were marginalized.

❖ ❖ ❖

The FBI's interest in Welles gradually diminished after it became clear that he was settled abroad. His 1946–47 activities on behalf of such groups as the Committee for the First Amendment, HICCASP, the Progressive Citizens of America, and the Baby Fund Campaign of the American Committee for Yugoslav Relief, as well as his advocacy of justice for

Isaac Woodard, were summarized in an eight-page August 1949 report from the FBI's Los Angeles office, which concluded about Welles: "Never identified as CP [Communist Party] member, but has permitted use of his name and has been active in CP front organizations. Literary and motion picture assistants identified as CP members." An informant told the FBI that Welles "did not even begin to know the goings[-]on taking place among his employees," some of whom allegedly were siphoning off his money to the Communist Party, "although [the informant] said he had no proof this was so."

Because "Welles has been in Italy for the past two years" with no further Hollywood political activities detected, he was removed from the Security Index in September 1949. FBI headquarters told the Los Angeles office that

> the Security Index card maintained for Welles at the Bureau is being canceled and you are instructed to similarly cancel the card maintained in your office.
>
> In the event subject again becomes active in CP [Communist Party] matters upon his return to the United States, consideration should be given by you to reactivate his Security Index card.

The FBI sporadically added to its Welles file until 1956, and the cloud hanging over his head never entirely lifted. Its persistence is indicated by the FBI's response when a White House staff assistant for security made an inquiry about him in 1976, during the Gerald Ford administration. Welles, the FBI replied on July 6, had been "the subject of a security-type investigation conducted by the FBI during the late 1940s based upon his name appearing in connection with the activities of Communist Party front organizations. Although Welles had never been identified as a Communist Party member, many of his associates and assistants were identified as such."

❖ ❖ ❖

Victor S. Navasky explains in his 1980 book *Naming Names* how the insidious system of show-business blacklisting worked from 1947 through the early 1960s: "Each naming went out like a burglar alarm to the freelance enforcer network, reminding them that there was a subversive to be fired, harassed, or embarrassed, a career to be derailed; reminding his children and their friends that they had a pariah for a parent; reminding neighbors that they had best keep their distance. The enforcers devoured the Committee's [HUAC's] annual indexes and supplements, reference manuals such as *Red Channels*, newsletters like *Counterattack*, and columnists like [Walter] Winchell and [George E.] Sokolsky. Their appetite for names was insatiable."

The clearest evidence of Welles's continued blacklisting or graylisting after his departure for Europe was his inclusion with 150 other show-business figures in the infamous 1950 "bible" of the blacklist, *Red Channels: The Report of Communist Influence in Radio and Television.* The pamphlet was published three days before the start of the Korean War by *Counterattack*, which billed itself as *"The Newsletter of Facts to Combat Communism." Counterattack* in turn was published by Aware Inc., a commercial enterprise run in New York by former FBI agent Theodore Kirkpatrick and TV producer Vincent Hartnett, described by Navasky as a "professional anti-Communist" whose company "cleared for a fee the performers it exposed."

Red Channels has been described by radio historian Eric Barnouw as "a list of 151 of the most talented and admired people in the industry—mostly writers, directors, performers. They were people who had helped to make radio an honored medium. . . . They had opposed Franco, Hitler, and Mussolini, tried to help war refugees, combatted race discrimination." Inclusion in *Red Channels* was tantamount to being blacklisted. *Counterattack* sent free copies of the pamphlet to employers in the entertainment industry as a way of alerting them to people who had not yet been blacklisted but needed to be. *Red Channels* acquired greater economic clout when a right-wing New York supermarket owner, Lawrence A. Johnson, organized a national boycott by supermarkets against firms that advertised on radio and television shows employing alleged Communists or Communist sympathizers. As Joseph Persico writes in his biography of Edward R. Murrow, "Thus it was that the networks and advertising agencies, before hiring anyone, began to check them out in *Red Channels* for possible Communist connections. *Red Channels* became the standard reference work on Communists, their sympathizers, and their dupes."

Those included in *Red Channels* had to clear themselves before HUAC or in some other way in order to keep working. Just as Welles never wanted to publicly confirm that he had been blacklisted or graylisted, out of an understandable need to maintain the hopeful posture that he was still available for hire in America, it was part of the insidious workings of the show-business blacklist that even its perpetrators, such as American Business Consultants and the Motion Picture Association of America, denied that the blacklist ever existed.

The allegations about Welles in *Red Channels* came mostly from the files of HUAC. His entry spans three pages and is a potpourri of Popular Front and progressive organizations and causes. Welles is listed as a member of the National Citizens Political Action Committee, the Motion Picture Artists' Committee, and the Negro Cultural Committee; an executive board member of the Theatre Arts Committee; a candidate for the executive board of the Hollywood Democratic Committee; and an "affiliate" of the American Committee for Protection of the Foreign Born, the American Student Union, the Coordinating Committee to Lift the Embargo, the Exiled Writers Committee, the Friends of the Abraham Lincoln Brigade, International Labor Defense, and *New Masses*.

Welles is also identified in *Red Channels* as a sponsor of the Citizens' Committee for Harry Bridges and the Sleepy Lagoon Defense Committee; a dinner sponsor for the Joint Anti-Fascist Refugee Committee; a contributor to the *Daily Worker*; a benefit patron for the Medical Bureau to Aid Spanish Democracy; a speaker to the National Council of American-Soviet Fellowship; and a signer of an advertisement appeal in the *New York Times* for Russian War Relief and of a call by the League of American Writers for the Fourth American Writers' Congress. He is listed as having presided over the 1942 Carnegie Hall event for the Artists' Front to Win the War. Welles collaborators and colleagues listed in *Red Channels* include Will Geer, Howard da Silva, Burgess Meredith, Ruth Gordon, Edward G. Robinson, Judy Holliday, and Arthur Miller. Other prominent show-business personalities whose dossiers appear in the pamphlet include Leonard Bernstein, Dashiell Hammett, Lena Horne, Burl Ives, Gypsy Rose Lee, Dorothy Parker, and Pete Seeger.

Guilt by association was one of the principal tools of the blacklist. Welles was vulnerable in this regard because he freely associated with many left-wingers, including some admitted Communists, during his days in the theater, radio, and films in the 1930s and 1940s. Several of his colleagues were blacklisted, and at least two became informers.

Actors who had worked for Welles on the New York stage and were later blacklisted in Hollywood included Geer, who played Mister Mister, the villainous Steeltown factory owner in *The Cradle Will Rock;* da Silva, union organizer Larry Foreman in *Cradle;* and Canada Lee, Banquo in Welles's "Negro *Macbeth*" and Bigger Thomas in *Native Son.* Georgia Backus, who acted for Welles on radio as well as in *Kane* and *Ambersons*, had her career ended by the blacklist, as did Dorothy Comingore, who played Susan Alexander Kane. John Berry, Welles's assistant director on

Too Much Johnson and stage manager on *Native Son*, was blacklisted after becoming a film director. Screenwriter-director Abraham Polonsky, who wrote radio shows for Welles in the 1930s, was also blacklisted.

Comingore was perhaps the most tragic figure among Welles's associates affected by the blacklist. She appeared in only three films after *Citizen Kane*. Her husband, screenwriter Richard Collins, was one of the Hollywood Nineteen. He named names to HUAC in 1951, but the following year, Comingore took the Fifth Amendment before HUAC and was blacklisted. Her children were taken away from her in a bitter custody battle with Collins in which she was accused of being an alcoholic and a Communist, and she was picked up on a prostitution charge some believe was a setup because of her political activities. Comingore never acted again and died in 1971.

John Houseman, like his former producing partner Welles, was never a Communist but often worked with party members and was active in many organizations later considered "Communist fronts." Houseman, by his own account, saved his producing career in the early 1950s by "weaseling." He wrote a seven-page letter to Nicholas Schenck, president of MGM's parent company, Loews Inc., stating, "I have not at any time supported or approved the Communist Party," and concluding, "I am sorry if, at any time, my efforts or the use of my name has been used to help further activities that were in any sense disloyal or subversive. I would do what I could to correct any such unfortunate results."

Four prominent actors who had worked with Welles were graylisted for their leftist affiliations but cleared themselves by cooperating with government investigators. Two gave friendly testimony before HUAC: Edward G. Robinson, who starred for Welles in *The Stranger*, and Lucille Ball, who appeared on several of Welles's radio programs and helped him make a brief Hollywood comeback in 1956. Judy Holliday, who was Judy Tuvim when she worked for the Mercury Theatre for two years in the late 1930s and appeared as an extra in Welles's lost 1938 film, *Too Much Johnson*, became a friendly witness before the Senate Internal Security Committee. Vincent Price, a cast member of the Mercury stage productions of *The Shoemaker's Holiday* and *Heartbreak House*, cleared himself of graylisting by cooperating with the FBI.

Two close associates of Welles, actor-producer William Alland and writer Elizabeth (Betty) Wilson, named names to HUAC to save their own careers. Neither, however, included Welles among the people they named in their testimony to the committee. Not only had Welles never been a Communist, but Alland and Wilson evidently retained a sense of loyalty toward the man who gave them their first important breaks in show business.

Best known as the newsreel reporter Thompson in *Citizen Kane*, Alland was Welles's factotum in the Mercury Theatre and was playfully dubbed "Vakhtangov" by Welles, a reference to the influential Russian stage actor-producer Yevgeni Vakhtangov. Alland recalled that around the time *Kane* was released and the FBI opened its file on Welles,

> The FBI gave me a questionnaire and asked questions of me. Weeks later, they called me back and said, "Now, look, you held out on us." "What do you mean, held out on you?" "Well, we know that you and Orson had a house in Hollywood, and you lived together there. Are you both homosexuals?" So I said, "Absolutely not." "Why did you rent it for Orson?" "Well, because he had a lady that he used to take there." "Who was the lady?" I said, "Well, I'd rather not say." "Well, you better tell us." I said, "It's Dolores Del Rio." They also asked me some questions about, "Is he a Communist?" You know, they asked me that. It told me that they were very much suspicious of Orson on every level.

Reuniting with Welles in the 1970s on *F for Fake*, Alland echoed his stentorian, tongue-in-cheek narration of the newsreel in *Kane* by narrating a faux newsreel about Howard Hughes.

Elizabeth Wilson worked as a production assistant on *It's All True* while accompanying her future husband, Welles's longtime associate Richard Wilson, to Brazil. She named forty-five names to HUAC in 1951. Although she had no screenwriting credits before then, she had an active career as a TV writer in the years that followed, notably for *The Waltons*. The former Betty Anderson had been a Communist Party member as well as secretary of two progressive organizations HUAC considered Communist fronts, the Hollywood Anti-Nazi League and the Motion Picture Democratic Committee. Richard Wilson stopped working regularly with Welles after 1948, when they finished revising *Macbeth*. Wilson said only half-jokingly that he had to choose between being married to Orson and being married to Betty. Richard Wilson worked with William Alland producing films at Universal-International in the 1950s. Despite Betty's capitulation to HUAC, Welles remained friendly with the Wilsons until his death, and the couple worked on the 1993 documentary *It's All True: Based on an Unfinished Film by Orson Welles*.

❖ ❖ ❖

It was ironic that Hollywood Communists were distrustful of Welles, despite his affinities with leftists and progressive causes. He observed in a 1964 interview with Spanish film critics:

> In American art the problem, or better, one of the problems, is the betrayal of the Left by the Left, self-betrayal. In one sense, by stupidity, by orthodoxy and because of slogans; in another, by simple betrayal. We are very few in our generation who have not betrayed our position, who have not given other people's names. . . . That is terrible. It can never be undone. I don't know how one starts over after a similar betrayal; that differs enormously, however, from this, for example, a Frenchman who collaborated with the Gestapo in order to save his wife's life; that is another genre of collaboration. What is so sad about the American Left is that it betrayed in order to save its swimming pools. There was no American Right in my generation. Intellectually it didn't exist. There were only Leftists and they mutually betrayed each other. The Left was not destroyed by McCarthy: it demolished itself, ceding to a new generation of Nihilists.

Welles engaged in the self-protective subterfuge of denying he was blacklisted. He insisted to Bogdanovich, "I wasn't run out of town," although that comment was made in the context of his commercial problems, not his political situation. Pointedly asked by British TV interviewer Michael Parkinson in 1974 whether he went to Europe because he was being investigated or because he needed to find work, Welles replied, "Not to avoid McCarthy, certainly not. Yes, really because the work's been in Europe. And because I like living on this side of the Atlantic very much. But I like living in America too. I'm not a refugee either politically or emotionally from my country. I'm neither very hot about—nationalistically inclined, because I hate that in anybody. I hate—I *do* truly believe that patriotism is the last refuge of the scoundrel. And I don't feel that way. But I'm very happy in America, but it happens that America is not as happy with me as I am with it."

❖ ❖ ❖

Welles sometimes attributed his expatriate status to tax disputes with the U.S. government. The excuse that his tax problems kept him abroad for most of the period between the late 1940s and the late 1960s has long been the standard explanation in Welles biographies, including the authorized biography by Barbara Leaming, published shortly before his death in 1985. That story does not hold up to scrutiny. Was this a cover for other, more overtly political problems? Press reports from the times when he was mostly living in Europe would seem to support that conclusion, for although Welles did have tax problems intermittently for many years, he sometimes exaggerated their severity and seemed to use his tax difficulties to deflect attention from his less tractable political status. At other times, he seemed to minimize reports of his tax difficulties in order to appear more employable in the States.

Welles said the tax problems began when he tried to deduct personal losses on his 1946 stage production *Around the World* as business expenses. When the Internal Revenue Service disallowed that claim, he said, he found himself with a tax debt he was unable to pay, variously reported at between $320,000 and $375,000. In September 1952, *Variety* reported that Welles had filed an appeal in U.S. Tax Court of an IRS ruling that he owed $24,302 in taxes from his 1947 return. The IRS said he had made excessive deductions on his 1946 film *The Stranger* in dissolving a corporation he owned with Rita Hayworth. *Variety* added that the government had reimbursed Welles $935 he had overpaid on his 1946 tax return. The article made no mention of any remaining dispute over deductions for *Around the World*, which evidently had been settled by that time, although Welles claimed in the late 1950s that it had taken him seven years to pay off that particular debt. Leaming's biography, in the face of all the contrary evidence, insists it was still a problem for him in the 1970s.

In January 1953, the government filed suit against Welles for $11,797.52, representing $10,192.56 in unpaid taxes it claimed he still owed for 1943, plus interest. A Los Angeles Superior Court judge agreed in July 1953 to extend for another year the deadline for serving a tax summons against Welles on that claim, since the government was unable to serve him while he was in Europe. It was also reported at the time that the IRS had attached $9,385.41 from Welles's earnings on *The Stranger*.

Those amounts would hardly have been unduly burdensome for Welles to pay if he thought it worth the effort to resettle in the United States. His first visit to the United States in the nearly six years since he had fled the blacklist came in the fall of 1953, when he visited New York to make his first television appearance in a live production of *King Lear*. Directed by Britain's Peter Brook and broadcast on October 18 by CBS, it was part of the *Omnibus* series, an arts anthology funded by the Ford Foundation's Television-Radio Workshop. Produced by Robert Saudek and hosted by Alistair Cooke, the lively and eclectic *Omnibus* was one of the exemplars of what is now considered TV's golden age. The Welles *King Lear*, which survived on kinescope, was severely cut (to only seventy-four minutes) to fit the series format. But Welles's performance as the anguished, befuddled king is eloquent in its uncharacteristic restraint.

Welles extended his New York visit to negotiate with CBS and the other networks for further television work, but nothing came of it, so he went back to Europe. There's some element of mystery about why he was able to return to work in New York, however briefly, while the blacklist was still in force. It's not known whether CBS had to pull any strings to help him return, or whether there was some kind of behind-the-scenes deal with the government about Welles's political status. The *New York Times* reported, "He denied that he had remained abroad to escape income taxes. To the best of his knowledge, his old tax problem with the United States Government was just about cleared up." Like John Houseman, Rita Hayworth and many others who wanted to keep working or return to work in that period had to write letters dissociating themselves from so-called "Communist front" groups. Almost certainly Welles at least would have had to write such a letter to work in network television or Hollywood studios in that period.

The blacklist was starting to show signs of weakening when Welles made his next comeback attempt in the United States in October 1955. Once again, to set possible employers' minds at ease, he put out the possibly coded message that his tax situation was under control. The *Los Angeles Times* told its readers, "While Welles remained abroad pending the settlement of income tax difficulties at one time, this is all smoothed out now, according to his associates, among them [producer] Harry Saltzman, who has been working on a big CBS deal with the flamboyant actor." Welles appeared in several more CBS-TV shows during that time. With his third wife, Italian countess and sometime actress Paola Mori, Welles was interviewed by Edward R. Murrow in November 1955 on *Person to Person*. He appeared twice on *The Ed Sullivan Show* in early 1956, once in an affecting scene from his staging of *King Lear* at the New York City Center. Returning to Hollywood that April, Welles starred with Betty Grable in a *Ford Star Jubilee* production of *Twentieth Century*, the Ben Hecht–Charles MacArthur farce about the theater. And in October, Welles had an amusing guest shot on Lucille Ball's comedy series *I Love Lucy*, sending up his public image while performing magic tricks and Shakespeare in "Lucy Meets Orson Welles."

The evidence indicates that Welles's tax problems were not the cause of his exile but a symptom or reflection of his greater problem; they were a sporadic form of harassment by the U.S. government that contributed to his staying abroad at various times in his career. During the Nixon era, Welles provoked another round of scrutiny by the IRS when he narrated a laboriously satirical record about Nixon told as a faux biblical tale, *The Begatting of the President* (1969). For a while that harassment drove him back overseas. Welles ran afoul of the IRS again in the early 1970s when it seized money paid to his company in Switzerland for an unfinished TV special he had been directing for CBS in 1968–70, *Orson's Bag*. He considered his company a production company, but the IRS ruled it a holding company. That tax problem led CBS to cancel the show and also caused difficulties with the funding of his feature *The Other Side of the Wind* (see chapters 5 and 6).

It's understandable that Welles would want to blame his tax problems for keeping him out of the United States from 1947 through the mid-1950s and deny or minimize the deeper reasons. He kept up the fiction not only during the blacklist era but also in later years, when the blacklist had been lifted and he was trying to reactivate his career in American films. Discussion of those old difficulties with the FBI and HUAC, still not common knowledge at the time, might have stirred fresh anxiety about Welles's penchant for controversy, a reputation he was trying to escape. But despite his denials, Welles occasionally made other remarks suggesting that he was keenly concerned with the political repression he had left behind in the United States.

During a discussion at the Cinémathèque française in 1982, a student asked Welles to comment on director Elia Kazan. "*Chère mademoiselle,*" Welles replied sharply, "you have chosen the wrong *metteur en scène*, because Elia Kazan is a traitor. He is a man who sold to McCarthy all his companions at a time when he could continue to work in New York at high salary, and having sold all his people to McCarthy, he then made a film called *On the Waterfront* which was a celebration of the informer." Welles paused, then conceded, "In other respects, he's one of our great directors." Welles's account of Kazan's informing contains some factual distortions. Kazan did not testify before Senator McCarthy, who never conducted hearings about Hollywood. Kazan testified before HUAC in January and April 1952 (first in executive session and then publicly), and he actually named a total of sixteen people to HUAC as Communists or former Communists, including eight colleagues in the Group Theatre. Kazan's act was shameful enough that it needed no exaggeration; the elements of dramatic heightening in Welles's account are a sign of how deeply Kazan's betrayal affected him and so many others. As Navasky writes in *Naming Names*, Kazan's "prestige and economic invulnerability" had put him in the best position to mount a "symbolic campaign" against the blacklist, so his capitulation made the left view him as "the quintessential informer."

When Welles was interviewed in 1950 by the British film magazine *Sight and Sound*, a publication that supported him enthusiastically over the years, he succinctly explained his expatriate status. He did so in terms that reflected his awareness of how inextricably intertwined are considerations of political and artistic freedom: "I came to Europe because in Hollywood there was not the slightest chance for me (or for anybody, at that) to obtain freedom of action. With *Othello*, I have now at least made a picture for which I can again accept full responsibility." Writing in *Esquire* in 1959 about his departure from Hollywood for Europe, Welles put it even more simply: "I chose freedom."

However, the maligning of Welles as a fellow traveler occasionally extended beyond the United States. After his stage production of *Othello* closed in London in December 1951, he went to see a play at Dublin's Gate Theatre, where he had begun his professional acting career twenty-one years earlier. He was taunted with cries of "Go back to Moscow, Stalin's star!" and "Stay out of Ireland!" The protesters from the Catholic Cinema and Theater Patrons' Association were, Welles recalled, "led by some insane priest." But such incidents were relatively rare in Europe. Welles would have been subject to far more harassment at home. And now, like John Huston, Welles was ceasing to think of America as home. He had always been a citizen of the world in spirit; now he was becoming one in fact.

Although the blacklist began to lift in the 1960s, some of its victims never returned to work, and most blacklistees found it hard to resuscitate their careers. For the hundreds of Hollywood people directly harmed by the blacklist, the fear never entirely went away. Even more pervasively, the trauma of that era has continued to exert a lingering, and largely unacknowledged, effect on Hollywood. There can be no doubt that the timidity toward controversial issues usually displayed in modern Hollywood, the tendency to favor mindless escapism over the kind of socially conscious material once on view in such films as *Mr. Smith Goes to Washington*, *The Grapes of Wrath*, *Citizen Kane*, and *The Best Years of Our Lives*, is a lasting legacy of the blacklist. The right-wing purge of Hollywood in the 1940s and 1950s was aimed at a wider target than the radical left. It was aimed at the much larger group of those who had, from time to time, espoused progressive ideas. As Hollywood Ten member Albert Maltz observed, "One is destroyed in order that a thousand will be rendered silent and impotent by fear."

In his later life, Welles was less visibly active in politics, no doubt for self-protection and also because he had become somewhat disillusioned about the efficacy of political involvement. "Politics still interest[s] me," he told Hedda Hopper in 1956, "but I'm more amused about it than I used to be. I used to take it very seriously. But that's the thing you do about both politics and love when you're very young." That may have been somewhat disingenuous, but his politics did seem more cautious and quirkier, though still firmly on the liberal/progressive side of the spectrum. Perhaps it was because of continued worries over political persecution that Welles destroyed a book he had been writing in the early 1950s about international government. During the cold war, a book on that subject could have derailed any hopes he had for a comeback in American show business. "I write in secret," he said in 1978. "I've got closets full of bad stuff."

A measure of Welles's continued anxiety over his precarious relationship to the American political establishment is a scene filmed in 1971 for *The Other Side of the Wind* revolving around the character described in the script as the "capo di tutti capi of the Hannaford mafia," Matt Costello. "I do all the dirty jobs," admits Costello, who shares his surname with a notorious Mafia boss of the 1950s, Frank Costello, and is played by Paul Stewart, the same actor whose sinister butler in *Kan*e knows "where all the bodies are buried." As Jake Hannaford's stooges ride to his birthday party on a yellow school bus with film critic Juliette Rich (Susan Strasberg), Matt Costello also admits to a larger role in Hollywood right-wing politics, like those played during the blacklist era by Ronald Reagan and John Wayne. Costello has just fired Zimmer (Cameron Mitchell), Hannaford's "Texas Jewish" makeup man, and Zimmer says bitterly, "Ol' Matt here, he knows about everybody." "Keep it quiet, Zimmie," snaps Costello, but Zimmer explains, "He's on that *Committee*, the one that decides if you're an American." Facing the film critic, Zimmer tells her, "Maybe you didn't know that these people are still in business." With a smug, sinister smile, Costello turns to a fellow right-winger in the Hannaford entourage, Pat (Edmond O'Brien), and says, "We're still in business, huh?" Pat uneasily toasts Costello with a bottle of whiskey, muttering, "And everybody and his fag commie brother is writin' a book about him—or somethin'." With his most wolfish grin, Costello assures the critic, "It's all right, Julie, you don't have to worry. You're *clean.*"

The film-within-a-film, Hannaford's unfinished pseudo-Antonioni art-house picture, also titled *The Other Side of the Wind*, has Oja Kodar playing "some kinda radical." Those are the words of Hannaford stooge Billy Boyle, played by Norman Foster, the Welles crony who directed the *My Friend Bonito* segment of *It's All True* and Welles's 1943 production of the Eric Ambler thriller *Journey into Fear*. Kodar's character, an American Indian ("a red, *red* Indian," Billy calls her), is involved in planting a bomb. She is being pursued not only by the young hippie motorcyclist John Dale (Bob Random), for reasons that are left unclear, but also by "others, besides him . . . like the FBI or something," says Billy. Hannaford rants against hippies and dope freaks and long-haired young filmmakers with the envious bile common to many older Hollywood hands in that period. Although played by one of the diehard liberals who fought the blacklist, Jake now represents all that is reactionary about the dying Hollywood. His rejection by the new Hollywood is partly attributable to his Neanderthal sociopolitical attitudes and partly due to his creative intransigence.

As Welles described Jake to director Paul Mazursky, a member of the cast, "Jake Hannaford has been living in Europe for some time. A director, filmmaker, someone who's been blackballed by Hollywood." Mazursky observed, "Jake sounds a lot like you, Mr. Welles." Laughing, Welles insisted, "He is not Orson Welles! . . . Even though he's back in Hollywood trying to raise money!"

❖ ❖ ❖

The eight years Welles spent largely in Europe from 1947 to 1955 were a time of peripatetic wandering and regrouping that left a permanent imprint on his evolving cinematic style. He completed only two feature films as a director, *Othello* and *Mr. Arkadin*, yet he evolved a freer, more European style while solidifying his role as an independent filmmaker *avant la lettre*. Welles's audacious cinematic experiments anticipated by several years the French nouvelle vague spearheaded by Jean-Luc Godard and François Truffaut and the American cinema verité movement led by documentary filmmakers Robert Drew, Richard Leacock, and D. A. Pennebaker and independent director John Cassavetes.

Making *Othello*, Welles admitted, was a "desperate adventure." His screen Iago and old friend Micheál MacLiammóir vividly described the transient production as a "chic but highly neurotic lumber camp." As he traveled to far places to suit up as Iago whenever Welles could find the money to pull the company together, "Strange sense of Eternity in relation to film of *Othello* overcame me," MacLiammóir writes in his witty diary of the experience, *Put Money in Thy Purse*. McLiammóir adds, "I am still wondering what all this cavorting through the air has to do with the art of the films." Welles's persistence in spending four years paying for and completing *Othello* was seen in the United States as a character flaw. By Hollywood standards, his raffish filmmaking adventures and scrambling for funds to shoot his shoestring production seemed an embarrassing, even shameful comedown for the maker of *Citizen Kane*.

Hollywood director Henry Hathaway told me he was not amused in 1949 when Welles, who was supposed to be playing an Asian warlord in *The Black Rose*, would spirit away a camera and crew to shoot scenes for *Othello* in the Moroccan desert. In Mogador that June, after dinner on an "orgiastic conversational level in five languages," Welles took MacLiammóir to see a fifteenth-century fortress and citadel he had discovered for a set. MacLiammóir recorded in his diary, "Pacing up and down under the moon, I learned of his endless difficulties about money, Italian wardrobe, and cost of labour: everything as I see it is against him before he starts, but his courage, like everything else about him, imagination, egotism, generosity, ruthlessness, forbearance, impatience, sensitivity, grossness and vision, is magnificently out of proportion. His position at the moment is grotesque in its lack of stability and even likelihood, but he will win through and all at the end will fall into his hands, the bright-winged old gorilla."

In one sense, *Othello*, Welles's first film made outside the United States since *It's All True*, deals with subject matter safely classical and outside the realm of contemporary sociopolitical controversy. But dealing with an interracial relationship, even a Shakespearean one with the jealous male played by a Caucasian in blackface, was touchy material for that era. The blackface helps account for Welles's stiff and unconvincing performance in the title role, although his woodenness is also attributable to production exigencies, including the problem of acting with other actors who weren't present and had to be inserted later. Welles no doubt identified emotionally with Othello, an exotic foreigner trying to hold on to his tenuous place in a strange new country. But playing the naïf, as he also does in *The Lady from Shanghai*, is not a natural role for Welles, who excels at playing flawed but powerful figures.

The interracial love story may partly explain why it took three years for *Othello* to find a U.S. distributor. As much out of necessity as choice, Welles hews to the theatrical tradition of having a white actor play the Moor. Paul Robeson's successful American touring production with Uta

Hagen in the early 1940s was an exception on the stage, but it took until late in the twentieth century for black actors such as Yaphet Kotto, Ted Lange, and Laurence Fishburne to be allowed to play Othello on the motion picture screen. Welles's defensiveness over his own performance—he agreed with the harsh judgment of critic Eric Bentley, "He never acts, he is photographed"—may help explain his mockery of Laurence Olivier's less restrained, outrageously hammy Othello. Welles told me that Olivier in his 1965 film of the play reminded him of Sammy Davis Jr. One day on the set of *The Other Side of the Wind*, Welles said, "Larry's acting is like getting a postcard from a foreign country. On one side is a beautiful landscape. And on the other side it says, 'Having wonderful time—wish you were here.'"

It's no accident that some of the dominant themes of blacklist-era politics appear prominently in Welles's *Othello*. Welles's interest in the play is primarily as a story of betrayal—betrayal of a friendship by an envious man spreading a false rumor about a nonexistent sexual betrayal. Betrayal is a constant theme in Welles films from *Kane* through *The Other Side of the Wind*. *Othello* is also a story about the poisoning of reputation, a theme that had attracted Welles in *The Magnificent Ambersons*. For a filmmaker whose good name was questioned loudly and widely, forcing him to leave his native country, there is a special poignancy in having a character (Cassio) lament in *Othello*, "Reputation, reputation, reputation! I have lost my reputation!" And there is an added personal dimension in a blacklisted filmmaker lamenting through his blackfaced screen character, "Othello's occupation's lost!"

"When Welles went to Europe," Pauline Kael argued, "he lost his single greatest asset as a movie director: his sound. . . . [Sound] became his worst problem as he began to work with actors who didn't speak English and actors who did but weren't around when he needed them. . . . Welles compensated by developing greater visual virtuosity." But it equally could be argued that Welles was freer with both sound and visuals when employing the European style of postsynchronized shooting. In Europe he was able to explore new levels of "musical" dissonance in filmmaking, displaying a modernism as trailblazing—and, to many traditionalists, as outrageous—as the experiments of Schoenberg and Stravinsky in the world of classical music. The soundtrack in *Othello* was entirely created in postproduction and often operates as a form of counterpoint to the action, increasing the film's density of expression. The sound multiplies the extreme sense of vertigo and disorientation conveyed by the visual style, expressing a loss of moorings both physical and spiritual, a feeling that was visible in earlier Welles films but intensified while he lived his rootless life in Europe. Nevertheless, there is no denying that even sympathetic audiences can find it jarring when important speeches in *Othello* are delivered in long shot or distractingly fragmented, with a fuzzy or vaguely synchronized soundtrack. It's also disconcerting to realize that many different characters all speak in the same voice—that of Orson Welles. But the film's flaws and strengths are inextricably linked, part and parcel of the unconventional new style Welles began exploring with *It's All True* and pursued with full vigor in his European exile. Although *Othello is* now widely accepted as one of his finest films, there's still a palpable uneasiness among critics toward it and his other European work for its ragged quality, which is viewed as somehow déclassé. But technical perfection is a chimera, and the soullessness of modern Hollywood films is directly linked to its cult of technical perfection.

Several versions of *Othello* exist, including three different cuts by Welles, two for Europe and one for the 1955 U.S. release. He also freely recut sequences for his 1978 documentary *Filming "Othello."* But the 1992 "restoration" of *Othello* sponsored by his daughter Beatrice and released by Castle Hill is a travesty of Welles's work. In a misguided attempt to clean up and modernize the film's imperfect soundtrack, sound effects were replaced, the splendid musical score by Francesco Lavignino and Alberto Barberis was rerecorded with fewer instruments, and some dialogue was replaced by new actors to bring lines into synchronization (one sequence was even reedited). Welles always preferred to sacrifice synchronization for a line reading. In reaction to the bastardized reworking of the film, the Criterion collection in 1995 released an unaltered laserdisc edition of Welles's American version.

❖ ❖ ❖

Several of Welles's projects in the 1950s offer an expatriate's implicit or explicit criticisms of the United States during the McCarthy era, portraying Europe in a more favorable light for its greater political, social, and artistic freedom. The first was his 1950 one-act play *The Unthinking Lobster*, which he staged in Paris and took on tour in Germany and Belgium with his abridged version of the Faust legend, *Time Runs.* Envisioned by Welles as a dry run for a film, *The Unthinking Lobster* spoofs Hollywood religious movies. A starlet playing Saint Anne in Hollywood (Suzanne Cloutier, Welles's Desdemona from his film of *Othello)* finds that she is able to perform real miracles. Heaven intervenes to make a deal with Hollywood to stop the miracles if the studios will agree to stop making religious movies. Welles made a short film, *La Miracle de Sainte Anne*, to start the show in a projection room à la *Citizen Kane*. Now lost, the film, shot in a Paris park, is designed as a series of rushes about cripples appearing in a Bible epic who are cured by the starlet. Welles played a crass Hollywood mogul named Jake Behoovian. *The Unthinking Lobster* contains digs at both Communists and McCarthy.

Welles also satirized anti-Communist hysteria in his unproduced screen treatment *V.I.P.*, based on a radio script, "Buzzo Gospel," that he wrote for the BBC radio series *The Adventures of Harry Lime*.* *V.I.P.* was novelized in French by film critic Maurice Bessy in 1953 as *Une grosse légume*, which translates as "A Big Vegetable" or "A Big Shot." The protagonist is an American soft-drink salesman. Welles explained, "It's about the Coca-Cola and Pepsi-Cola empires—a farce about capitalist imperialism, the communist menace, and all that. It's set in one of those mythical kingdoms, some place about the size of Luxembourg but in the Mediterranean—the last place on earth without either a Pepsi or a Coca-Cola concession. It's about competing imperialism and the Cold War. They have been living off American aid ever since the war in order to keep off the communist menace. The truth is, they have no Communists—but that's their own well-kept secret." The story anticipates Billy Wilder's 1961 cold war farce about a Pepsi-Cola executive in Berlin, *One, Two, Three*.

Mr. Arkadin (1955), Welles's most surreal feature, evolved from "Man of Mystery" and two other plays Welles wrote for the *Harry Lime* radio series. Welles's title character in the film commissions a J. Edgar Hoover–style dossier on himself, hiring an American "petty adventurer" to dig up whatever dirt he can find, sending him around the world to snoop around his old colleagues. The thuggish Guy Van Stratten (Robert Arden) doesn't realize he is being used as a cat's-paw for Arkadin to find out who knows what about him and to have each knowledgeable party killed. The British title of this dark parody of FBI and HUAC methodology was

---

* Loosely based on his *Third Man* film character, though considerably sanitized, the series was a popular success. Ironically, the character Welles considered the most despicable he ever played caught the public's fancy, and he was portrayed on radio as a charming rogue rather than the truly sinister charmer of the movie. Whenever he entered a restaurant in those years, the band would strike up Anton Karas's "*Third Man* Theme."

Confidential Report (the film was first announced under the title *X*, and its working title was *Masquerade)*.

As James Naremore first pointed out in the 1978 edition of his insightful critical study *The Magic World of Orson Welles*, Arden, with his beady eyes, heavy eyebrows, and five o'clock shadow, "bears an uncanny resemblance" to Richard Nixon, a former member of HUAC who was then the vice president of the United States. But I question whether this happened "quite by accident," as Naremore supposes; Arden seems deliberately cast and directed as a crude and dopey figure, a gangster functionary, the way the left regarded the members of HUAC and Hoover's FBI in that era. Welles said that his own character, the mysterious international tycoon Gregory Arkadin, was based on Joseph Stalin, who was also a Georgian living under an assumed name. Although Arkadin "runs the greatest private spy service on Earth," he tells Van Stratten he is worried about something in his past coming back to taint him during a security check by the Americans; he is trying to get a contract to build an American military base in Europe. "You've heard of a thing in the army called 'intelligence check'? These army people are thorough—they look under the wallpaper, they turn up the carpets." Even though that proves a red herring, the film can be seen as a cold war allegory of the ideological battle between Stalin and Hoover, or Stalin and Nixon, a clash in which there is no hero, reflecting Welles's growing cynicism about both the United States and the USSR. "In another epoch such a man might have sacked Rome or been hanged as a pirate," another character, Sir Joseph, "a retired intelligence chief," reflects on Arkadin. "Today we must accept him for what he is—a phenomenon of an age of disillusion and crisis."

Playing the sinister Arkadin demonstrates Welles's penchant for irony. Arkadin exists largely as a visual conceit, a set of disguises, false beards, wigs, and masks, embodying Welles's own obsession with self-obliterating theatrical makeup. A man in hiding from his past—concerned that his daughter will learn that he began amassing his fortune in the white-slavery racket—Arkadin, notes Van Stratten, "was once somebody like me," and the old man is paranoid to the point of obliterating friends who knew him and his secret in his earlier days. Welles constructs a cautionary tale about the vulnerability of even one of the world's most powerful figures to investigative harassment and blackmail. Further reflections of blacklist-era concerns can be seen in the film's emphasis on false names and fabricated papers, and in Arkadin's asking in Hoover-like fashion, "Is Van Stratten a Communist?" Arkadin's own political record is fascist, including collaboration with the Nazis in Vichy and road building for Mussolini in Ethiopia. Critics' complaints of the film's unreality and caricaturish performances are beside the point, for *Mr. Arkadin* is a fable about identity and guilty subterfuge. The atmosphere of anxiety, disorientation, absurd frenzy, and endless traveling from country to country and hotel room to hotel room reflects Welles's peripatetic life in the 1950s. Welles proudly called himself "a migratory worker. I go where the jobs are, like a cherry picker." The simile is richly suggestive, with echoes of his Popular Front period, equating the American artist with a peasant laborer exploited by those holding economic power.

The executive producer of *Mr. Arkadin*, Louis Dolivet, was a Romanian, a longtime political activist, a fellow exile from the United States during the blacklist era, and one of Welles's political mentors in the 1940s. Dolivet may have served as a partial model for Kim Menaker, the mentor of political candidate Blake Pellarin in the Welles–Oja Kodar screenplay *The Big Brass Ring*. In the 1940s, Dolivet helped promote the cause of the United Nations through his organization, Free World, with Welles serving as Free World's voice in print and on radio; Dolivet was among those urging Welles to run for the U.S. Senate. But despite their long association, they clashed over *Mr. Arkadin*. Because Welles missed a postproduction deadline, Dolivet took the film away from him. "*Arkadin* was destroyed," Welles felt, "because they completely changed the entire form of it: the whole order of it, the whole point of it."

Five versions of the film were released, all with variant scenes, including the British version, *Confidential Report;* two Spanish versions, with different actors in some roles and "temp" versions of some scenes corresponding more closely to Welles's plan; the Corinth Films edit for the American release in 1962; and a television/home-video version that removes Welles's intended flashback structure to tell the story in linear time. The new "comprehensive version" assembled by Stefan Drössler of the Munich Film Museum with Claude Bertemes, managing director of the Cinémathèque municipale de Luxembourg, was released in 2006 on DVD by the Criterion Collection in a three-disc set that also includes *Confidential Report* and the Corinth version. The new cut, described by Bertemes as "a kind of ideal version, a daring project," strives to be the fullest assemblage of scenes shot for the film. Its structure takes into account Welles's comments in interviews and other documentation of his intentions, although it cannot resolve all the differences in editing among the various versions, and it is not a "director's cut" because Welles never was allowed to complete one. Nevertheless, Welles's multilayered conception of *Mr. Arkadin* comes across more richly in the new version, which elaborates on the moral complexities of the Arkadin–Van Stratten relationship, adds further levels of irony, and makes some of the transitions from place to place and country to country fuller and more intelligible, which serves to enhance rather than diminish the film's vertiginous, nightmarish style.

❖ ❖ ❖

Welles's profligate creativity and migratory career outside the United States in that period contributed to what I see as the "air of frenzy" school of commentary on his life and work. The phrase is David Thomson's, a clichéd journalistic device that uses the constant whirlwind of activity surrounding Welles as a not-so-subtly coded way of suggesting that he was crazy—an even more effective slur in the long run than calling him a Red. The locus classicus is John Houseman's 1972 description, in his memoir *Run-Through*, of Welles's Mercury radio rehearsals: "Sweating, howling, disheveled, and singlehanded, he wrestled with chaos and time—always conveying an effect of being alone, traduced by his collaborators, surrounded by treachery, ignorance, sloth, indifference, incompetence and—more often than not—downright sabotage." This seems a defensive comeback on the part of Houseman, who holds himself up as Welles's antithesis, the sober producer-businessman-artist who kept Welles under control so that he could do his best creative work. There are some elements of truth in this picture, but it is a caricature nonetheless and a highly damaging one, revealing the biases and values of those who promote it.

When I had lunch with Houseman in the 1970s, he refused to speak about Welles, having become gun-shy as a result of helping Pauline Kael on her Welles demolition project. But Houseman made a revealing comment when I asked why he thought the British director Ken Russell, who made such great work on television, had not lived up to that high standard in feature filmmaking. Houseman said the answer was simple: Russell no longer worked with Huw Wheldon, who had produced his work for BBC TV. Houseman said Russell needed a strong producer to restrain his wilder tendencies, which went out of control when he started making features. Welles's name was not mentioned, but the subtext was unmistakable.

As Houseman knew, Welles also collaborated with Wheldon, who produced Welles's BBC TV documentary series *Orson Welles' Sketch Book* in 1955 and conducted thoughtful interviews with Welles on BBC's *Monitor* in 1960 and 1962. Houseman's point has some validity—Welles certainly benefited from collaborating with a strong producer—and it's a shame that he and Welles couldn't have continued to work together fruitfully, but their own considerable egos prevented it. Yet as Houseman himself noted, Welles had a "surprising capacity for collaboration. For all the mass of his own ego, he was able to apprehend other people's weakness and strength, and to make creative use of them."

❖ ❖ ❖

Orson Welles' Sketch Book is an entertaining series of fifteen-minute talks by Welles, punctuated by shots of his hands sketching cartoons. The six-program series has never been released in the United States, although clips have appeared in documentaries on Welles. In addition to light-hearted shows about false noses, John Barrymore, critics, and *The War of the Worlds*, the *Sketch Book* deals with such weighty themes as the abuse of police power, the indignity of passports, and American racism. It's a good example of how Welles was able to adapt a format he had used successfully on radio—the intimate, wide-ranging chat, such as was heard in his 1940s shows *Orson Welles' Almanac* and *Orson Welles Commentaries*—to the needs of a new medium.

His more ambitious 1955 British TV documentary series *Around the World with Orson Welles* consists of seven half-hour programs (one uncompleted), each giving his idiosyncratic take on a European country, city, or culture. Five were released on DVD in the United States in 2000. They deal with the bohemian life of the St.-Germain-des-Prés section of Paris, old-age pensioners in London, bullfighting in Spain, and the people of the Basque country (in two parts). The unfinished program, "The Tragedy of Lurs," about a controversial 1952 French murder case in which a peasant farmer named Gaston Dominici was accused of killing a British tourist family, was partially restored for French television in 2000 and released with a new documentary written and directed by Christophe Cognet, *The Dominici Affair*. One *Around the World* program unfortunately is missing, the tantalizingly titled "The Third Man in Vienna."

Welles takes an unabashedly personal, even whimsical, approach to the travelogue format in *Around the World*, seizing on whatever aspects of a subject interest him and dwelling more on obscure people and places than on famous faces and tourist attractions. (The cameos in the Paris segment for Jean Cocteau, Simone de Beauvoir, Juliette Greco, and Eddie Constantine were added after Welles turned in his cut.) As always, Welles experiments with narrative formats. The poetically structured program "St.-Germain-des-Prés" eschews the expected voiceover narration by Welles and is framed instead around Art Buchwald writing his "Paris after Dark" column for what was then the European edition of the *New York Herald Tribune*. The most conventionally filmed program is "Spain: The Bullfight," a Hemingwayesque primer on the corrida. But even that show is given offbeat framing by a pair of young British aficionados, drama critic Kenneth Tynan and his actress-writer wife Elaine Dundy, who narrate until Welles takes over the hosting chores from his seat in the stands during the actual corrida.

The series is united by its concentration on themes critical to Welles in that period: independence, eccentricity, and expatriation. The clearest exposition of those themes comes in Welles's lengthy interview for the Paris program with another expatriate, Raymond Duncan, a bohemian who fled the United States in the 1930s after being arrested for allowing his five-year-old son to wear sandals on New York's Fifth Avenue. Now a successful sandal maker as well as an artist and printer, Duncan dresses in a makeshift toga and espouses a philosophy of Thoreauvian self-reliance. A colorful eccentric who anticipates the American beatnik movement of the late 1950s, Duncan is treated with loving indulgence by Welles, who clearly finds in him a kindred spirit. "Independence is the greatest thing in the world," Duncan declares, to which Welles responds, "Well, I say, 'Hear, hear!' . . . You know, there's a growing fear among some people in America that the old American spirit of independence is giving way to a new tendency toward conformism."

Independence is also the theme of "London," a touching and humorous meditation on old age by a filmmaker whose lifelong reverence for the elderly was among his most endearing traits. This small gem recalls the lost ending of *The Magnificent Ambersons.* Welles described that sequence in a shabby rooming house as being about "the deterioration of personality, the way people diminish with age, and particularly with impecunious old age." But Welles does not see the old Londoners he visits as tragic figures; he sees them as gallant survivors revered and cared for by their more traditional society. Welles has a delightful exchange with a group of six elderly widows living comfortably in a London almshouse endowed by a vicar in the seventeenth century. The filmmaker's attitude during this conversation is suffused with warmth and utterly without condescension. "Growing old is no joke," Welles muses. He draws an implicit contrast with American retirement homes: "To be old and indigent is not just an economic problem, it can be a tragedy in human terms, a tragedy of loneliness, a loss of dignity, a loss of the sense of individuality. And that's why I admire, and I think British people should be so proud of, institutions like this almshouse."

Equally moving is a segment with dignified old soldiers living in retirement at the Royal Hospital in Chelsea. On their parade grounds and later in a nearby pub, Welles draws them out on the reasons they feel such abundant dignity and pride. The old men's faces have the Rembrandt-like grandeur displayed by Richard Bennett's Major Amberson. Watching two old soldiers march slowly back to their barracks to the accompaniment of stirring martial music, Welles quotes their proud statement that they are passing "the evening of life in independent retirement."

The two shows on the Basque country, "Pays Basque I and II," offer the anachronistic simplicity of an unspoiled primitivism as an antidote to the overcivilized, overmechanized nature of life in the twentieth century. Welles's fondness for the Basques, who resist the idea of borders and stubbornly persist in their idiosyncratic ways, reflects his characteristic preference for the medieval over the modern. Here again the point of view is largely that of expatriate Americans rejecting their own country, represented not only by Welles but also by journalist and author Lael Tucker Wertenbaker, who finds in the Basque country a more authentic, "independent" existence for herself and her young son, Christian. Only in "The Tragedy of Lurs," which remained unfinished because of pressure from the French government, did Welles qualify this positive view of the peasantry by exploring the possibility that Gaston Dominici, widely considered innocent of murder, was actually guilty.

❖ ❖ ❖

The same year Welles filmed his program on bullfighting in Spain, he took the opportunity to begin production on his adaptation of Cervantes' *Don Quixote*, which would continue to be in the works off and on for the next thirty years. While in Paris directing *Mr. Arkadin*, Welles shot some color footage in the Bois de Boulogne with Mischa Auer as the knight errant Don Quixote and Akim Tamiroff as his devoted squire, Sancho Panza. Esteve Riambau reports in his book on Welles and Spain that the project was originally titled *Don Quixote Passes By* and would have been a multipart "view of Hispanic culture, which also included such characters as Don Juan, Goya, and the Dutchess of Alba, as well as a reconstruction of the story of a bull saved from death by its friendship with a child, pre-

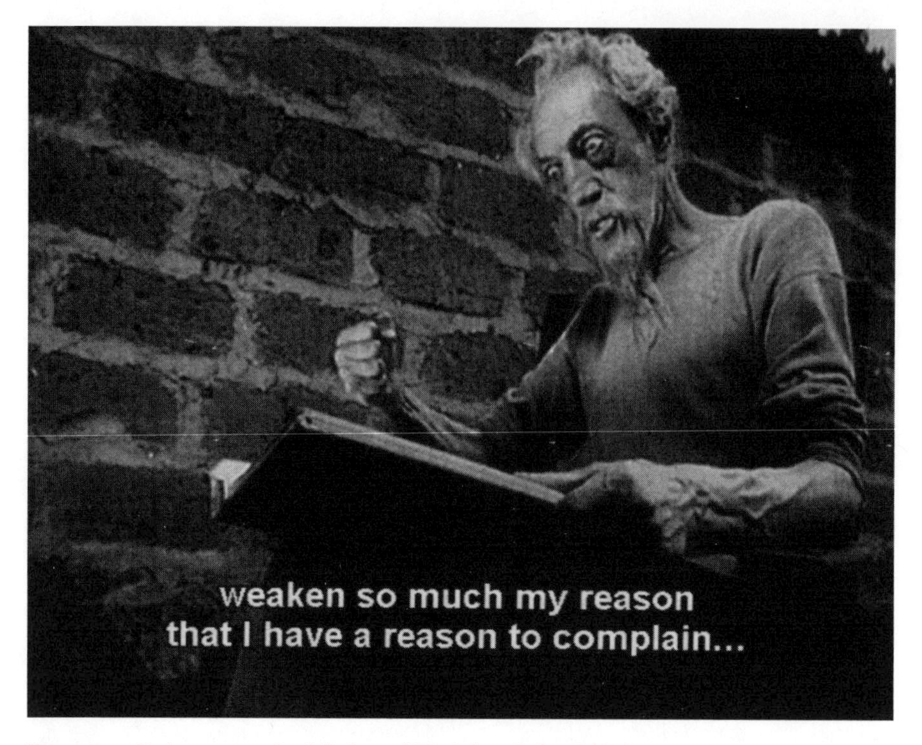

Francisco Reiguera as the blinkered Knight of the Sad Countenance, Don Quixote, in Welles's unfinished film adapted from the Cervantes novel: a frame enlargement from the 1992 version of *Don Quixote* assembled by Jesús Franco. *(El Silencio)*

viously developed in the Mexican episode of *It's All True* [the story *My Friend Bonito* by Robert Flaherty]." Welles hoped to package *Don Quixote Passes By* into a TV program, but the project was rejected by CBS; the original color footage has been lost.

Another version of his *Don Quixote* began filming in Mexico in July 1957. Welles started with $25,000 in funding from his old friend Frank Sinatra, hoping Sinatra would show part of it that fall on his new ABC-TV series *The Frank Sinatra Show.* Francisco Reiguera, a political exile from Franco's Spain, replaced Auer in the title role (Welles had also considered his *Touch of Evil* costar Charlton Heston). Mexican producer Oscar Dancigers backed the shooting for eight weeks before pulling the plug, blaming the director for going over budget (although by only about $5,000). Eventually the project turned into what Welles called "my home movie . . . an experimental film." Shooting continued sporadically in Mexico, Italy, and Spain into the early 1970s, with his own money.

To help pay for his *Quixote* feature, Welles also worked on a documentary series for Italy's RAI-TV, *Nella Terra di Don Chisciotte (In the Land of Don Quixote).* This 16mm travelogue with Welles, his wife Paola Mori, and their little daughter, Beatrice, jaunting around Spain was begun in 1961 but not shown until 1964, and then with a narration written and delivered by others. Like his *Quixote*, the series enabled Welles to experiment with on-the-fly, handheld, nouvelle vague filming techniques. But the TV episodes never transcend their casual, rambling, touristy approach, which is most obvious in a segment about Beatrice learning the flamenco, so much like any other indulgent father's home movie that RAI wouldn't show it ("Flamenco Lessons" has been restored by the Munich Film Museum).

Welles's modern-day gloss on Cervantes, with the Don and Sancho as anachronistic figures in twentieth-century Spain, has strongly autobiographical overtones, devoted as it is to glorifying the ultimate symbol of rebellious independence and living life outside one's own time, surviving defiantly in a world largely indifferent to impractical dreaming. As *Around the World with Orson Welles* also shows, far from feeling defeated by his circumstances, Welles reveled in the newfound freedom of European independent filmmaking, approaching it in a quixotic spirit of picaresque adventure. He enjoyed the process of filming *Don Quixote* so much that he kept wanting to embellish on what he had filmed or shoot new footage, changing his concept to reflect the tentative steps toward modernization in Franco's Spain. He viewed that process in a largely negative light, much as he did the coming of the automobile in *Ambersons*, as a force despoiling an Eden all the more precious for being largely imaginary.

❖ ❖ ❖

When he made his attempt at a Hollywood comeback in 1955–58, Welles devoted much of his creative energy to continuing to conquer the television medium. In addition to appearing on *I Love Lucy* and other TV shows, Welles directed three half-hour TV pilots for the American audience in that period, but none resulted in a series. His innovative approaches to television narrative were rejected as too unconventional for a medium already ossifying as networks and sponsors in the United States turned their backs on TV's early creative energy to gratify a lowest-common-denominator audience.

But Welles's playful approach to the medium allowed him a welcome sense of creative freedom, with less pressure than he felt in his rare opportunities to direct features. His vision of the potential of television regarded it as a means of dealing halfway with the increasingly unavoidable fact that he was not a mainstream commercial filmmaker. In a prescient lecture at the Edinburgh Film Festival in 1953, he said:

> There is nothing wrong with popular art; some of the greatest artists in the world have been popular artists. But the trouble with films is that they cost too much. . . . I think movies are dying, dying, dying. . . . So we have to find some ground between the experimental 16mm avant-garde [film]—although that medium is important—and the commercial production—which is, anyway, dying from an economic point of view. . . . [W]e have to find a way of making films—and here television may help us—by which, if two or three million people see them, we have a return for our money; which involves the creation of a true international audience, and a struggle with the mysterious national forces in the world which call themselves governments.

The only Welles pilot that reached the air in the United States during the 1950s was *The Fountain of Youth*. It was intended to inaugurate a series of short stories Welles would narrate and direct in the *First Personal Singular* style of his *Mercury Theatre on the Air* and *Campbell Playhouse* radio series, but with his innovative radio techniques adapted for the visual intimacy of the newer medium. Filmed in May 1956, Welles's adaptation of John Collier's story "Youth from Vienna" was honored with a Peabody Award after its single network screening on ABC's *Colgate Theater* in September 1958. Making gold from Welles's paucity of means, *The Fountain of Youth* combines minimalist settings and process-screen backdrops with live-action scenes, stills, and freeze frames. Welles described it to me as his only "film conceived for the box." The vaudeville-show tone and blackout style, suited to the 1920s setting, lend unsettlingly dark humor to this fable about human vanity, personified by a narcissistic young couple (Joi Lansing and Rick Jason) who fall for a quack eternal-youth potion given them in revenge by the woman's jilted middle-aged lover (Dan Tobin). As the faintly sinister host, Welles is so ubiquitous a presence, sometimes even mouthing the characters' words, that he becomes their puppet master, darkly amused by their self-destructive foibles. The best measure of how far ahead of its time this experimental but unpretentious program was in 1958 is that it *still* seems avant-garde compared with anything yet seen on American commercial television.

Contrary to myth, Welles easily adjusted to the tight schedules and low budgets of television. The cost of *The Fountain of Youth* was only $54,896, $5,064 over budget, and it was shot in just five days, according to information found in the Desilu files by Welles scholar Bill Krohn. But rather than being celebrated today for the innovative, delightful achievement it is, *Fountain* has been held up against Welles as yet another (false) example of his profligacy.

Also in 1956, with a mere $5,000 he had earned from appearing on the *Lucy* show, Welles spent a day at a Poverty Row studio in Hollywood shooting a half-hour film about Alexandre Dumas. Never shown in public and now lost, *Camille, the Naked Lady, and the Musketeers* was the pilot for a planned series called *Orson Welles and People.* Using stills and drawings, it was an early example of the "essay film," a documentary genre that would increasingly preoccupy Welles.

A more elaborate excursion into that field was a film variously known as *Viva Italia!* and *Portrait of Gina* but lacking a title onscreen. This fast-paced, jocular documentary, completed in 1958 as the pilot for a planned ABC series, *Orson Welles at Large,* is Welles's tribute to the vitality of Italian culture, seen through its flamboyant movie stars. Using the same kind of bricolage style he later pushed even further in *F for Fake,* this whirlwind cinematic tour of the country where he had been spending much of his exile is a whimsical blend of stills and headlines, documentary shots of streets and country villas, and interviews with Gina Lollobrigida, Rossano Brazzi, and actor-director Vittorio de Sica. Welles's wry commentary is delivered on camera as unifying material, as in *Around the World with Orson Welles,* but this show's more free-form visuals make it more akin to the work of what were then known as "underground" (i.e., experimental) filmmakers. At the same time, paradoxically, Welles was trying his damnedest to be droll, diverting, and popular in tone. He later admitted, "I don't think it was very good. . . . I worked very hard on it and the result was a show that looked like it had been worked on very hard."

The network predictably failed to appreciate his idiosyncratic approach to the travelogue genre. An indication of just how warily Welles was viewed by the "suits" who ran the entertainment business in that era was offered by ABC president Leonard H. Goldenson, who recalled that the network was "desperate for programming and experimenting with all sorts of strange ideas. We were trying to come up with something totally different. One of our worst ideas was giving Orson Welles $200,000 to do a pilot. . . . Welles was vague about what he planned to do. But he was *the* Orson Welles, and nobody pressed him too hard. I should have known better." More than a year later, "Welles turned up with a single reel of 16mm film." Goldenson seems not to remember *Viva Italia! / Portrait of Gina* accurately, describing it as "very poorly done . . . little more than a home movie of splendid homes and ostentatious yachts belonging to obscure European royalty." Perhaps his fuzziness bears out Welles's recollection that the executive who watched and rejected the film was not Goldenson but his head of programming, the notorious Jim "the Smiling Cobra" Aubrey. But Goldenson leaves no doubt about the contempt in which Welles's work was held by the network: "In plain language, Orson Welles conned us out of $200,000."

Left behind by Welles in his room at the Ritz Hotel in Paris, the documentary was rediscovered nearly thirty years later in a storage room. It received its first full public screening at the Venice Film Festival in 1986. But Lollobrigida, who talks frankly to Welles about her negative views of the Italian tax authorities and her public, was offended by the film and obtained an injunction against further public screenings. Nevertheless, the film later was shown in its entirety on German television and again in 2005 at the Locarno International Film Festival in Switzerland, delighting the audience that had the rare chance to see this adventurous jeu d'esprit.

❖ ❖ ❖

It's understandable that even such a sophisticated and experienced student of Hollywood as Welles fell for the hopeful notion that the filmmaking process in America had radically changed for the better when the studio system began breaking down during the 1950s. It was a common view among independent-minded filmmakers that whatever replaced the studio system would have to be an improvement. During that uncertain period, the system was crumbling from the impact of the post–World War II Paramount consent decree that divorced the major studios from their theater chains. The concurrent rise of television was another cause of the drastic changes affecting Hollywood. As a result, independent companies sprouted all over town and in time became the dominant suppliers of most studios. The 1950s also saw the rise of agents who "packaged" movies for their clients. The system pioneered by United Artists, giving creative control to the star-producer or the star who commanded a percentage of the gross, became the preferred route to Hollywood success. But for Welles and some other major filmmakers, such independence was illusory.

When Liberty Films was formed in 1945 by directors Frank Capra, George Stevens, and William Wyler and production executive Sam Briskin to release its "independent" films through RKO, "some saw this as the wave of the future," film historian Douglas Gomery writes.

> But it was not: the important companies remained firmly in control of world-wide distribution, which any independent needed to survive. . . . United Artists, after 1952, made independent production a common practice. But what this company wanted were producers who could make profitable packages of cost-effective films, not the kind of idiosyncratic visions conceived by Welles or Capra. . . . Ironically, Welles, because of the prestige he enjoyed in the early Forties, had a greater chance to be independent in Hollywood *prior* to the war rather than later in the so-called era of the independent. . . . He would struggle in Europe to see if he could make independent films that fit his vision. Hollywood was closed to him.

Although one film would prove an exception to that rule, Welles came to understand the reasons for his new dilemma, admitting to Kenneth Tynan in 1967:

> It was the rise of the independents that was my ruin as a director. The old studio bosses—Jack Warner, Sam Goldwyn, Darryl Zanuck, Harry Cohn—were all friends, or friendly enemies I knew how to deal with. They all offered me work. . . . The minute the independents got in, I never directed another American picture except by accident. If I'd gone to Hollywood in the last five years, virgin and unknown, I could have written my own ticket. But I'm not a virgin; I drag my myth around with me, and I've had much more trouble with the independents than I ever had with the big studios. I was a maverick, but the studios understood what that meant, and if there was a fight, we both enjoyed it. With an annual output of forty pictures per studio, there would probably be room for one Orson Welles picture. But an independent is a fellow whose work is centered around his own particular gifts. In that setup, there's no place for me.

❖ ❖ ❖

The American picture Welles directed "by accident" was *Touch of Evil.* A daringly expressionistic nightmare vision disguised as a B-movie crime thriller, *Touch of Evil* was reworked and tossed away by Universal-International in 1958. It was the last film Welles directed for a Hollywood studio.

It's no coincidence that Welles's first feature after his return to work in the United States deals explicitly with an abuse of American governmental power, with a policeman in a town bordering on Mexico framing a suspect through the use of planted evidence. The crime has to be exposed by a foreigner (Vargas, a Mexican official played by Charlton Heston) since the locals are too cozy with the corrupt modus operandi of Captain Quinlan (memorably played by Welles). Welles presents this

Welles's experiences with the injustices of the American "justice" system during his years on the blacklist were reflected in his first American film as a director in ten years, *Touch of Evil* (1958). His brutal cop, Hank Quinlan, interrogates a murder suspect, Manolo Sanchez (Victor Millan), as detective Pete Menzies (Joseph Calleia) and Mexican official Mike Vargas (Charlton Heston) skeptically observe his third-degree methods. *(Universal/International)*

scathing exposé of police criminality with his characteristic ironic slant and an extremely baroque (even for him) visual style. Welles had dealt with the abuse of power in his crusade to bring to justice the police chief who assaulted Isaac Woodard Jr. He had reflected further on the subject on *Orson Welles' Sketch Book*. But the theme was first raised in Welles's film world comedically in *Citizen Kane*. Kane and Jed Leland joke about harassing a Brooklyn man named Harry Silverstone, whose wife has gone missing and is suspected to have been murdered. Kane cynically instructs the indignant *Inquirer* editor, Herbert Carter (Erskine Sanford), to tell Mr. Silverstone that "if he doesn't produce his wife, Mrs. Silverstone, at once, the *Inquirer* will have him arrested." The fusty old editor is treated as a comic foil, sputtering indignantly in close-up reaction shots. But on reflection, the viewer would have to concede that Mr. Carter is right and it *is* outrageous for Kane to turn his newspaper into a ruthless arm of the police.

In *Touch of Evil*—adapted by Welles from *Badge of Evil*, a novel by Whit Masterson, the pseudonym of San Diego writers Robert Wade and Bill Miller—Welles takes the same ironic approach when Vargas utters the lines that in fact represent Welles's "author's message": "A policeman's job is only easy in a police state. That's the whole *point*, captain. Who is the boss, the cop or the law?" Welles avoids the self-righteousness of the indignation Vargas displays by having Quinlan, in a tight two-shot with a man he considers "one of these here starry-eyed idealists," ostentatiously roll his eyes and mutter. Welles said in 1964, "I do not want to resemble the majority of Americans, who are demagogues and rhetoricians. This is one of America's great weaknesses, and rhetoric is one of the greatest weaknesses of American artists; above all, those of my generation. [Arthur] Miller, for example, is terribly rhetorical."

The evidence against Quinlan is gathered with a "bug," a concealed recording device worn by Quinlan's oldest friend, police detective Pete Menzies (Joseph Calleia). Menzies has finally become appalled enough by Quinlan's crimes to trap him into confessing. In a scene cut by the studio from the original release version but later returned to the film, the director makes clear his own revulsion, and Vargas's, toward this method of entrapment. Welles went so far as to say that "the theme of the scenario is betrayal" because Vargas induces Menzies to betray Quinlan. By introducing such morally complex elements into what could have been a straightforward melodrama about the exposure of a corrupt policeman, Welles questions basic premises of the Hollywood police movie and the ends-justify-the-means mentality of the American justice system under Hoover.

In his extended interview with Bogdanovich beginning in 1968 for *This Is Orson Welles*, Welles frequently chafes at what he considers intrusive questions and calls his young interviewer "Mr. Hoover." Welles mocks Bogdanovich's scholarly use of tapes and documents as tools of interrogation. That anxiety about protecting his secrets was part of Welles's often-expressed ambivalence toward those pests he called "bee-ographers," an attitude no doubt intensified by his awareness of being investigated by HUAC and the FBI.

Most contemporary American reviewers were too fixated on the B-movie aspects of *Touch of Evil* to regard it with the seriousness it deserved, but the provocative nature of Welles's analysis of police corruption was not lost on the right-wing magazine *Films in Review*, which attacked *Touch of Evil* for summing up "all the negative characteristics which appeal to Welles. . . . He must return to the moral values of America if he is ever to be the artist he could be."

Welles admitted it was a "terribly traumatic experience" when Universal-International, which had been talking with him about a multipicture contract, barred him from the lot during the final stages of postproduction. The film was reedited by the studio and partly reshot by studio director Harry Keller. Welles wrote a fifty-eight-page memo imploring the studio to make many small but often crucial fixes in that version, but the memo was largely ignored. It was not until 1998 that Welles's suggested changes were implemented, when editor–sound designer Walter Murch reedited the film for a new version produced for Universal by Rick Schmidlin. Among Murch's fifty revisions were removing the credits from the bravura opening tracking shot, restoring Welles's intricate crosscutting in the sequences following the car's explosion, shortening a gruesome close-up of the strangled Grandi (Akim Tamiroff), and following Welles's revolutionary sound design by using source music from nightclubs and car radios under the opening shot rather than Henry Mancini's score.* Discussing what Welles wrote in the memo about his plans for the sound design for the opening shot, Murch said, "Here was something I thought I had invented myself [for George Lucas's 1973 film *American Graffiti*]. It was great to read this and to realize that I was just kind of following in his footsteps." Murch added, "*Touch of Evil* was going to be the film with which he came back to Hollywood with a vengeance."

Barbara Leaming contends that Welles made a serious mistake by going to Mexico when the studio took over the film and by delaying his comments on the revised version, thus playing into the hands of his opponents and allowing them to claim he was "walking away" from *Touch of Evil*. His self-protective response was to move on to a film he thought represented his future and the chance to freely exercise his art, *Don Quixote*. For a filmmaker who had repeatedly suffered such devastating blows in Hollywood, that reaction was understandable but self-defeating. All Welles could assume was that *Touch of Evil* "was just too dark and black and strange for them." But he considered the studio's reaction "a mystery. There's some-

---

* I am among the people given "special thanks" in the end credits of the 1998 reedited version of *Touch of Evil*. Other than approving of the project as a closer approximation of Welles's artistic vision, my contribution was to suggest that the volume of the music be raised slightly in the opening shot when the bomb-laden car is approaching the camera from the distance. Murch agreed with my argument that a heightened volume level was needed to emphasize the car's presence in the shot, previously obscured by credits.

thing missing there that I don't know about, that I'll never understand. It's the only trouble I've ever had that I can't begin to fathom."

❖ ❖ ❖

The year after *Touch of Evil* was dumped so contemptuously onto the market, Welles's jaundiced attitude toward Hollywood was given full public venting. In an apocalyptic March 1959 article for *Esquire*, "Twilight in the Smog," he wrote:

> Is Hollywood's famous sun really setting? There is certainly a hint of twilight in the smog and, lately, over the old movie capital there has fallen a grey-flannel shadow. Television is moving inexorably westward. Emptying the movie theatres across the land, it fills the movie studios. Another industry is building quite another town; and already, rising out of the gaudy ruins of screenland, we behold a new, drab, curiously solemn brand of the old foolishness. . . .
>
> The feverish gaiety has gone, a certain brassy vitality drained away. TV, after all, is a branch of the advertising business, and Hollywood behaves increasingly like an annex of Madison Avenue. . . . The town's new industry threatens its traditional cosmopolitanism and substitutes a strong national flavor. This could not be otherwise since our television exists for the sole purpose of selling American products to American consumers. . . . One of our producers, by way of explaining the school of neo-realism in the Italian cinema, told me that over there, instead of actors, they use people. For good or evil it's certain that the town [Hollywood] is overrun with characters who are quite reasonable facsimiles of today's people. It's a solemn thought, but maybe that's what's wrong with Hollywood.

When that parting volley appeared on the newsstands, Welles had already returned to Europe, embracing what Truffaut called his "position as an avant-garde director." But even in Europe it took him four years to find funding for another feature.

❖ ❖ ❖

Welles's 1962 adaptation of Franz Kafka's novel *The Trial* is his most extravagantly stylized picture, a European "art film" as experimental in its rejection of conventional movie "realism" as Alain Resnais's 1961 film *L'année dernière à Marienbad (Last Year at Marienbad).* Although Welles always remained defiantly fond of *The Trial* in the face of disdain from many critics and filmgoers, he recognized that its nightmarishly distorted perspectives put a strain on the audience. "I carried wide angles to the

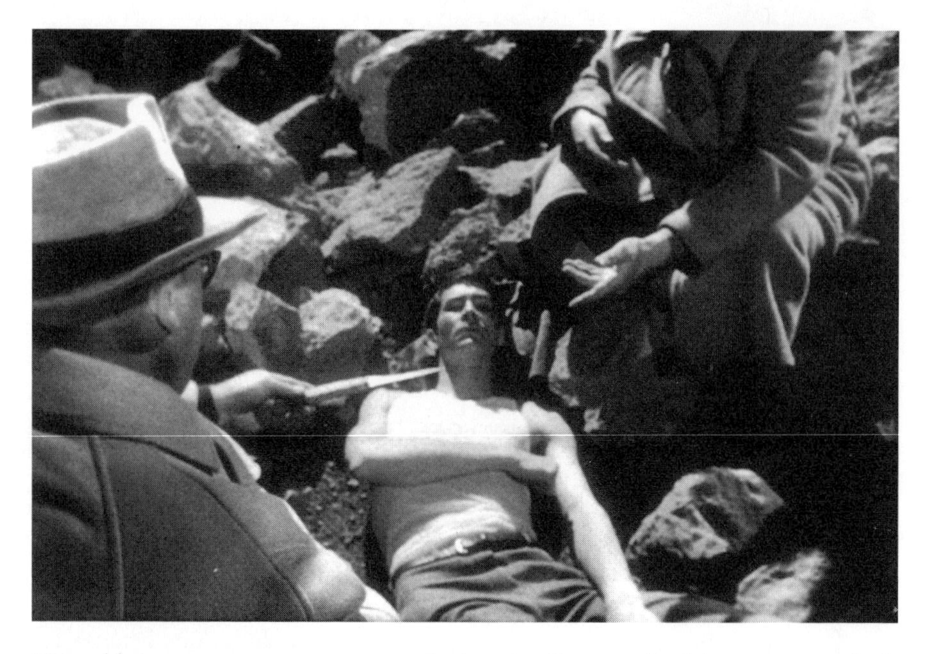

"I couldn't put my name to a work that implies man's ultimate surrender": Welles's 1962 adaptation of Franz Kafka's novel *The Trial*, starring Anthony Perkins as Joseph K., made Kafka's Everyman seem both more defiant and more truly guilty. *(Paris-Europa Productions/Hisa Films/FI-C-IT/Globus-Dubrava)*

point of madness in *The Trial,*" he reflected in 1978. "The wide angle is a marvelous instrument, but you have to use it carefully, because it can get away from you. One thing that doesn't work is to mix wide angles and close-ups. It's too much of a difference in style. Your whole psychological sense is distorted." In its hellishly expressionistic depiction of life in a contemporary totalitarian state, *The Trial* offers an even more explicit reflection than *Touch of Evil* of Welles's experience with political persecution. He pointedly used "American English" vernacular in adapting Kafka, while keeping the novel's European setting. The police investigators who burst unannounced into the bedroom of Joseph K. (Anthony Perkins) look like petty gangsters. Wearing homburgs and tacky raincoats, talking with broadly comical, guttural illiteracy, these thuggish characters represent another Wellesian dig at Hoover's flatfeet.

"Just exactly what is it I'm charged with?" asks K., insisting, "My papers are in perfect order" and wondering if his arrest is "an elaborate practical joke by some of my friends in the office." When he finds three office mates in the next room, K. demands, "What are you anyway, informers? What would you have to inform about?" To the policemen, K.

protests this "invasion of privacy and rank abuse of basic civil rights." Telling them sarcastically, "I'm sorry to disappoint you, but you won't find any subversive literature or pornography," he turns somber when he realizes they aren't joking: "But the real question is, Who accuses me?" K.'s neighbor Miss Bürstner (Jeanne Moreau) seems sympathetic at first but quickly flies into a panic: "Jesus! I hope it's not *political!* Politics! Don't go dragging me into it!"

Welles's K. is more defiant than Kafka's. Welles characteristically uses Brechtian alienation effects to avoid simple audience identification with the protagonist and keep the emphasis on the ideas behind the story. Welles's K. is a self-pitying, officious bureaucrat who revels in his own ability to keep people waiting in his office. Welles consciously portrayed K. as guilty, believing that K. "is not guilty as accused, but he is guilty all the same." This is an adaptation at war with the original text, which leaves the question of K.'s guilt more ambiguous, but Welles said that in the post-Holocaust era, "I couldn't put my name to a work that implies man's ultimate surrender. Being on the side of man, I had to show him, in his final hour, undefeated." The result is a striking but strained film that succeeds only intermittently in its mission of modernizing Kafka's vision of totalitarianism.

❖ ❖ ❖

Even though Welles managed to find funding in Spain in 1964 to direct his long-cherished Falstaff film, *Chimes at Midnight*, his frustrations over his endless struggles to exercise his craft renewed his ambivalence about staying in the movie business. Interviewed that year in Madrid, he was asked: "You said one day that you have a great deal of difficulty finding the money to make your films, that you have spent more time struggling to get this money than working as an artist. How is the battle at this time?"

"More bitter than ever," Welles replied.

> "Worse than ever. Very difficult. I have already said that I do not work enough. I am frustrated, do you understand? And I believe that my work shows that I do not do enough filming. My cinema is perhaps too explosive, because I wait too long before I speak. It's terrible. I have bought little cameras in order to film if I can find the money. I will shoot it in 16mm. The cinema is a *métier* . . . nothing can compare to the cinema. The cinema belongs to our times. It is 'the thing' to do. During the shooting of *The Trial*, I spent marvelous days. It was an amusement, happiness. You cannot imagine what I felt. . . ."

Welles's greatest film performance, as Shakespeare's bounteous rogue Sir John Falstaff in *Chimes at Midnight* (1966). The director's masterpiece, acclaimed in Europe, has seldom been seen in America. *(International Films Española/Alpine/Peppercorn Wormser)*

> "Are you thinking of returning to Hollywood?"
>
> "Not at the moment. But who knows what may change at the next instant? I am dying to work there because of the technicians, who are marvelous. They truly represent a director's dream."

When he attempted his final Hollywood comeback in 1970, it seemed a more propitious time than the late 1950s. With the loosening of censorship restraints, the freedom desperate executives were granting to "auteur" filmmakers, and the wholesale hiring of untried young talent, the "New Hollywood" seemed to many observers a fresh wind blowing away the rubble of the crumbling studio system. But the "thaw" Welles hoped for ultimately proved to be just another big chill. His penchant for dangerous material and reputation as a troublemaker and spendthrift preceded him and continued to shadow his every move. As a result, in later years he tended to avoid any involvement with studios on his own projects, with the exception of some brief flirtations that never led to consummation. "The pictures I like to make are not the pictures Hollywood producers, and particularly modern Hollywood producers, want to make," Welles admitted in 1982. When he realized this situation was not going to change, he didn't give up or sit around bitterly waiting for the phone to ring, as many older directors were doing. Instead, he ventured farther down the independent path, opting to work with small budgets and young nonunion crews. Sometimes he even used those little 16mm cameras he had earlier dismissed as too avant-garde, and at the end of his life he was planning to make a feature partly on video.

Surveying the chaotic contemporary Hollywood scene in his November 1970 article for *Look*, "But Where Are We Going?" Welles expressed guarded hope for his future and that of American movies. He noted that the Hollywood studios, in a state of collapse because of the country's radically changing social conditions, were desperately trying to exploit the youth audience. As a result, the Hollywood establishment was now happiest, he observed, when a director had no experience: "Like a nervous old lady, Hollywood is suddenly afraid of the traffic. She needs youthful hands to guide her. This trust is rather touching, slightly ridiculous, and very hopeful for the future of American films."

Providentially, when Welles wrote those words, "youthful hands" were reaching out to him.

Welles and the indispensable cameraman of his last fifteen years, Gary Graver, whom he affectionately called "Rembrandt." *(Gary Graver)*

Chapter Four

"TWILIGHT IN THE SMOG"

Look, I like this boy. And we have that story—let's see if we can make it.

—Welles talking to Oja Kodar about Gary Graver, 1970

On July 4, 1970, the young cinematographer Gary Graver, who had been working on low-budget exploitation movies, read a brief item that had appeared two days earlier in Army Archerd's *Daily Variety* gossip column: "Orson Welles, looking very well, visiting friends here and in San Fran, says he soon returns to film his yarn, 'The Other Side of the Wind,' in Italy and Yugoslavia." What happened next transformed both Welles's and Graver's lives and enabled Welles to continue pursuing his art for his remaining fifteen years.

Welles spent part of the summer of 1970 in New York playing an old Jewish magician in *A Safe Place* for the young independent filmmaker Henry Jaglom, who would become a longtime friend. Then, with his companion, Yugoslavian actress-sculptor-writer Oja Kodar, Welles went to Hollywood in July to appear on *The Dean Martin Show* and to discuss the possibility of directing a film for Columbia Pictures. Peter Bogdanovich was about to film *The Last Picture Show* for Columbia and the independent company BBS, which had scored a huge success the previous year for Columbia with Dennis Hopper's countercultural biker movie, *Easy Rider*. Bogdanovich put Welles in touch with BBS partner Bert Schneider, a bright and politically radical young producer whose father, Abe Schneider, was Columbia's chairman. Welles was hired by BBS to adapt Gavin Lyall's 1965 novel, *Midnight Plus One*. Set in post–World War II France, it deals with former comrades who have fallen out because of wartime betrayal. Welles was considering Robert Mitchum, Yves Montand, and Jack Nicholson for leading roles. Columbia paid for

Welles's bungalow at the Beverly Hills Hotel, but according to Kodar, the studio lost interest in the project. Bert Schneider, on the other hand, told me in 1976 that Welles ran up a $30,000 bill in his two months at the hotel, never finished the script, and absconded with the portable typewriter the studio had rented at his request.

❖ ❖ ❖

Oja Kodar was born Olga Palinkas in Croatia in 1941 but took her new surname at Welles's Svengali-like suggestion. It happened one night in France when she and Welles had dinner with a school friend of hers, "and this friend of mine asked Orson how he saw me and what I meant to him. And Orson said I was a present from God to him. I translated that into Croatian, and when he heard the word *kodar* he asked what that meant. And I said, '*as a present.*' Ko-dar! *Dar* is present and *ko* is *as—as a present.* And he said, 'Well, that's what you should be called: *Oja as a present.*'"

The worldly, intelligent, voluptuous, exotically beautiful young woman was working as a television news anchor in Yugoslavia when she met Welles in a nightclub during the filming of *The Trial* in 1962. He remained married to Paola Mori for the rest of his life but settled into a *Captain's Paradise* kind of existence, shuttling between his wife and Oja, though not always in such a carefree fashion. It was not until nearly the end of Welles's life that Paola realized the truth about his mistress. "We didn't publicize our relationship," Oja recalled. She explained, "I think it was very important for Orson's wife to be Mrs. Orson Welles. But I didn't care to be Mrs. Orson Welles. I was with the man I wanted to be with, that was enough. I've always been a bit against marriage. . . . When we were in Spain, Orson asked me if we shouldn't marry, but I said that everything was fine as it was." Kodar said one of the reasons her name rarely appeared as coauthor of Welles's later scripts was that she "didn't want Orson to encounter difficulties with his wife."

Welles began working with Oja in 1963, giving the neophyte actress a substantial role, albeit with minimal lines and costuming (a tiny bikini and a large hat), in his psychological thriller *The Deep.* Set on a pair of yachts stranded in the sea, it was adapted from Charles Williams's novel *Dead Calm* and began filming off the coast of Yugoslavia as *Deadly Calm* or *Dead Reckoning.* Also in the cast are Welles, Jeanne Moreau, Laurence Harvey, and Michael Bryant; the film was left uncompleted after further shooting in 1967–69 but is being assembled by the Munich Film Museum, which has screened its restoration in progress at Welles conferences in Europe.*

Oja was to have starred for Welles in the late 1960s in a short film based on Isak Dinesen's story "The Heroine." Welles intended it as part of a Dinesen anthology film for which he also considered "The Deluge at Norderney," featuring himself as the bogus cardinal, and "A Country Tale." Eventually those stories were to have been replaced in the anthology film by Dinesen's "Full Moon" and her novella *The Immortal Story*. But shooting on "The Heroine" in Budapest was canceled after a single day when Welles discovered that his financier was broke. Welles also learned he was being stuck with the hotel bill, so he fled the scene with Kodar at 4:00 A.M. *The Immortal Story* stood alone as the first Dinesen tale Welles brought to the screen, appearing in 1968 as a short feature released simultaneously on French television.

Welles and Kodar wrote scripts together for other projects in the late 1960s, including *The Masque of the Red Death*, combining that story by Edgar Allan Poe with another of his tales, "The Cask of Amontillado." Welles had been asked to direct *Masque* for the 1968 anthology film *Histoires extraordinaires (Spirits of the Dead)*. Federico Fellini, Louis Malle, and Roger Vadim directed segments of that film, but the production company rejected the richly expressionistic Welles-Kodar script, perhaps because it was too long at sixty pages, or about an hour in screen time.

❖ ❖ ❖

What could be called Welles's "Oja period" lasted until his death in 1985, and it marked profound changes in his filmmaking style. Under Kodar's influence, Welles's work underwent a Picasso-like late flowering of sexual themes and imagery. *The Immortal Story* contains an actual lovemaking scene; although filmed obliquely, it's arguably more erotic for its concentration on suggestive details. The connection between Welles and the older Picasso is drawn explicitly in *F for Fake*, with Welles ingeniously

* The production dates for *The Deep* usually are given as 1967–69, based on information Bogdanovich supplied for my first book on Welles. But according to a January 1964 item in *Variety*, "At Bavaria-Geiselgasteig, Orson Welles edited 'Deadly Calm,' the film he had produced, directed, and enacted late last year on a yacht off the Yugoslavian coast." Footage shot by two different cameramen during the two periods of shooting was combined by Welles in his rough cut (see chapter 6 for further discussion of the film).

"directing" the artist by intercutting still photographs of him seemingly ogling Oja as she strolls past his window in skimpy outfits. As "Picasso" paints nude pictures of Oja, Welles intercuts ravishing shots of her body in sensuous poses and rhapsodizes about the artist's reaction to her lush figure: "Was he . . . tempted? Perhaps he was *inspired*. . . . [T]he results of this encounter were, to say the least of it, extremely fruitful. Figs sweetened on the trees—grapes burst into ripeness on the vines—and twenty-two—twenty-two!—large portraits of Miss Oja Kodar were born under that virile brush."

Kodar said of *The Other Side of the Wind*, "When you see the film, you will feel that somebody else worked with [Welles], because there are things that he never would have done alone and never did before. He was a very shy man, and erotic stuff was not his thing. And in this film, you will see the erotic stuff. He kept accusing me with his finger: 'It's your fault!' And he was right—it's my fault! . . . Not only did I write the script [with him], I practically directed some of those erotic scenes, because Orson was a very shy person."

Because of Oja's limited acting skills, their working relationship on many film and television projects could be compared unkindly to Charles Foster Kane's building an opera house for his reedy-voiced mistress, Susan Alexander. But Kodar, whose greatest passion is sculpting, did not need Welles to give her ambition. She was a vivid screen presence who photographed well in the relatively undemanding ensemble roles he usually gave her. François Truffaut, who had considered Welles "the most Catholic of all directors," told me in the 1970s that he found Kodar's sensuality in Welles's films a stimulating new element in his artistic development. More crucially, she was an indefatigable creative partner who served as a goad and inspiration to keep him working on new projects, often of a daringly contemporary nature, throughout his sometimes dispiriting final decades.

Kodar recalled what happened in the summer of 1970:

> Orson and I were sitting in a bungalow at the Beverly Hills Hotel, with our living expenses being paid by Columbia. Orson said, "We can both write, I'm a director, you're an actress, let's think of a film to make while we're here in Hollywood." We had two stories. Orson had one called *Jake*, which is the name of the main character played by John Huston, and I had a story called *The Other Side of the Wind*. . . . [W]hen Orson was planning on doing *The Merchant of Venice* in Italy, we were looking for sets, and we were at Cinecittà Studios looking at the sets for Zeffirelli's *Romeo and Juliet*. Orson was wearing his big black cape, and there was a big gust of wind and his cape

A new eroticism bloomed in Welles's later work, a development for which his personal and professional relationship with actress Oja Kodar, from 1962 until his death in 1985, was largely responsible. Frame enlargements from *The Immortal Story* (1968), with Jeanne Moreau as Virginie Ducrot, and *F for Fake* (1974), with Kodar as a model for Pablo Picasso. *(ORTF/Albina Films; SACI/Les Films de l'Astrophore/SACI/Janus Film und Fersehen)*

> flew up, and I thought, "Orson is so multifaceted . . . I'm going to write something and call it *The Other Side of the Wind.*" . . . So we mixed the two stories together and started working on it, until finally we had a script for *The Other Side of the Wind.* Of course Orson was the main writer, I in a minor capacity. Then Gary came into the story.

❖ ❖ ❖

When Gary Graver made his providential appearance in Welles's life, he was an ambitious young man working on the fringes of Hollywood. A native of Portland, Oregon, Graver followed an eclectic path to the movie business. In his youth, he ran a 16mm movie theater in his basement and was a magician, a circus clown, a radio personality, a still photographer, and an aspiring actor. After moving to Hollywood, he became a self-described "film snob," studying the work of Truffaut, Godard, and Bergman and devouring British film magazines such as *Sight and Sound* and *Films and Filming* for information about European cinema. He studied acting with Jeff Corey, Lee J. Cobb, and Lucille Ball, but, with the old-line studio system still functioning in extremis, found it nearly impossible to break into the business. He recalls, "I parked cars and worked in a movie theater for ten years before I got a job on a movie."

Graver was as an usher at the Vogue Theater on Hollywood Boulevard and spent weekends in 1963 as assistant manager of the first-run Beverly Theater in Beverly Hills. In an early sign of his reverence for older filmmaking masters, he would spot Alfred Hitchcock and Jean Renoir waiting in line to buy tickets and wave them in for free. Graver was drafted by the U.S. Army in 1964 but joined the navy instead because he thought it might help him meet the director John Ford, a retired rear admiral who was known to visit naval facilities in Los Angeles to help train cameramen. Graver didn't get to meet Ford, but the navy made him a cameraman.

In two years with the Combat Camera Group in Vietnam, Japan, and the Philippines, Graver photographed battles from land, sea, and air, as well as medical operations, training, distinguished visitors, and anything else the navy wanted him to shoot. His filmmaking baptism of fire served him well when he returned to Hollywood. He soon found jobs as an assistant cameraman and eventually became a director of photography on low-budget exploitation films such as *The Girls from Thunder Strip* (1966) and *Hell's Bloody Devils* (1970); he made his own short movies and began directing features in 1970 with *Sandra, the Making of a Woman.* But if he had to earn his living grinding out formula pictures, he was determined to realize his higher aspirations.

While still in high school, Graver saw his first Welles film, *Touch of Evil*, in a theater and was "blown away by the moving camera, the weird angles, the shadows, the choreography, the opening scene, *everything*. I love how there's an empty picture and the camera is still, and a guy rushes in and says, 'Look over here, fellas,' and then as the actor moves the camera moves with him. Rather than have people come toward the camera, Welles would have people walk in from *behind* the camera—I'd never seen that before." At a time when few in America were paying attention to Welles's career or his truly radical style, Graver continued to follow it closely. When he watched *Chimes at Midnight* on Hollywood Boulevard in the late 1960s, he was the only person in the theater. "I'd only ever really been interested in meeting or working with one director, and that was Orson," Graver told me.

> When I heard he was going to start a new picture, I thought maybe I could shoot it, because he worked independently.
>
> On the Fourth of July, 1970, I was sitting in Schwab's drugstore in Hollywood with my wife, Connie, having a cup of coffee reading *Variety*. It said that Orson Welles is in town. I thought, I bet he's at the Beverly Hills Hotel. So I just made a cold call to the hotel: "Orson Welles, please." The operator put me right through to him—I couldn't believe it, no screening or anything.
>
> I said, "My name's Gary Graver. I'm an American cameraman and I know you have some projects. I'd sure like to be involved with you as cinematographer." He brushed me off, saying, "Well, you know, I'm kind of busy right now, I've got to go to New York and do a picture. Give me your name and your phone number." So I thought, "Well, that's the end of it, I won't hear from him."
>
> I said to Connie, "Let's go home." We had a home in Laurel Canyon. As I pulled the car into the driveway, I heard the phone ringing, and it kept ringing. I answered and he said, "Gary, this is Orson, get on over here to the Beverly Hills Hotel, I've got to talk to you right away." So I drove right over, went to his bungalow, and there he was. He had a robe on, and I remember seeing a woman in the background close the door as I came in. That was Oja—I didn't meet her that day.
>
> Orson said, "My plane's leaving later tonight. I've got some time now, let's talk. You're the second cameraman who ever called me up and said he wanted to work with me. The first one was Gregg Toland. Since then no technician or crew member has ever called me up and said they wanted to work with me, so it seems like pretty good luck. I'm looking for an Ameri-

can cameraman. I want to make a picture in Hollywood." So Orson and I were chatting for a while and having coffee. All of a sudden he grabs me by the shoulders and throws me on the floor and keeps his hands on top of me—he's a big guy, and I can't get up. I say, "What's wrong?" And he said, "Shhhh—quiet, don't talk." He's holding me down, this guy in his bathrobe, and I wonder what the hell did I get myself into here. It's a little weird, I'm lying on the floor with Orson Welles in a bungalow on July Fourth. Finally he let me up and said, "OK, come on, get up and sit down." I said, "What's wrong?" He said, "The actress Ruth Gordon is outside the window, she's kind of looking in here, and if she sees me she'll come in and talk and talk and talk. I want to talk to you."*

We talked about everything. I said, "I can get you a crew, very inexpensive." I told him I could make a film with him for $10,000. After he met me, he stayed here, because he saw I could help him get the film made, save money on equipment, use a small, young crew, pay everyone flat rate. Guys were getting $200 a week; we worked nights a lot, and if people got better-paying jobs, they'd leave. I had my own camera. I knew a lot of stuff he didn't know. I knew how to get permits, how he could buy short ends [the unexposed ends of used film rolls].

He went to New York for a few weeks on *A Safe Place.* When he came back, I went to his bungalow every night for about a week and brought my tripod and camera and lighting to do test shots of him. The first night, I didn't bring the top of the tripod or something, and then I brought the wrong lens. I was screwing it up, I was very nervous. He knew all the equipment, he read *American Cinematographer*, and he was always up on everything before I knew about it. He said, "Let's get this, let's use that." Finally we did commence shooting and we shot for four months straight. We never had a budget, we just started filming. What I didn't fully understand was going to happen was that Orson worked seven-day weeks, every single day, and the only way to get out of it was to say you didn't feel good, you had a touch of the flu or a cold or something. Then he didn't want you around.

When I called Orson, I felt that he wasn't making enough movies. I wanted there to be more Orson Welles movies. I wanted to make myself available for free or for very little money, so he didn't have to have money pressure. That is the centerpiece of my life, of my career, that I was able to enable Orson to make more movies and projects easily and freely. I didn't know it was going to be so long, but that's the way it was. I wanted it more for Orson than for me. I sacrificed everything I could. I was married and divorced two times during the making of *The Other Side of the Wind.* It was

---

* Gordon acted with Welles in a 1941 radio adaptation of Ring Lardner's short story "The Golden Honeymoon." Welles and Graver filmed the director's arch reading of the nostalgia piece against a discordantly gaudy backdrop in 1970.

> hard on my marriages. I was with Orson all the time, more than with my wives. Orson was good about it, he included both my wives, Connie and April, they worked on the film, but they were bored. It was slow going if you were not totally into it.
>
> It was like going to a film school for fifteen years. Very demanding; he was gruff. But a lot of fun. The work process was great. He was my favorite director and my favorite guy, and like a father figure at the time, older, wiser, smarter than me.

At the Locarno Welles conference in 2005, Graver displayed a modesty that underrates his contribution to Welles's work but helps explain why they functioned so well together: "I never said no to him. The visuals were all Orson. My job was to implement everything he wanted. He was boss. I was there to make sure it was exposed right, that it was in focus, that it was framed right." But Graver acknowledged that when he presented himself to Welles as a collaborator, "I was brazen about it. I knew that Orson and I were the kind of personalities who would get along. We had the same sense of humor."

Their meeting began a filmmaking collaboration that would last to the end of Welles's life—and beyond. Almost twenty years after Welles died, Graver told me, with weary amusement, "I'm *still* working with Orson. I never stopped."

❖ ❖ ❖

In August 1970, Peter Bogdanovich was getting ready to leave for Texas to begin filming *The Last Picture Show* when Welles called him to announce, "I've started shooting a movie."

"You *have*?" replied Bogdanovich.

"Yes. It's a dirty movie. If you can make one, I can."

Since Welles and Bogdanovich had begun work on their interview book in 1968, Bogdanovich's filmmaking career, temporarily stalled by the commercial failure of *Targets*, had begun to accelerate with his hiring in January 1970 to direct *The Last Picture Show*, from the 1950s Texas coming-of-age novel by Larry McMurtry. To heighten that film's sense of nostalgia and allow a greater range of depth-of-field imagery, Welles suggested that Bogdanovich make his picture show in black-and-white, a radical idea at the time. Initially resisted by Columbia, it helped make the film successful and led to a modest revival of black-and-white cinematography. Bogdanovich subtly borrowed from the lost ending of *The Magnificent Ambersons* for the mordant ending of his picture, in which Sonny

(Timothy Bottoms) visits the dismal home of his discarded lover, Ruth Popper (Cloris Leachman), as a raucous commercial jingle plays in counterpoint on an offscreen television.

(After Welles's relationship with Bogdanovich had soured in the mid-seventies, Welles was interrupted during the shooting of *The Other Side of the Wind* in Arizona by a phone call from Bogdanovich in Hollywood. Bogdanovich told Welles he was planning to make a musical set in the 1930s using Cole Porter songs. That sounded like a good idea, Welles said impatiently. Bogdanovich then asked Welles if he thought he should shoot the picture in black-and-white. Welles thought for a moment and replied, "Yes, yes, Peter, *great* idea. Shoot it in black-and-white." He hung up, turned to the crew, and burst into uproarious laughter: "*Black-and-white!* Haaahaaahaah!" Bogdanovich didn't follow his advice for the cinematography of *At Long Last Love* but used a black-and-white motif for the sets and costumes. Would that notorious, if elegantly filmed, flop have been more or less disastrous if he had taken Welles's advice?)

Welles thought there was too much sex in the script Bogdanovich and McMurtry had written for *The Last Picture Show*. But Welles coveted the role of Sam the Lion, the grizzled owner of the local pool hall and diner who serves as a mentor to the local boys and embodies old-fashioned cowboy chivalry. Welles told me, "Anybody who plays that role will win an Academy Award." But Peter said, "I didn't want a movie star in the role." Instead he cast the veteran character actor Ben Johnson, whose weathered face spoke volumes about western values and his own sense of disillusionment. Just as Welles predicted, Johnson won the Oscar for best supporting actor. Judging from the hammy southern accent and makeup Welles used in the 1958 William Faulkner adaptation *The Long, Hot Summer* and his remoteness from the kind of simple dignity Sam the Lion represents, his casting might have ruined Bogdanovich's film single-handedly.

Peter was in the final stages of the casting process when we spent three hours that August talking in the study of his small home in Van Nuys. Graciously answering my questions about some of the mysteries of Welles's career, Peter was also, in effect, auditioning me for *The Other Side of the Wind.* The phone rang in the midst of our conversation. As I sat there vainly trying to pretend I wasn't listening to Peter talking with Welles, I couldn't help thinking it sounded like a lovers' conversation, all low-pitched bantering with an intimately elliptical way of completing each other's phrases.

At the end of the evening, I passed Peter's exhausted-looking wife,

Polly Platt, in the hallway. She was pregnant with a daughter who would be named Alexandra Welles Bogdanovich. Polly was working as production designer on *The Last Picture Show,* the movie that would destroy their marriage. Peter's Welles homages unfortunately would extend to imitating the Kane–Susan Alexander relationship by falling in love with the blonde model he cast as his ingenue, Cybill Shepherd. Welles would watch the meteoric rise of his young acolyte with some bemusement and barely repressed jealousy, feelings that would find their way into the storyline of the movie Welles was about to start shooting.

The Last Picture Show was an ironic title for a young director's breakthrough film. And it would have been a good title for Welles's film about an old director's disastrous attempt at a Hollywood comeback.

❖ ❖ ❖

Welles had been thinking intently about the dilemma of old directors in the New Hollywood since the summer of 1969. While he was in Guaymas, Mexico, acting in Mike Nichols's film of *Catch-22,* Bogdanovich was interviewing him for their book. Bogdanovich told him about John Ford and other great veterans who were having trouble finding work. The next evening they were getting "a bit soused in an elegant bar," Bogdanovich recalled, when Welles launched into an eloquent, melancholy monologue:

> "You told me last night about all these old directors whom people in Hollywood say are 'over the hill,' and it made me so sick, I couldn't sleep. I started thinking about all those conductors—Klemperer, Beecham, Toscanini—I can name almost a hundred in the last century—who were at the height of their powers after seventy-five. And were conducting at eighty. Who *says* they're over the hill!
>
> . . . "It's so *awful.* I think it's just terrible what happens to old people. But the public isn't interested in that—never has been. That's why *Lear* has always been a play people hate."
>
> "You don't think Lear became senile?" [asked Bogdanovich].
>
> "He became senile by giving *power* away. The only thing that keeps people alive in their old age is power. . . . But take power away from de Gaulle or Churchill or Tito or Mao or Ho or any of these old men who run the world—in this world that belongs only to young people—and you'll see a 'babbling, slippered pantaloon.'"

"The day after," reports Bogdanovich, "Orson told me he planned to make his next picture on precisely this subject: the last days of an aging director, which eventually became *The Other Side of the Wind.*"

Hearing about the problems experienced by Ford, whom he considered the greatest of all directors, crystallized Welles's ambivalence about returning as an "old" man (he was actually only fifty-four at the time) to a Hollywood suddenly crazy for youth. Once he had been the youngest director in a profession dominated by older men. But now, with the Hollywood studios crumbling and back lots being sold for real estate development, the dilemma of an old director trying to make a comeback in the New Hollywood seemed a powerful metaphor for the downfall of a business that Welles and other filmmakers had tried to make into an art. Welles had been down the comeback road before, while making *Touch of Evil*, and had found only a mirage. By the summer of 1970, the "twilight in the smog" he had warned about was threatening to blot out the Hollywood sun entirely. In his first conversation with Graver, Welles said the film he wanted to make was inspired by his 1959 *Esquire* article of that title.

The apocalyptic view of Hollywood decadence expressed in "Twilight in the Smog" reflected Welles's jaundiced feelings upon returning to town from his long European exile. He later told Bogdanovich that during the making of *Touch of Evil* in 1957, "I decided to throw a party for all the little Hollywood grandees from the old days who'd been friends and whom I hadn't seen in so long, having been in Europe for almost ten years, to show that I still remembered my friends—Sam Goldwyn and Jack Warner and those kind of people. And I was late. I'd been shooting *Touch of Evil* and I thought, 'I won't take time to remove this terrible, enormous makeup that took forever to put on'—padded stomach and back, sixty pounds of it, and horrible old-age stuff. When I came into my house, before I had a chance to explain that I had to get upstairs and take my makeup off, all these people came up and said, 'Hi, Orson! Gee, you're looking great!'"

During the party, Welles showed his guests *The Fountain of Youth* and the other short film he had made the previous year, *Camille, the Naked Lady and the Musketeers*, "and Sam Goldwyn walked out of the first one and said, 'I didn't come here to see a lot of shorts.'" It's likely that the grotesquely comical memories of that "comeback" party provided the inspiration for the disastrous party the Dietrich-like actress Zarah Valeska (Lilli Palmer) throws in *The Other Side of the Wind* to celebrate her old friend Jake Hannaford's comeback attempt.

❖ ❖ ❖

At noon on Saturday, August 22, 1970, I went to Welles's rented ranch house on Lawlen Way, high in the hills above Sunset Boulevard, for our

"The high priest of the cinema" was Welles's sarcastic description of the character Joseph McBride plays in *The Other Side of the Wind*, a film critic named Mister Pister. Exasperated by his malfunctioning tape recorder, Pister rides on a bus to director Jake Hannaford's birthday party, amid dummies representing Hannaford's leading man, John Dale (a frame enlargement from a scene shot in 1971). *(SACI/Les Films de l'Astrophore)*

first meeting. He was typing on a portable typewriter in the foyer, swathed in a massive white silk dressing gown that made him look like a polar bear. I was waiting to hear his laugh—that immense, intimidating, chilling laugh so familiar from the screen—but when it came, I was surprised. When Welles laughed, he started slowly, cocking an eye toward his companion, watching his response. When the response was encouraging (how couldn't it have been?), the laugh swelled and began to gather force, like a typhoon, until his features were dissolved in a mask of Falstaffian delight. "When I met Orson, I thought he was very handsome, but I was enchanted by his laugh," Jeanne Moreau recalled. "He had an incredible way of laughing—you know, something like the Sun exploding." Welles's laugh was ingratiating, not intimidating, for he kept a slight portion of that eye fixed on his companion.

Seeing him up close, I sensed a surprising vulnerability. The wariness and tension lurking behind Welles's bonhomie became even more apparent when we sat down to lunch. The meal itself was the picture of California healthfulness—just a salad, tossed by Welles himself in a big wooden bowl—but I was surprised to find him knocking back large belts of whiskey. More of a beer drinker myself at the time, I reluctantly joined him in a whiskey, wondering why he was drinking so heavily that early in the day.

"In the first few days of filming," Graver recalls, "Orson was drinking bourbon or something. He'd get a little buzz on, get a little excited, put things in front of the lens: He was having a good time and being very creative—stuff I wouldn't do. One night, we were all sitting in the house, and he said, 'Bring the crew in, we're going to watch *Dean Martin*, I'm on it tonight.' He looked at it and said, 'God, I'm fat,' and stopped drinking. That was September 17, 1970, and I never saw him take a hard drink again. Just wine, but only in Europe. I never saw him drink in America again, except in the eighties, I guess he would have some wine at lunchtime at Ma Maison [the West Hollywood bistro that became his haunt]."

Welles's drinking in the early days of *The Other Side of the Wind*, and perhaps his intermittent eating binges, were signs of an anxiously driven, addictive personality, a legacy of the alcoholism that helped kill his father. *Touch of Evil* has a memorably comic exchange on the subject of addiction: When Marlene Dietrich's Tanya tells Hank Quinlan, "I didn't recognize you—you should lay off those candy bars," Quinlan grunts, "Well, it's either the candy or the hooch. I must say I sure wish it was your chili I was getting fat on. Anyway, you're sure looking good." Tanya reacts with the bluntness of an AA counselor: "You're a mess, honey."

Along with the whiskey, I was offered a Wellesian cigar (seven inches long, by my measure) from a box on the piano. I lit one and sat down to talk with a man whom, a few hours before, I had known only as a figure of legend. Welles kidded me about the fanatical love of movies I shared with Bogdanovich. Pointing out that people had been living on earth for thousands of years before being able to watch movies, Welles reminded me of his many other interests, from magic to painting to politics. But I wanted to hear his opinions about some contemporary filmmakers. Remembering that he had said of Stanley Kubrick in 1964, "Among those whom I would call 'younger generation,' Kubrick appears to me to be a giant," I asked what he thought of *2001: A Space Odyssey*. Welles surprised me by saying he had no desire to see it: "I'd rather spend the two hours talking to you."

Welles explained that he only saw movies when he was seized with a fit of guilt over being out of touch with the contemporary moviemaking scene. He would spend two or three days going to see several movies a day but would walk out after the first twenty minutes unless he found a rare one that intrigued him.

Another film he didn't plan to see was *Catch-22*. Welles grumpily plays the oafish Brigadier General Dreedle in that disastrous, overpriced botch, which substitutes gargantuan production values for the wry black humor of Joseph Heller's novel. Welles had tried to obtain the film rights and was disappointed to have such a small part in the making of the film. He asked what I thought of *Catch-22*, which had opened a month earlier. I told him that Mike Nichols's visual style was hysterical and overheated, when it should have been cool. "*Very* cool," he agreed.*

Welles went on to express astonishment at my obsession with *Citizen Kane*. "You've seen *Kane* sixty times?" he asked. "How could you see *any* movie sixty times?"

"Well," I replied, "you watched [Ford's 1939 Western] *Stagecoach* forty times in one year while you were preparing to make *Kane*. I was emulating you."

"Yes," said Welles, "but I didn't really *watch Stagecoach* every time. Every night for more than a month, I would screen it with a different technician from RKO and ask him questions all through the movie."

Welles chided me half-jokingly for unearthing his early amateur film *The Hearts of Age*. I was tipped off to its existence by film historian Russell Merritt, one of my professors in Madison, who had discovered the original 16mm print in the William Vance collection at the Greenwich, Connecticut, Public Library. A future producer-director of television commercials,

---

* In his DVD commentary on the film, Nichols admits he "knew all the time that something was wrong" with his approach to *Catch-22*. Nichols adds, "This is not my kind of movie because it's not about interpersonal things at all." Welles, he says, "was not wonderful on the set. . . . What I never knew until I read a book twenty-some years later was that he, Welles, had tried to get *Catch-22* to make himself. And no wonder he was annoyed that this squirt was doing it when he couldn't. . . . I was already semi-paralyzed at the idea that Orson Welles was there and I was supposed to tell him what to do. But if I knew that he wanted to do *Catch-22*, it would have been [a] disaster."

Vance codirected the short with Welles during the 1934 Summer Festival of Drama Welles conducted with Roger Hill in Woodstock, Illinois. Parts of the tongue-in-cheek, heavily "symbolic" allegory of death (eventually preserved by the Library of Congress) have the goofy flippancy of a student movie made hastily on a lark, but some of the compositions and moody expressionist lighting are startlingly sophisticated and evocative of the mature Welles visual style. Welles seemed bemused and somewhat irritated that I had reported on the discovery of *The Hearts of Age* in the spring of 1970 in a *Film Quarterly* article, "Welles before *Kane*."

Like a magician perpetually pulling wonders from his hat, Welles wanted people to think he had started making movies as a full-blown master with *Citizen Kane*, not with what he called "a Sunday afternoon home movie." Welles told me *The Hearts of Age* was intended as a parody of the pretensions of avant-garde cinema, particularly Jean Cocteau's surrealistic 1930 film *Le sang d'un poète (Blood of a Poet)*. To a subsequent interviewer, Welles bemoaned the discovery of this work of juvenilia: "I don't know how it has entered the *oeuvre*." And Graver told me many years later, "Orson kept saying, 'Why did Joe have to discover that film?'"

My article also discussed the little-known silent movie Welles filmed (but did not complete) in 1938 to accompany his stage production of William Gillette's farce *Too Much Johnson*. The only print was destroyed in a fire at Welles's villa outside Madrid shortly before we met, along with several unpublished books and unproduced scripts. The fire occurred while the Irish actor-writer Robert Shaw was renting the home. "It's probably a good thing," Welles told me. "I never cared much for possessions, but over the years I accumulated a few. Now I can tell everybody how great those scripts were! I wish you could have seen *Too Much Johnson*, though. It was a beautiful film. We created a sort of dream Cuba in New York. I looked at it four years ago and the print was in wonderful condition. You know, I never [fully] edited it. I meant to put it together to give to Jo Cotten as a Christmas present one year, but I never got around to it."

Despite his gibes at my fanatical scholarship, Welles expressed appreciation that I wrote about him seriously and sympathetically. Today, when there are many more books about Welles than there are completed Welles movies, it's hard to remember the days when the bookshelf on the man and his work was small indeed. Asked by Huw Wheldon in a 1960 BBC *Monitor* interview how he wanted people to remember him, Welles said he hoped they would forget the derogatory things that had been written about him in American books, because "almost every American book on the cinema pricks the bubble and proves that what is said about me is a lie and I am no good. . . . I really wish there was something nicer that they could read about me." He added in 1964, "What is serious is that in countries where English is spoken, the role played by criticism concerning serious works of cinema is very important. Given the fact that one cannot make films in competition with Doris Day, what is said by reviews such as *Sight and Sound* is the only reference." *Sight and Sound* was one of the journals that was publishing the chapters of my work in progress on Welles. After the book appeared in 1972, I told him I thought the color tinting of his face on the cover (a still from *The Immortal Story*) made him look "like a carrot," but he told me firmly, "You should be very proud of it."

We talked awhile in 1970 about his difficulties raising funds for film projects and about the endless vagaries of production and distribution. I told him of my great admiration for *Chimes at Midnight* and described my experiences trying to help find an audience for the film in the United States. In March 1967, I watched it three times in one night at a Chicago theater, the Town Underground, where it played for only five days (accurately billed as "A Spectacular Triumph for Orson Welles") before the theater was changed back into a soft-core porno house. The elderly winos and scattered film buffs who made up the small Chicago audience found it entertaining and accessible. But the film's abbreviated run in one of America's major cities was typical of the insulting treatment *Chimes* received from its U.S. distributor, Peppercorn Wormser.

I called the eponymous Carl Peppercorn in New York that summer to register my concern. When I asked why he would dump such an important film so unceremoniously, he was irritated and dismissive. But he admitted losing faith in the film's commercial potential after it was panned in the *New York Times* by Welles's longtime nemesis Bosley Crowther, writing from the Cannes Film Festival. Fearing another blast, the distributor opened the film cautiously in Ann Arbor, Michigan, before letting the national critics see it. *Chimes* arrived in New York with, as *Newsweek* put it, "all the advance publicity of a Federal raid on a moonshine still." Crowther repeated his complaints, proclaiming it a "fatal" mistake for Welles, "with the record he has!" to have been allowed to both direct and star in *Chimes* and to "spread himself so extensively and grotesquely as he conspicuously does in this picture." The distributor's resulting lack of support doomed *Chimes at Midnight* to oblivion.

After hearing about my efforts on behalf of the film, Welles said he had recently received a telegram from Charlton Heston. Heston was planning to make a film of Shakespeare's plays about Prince Hal and Falstaff. Falstaff, declared Heston, was the part he had always wanted to see Welles play. Would Welles be interested in starring in the movie with him? With a rueful smile, Welles showed how astonished he was that Heston didn't even know *Chimes at Midnight* existed. I could see that Welles wanted to burst out laughing at the absurdity of the situation, but the laughter died in his throat.*

Then I asked why, in recent years, his movies had less and less of the razzle-dazzle of his youth. Was it a kind of growing serenity?

"No, the explanation is simple," he said. "All the great technicians are dead or dying. You can't get the kind of boom operator I had, for example, on *Touch of Evil.* That man, John Russell, is now a lighting cameraman. I have to make do with what I can get."

Welles surprised me by spending a full half hour of our conversation vehemently denouncing a student film he had watched at the American Film Institute in Beverly Hills. He called it the worst movie he had ever seen, pretentious, obscure, an indulgent waste of celluloid he had been forced to sit through despite an almost uncontrollable impulse to walk out of the screening room. His complaints were like those he made against Michelangelo Antonioni's ennui-ridden films, then highly fashionable on the art-movie circuit. Antonioni was his cinematic bête noire, an exception to his general rule about not publicly denouncing other directors. Welles no doubt was annoyed that Antonioni had been given a big budget by MGM in 1969 to make his radical-chic art movie *Zabriskie Point,* a resounding flop that Welles would parody with the film-within-the-film in *The Other Side of the Wind.* But I was dismayed to hear Welles spending so much time and energy attacking the work of a lowly film student (who has since gone on to a successful career as a critically praised Hollywood director).

I suspected that in spite of his disclaimers about welcoming the New Hollywood youth boom, Welles deeply resented that the AFI and the studios were giving youngsters the chance to make movies when he still

---

* This was not a unique occurrence. Near the end of his life, "Orson came home and said he was very upset," Oja Kodar recalled. "He had just met with Anne Baxter [his Lucy in *The Magnificent Ambersons*]. She said, 'Orson, I have a great idea. I am going to produce and play in a story by Isak Dinesen called *The Immortal Story.*' She didn't even know that he had made the film."

had to scramble for funds thirty years after making *Citizen Kane*. His diatribe casts a darker light on his sarcastic gibes three months later in his *Look* article about the studios desperately turning to neophytes to save them from bankruptcy. Welles's comments on the overrated nature of directors and his attack on the tendency to romanticize artists as "geniuses" were partly a reaction against Federico Fellini's acclaimed 1962 fantasy about a director's inner life, *8 1/2*, which Welles felt made it seem "as though the Duce's balcony has risen again from the ashes in the form of a camera crane." Never one to let himself off the hook, Welles was also exploring in that article, as well as in *The Other Side of the Wind*, his own oscillations between narcissism and self-criticism, perfectly expressed in the correction he once offered when someone described him as vain: "I am *conceited*, but I am not vain."

He told me the story of *The Other Side of the Wind* that first day, and I observed that it sounded like his early 1960s project *The Sacred Beasts*. He said the new project was a "permutation" of the earlier idea. I asked Welles if he had been working on the script when I walked in. He laughed and said there wasn't any script; the film would be improvised. Seeing my surprise, he said he had written a script that would have run for nine hours on-screen but put it aside because he realized he was writing a novel. "I'm going to improvise out of everything I know about the characters and the situation," he said. He had a large cardboard box crammed with notes sitting next to the typewriter.

❖ ❖ ❖

Our discussion continued through the afternoon and into dinner when several other people arrived, including Kodar, Bogdanovich, and Gary and Connie Graver. But after that first day, Welles partly seemed to shut down with me, resisting my attempts to engage him in lengthy discussions. Perhaps he felt one freewheeling talk satisfied his obligation to charm me. Or perhaps I was too opinionated or naive for his liking. I was aware that some of my remarks at dinner irritated him.

The name of the British director Tony Richardson came up, and I said something to the effect that he was a terrible director who didn't know how to use a camera. Welles, who had acted for Richardson in the awful 1967 film *The Sailor from Gibraltar*, reacted with annoyance. Glowering vaguely in my direction, he declared, "Tony Richardson is a *major* director."

There was an uncomfortable silence at the table. I realized that I had committed a faux pas. After that day, I was more reticent about expressing my views. I always felt somewhat uncomfortable around Welles. I initially spoke up because I felt the need to assert myself, to cover up my nervousness and inexperience, and to stake out a bit of intellectual independence from the overbearing host. I had the impression that Welles was not a man who welcomed spirited disagreement.

Our sharpest difference of opinion that first afternoon came when we talked about President Lyndon B. Johnson and the student antiwar movement. I criticized Johnson's handling of the war and assumed that Welles, as a lifelong progressive, would agree with me. After all, he had told Kenneth Tynan in the spring of 1966 in their *Playboy* interview, "America doesn't have a history of losing wars and it has only a few bad wars on its conscience: this is one of them."

But in our conversation, Welles insisted with surprising vehemence that Johnson was one of America's greatest presidents. Why, I wondered? Because of his civil rights legislation guaranteeing blacks the right to vote and his Great Society programs to help the poor and disadvantaged, Welles said. I agreed that Johnson had done much in those vital areas but insisted that his record on Vietnam had to be weighed heavily against his domestic achievements (which ultimately would be undone by his war and its ruinous economic cost). Welles huffily refused to take my point. I realized that his high opinion of LBJ was a reflection of his own lifelong commitment to civil rights, but I was surprised by what I took to be his cavalier dismissal of the relative importance of the war.

I ventured a criticism of some of the Madison antiwar radicals. I had been covering their increasingly violent protests for the *Wisconsin State Journal*, and I told Welles that they were getting crazy: "They're going to kill somebody pretty soon." Welles angrily disagreed: They *weren't* crazy and they certainly weren't out to kill anybody. Now he seemed offended that I had introduced a note of ambiguity to a discussion of opposition to the war. Again I was mightily surprised at such a simplistic reaction from a filmmaker whose work I revered for its moral complexity.

I had the impression that Welles was out of touch with the reality in the streets and took an old-fashioned liberal idealist's view of the antiwar movement. He didn't seem to realize, or wouldn't accept, that a significant part of the antiwar movement had gone beyond its blithely inhuman rhetoric about "killing the pigs" and begun its fatal descent into nihilistic, self-defeating violence. Welles seemed to feel that since the protesters were right about the war, they couldn't be wrong about the way they went about attacking it. I was less concerned that Welles disagreed with me than I was by his condescension in dismissing my viewpoint. He obviously was unaware of the firebombings carried out in recent months by a small group of Madison radicals who had become known as "the New Year's Gang." I knew it was only a matter of time before such reckless violence would reach its inevitable climax; I had covered most of these events for the *State Journal.*

When I flew back home from Los Angeles the next night, arriving at the Madison airport at about 7:30 in the morning, I asked the cab driver what had been happening in town since I had left.

"The students just blew up a building," the cabbie said.

Thirty-six hours after I told Welles that the students were about to kill somebody, the New Year's Gang ignited a bomb that destroyed the Army Mathematics Research Center on the UW campus, where research for the war was being conducted. The bomb killed a graduate student, Robert Fassnacht, who was working late on a physics research project. I wrote the lead story about the event for the following day's *State Journal.* Although the bombing sickened me, I couldn't help feeling vindicated in my argument with Welles. (I never asked him how he had reacted to the news.)

My realization that Welles would not engage me in serious discussion on the subject, that he would not treat me as an intellectual equal (or even as someone within hailing distance of his intelligence), chagrined me. So did his responses to my screenplay ideas.

❖ ❖ ❖

When I told Welles that I hoped to write and direct a film by the time I was twenty-five, as he had, he kindly replied, "You *will.*" He asked what I was working on. I described a script project I was calling *I'm Nobody*, an intimate portrait of the life of the reclusive nineteenth-century poet Emily Dickinson.

I wanted Welles to play a small but crucial role, that of her literary mentor, the writer and editor Thomas Wentworth Higginson. Putting myself in something of the same position toward Welles as Dickinson assumed toward her bearded, gruff, sympathetic but only partly comprehending "Preceptor," I said I was having trouble writing the story of someone who has been described as "having thought more and done less" than any other human being. And I wondered where I could find backing for such an unfashionable film.

Welles replied that the only place to do *I'm Nobody* would be the BBC. I laughed reflexively, thinking he was belittling my idea by discounting its possibilities as a theatrical film. "No, I'm serious," he said: I should offer it to the BBC because they were receptive to serious biographical films about artists. He was right, but I had only vaguely heard of the brilliant films Ken Russell and Huw Wheldon were making for the BBC about composers and other artistic figures. Welles asked me to send him one of my completed screenplays, promising to help me sell it.

So I sent him *Hell*, about a middle-aged midwestern religious fanatic torturing to death a teenaged girl. What makes the torture particularly horrifying is not only that it takes place over a period of months but also that it involves several neighborhood children as torturers, including the victim's crippled younger sister, who is forced to participate. I based *Hell* on the true story of sixteen-year-old Sylvia Likens, who was tortured to death in 1965 in Indianapolis by a middle-aged woman named Gertrude Baniszewski and a group of neighborhood children. The feminist author Kate Millett later wrote a poetically moving, deeply compassionate book about the incident, *The Basement: Meditations on a Human Sacrifice* (1979).

The next time I saw Welles, for another round of shooting in the spring of 1971, he told me what he thought of *Hell.* With palpable anger, he declared, "If it weren't you who had written this script, I would do *everything in my power* to prevent it from being made." He said he was morally opposed to depicting torture on-screen in such graphic detail, particularly if a child is involved. Stunned, I tried to engage him on the issue. I argued that the validity of such a cinematic representation of torture depends on whether the film is morally serious, as I believed mine would be. Oja Kodar, who also had read the script, more gently asked what led me to write it; she always treated me more like an individual, asking me about my daughter and other personal matters to which Welles seemed oblivious. I told Oja that the themes and emotions I explored in *Hell* were reflections of my childhood experiences with Catholicism and my conflicts in adolescence over the church's sexual teachings. Intensifying the religious themes of the story of the girl's torture, I explained, was my way of trying to make sense of what can cause such abuse.

Oja listened with apparent sympathy to my explanation, but Welles wasn't having any. Nor was he pleased when I cited Alfred Hitchcock's *Psycho* as an example of a film showing a graphic murder in a serious context. He called *Psycho* "a sick film." *Psycho*, he insisted, has had a damaging effect on the cinema and the film-going audience by encouraging directors to exploit murder and psychological illness for quasi-pornographic effect. I didn't mention to Welles that *Touch of Evil* seems to have been a major influence on *Psycho*, or that *Touch of Evil* has been subjected to some of the same criticisms he leveled against the Hitchcock film—criticisms I considered narrow-minded and shortsighted, as well as surprisingly unsophisticated coming from an artist of Welles's stature. ("Welles was annoyed at Hitchcock," Walter Murch observed, "because he felt Hitchcock sort of took *Touch of Evil*, which was a failure, and re-packaged it [as *Psycho*] and made it a success.")

Probably Welles was right in thinking that the subject matter of my screenplay was too horrible to be shown with graphic accuracy in such a public and realistic medium. But saying that if it weren't my work, he would "do *everything in* [his] *power* to prevent it from being made"? I thought Welles was against censorship. Hadn't he barely saved *Citizen Kane* from being burned as an act of political censorship? Welles often spoke of how, for him, the concept of evil was very real, how he believed evil actually exists. And if he felt "the horror" should have remained only on paper, how did he justify wanting to convey on film the sense of evil Joseph Conrad evokes so powerfully in *Heart of Darkness?* Welles could be surprisingly censorious, particularly where sexuality was involved. On Dinah Shore's TV talk show in the 1970s, he erupted at actress Dyan Cannon for saying that there were now "no rules" governing sexual conduct. "You are wrong—there are rules," he told her. "You are profoundly wrong. That is a very dangerous line of thought. . . . There have to be taboos. We have to live by rules. Her idea of what is guilt may be my idea of what is sin."

Trying to find another way of exploring the subject of cinematic violence with Welles in our 1970 meeting, I brought up the Manson family murders of the previous year. I told Welles I was "obsessed" with the Manson murders. My wife Linda was pregnant with our first child, Jessica, when the Manson family killed the nine-months-pregnant Sharon Tate and several other people in Los Angeles in August 1969. I also felt an affinity with Tate's husband, Roman Polanski, one of the younger directors whom I (like Welles) most admired. With *Hell*, I was consciously emulating Polanski's desire to make the movie audience deal unflinchingly with horrific subjects.

Welles replied gruffly, "*I'm* not obsessed with the Manson murders."

I wondered why he was so dismissive of the subject: Hadn't he made *Macbeth*, about a mass murderer who kills, among others, Macduff's wife and children? The very play Polanski was filming that year in the UK, his first film since the Manson murders?

But as we talked about the case, Welles began to show a creative interest in it. He described how he would film the story of hippie guru Charles Manson and his crazed followers. He said he wasn't interested in the grisly details of the Tate–La Bianca murders but in understanding "how this man got control of the minds of all those girls"—a truly Wellesian theme. Welles had a particularly chilling ending in mind. He said he would take it right up to the point of the Tate killings but would not actually show them. Instead he would show Tate and her friends casually sitting in the house when the patio doors suddenly fly open to reveal the murderers—with a quick fade to black. Just *typing* these words gives me the creeps.

So Welles was no stranger to evil and the need to explore it on-screen. That made his vehement reaction against my screenplay seem all the more illogical. By implying that *Hell* was "sick" and by not respecting that I too might have been trying to explore serious themes, however clumsily, Welles seemed to be leveling a personal attack.

❖ ❖ ❖

After those disheartening early experiences with Welles, I decided not to continue provoking him and to confine myself instead to being putty in his directorial hands. Something vital had been forcibly taken from our relationship. My idol had stepped down from his pedestal to slap me in the face. Part of me shut down emotionally with him. I contented myself with entering and reentering the foolish persona of Mister Pister whenever Welles called on me to do so. I stopped talking about what I was writing. I asked Welles less abrasive questions and avoided confronting him with contrary opinions. I let him initiate most discussions and cautiously raised safer subjects.

My initial forthrightness seemed to have left Welles permanently wary of me, just as I had become of him. He understood that I was a person of strong opinions and an investigative reporter by nature, not the flattering kind of interviewer who made him comfortable. Bogdanovich personified that kind of malleable acolyte, at least until he became (for a time) a highly successful director and his relationship with Welles became more complicated. I felt Welles did not care to know me as I really was, with artistic ambitions of my own, but regarded me only as an acolyte he could flatter and manipulate. The limitations Welles imposed on our relationship sadly put me in mind of screenwriter Ben Hecht's wise insight from the early 1940s: "Orson has no friends, only stooges." Coupled with Welles's habitual bullying methods of directing me, his arm's-length attitude kept me in a tense, intimidated state for the first few years of the film's production.

Sometimes during the prolonged shooting of *The Other Side of the*

Wind, Welles seemed to preempt what he feared I might say or write about him in my other, non-Pister, persona. One night I was in another room at Bogdanovich's house and heard Welles's voice suddenly booming out: "*Joe* would like Christopher Plummer—*he* doesn't like my Shakespearean performances either!" Hastening to Welles's presence, I lightly assured him I considered Falstaff in *Chimes at Midnight* his greatest performance, even if I had reservations about his Othello and, to a lesser extent, his Macbeth. Welles was not assuaged. I let the discussion drop.

That's how it usually went on topics that were sensitive to him. I was disappointed by his preference for treating me as a sounding board for pontifications and wisecracks, but figured it was the price I had to pay for being in his presence; and, of course, I was grateful for that. And perhaps the sense of aloofness I felt from him had a positive effect in the long term by enabling me to see more him more clearly, with less hero worship.

In 1979, during the American Film Institute's two-month "Working with Welles" seminar at the Directors Guild Theater in Hollywood, Welles discussed *The Other Side of the Wind* with, from left, cast members Joseph McBride and Susan Strasberg and *Los Angeles Times* film critic Charles Champlin. *(Joseph McBride Collection)*

Chapter Five

"YOUR FRIENDLY NEIGHBORHOOD GROCERY STORE"

Orson does everything. He lights the scene. Holds the camera. He wrote the script. My God, he even makes the sandwiches!

—John Huston, on filming *The Other Side of the Wind*

Looking back over Welles's career, his longtime associate Richard Wilson remembered the mood that prevailed when shooting began on *It's All True* in the early 1940s: "All the struggles and the frustrations and missed opportunities that we associate with Orson now—none of that had happened yet. And nobody would have believed it would. After all—in those days, working with Orson, anything seemed possible." That spirit was renewed for a time with the launching of *The Other Side of the Wind.* On the day in 1970 when that adventure began, whatever worries I had about Welles's future and his prospects for making a new film in Hollywood were quickly eclipsed by his enthusiasm for the project. Once again for Welles, anything seemed possible. But like almost everything about his career, it didn't turn out the way it started.

Micheál MacLiammóir's wry observation of the "Strange sense of Eternity" that envelops a Welles movie overcame me too. *Othello* sounds like a day in the park in comparison with *The Other Side of the Wind.* I worked from the first day of shooting to the last as the callow young film scholar Mister Pister. Since the first day was spent filming what Welles called "test scenes," I can truthfully say, like Everett Sloane's Bernstein in *Citizen Kane*, that I was there "From *before* the beginning, young fella. And now—it's after the end."

❖ ❖ ❖

As we assembled at Welles's house on August 23, 1970, to begin filming *The Other Side of the Wind* (whose title on the clapperboard was abbreviated to *Other Wind*), we were supposed to shoot scenes in Tijuana of Jake Hannaford's followers attending bullfights with him. But Welles changed plans abruptly when he learned that legal restrictions prevented him from taking cameras across the Mexican border. So instead we spent the day inside, shooting scenes of Peter Bogdanovich and me playing a pair of squabbling film critics at Hannaford's birthday party and scenes in his car en route to the party, as we pepper him with silly film-buff questions. Welles's nonchalant volte-face in switching the locale was characteristic of his ability to throw out his planning and take off in another creative direction. "Welles doesn't play it safe," Gary Graver said admiringly as we wrapped that night after completing an astonishing twenty-seven shots in twelve hours of work.

Bogdanovich eventually played a hotshot young director in the film, but he originally was cast as an arrogant, slickly dressed, social-climbing, supercilious critic vaguely reminiscent of Rex Reed, with an overlay of Peter's own personality. The character was named Charles Higgam in a calculated dig at Charles Higham, the British author whose vitriolic and highly inaccurate critical study *The Films of Orson Welles* had been published earlier that year, angering and depressing Welles and making it more difficult for him to raise financing for *Other Wind.* No one was playing Hannaford when we began shooting. Since Welles hadn't decided whom he wanted in the part, he simply shot around the central character for the first three years of production.

I learned a valuable lesson on the first day from Welles's sensitive treatment of his new young cameraman. When we went out in the convertible, Welles took the place of Hannaford in the front seat while Peter and I sat in the back. Also riding along were Eric Sherman and Felipe Herba, playing a pair of documentary filmmakers shooting a faux BBC program called *Closeup on Hannaford.* Sherman was filming Hannaford with his 16mm camera, and Herba, the soundman, clung to the trunk of the car as he anxiously thrust his microphone toward us. Welles dubbed them "the Maysles brothers" after the noted documentarians Albert and David Maysles, who had made a short film with Welles to promote this very project in 1966.

As we began driving along the circular road outside Welles's house, Graver stationed himself at the side of the road to shoot our passing car with his handheld camera. "He's in the wrong place," Bogdanovich pointed out to Welles. "He should be shooting the scene from the front seat of the car." "I know," said Welles. "But this is the first day of shooting, and if I correct him, he may never want to suggest anything to me again. Let's let him do it his way." I was impressed that Welles would sacrifice the quality of a shot for the sake of his still-fragile relationship with his new cameraman. What a wise decision that turned out to be. Graver became the indispensable man, enabling Welles to keep working for the rest of his life. They worked together so closely that, as Graver recalled at Welles's memorial service, "Once, I had my eye on the eye-piece and I was shooting, Orson was right behind me, leaning over me, I could feel him there—and I felt this sort of a little pain in the back and all of a sudden, *Gaaahh!* His cigar had burnt right through my shirt!"

We wound up reshooting the car scene anyway two years later. Bogdanovich, who had become one of Hollywood's leading directors with the release of *The Last Picture Show* in 1971, was recast as the phenomenally successful director Brooks Otterlake; a production assistant, Howard Grossman, replaced Peter as Higgam. Graver shot from *inside* the car the second time around. I waited almost thirty-two years to tell Gary what Welles and Bogdanovich said about his first-day camera position. Gary smiled when he finally heard the story.

The Otterlake character originally was played by the gifted mimic Rich Little. As I discovered while looking through the script Little left behind when he quit the film, Welles and Little planned to have his character deliver every line in the voice of a different celebrity, a gag that probably would have become tiresome. I played a scene with Little, conducting a mock interview with him, and that conceit for the Otterlake character at the time struck me as uncomfortably labored. It has been reported that Welles fired Little, but according to Graver, this is what happened in 1973 during shooting on the former set of *The New Dick Van Dyke Show* at Southwestern Studios in Carefree, Arizona: "We were sitting there and all of a sudden we heard, 'Goodnight, everybody, nice working with you.' Rich Little was standing there with a suitcase, and he left. Orson just looked at me. Didn't get mad, just couldn't believe the guy walked. Little didn't know about a part not being over, he wasn't used to being in the movies, he just left with no explanation. He wanted to get back and see his wife. Orson was too stunned to contact him." Little also had a busy work schedule, but Welles may have recognized that as clever as his mimicry was, the concept and execution of the character would have remained largely on the surface.

Bogdanovich, who loves doing mimicry, is no Rich Little in that department and does impressions only intermittently as Otterlake. But Hannaford says slyly, "That's what's so nice about Brooksie—I don't have to repeat myself, he does it for me." With Bogdanovich playing the part, there's more of an edge to the Otterlake character and there are deeper, richer nuances in his relationship with Hannaford.

When I asked Welles in 1970 who would be playing Hannaford, he replied, "It's either John Huston or Peter O'Toole doing his imitation of John Huston." O'Toole didn't know Welles had thought of him for the role until I told him that in 1981. The Irish actor dissolved with laughter and launched into an instant, unerring Huston impersonation ("Everything will be *fine*"). O'Toole remembered "beautiful footage of Orson Welles and I together doing a chat show in England discussing *Hamlet.* We had an eating competition once. Yes, we rolled around together a great deal." They had talked about doing "several" films together, said O'Toole, including *The Deep*, "a script that I thought was beautiful." Another was "A Country Tale," the Isak Dinesen story that would have been a companion piece to *The Immortal Story.* O'Toole hinted at a reluctance to get involved with Welles's protracted projects: "Akim Tamiroff had been playing Sancho Panza in a film of *Don Quixote* for Orson for fifteen years when I met Akim first. Then we worked together again three years later and he was *still* doing bits of Sancho Panza. Then Akim died."

❖ ❖ ❖

While Bogdanovich and I were talking at his home in Van Nuys before shooting started on *Other Wind*, he asked why I had pen marks all over my hands and arms. I said I'd run out of notepaper that afternoon while watching Fellini's *Satyricon* at a theater in Beverly Hills. Peter reported this to Welles, who thought it hilarious and had me jot such phrases as "Oedipus Complex" and "Mother Fixation" on my wrists. When shooting ended that day, Welles paternally insisted I wash off all the marks, even though I was too tired to lift a bar of soap. I had to keep applying those words to my hands and arms for the next six years.

Four separate times, I had to shave off my beard and long hair to get back into character. I had gone clean-shaven originally because I wanted to make a favorable impression on John Ford, whom I interviewed four days before I began working with Welles. So there I was in front of the camera with my short bowl haircut, black horn-rimmed glasses, dark green J. C. Penney's suit, and green trench coat. The stovepipe pants and tight jacket accentuated the gauntness of my six-foot-two, 150-pound frame. I looked like an anorexic version of Anthony Perkins's buttoned-down clerk Joseph K. in *The Trial.* (After I met the film critic Robin Wood in 1972, he wrote me, "How surprising, when expecting Orson

Welles, to meet Tony Perkins!") The pockets of my shirt and coat were stuffed with pens, notepaper, and cheap cigars, and I was weighed down with a large reel-to-reel tape recorder. My favorite among all the scenes I did for the film is a mocking montage of multiple angles on a bus as I frantically try to thread a tape onto the recorder and finally give up, utterly despondent.

After being away from *Other Wind* for two years before the 1973 filming at an isolated house in Carefree, I arrived on the set twenty-five pounds heavier, and Welles exclaimed, "My God! He's matured!" He advised me to keep a day's growth of stubble on my cheeks to make them seem less filled out—a trick I'm sure he had often used in his younger days as a movie actor while still struggling with his weight. Welles joked in 1975 that if the filming went on much longer, he might have to let me take over the Bogdanovich part "and find a younger Mister Pister."

Welles had me take the lenses out of my glasses to avoid reflections, which meant that other than in tight two-shots I couldn't see what was going on around me in a scene, making my character seem even more out of it. One night I arrived on the set at Bogdanovich's house in Bel-Air just as Welles was about to start filming a musical number that wasn't in the script. The lights go out at the party, and John Carroll, the old Republic Pictures star from the 1940s, sarcastically leads the partygoers in a rendition of "The Glow-Worm" (Carroll, naturally, wasn't present at the time but would be filmed later). Welles ordered me to stand in the front row and sing. I told him I didn't know the words to the song. He said I could read them from the cue cards. I said I couldn't see the cue cards. He said it didn't matter, I should just move my mouth in time with the other people's singing. So that's what I do on-screen, looking genuinely baffled.

❖ ❖ ❖

Welles began molding my character on the first day while directing from a thronelike chair at his typewriter table ("because this is an auteur film"). As he would throughout the production, he encouraged me to throw out ideas for Mister Pister's questions, and we would reshape them before he wrote the final versions. Among those questions are "Mr. Hannaford, is the camera eye a reflection of reality, or is reality a reflection of the camera eye? Or is the camera a phallus?"

The part about the "camera eye" came from my suggestion to ask Hannaford about the work of Dziga-Vertov. "You're kidding!" exclaimed Welles. "Who's that?" "Dziga-Vertov, the Russian director of the 1920s.

He made newsreels known as *Kino-Pravda.*" Welles laughed uproariously before saying, "Come on, now. You're supposed to be playing a serious character." As for the camera being a phallus, I borrowed that phrase, without telling Welles, from a comment in *Esquire* by Peter Fonda on his brother-in-law, the notoriously womanizing French director Roger Vadim. Fonda told Rex Reed in a 1968 profile: "And then there's also the possibility of doing something with my sister. Listen, Jane and me in a film, right? Directed by Vadim, right? Who's got one of the greatest love cameras I've ever seen, a *phallus!* Jane and I as brother and sister who make nude pornographic movies directed by her husband, who is a porny moviemaker." Giving a phallic dimension to the camera delighted Welles since it slyly reinforced his mocking take on auteurist megalomania and Hannaford's old-fashioned machismo and on his own use of seductiveness as a directing tool. I did the line a second time in the footage with Grossman replacing Bogdanovich in the car. Bogdanovich must have liked the "phallus" line, because he later claimed that *he* delivered it.

Although Welles said "the answer to getting great performances in a movie is to have great actors," he coaxed brilliant performances from a wide range of performers throughout his career, from such great actors as John Gielgud, Agnes Moorehead, and Jeanne Moreau to more limited ones such as Dorothy Comingore, Tim Holt, and Charlton Heston. Welles directed each differently, with a masterful psychological skill, treating the actor with the degree of tenderness or intimidation that would bring about the desired result. Many actors were able to express deeper aspects of their personalities for Welles than they have shown on-screen for any other director. "There are two ways of working with actors in movies," Welles said during the taping of his TV talk show pilot *The Orson Welles Show* in 1978. "One way is giving them hell so they can't sleep at night and tremble at the sound of your voice—what they call the Teutonic school. And the other is keeping them happy, because the great enemy of actors is boredom. I'm of the happy school, although God knows you can't always have a good party."

Although Welles also said that his method with actors was to seduce them, I had already been seduced by his films, so he could skip that phase in our relationship and move on to another directing technique: browbeating. Since I was no actor, and since the character I was playing was supposed to be an intimidated nincompoop with occasional flashes of cockeyed insight, Welles must have decided that the best method was to bully me into submission. His usual mode of addressing me was bellowing (though sometimes with a glint in his eye), and he barked unmercifully if I fumbled a line or piece of action. He would often give line readings (not just to me), usually prefacing them by saying, "It's terrible when a director gives line readings, but . . ." Many times over the six-year period, he would tell me, "Don't act!" explaining that I was usually better with spontaneous reactions on the first take. When I asked him once how to play a scene with Susan Strasberg, he replied, "How should I know? Just do it." I felt better when I learned that he told Tim Holt during the filming of *The Magnificent Ambersons*, "That was bad. It sounded like movies. Do it again—and don't act." When I read several lines without sufficient inflection in a difficult scene filmed in a moving car on a Los Angeles freeway, the director reacted with understandable frustration: "You sound like you're reading from the telephone book. *Think* about what you're supposed to be saying!"

Making me feel I was shamefully letting him down and impeding the hard-won progress of his movie with my exasperating incompetence, he would glower and seldom say an encouraging word. But he must have liked what I was doing, because he kept calling me back and coming up with new scenes for me to play. I appeared before the camera and was given lines to speak on every one of the forty-five days I was present on the set, even when I showed up unexpectedly, as I sometimes did at Bogdanovich's house during two months of production in the spring of 1975. When I posed for a portrait with Welles three years later on the set of *The Orson Welles Show*, I stood on the wrong side of him, in the wrong light, and Graver had to move me. Giving me an impish look, Welles asked, "Where's your training?"

❖ ❖ ❖

Welles remarked early in the shooting that *Other Wind* was the most democratically cast movie ever made, because the many major roles (with the possible exception of Hannaford's) would all have the same amount of screen time. That Altmanesque, or Renoirian, approach encouraged a spirit of camaraderie among the cast, which I particularly appreciated from the older actors, who never showed any impatience with me and were always generous with sympathetic advice. Perhaps Welles wanted to evoke that kindness from the other actors by his relentless bullying, as Ford famously did with the young John Wayne in *Stagecoach*.

"Every one of Orson's pictures involved ensemble acting," Joseph Cotten observed. Cotten felt that "in his whole career as a director [Welles] never led an actor or even allowed an actor to make a move alien to his own nature or utter a self-conscious line of dialogue. This is one of the reasons, I'm sure, that all actors felt safe in his hands. He was uncanny at instant personality perception. I have seen him change the whole concept of certain characters to take advantage of an inspirational, on-the-spot discovery of a natural human quirk."

I was flattered that Welles allowed me to collaborate on my dialogue, but that collaboration ended once a scene came out of his typewriter. Perhaps his most intimidating tactic was his rigid control of how I was allowed to behave on-screen. Keith Baxter, who gives a magnificent performance as Hal in Welles's *Chimes at Midnight*, observed, "Most directors either move the actors or move the camera. Orson would move both at the same time, and that is tricky." I had to move strictly within the confines of his blocking, however complex that choreography might be, and avoid any unexpected gestures. Early in the shooting, I foolishly thought I should prove my newfound acting skill by venturing a bit of improvisation without telling the director. The camera was in tight as I reacted silently to another actor's lines. My finger slowly rose to my face and began scratching my nose in what I thought was a pensive, Brandoish gesture.

"*Cut!*" roared Welles. "What on earth do you *think* you're doing?"

I mumbled something vaguely apologetic, and Welles ordered me never, *never* to add anything to a scene.

I often felt abjectly guilty over my inexperience. One day in 1971, Welles angrily called off the shooting because I showed up in a black trench coat that didn't match the green one I had worn earlier. Frank Marshall, a Bogdanovich aide who later became a director himself and one of Steven Spielberg's producing partners, was a production manager on *Other Wind.* Frank spent that day fruitlessly running around Hollywood costume houses trying to find me a suitably (or even roughly) matching coat. I hadn't realized that on a Welles shoot, as Mercedes McCambridge later explained to me, "You keep your costume in a box in the attic."*

On the bus where he was trying to set up the scene, Welles railed at me in front of the cast and crew, and I walked away in tears. Two cast members, documentary filmmaker Joan Churchill and actress-model Janice Pennington, kindly tried to cheer me. But I was inconsolable for hours, wandering around the Sunset Strip in a daze that night, crestfallen that I had cost the great director a day of filming. Later I realized Welles

* One morning a few years ago my telephone rang, waking me. I heard Graver's voice: "Joe—it's Gary. We need you for some shooting on *The Other Side of the Wind.*" Automatically, I replied, "Sure. When do you need me?" Graver cracked up and said, "*Joe!* I was just kidding!"

probably just wanted a day off; he sometimes threw a fit when he became tired, blaming a production shutdown on someone else so he could justify taking a nap. Only Chaplin, who owned his own studio, and Welles had the luxury of making movies when they *felt* like working. Welles finally said the coat didn't matter; he would simply tint the scenes in which I appeared to match the color of the original coat.

I also was missing the large prop I had carried in my first day's scenes. "We shot you with the tape recorder," Graver remembers, "then you came back from Wisconsin without the same tape recorder. Well, why would you have it? But Orson expected you to keep everything. He said you told him a story: 'Maybe I drop the tape recorder in a service station parking lot, and I buy a new one.' He said, 'Well, I'm not going to shoot a sequence of Joe buying a tape recorder!' He thought that was really funny. He laughed and laughed."

A couple of weeks after I returned home to Madison, my pay for my work in *The Other Side of the Wind* arrived in the mail: two boxes of cigars. I treasure those still-unsmoked cigars and, even more, the letter Welles sent with them:

> Dear Joe,
>
> We didn't get to say a proper goodbye, and I certainly didn't begin to say a proper thank you.
>
> Yours was a very real and valued contribution. We hope to make you proud to have been a part of our picture.
>
> All my most affectionate regards
>
> Orson

❖ ❖ ❖

Somewhat masochistically, I compensated for my limitations by playing along with Welles's mocking approach to Mister Pister, enthusiastically accentuating the character's geekiness. But one night about four years into the shooting, a crew member confided what Welles had said that afternoon while watching the rushes of a scene at a foggy drive-in theater. As I was shown walking slowly toward the camera, holding my tape recorder to my chest and gazing at the unseen movie, Welles said: "Joe looks good up there on-screen. But then he *always* looks good on-screen." As if by magic, when I heard those words I immediately felt relaxed and confident and began enjoying the experience of acting in the film. That enjoyment lasted for the following two years. *Other Wind* became what Huston told me the picture was for him: "a lark."

Dear Joe,

We didn't get to say a proper goodbye, and I certainly didn't begin to say a proper thank you.

Yours was a very real and valued contribution. We hope to make you proud to have been a part of our picture.

All my most affectionate regards Orson

Letter from Orson Welles to Joseph McBride

The other side of my screen character was the comically bumptious careerist. In a scene shot in 1971 on the shabby back lot of Producers Studio (since renovated as Raleigh Studios), Welles has me identify myself to a documentary camera crew by shouting that I'm "Pister—Pister from the Film Institute!" Actually, it was Bogdanovich who had been commissioned by the American Film Institute to conduct oral histories with such veteran directors as Allan Dwan, Raoul Walsh, and Leo McCarey (his Welles interview book was not done for the AFI). But Mister Pister's self-description proved prophetic when I went to work for "the Film Institute" from 1980 through 1984, writing the AFI's Life Achievement Award specials on CBS-TV with producer George Stevens Jr.

Mister Pister's intrusive interviewing style resembled both mine and Bogdanovich's. John Ford would say to Peter, "Jesus *Christ*, Bogdanovich! Can't you ever end a sentence with anything but a question mark? Haven't you *heard* of the declarative sentence?" Peter tended to ask even more softball questions than I did with Welles after our contentious beginning. My own personality then was an uneasy, somewhat immature mélange of the deferential and the confrontational. The abrupt transitions I was prone to make between those two modes of behavior must have seemed rather jarring, if also bemusing, to Welles.

Even though I was thoroughly intimidated by Welles, his bullying enabled me to do what he intended, which was to forget about "acting," stop being self-conscious, and just *do* the scene. Welles's explanation of how he handled actors was: "I give them a great deal of freedom and, at the same time, the feeling of precision. It's a strange combination. In other words, physically, and in the way they develop, I demand the precision of ballet. But their way of acting comes directly from their own ideas as much as from mine. When the camera begins to roll, I do not improvise visually. In this realm, everything is prepared. But I work very freely with the actors. I try to make their life pleasant."

Welles was often in a playful mood. He liked to direct in a purple or white bathrobe that gave him a regal air, waving his cigar like a scepter, with a can of Fresca always nearby. His feet were encased in huge tennis shoes, unlaced for comfort, and his graying, leonine hair and beard were often casually disheveled, making him look like a beat poet. I realized that Welles was happiest when he was actually making a movie. The end result meant less to him than his joy in the process. A constant stream of banter, stories, jokes, and uproarious laughter issued from his director's chair, making the movie seem like a floating party. He would call Graver "Rembrandt" or "Billy Bitzer" (after D. W. Griffith's cameraman). Graver would reciprocate by calling Welles "D. W."

Early in the shooting, Welles gave Graver some money to take the crew to lunch, saying, "Take your time. Have a proper meal." Graver relates, "We went to the Hamburger Hamlet on Sunset. We came back an hour and a half later, and he was really pissed off. I said, 'You told us to take our time.' He said, 'Not *that* long.' I said to the crew, 'From now on, it's just grab a sandwich.' My nickname became 'Grab a Sandwich.' Oja changed that into the Slavic name of Grabaslov. She still calls me Grabaslov, never calls me Gary."

Welles had other pet phrases. "*Run*, do not walk!" was one of his favorite commands, especially to the crew. And if an actor was taking too long to make an exit, he would bellow, "Just pick up your cloak and go!"—a Shakespearean prompt that became a running joke between him and MacLiammóir on *Othello.* Often when Welles was getting ready to shoot a close-up on *Other Wind*, he would announce, "*Und now a big head of Pola!*" Akim Tamiroff had told him that that was how the silent-movie actress Pola Negri would call for her close-up. Another Tamiroff line Welles often used, and put into the film, was "The Box likes him," meaning that the camera can summon up magic from an actor it mysteriously favors. Welles and Graver often communicated privately in shorthand: "YP" meant "your problem"; "TP" was "their problem"; and "MP" was "my problem." Welles's "rule number one," Graver relates, "was 'Never assume anything on a film set. Don't assume it, know it.'"

When Welles felt in a particularly festive mood, or wanted to cheer up his sluggish actors, he would burst into a favorite song. It came from *Finesse the Queen*, a musical comedy revue he had starred in as an eleven-year-old boy at Todd School in the 1920s. Hearing him warble the tune in a tone of innocent sincerity took the listener back to Welles's semi-mythological youth:

> Everyone loves the fellow who is smiling,
> He brightens the day and lightens the way for you—
> He's always making other people happy
> Looking rosy when you're feeling awful blue. *

❖ ❖ ❖

The Other Side of the Wind is a satire of the shattering clash between the new and old Hollywood, which Welles's narrative and shooting style conveys in a visceral way. Welles employs *two* unconventional filmmaking styles, cinema verité for the framing scenes of Hannaford and his followers at the birthday party and elegantly "arty" framing for the film-within-the-film.

Hannaford's work in progress, shown in fragments throughout the story, is the old director's misguided, somewhat incoherent attempt to appear "with it" in New Hollywood terms. Lavishly filmed in 35mm color, Hannaford's Antonioniesque footage was described by Welles as "the old man's attempt to do a kind of counterculture film, in a surrealist, dreamlike style." The party footage, on the other hand, is filmed as a faux documentary with handheld cameras in both color and black-and-white, on 16mm and Super 8 film, on video, and in stills. This kind of collage style has since become familiar in the films of Oliver Stone and many other directors, who picked it up from rock videos on MTV. But Welles was there first, as he so often was, experimenting and blazing trails, even if those trails remained partially hidden.

---

* I learned from MacLiammóir's *Put Money in Thy Purse* that Welles would sing the song and talk about "a big head of Pola" on the set of *Othello* as well.

"A film about death, the portrait of a decadence, a ruin": Jake Hannaford (John Huston) in the car that will take him to his rendezvous with death in *The Other Side of the Wind.* Welles directs Huston in an ending partly inspired by James Dean's fatal car crash and partly by Ernest Hemingway's suicide. *(Gary Graver)*

"I've assumed that the party is being covered by a documentary crew from the BBC and another from West Germany and by a whole lot of amateurs with cameras," Welles explained. "You'll see only what they've recorded of this evening. It's a device that would only work once, I suppose, but, God, it's fun, using three and four cameras at once." By capturing and parodying these two styles of filmmaking, *Other Wind* serves as both a time capsule of a pivotal movement in movie history—an "instant" piece of period nostalgia set in the early seventies—and a meditation on changing political, sexual, and artistic attitudes in the United States during that period.

The frenetic style of the cinema verité scenes is Welles's way of spoofing the voraciousness of the media and how they can swallow up their subject/victim. The power of the media has always been a central focus of Welles's work, from the time he made his mark with a spoof of radio in his *War of the Worlds* broadcast, spotlighting the vulnerability of the

American public to radio demagoguery and scare propaganda. *Kane* takes the media for its subject matter; the framing device of a newsreel reporter investigating the dying words of the "great yellow journalist" foregrounds the problem of getting at the "truth" about the life of a famous man—or about anyone's life. As someone considered a "legend" since childhood, Welles was acutely aware of the factual distortions of the media (many of which he cheerfully fostered) and how such exaggerations and outright fabrications can affect an artistic career both positively and negatively. In a 1967 interview, Welles said he worried about his own legend taking over public perceptions: "You get to be like Hemingway, nothing but people writing about you."

❖ ❖ ❖

The Other Side of the Wind bears similarities to Thomas Mann's novel *Death in Venice*, filmed in 1970–71 by the Italian director Luchino Visconti, with Dirk Bogarde starring. Both stories tell of an aging artist who becomes enraptured with a beautiful young boy in a crumbling artistic capital and pursues that self-destructive passion to his death. The figure of the beautiful, long-haired young man in *Other Wind*, John Dale, played by Jim Morrison look-alike Bob Random, is the rebellious, motorcycle-racing leading man of Hannaford's movie and the director's fatal sexual attraction. Welles explained the backstory for me: In carrying out his habitually sadistic, sexually based domination of his male stars, Hannaford has always made a point of seducing the leading lady or the wife or girlfriend of the leading man, but Hannaford's underlying interest has always been in the leading man himself. In the desperation and abandon of his old age, the macho mask slips away and Hannaford becomes openly smitten with his somewhat androgynous-looking "hippie" leading man.

Welles based the Hannaford-Dale relationship in part on the clash between James Dean and George Stevens, the veteran director of the mercurial young actor's final film, *Giant*. After quarreling with Stevens throughout the shooting, Dean drove to Warner Bros. to show Stevens his new Porsche, which he had been forbidden to race until completing his part. Stevens tried to persuade Dean not to drive the car to northern California but to have it towed on a trailer. Dean ignored his advice and was killed that afternoon in a highway collision. At the end of *Other Wind*, Hannaford drunkenly rides off to his death in a Porsche he had been intending to give to John Dale. In an earlier version of the story, both men were supposed to die in the car.

"Oh, it's the sickest story I've ever thought up in my life," Welles told Bogdanovich. The story, Welles related, "begins with this wrecked car and then, at the end, the boy that [Hannaford] has lost is in a car and he says to the director, 'Come on, Fatso, want to get in the car? Are you chicken?' That's what Jimmy Dean used to call George Stevens—'Fatso'—and Stevens hated it. And Dean is going off to kill himself in that car, and the director gets into the car to show that he's a man. A terrifying story. Boy, you don't know where you are, it's so complex."

Like the plane crash at the end of *Mr. Arkadin*, the car crash was to be shown as smoke in the distance. Welles's voice would have been heard at the beginning of the film, telling the audience about the crash as still photographs of the wreckage flash onto the screen. Since I was working in 1973 as a reporter for the *Riverside (California) Press-Enterprise*, Welles asked me to find pictures of crashed cars without bodies visible, and I obtained some stills of twisted wrecks from the California Highway Patrol.

The older generation of Hollywood is also represented in *Other Wind* by Hannaford's gallery of stooges, most of whom have social views verging on the fascistic. They include such old Welles cronies as Norman Foster (playing Billy Boyle, perhaps the film's best performance other than Huston's), Paul Stewart (Matt Costello), Edmond O'Brien (Pat), Mercedes McCambridge (Maggie), and George Jessel and Richard Wilson (as themselves). The younger crowd includes several filmmakers and critics playing themselves or thinly disguised versions of their own personas, among them Dennis Hopper, Henry Jaglom, Paul Mazursky, Curtis Harrington, and Claude Chabrol.

Other characters in this eclectic roman à clef gathering include takeoffs on Pauline Kael (Susan Strasberg as film critic Juliette Riche), John Houseman (Tonio Selwart as the Baron, "in charge of metaphysics"), hot studio executive du jour Robert Evans (Geoffrey Land as Max David), young macho blowhard director John Milius (Gregory Sierra as Jack Simon), veteran agent Abe Lastfogel (Benny Rubin as Abe Vogel), and Bogdanovich's blonde flame Cybill Shepherd (amateur actress Cathy Lucas as Mavis Henscher, a surprisingly touching performance from a nonprofessional). Oja Kodar plays the mysterious "red, *red* Indian" leading lady of Hannaford's film, a largely silent role, always semiclothed or nude. (The right-wing character actor Pat O'Brien turned down the part tailored for him, which was given to Edmond O'Brien, and Joseph Cotten and Gilbert Roland passed on the role played by Selwart, whom Welles remembered from his youth, when he saw Selwart starring in a play.)

In addition to the running exposure of Hannaford by Juliette Riche and the other media people attending his birthday party, Hannaford's old cronies serve as choral commentators. Their exchanges about Hannaford and their own lives—amusing and touching, insightful and appalling—are reminiscent of Welles's use of the townspeople as a chorus in *Ambersons.* With this device, Welles deftly sketches a portrait of Hannaford's past and his reactionary sociopolitical views. Hannaford bears little affinity with Welles's progressive views or Huston's lifelong liberalism. At least in his politics, Hannaford represents what Welles and Huston left the country to escape.

❖ ❖ ❖

Hannaford resembles such he-man Hollywood directors as Ford, Rex Ingram, Howard Hawks, Henry Hathaway, Raoul Walsh, and Huston himself. Welles described Hannaford to me in even more expansive terms, saying that he was "the kind of director America should have had but never has had," combining the temperaments of Ford and Ernest Hemingway, but with the rough, overflowing dexterity of Mark Twain. Hannaford, Welles explained, would not have been content to film actual combat, as Ford did in World War II and Korea, but would have joined in the combat, as Hemingway did while serving as a war correspondent. The audience could use "keys" like these to understand Hannaford, Welles said. Hannaford's Mark Twain–like philosophy has made him a favorite with the young, but when the old filmmaker tries to make his Hollywood comeback by pandering to what he thinks the youth audience wants, he falters, producing a beautiful but obscure mess. Not all of this backstory about Hannaford comes across on-screen; Welles could have said about him what he said to Bogdanovich when asked why Charles Foster Kane on-screen wields power with more charm than he does in the script: "I found out more about the character as I went along."

Welles called Hannaford "Jake" because that was the nickname Welles was given by his friend Frank Sinatra. They became acquainted while campaigning for Franklin D. Roosevelt's fourth term in 1944. Sinatra provided some of the funding for Welles's unfinished film *Don Quixote*, was his daughter Beatrice's godfather, and hosted his 1975 AFI Life Achievement Award tribute. A suitably crass-sounding name for a figure of Hollywood macho swagger, "Jake" may have been applied ironically to Welles by Sinatra or could have been bestowed in its hipster meaning of "OK." Jake was also the name Welles used for the producer (Jake Behoovian) he played in his satirical 1950 play about Hollywood religious movies, *The Unthinking Lobster.* "Hannaford" is an Irish name that evokes and incorporates Ford as well as some of the sounds and rhythm of "Hemingway." It's worth noting that there was an obscure crew member named Hannaford—Frederick S. (Fred) Hannaford, a generator operator—who accompanied Welles to Brazil in 1942 for the making of *It's All True.*

Unable to decide whether to give the plum role to Huston or O'Toole, Welles kept hesitating. He said he didn't want to play it himself because he didn't want people to think of the role as autobiographical. Despite the distanciation offered by Hannaford's machismo, right-wing politics, and absurdist venture into Antonioniesque filmmaking, the root of the character, the sexual ambiguity, was what the protective coloration was intended to cloak in Hannaford's persona and perhaps also in that of Welles-as-author. If Welles had played the role himself, the audience would have been handed a "key" much easier to use to open the autobiographical lock. Welles no doubt also realized he could not have played the other aspects of Hannaford as convincingly as Huston.

According to Huston, it was during the shooting of his film *The Kremlin Letter* in 1969 that Welles, who was playing a Soviet diplomat in that baroque spy movie, first broached the idea of Huston starring in what became *The Other Side of the Wind.* Huston immediately accepted, but Welles hesitated for years, keeping him wondering what was happening with the project. Even in those pre-*Chinatown* days, Huston was regarded as a delightfully colorful character actor, having proven his chops with his Oscar-nominated role in Otto Preminger's film *The Cardinal* (1963). But no matter how inevitable a choice Huston seems in retrospect for Hannaford, Welles no doubt was concerned about the somewhat narrow acting range of his longtime writing and directing crony. While shooting around Hannaford, Welles played the role on the other side of the camera as we all pretended to be talking to the elusive Jake. When difficulties arose in 1973 over a salary demand from Huston's agent, Paul Kohner, Welles, perhaps as a bargaining ploy, briefly considered giving the role to Dean Jagger, the veteran star of such films as *Brigham Young* and *My Son John* (and a cast member of *The Kremlin Letter).* Huston agreed to play Jake for a lesser amount, $75,000.

❖ ❖ ❖

Richard Wilson, during the shooting of *Other Wind,* asked Welles what the film was about, and Welles replied that it was "an attack on machoism."* Hannaford the hairy-chested ladies' man is exposed in the course of the story as a latent or perhaps closeted homosexual. His personality, Welles told me, was largely based on Hemingway's. It's not coincidental that the film takes place on July 2, the anniversary of Hemingway's suicide. That shocking 1961 event probably provided the dramatic framework for the first version of the script, *The Sacred Beasts*, which was set not in Hollywood but in Spain, where Welles was then living; syndicated columnist Leonard Lyons reported from Madrid in August 1961 that Welles had "just finished writing a screen play about a bullfighter." The title of that early draft has a double meaning, referring to bulls killed ritualistically in the ring and to the celebrities like Hemingway—the "*monstres sacrés*"—who follow bullfights. (Welles's friend and fellow filmmaker Jean Cocteau wrote a 1940 play called *Les monstres sacrés*, published in the United States in 1961.)

The seed for Welles's story was planted in 1937, when he had his first encounter with Hemingway. Welles recorded the narration Hemingway wrote for Joris Ivens's documentary feature on the Spanish Civil War, *The Spanish Earth*. When Welles and Hemingway met at a preliminary screening, Welles suggested eliminating some lines and letting the pictures speak for themselves. Hemingway snarled, "Some damn faggot who runs an art theater thinks he can tell me how to write narration." Welles put on a mocking swish act ("Oh, Mr. Hemingway, you think because you're so big and strong and have hair on your chest . . ."), and they had a fistfight in front of the images of people fighting and dying on-screen. Hemingway replaced Welles as narrator, but the Welles soundtrack was rediscovered and released in 2000 on a double-track DVD. His narration, though hardly effeminate, sounds a bit studied and theatrical. His transatlantic stage accent comes off second-best compared to Hemingway's gruff, biting delivery but is eloquent and serious nonetheless. Welles and Hemingway were able to laugh about their fight over a bottle of whiskey after the screening, beginning a long if sometimes strained friendship. Welles said he "never belonged to [Hemingway's] clan, because I made fun of him," but though he continued to needle the writer posthumously through the character of Hannaford, he always considered Hemingway "a great, great, great artist."

---

* "Machismo" would be the correct word, of course. Welles would have known that from living in Spain. But "machoism" was a term widely in use in the United States during the early 1970s, when the concept was just beginning to penetrate the national consciousness, thanks to the women's liberation movement.

The Sacred Beasts was to have been "a picture about the love of death," Welles said, revolving around the bullfight aficionados following "a pseudo-Hemingway, a movie director . . . a fellow that you can hardly see through the bush of the hair on his chest. And he was frightened by Hemingway at birth." Welles had witnessed the spectacle of Hemingway's entourage at corridas in Spain. The script also may have been influenced by Hemingway's account of the 1959 bullfighting rivalry between the brothers-in-law Antonio Ordóñez and Luis Miguel Dominguín; Hemingway has been criticized for being biased in favor of Ordóñez, but Welles said their mutual respect for Ordóñez was one of their few areas of agreement about bullfighting.

Parts of Hemingway's manuscript of *The Dangerous Summer* were published in *Life* in 1960, but the work was not published in book form until 1985, when James A. Michener described it as "a book about death written by a lusty sixty-year-old man who had reason to fear that his own death was imminent." The suicide of the man whose credo was "grace under pressure" was a moment of truth for many of the writer's admirers; some were disillusioned, but others understood it as a manifestation of mental and physical decline. "He was sick," Welles realized. "But he did talk about suicide. You know, his father killed himself with a gun in the same way. And he talked to me about it several times in a sort of obsessive way. . . . He's not to be judged as himself. In other words, the Hemingway we are talking about did not choose his death. He *might* have. But he wasn't that man." Hemingway's macho bluster was only a thin cover for the perilous emotional vulnerability he always explored in his characters. In that light, his own suicide does not seem out of character.

When Hannaford drives Mister Pister and other followers to the party in *Other Wind*, I find myself thrown out of the car, partly because it's overloaded but mostly because, from my perch in the back seat, I ask him a supremely irritating question: "To assess, Mr. Hannaford, how your films would relate the trauma of your father's suicide?" When the scene was filmed, the car, driven by a Huston double, halted in the Coldwater Canyon area of Beverly Hills. Welles said he would shoot from inside the car as it pulled away from me. I remembered a shot in the *Ambersons* screenplay that wasn't included in the film's release version: George Amberson Minafer standing forlornly as an automobile pulls away from him, his rapidly receding figure pathetically expressing his helplessness in the face of "progress." So as the car moved off, I quickly set down my tape recorder, held my breath, and stood statue-still for the duration of the shot.

My offending question raises an issue Hannaford has spent his life avoiding, and it was one I suggested to Welles. I drew it from my awareness of the chilling effect of Hemingway's father's suicide on the writer's life and work. But the question also reflects Welles's guilty conscience over his own father's death—a fact of which I was unaware when we shot the scene. In tantalizing autobiographical fragments he published in the Christmas 1982 issue of *Paris Vogue*, Welles confessed that as a child he was "convinced—as I am now—that I had killed my father." Welles's father, Richard, a retired inventor, industrialist, and playboy, essentially drank himself to death in a Chicago hotel room in 1930. His death certificate says he died of chronic heart and kidney disease, but according to Barbara Leaming's biography, "the young Orson told people that he was present at his father's suicide." She believes that this didn't literally happen and that his claim probably was a projection of his acute guilt over abandoning his father in a last attempt to get him to stop drinking. Welles felt his desperate maneuver pushed his father over the edge. Welles called his behavior toward his father "inexcusable," telling Leaming, "I don't want to forgive myself. That's why I hate psychoanalysis. I think if you're guilty of something you should live with it."

Probably that devastatingly traumatic event helps explain why Welles so fiercely guarded certain secrets about his emotional life; why, despite fits and starts, he could not bring himself to write a full autobiography but only participated in elliptical as-told-to books with controllable acolytes such as Bogdanovich and Leaming. One of the few points in my writings about which Welles took issue was my statement that he had an overly protected childhood, with a doting mother and father. In fact, he said, his was the opposite of a smothering childhood: his parents seemed aloof and distant. When he offered this painful revelation, his affect was both gentle and sad.

From Welles's description of his *Sacred Beasts* project in 1962, it's evident that while the setting and other details of the story evolved, the Hannaford character remained essentially the same: "There will be a confrontation between my hero, an aging American romantic who is having trouble supporting himself, and an anti-romantic young man of the new generation, 'cool,' who ends up subscribing to romanticism himself and defending the bullfight. This will be a film about death, the portrait of a decadence, a ruin. I will play the part. But don't look for a self-portrait in it. For example, he will be a sadist, and I don't want to be one." In the same interview, he observed, "Hemingway and Fitzgerald thought that genius disappears with old age. At the end of his life,

Hemingway always tried to prove that he was still young. Fitzgerald, even before he turned forty, was rotted with the same anguish. That attitude is death. It's not something that bothers me." However, when Welles turned sixty in May 1975 during the shooting of *Other Wind* and several crew members surprised him with a birthday cake, he moaned, "Oh, God," and locked himself in his room for the rest of the day.

Welles had already become critical of bullfighting by the time he began writing *The Sacred Beasts*. He explained a few years later: "I've turned against it for very much the same reason that my father, who was a great hunter, suddenly stopped hunting. He said, 'I've killed enough animals and I'm ashamed of myself.' . . . I've seen too many hundreds of bullfights, thousands of 'em, I suppose, and wasted a lot of my life, now that I look back on it. And although it's been a great education to me in human terms and in many other ways, I begin to think I've seen enough of those animals die. . . . [W]asn't I living secondhand through the lives of those toreros, who were my friends? Wasn't I living and dying secondhand? Wasn't there something finally voyeuristic about it? I suspect my *afición*."

The Maysles brothers' short promotional documentary for *The Sacred Beasts*, *Orson Welles Madrid Juin 1966*, shows Welles talking to a group of admirers in a Madrid bullring about his plans for the filming. Welles says that his "*muy macho*" filmmaker protagonist would follow a matador, "living through him. He's become that lovely young fellow in the beautiful costume . . . he's become obsessed by this young man, who has become, in a way, his own dream of himself. He's been rejected by all his old friends. He's finally been shown up to be a kind of voyeur, a peeker, a secondhand guy, a fellow who lives off other people's danger and death." Welles describes the jet-set bullfight aficionados in his story as "those people who are lightheaded and nonsensical and *seriously* evil, living off the idea of death."

Welles explains the unusual shooting method he has in mind:

> We're going to shoot it without a script. I've written the script. I know the whole story, I know everything that happens. What I'm going to do is get the actors in every situation, tell them what has happened up to this moment, who they are, and I believe that they will find what is true and inevitable from what I've said. . . . We're going to make the picture as though it were a documentary. The actors are going to be improvising. . . . Nobody's ever done it before. . . . Because we've been cranking along in movies too long the same way. You know, it's the most old-fashioned business on earth. It's a wonderful medium, but nobody's done anything *new* in it. They're be-

ginning to now in France and so forth—but they take a basic situation and they let—you know, there's a certain kind of freedom—but I would like to take a *whole story*, a given group of people, and see what happens within that. . . . The greatest things in movies are divine accidents.

In words that would seem sadly ironic in retrospect, Welles assures his listeners that the shooting "can't take too long. I think the whole thing is eight weeks at the most." In the event, the *Other Side of the Wind* filmmaking process that began four years later involved what could be called "planned improvisation." Not just mine but much of the film's dialogue indeed was improvised between Welles and the actors, the improvisation occurring before the cameras rolled. With the exception of Huston, who was given more freedom because of the size and complexity of his part, the actors, celebrated or obscure, had to follow the fresh script pages agreed upon with Welles. For Huston's big speeches, Welles had his lines written on a blackboard. When Huston insisted on learning them anyway, Welles said, "John, you're just causing yourself unnecessary agony. Just read the lines or forget them and say what you please. The idea is all that matters." But Welles's method allowed the actors to feel like creative collaborators in telling the story. He followed the dictum of Jean Renoir: Always change your script to fit your actors, not your actors to fit your script.

Despite Welles's disclaimers about not wanting the film to be seen as autobiographical, he clearly put much of himself into Hannaford. There was some sadism in him and something that was ruined. There was an ambiguity about his own sexuality. And how much did Welles identify with Hannaford's sense of failure and decline, his frustration at seeing younger directors crowd him out of the picture? There's no doubt Welles was exploring his own feelings about aging and obsolescence through Hannaford. But Welles had a healthy respect for older artists and was telling the truth when he insisted he was not "rotted with anguish" about losing his powers.

American critics tend to assume that directors gradually lose their power as they age; this prejudice is a corollary of the American obsession with youth. The French critics who championed Welles and other American directors in the 1950s for *Cahiers du Cinéma* took the opposite point of view. "What kind of absurd discrimination has decided that filmmakers alone are victims of a senility that other artists are protected from?" asked André Bazin. "There do remain the exceptional cases of dotage, but they are much rarer than is sometimes supposed. . . . A great talent matures but does not grow old. . . . The drama does not reside in the growing old of men but in that of the cinema: Those who do not know how to grow old *with* it will be overtaken by its evolution."

Welles's later work was fecund with inspiration and constantly set out in new directions; he knew how to grow old with the cinema. Hannaford, on the other hand, makes a fool of himself by imitating the young and trying to adapt his style to suit the changing times. That was a mistake Welles always studiously avoided, even if, in parts of *Other Wind*, he deliberately mimicked the mannerisms of the New Hollywood. With his tragicomic portrait of Hannaford, Welles was constructing a cautionary tale for aging directors.

❖ ❖ ❖

When *Other Wind* was described in the press as Welles's "first erotic movie," he joked, "All I can say is that compared to *Last Tango in Paris*, which incidentally I liked very much, my production will be a nice family picture." But in fact *Other Wind* offers an especially searching and complex portrait of sexuality for a director whose earlier work had tended to treat sex discreetly. When Welles turned down on moral grounds an offer to appear in Gore Vidal's screenplay for *Caligula*, because he correctly suspected that the Penthouse production would become a pornographic extravaganza, Kenneth Tynan told Vidal, "You must never forget what a Puritan he is when it comes to sex." Welles told me he had always wanted to shoot erotic scenes but was uncomfortable doing so until he found a way he could pass them off as somebody else's work; no doubt that was the game he had to play with himself in order to liberate the repressed side of his directorial personality.

In a 1982 interview with Bill Krohn for *Cahiers du Cinéma*, Welles said that in his later work he was consciously trying to deviate from what was expected of him: "I got fed up with that about the time that people told me *The Trial* was an 'anthology of Wellesian visual ideas.' At that moment, I thought, well, we've had enough Wellesian ideas! . . . I think it was a general revulsion against the whole auteur business. . . . On camera, at eye level, I did nothing that you could parody as Wellesian at all in *F for Fake*." (Except, perhaps, that brief, flashily composed shot of Welles walking between swaying circular mirrors in an art gallery, murmuring the word "Pretentious?" as he parodies his own penchant for visual flamboyance.) Welles regarded the employment of other styles as a "mask . . . I'm very interested in masks. . . . [And] you had, when I started *The Other Side of the Wind*, a kind of fanaticism about the greatest man in the art

One of the greatest sequences Welles ever directed and a striking departure for a filmmaker who for many years approached sex puritanically, this bravura seven-minute segment of the film within the film in *The Other Side of the Wind* features virtuosic lighting by Gary Graver. Welles's rapid editing conveys the feeling of orgasm as Oja Kodar's character straddles a young man in a moving car during a rainstorm (frame enlargement). *(Orson Welles: The One-Man Band; Medias Res/The Criterion Collection)*

world being the 'master auteur.' And that was what I was going to knock on the head."

Welles's interest in exploring other styles helps account for the extraordinary creative leeway he allowed his two principal collaborators on *Other Wind*, Kodar and Graver, particularly in the treatment of sexuality. Welles sometimes even encouraged them to go off and shoot material by themselves for the film-within-the-film. Kodar was actively involved in the conception and staging of the erotic scenes, and the characteristically sensual and romantic texture of Graver's lighting is related to his sideline as a maker of erotic films, which helped support his largely pro bono work for Welles. Welles reciprocated by working without credit on one of Graver's hard-core films, *3 A.M.* Fuming that Graver was busy editing it instead of working on *his* projects, Welles volunteered to cut a sequence to speed the film's completion. The star of *3 A.M.*, Georgina Spelvin, proudly told me that Welles was responsible for the dynamic editing of her masturbation scene in a shower, which also contains several Wellesian low-angle shots that help raise the temperature.

Other Wind is a veritable riot of the id, a dark carnival of sexual themes and imagery. The film's greatest tour de force is the seven-minute sex scene in the moving car. A passive male (Random) sits stunned in the front seat as an energetically determined woman (Kodar) strips and bounces atop him, doing all the work. The stolid driver is played by Robert Aiken, from the cast of Russ Meyer's raunchy soft-core sex films *Vixen!* and *Cherry, Harry, & Raquel!* Welles gleefully exclaimed while shooting the sequence, "Russ Meyer rides again!" The silent, voyeuristic presence of the third party plowing the car through a rainstorm adds a further level of kinkiness to this comically grim coupling, which becomes increasingly baroque with colored lights, waves, and shadows flashing stroboscopically across Oja's frenzied face until she's thrown out of the car into a mud puddle at the moment of climax. Rather than simply depicting a sexual encounter, the visual rhythms actually capture the feeling of orgasm. Why Oja's character has sex with another man in front of the increasingly incensed driver (described by Aiken as her fellow "left-wing radical") is not clear, but this is yet another tantalizing riddle from Hannaford's unfinished film.

What makes the sequence even more astonishing is the way Welles filmed it in two countries, with low-budget camera trickery. "We shot a lot of it in the driveway at Lawlen Way, at night only, and we finished it years later in France," recalls Graver.

> We started on September 6, 1970, with my car, a '67 Mustang. To protect ourselves from the water from the hoses, Orson put a big tarp over one side of my car and attached it with gaffer's tape. I didn't know it then, but the gaffer's tape pulled the paint off my car. We started with "poor man's process," where you shake the car [with moving lights seen through the windows]. Orson had a trio of friends helping—Ed Scherick, a producer; the actor Bud Cort; and Rift Fournier, a TV writer-producer. Rift's in a wheelchair, so we gave him two sun guns and pushed him, and he looked like headlights coming toward the car. Everybody was outside waving lights and things, and we had the hoses on the car. I was sitting really close to Orson in the car, there was hardly room; we were touching each other. We shot it without sound, so he was yelling to the crew where to put the lights, put a green gel on, put on a red gel—and we'd do different takes, change the angles over and over again.
>
> Then I said to Orson, "We should get some shots driving on the street." So we got a water truck, and on a Sunday morning we went down Santa

Monica Boulevard in Beverly Hills with the cameras going. I was inside the car, and because of the rain we didn't see the water truck. We saw the dailies, and it didn't work. We went back to the poor man's process again.

Years later, Orson and Oja had a house in Orvilliers, outside of Paris, with a big backyard. Orson bought a Volkswagen Beetle. He said to me, "Take the camera and go through Paris at night. Have some girl driving." I had an all-girl crew in France. So I went all through Paris filming the streets, the City of Lights, in 16mm. We developed it. Then in the backyard of his house, we built three big screens, like billboards or drive-in screens. He had a carpenter do it, painted them all white. Then he got three projectors and had three French girls running them, so now we could look out the windows of the car and see streetlights going by, rather than actually going out in the street filming it. We could control the rain, control the lighting, and the backyard was big enough to actually drive cars around in it. We had his film editor, his accountant, even a conductor from the London Symphony Orchestra, anybody we could get, driving cars past.

The final sacrifice I made for that sequence, besides being wet, came because we didn't have Bob Random. We had finished with him in California, in one session. But I was the same build and had the same hair, and it was dark. Orson got in the back seat with the camera and had me focus it and expose it. I took off my shirt and sat in the front with Oja sitting on top of me. I leaned my head back, and all of Oja's close-ups were made of me, the back of my head.

Another nude scene, with Oja's character pulling John Dale through a doorway on the crumbling film studio back lot, deep shadows casting prison stripes across their bodies, evokes the funhouse sequence of *The Lady from Shanghai.* Filmed with flats set up on the patio at Lawlen Way, it was seamlessly cut into footage shot on the MGM back lot in the declining days of that once-great studio. A sadistic sex scene follows with the unseen Hannaford directing the naked actress to cut the love beads from the neck of the equally naked John Dale with a large pair of scissors—"Snip snip snip," Hannaford commands with wicked glee—a piece of business uncomfortably suggesting castration. Most of the sequence was filmed in the backyard at Orvilliers, with Graver doubling again for Random on the bed. But it is Random walking away naked down an MGM street at the end of the sequence. Such filmmaking sleight of hand had become habitual for Welles, and Graver, the magician's apprentice, makes it believable. Graver recalls his most difficult task for that sequence:

Orson had to have me totally naked for the wide shots on the bed, with Oja on top of me, naked. I said, "Orson, don't ask me to do this." "You gotta

> do it, Gary, there's nobody else." I said, "I really don't want to. Let me just be the cameraman." He said, "Oh, I'll operate." But his fingers were big and they would hit the aperture, and the exposure would go up, so we had to print it down when we made the final print. There I did take off all my clothes and got up on the bed, in front of my French girl crew.

❖ ❖ ❖

Homosexuality became an increasingly overt theme in Welles's later work: the Hal-Poins relationship in *Chimes at Midnight* has gay overtones, and the king scorns Hal as a "young, wanton, and effeminate boy"; the disturbed painter Hughie Warriner (Laurence Harvey) in *The Deep* is mocked as a "fag" by Welles's character, Russ Brewer, a macho buffoon who falsely accuses Hughie of murder; *F for Fake* has a gay protagonist, the art forger Elmyr de Hory, whose young lover talks about their relationship; and the central characters in Welles's screenplay *The Big Brass Ring* were once gay lovers. But the sensitive question of Welles's possible bisexuality has largely been avoided in the critical literature on his work.

Welles was always coy on that subject, never more so than in his interviews near the end of his life with Barbara Leaming: "From my earliest childhood, I was the Lillie Langtry of the older homosexual set. Everybody wanted me. I had a very bad way of turning these guys off. I thought it would embarrass them if I said I wasn't homosexual, that that would be a rebuke, so I always had a headache. You know, I was like an eternal virgin." His denials in the Leaming biography are so obsessive and insistent that it seems he doth protest too much. Another biographer, Simon Callow, more plausibly suggests that Welles, in addition to his many heterosexual liaisons, may have had homosexual experiences during his time in the New York theater in the late 1930s.

Welles shed some light on his attitudes toward homosexuality in casual remarks on the set of *Other Wind.* Recounting his youthful disillusionment while trying to court a certain glamorous female star, Welles said he had shown up at her door with a bouquet of flowers only to find that one of her lesbian admirers had also arrived with flowers. "Many beautiful women, in my experience, go both ways," he mused. "It's not like a man, who has one homosexual experience and it corrupts him for the rest of his life—they do it for the simple pleasure of the thing, and they don't think about it afterwards. Now, I'm not talking about your hard-core bull dykes, you understand." Welles's view that a man is permanently corrupted by one homosexual experience helps explain his portrayal of Hannaford as tormented and driven to self-destruction by his secret feelings toward John Dale. Although today such anxiety over one's sexual nature seems benighted, if still unfortunately widespread, it was a more common fear when Hannaford (and Welles himself) were constructing their images as Don Juan directors by hiding less conventional sexual impulses for which that persona is now seen as a cover.

During the year Welles spent in Madison, attending Washington School, he was studied as a child prodigy by a University of Wisconsin psychologist and lived with the man and his family in their apartment near the campus. The psychologist helped run Camp Indianola, a boys' summer camp, directly across Lake Mendota from the university. Remembering Madison as "a wonderful city," Welles told me, "I'm not ashamed of being from Wisconsin. Just of being from Kenosha. It's a terrible place." Hearing him say that, Oja Kodar interjected that all Welles remembered from his boyhood in Kenosha was the day of his mother's funeral, when he was nine and the rain fell all day long. "*Of course* you would remember it as a terrible place if that's all you can remember," she said, and he grunted his assent. The ten-year-old Orson must have enjoyed putting on his solo show of *Dr. Jekyll and Mr. Hyde* to amuse the boys at Camp Indianola during the summer of 1925. But he told me he had to flee in the dead of night when the psychologist came into his cabin and made a pass. Welles recalled that he climbed through a window, paddled across the lake in a canoe, and ran to the train station to escape to Chicago.

Welles made an even more telling remark at the "Working with Welles" seminar I helped conduct for the American Film Institute in the late seventies. For an evening on Welles's work in the theater, we began with his apprenticeship at the Todd School to Roger Hill, who was also part of our panel discussion. Welles looked lovingly at his octogenarian schoolmaster, saying, "I'm the boy you could have had." Telling the audience—as he did that year in his filmed interview with Hill—that his interest in the theater arose from a need to attract Hill's attention, Welles declared, "If he had been gay, I would have been gay." In *Other Wind*, there's a prolonged, acutely uncomfortable sequence of Hannaford revealing his vicious homophobia by gay-baiting his young leading man's elderly schoolmaster, Bradley Pease Burroughs, played by Dan Tobin, the star of Welles's TV pilot *The Fountain of Youth*.

Among the most significant of Welles's close male friendships was that with John Houseman. Welles told Bogdanovich he thought House-

Welles and Jeanne Moreau, seen in a frame enlargement from his unfinished thriller *The Deep* (1963–69), were good friends and collaborated fruitfully in *Chimes at Midnight* and *The Trial*, but this film strained their relationship. Moreau was given a secondary role to Oja Kodar, offering her little to do besides watching Welles ham it up in what he considered "the funniest part I've ever played." *(Orson Welles: The One-Man Band; Medias Res/The Criterion Collection)*

man had been in love with him and that their violent split in 1939 was the result of Houseman feeling jilted. Or perhaps toyed with and let down? Even if they may not have been lovers, there's no doubt of the intense erotic feelings Welles stirred in Houseman from the beginning. Houseman's first glimpse of Welles came in December 1934 when Welles played Tybalt in the Katharine Cornell company's production of *Romeo and Juliet.* Describing Welles's stage presence as that of "a monstrous boy . . . obscene and terrible," Houseman writes in his memoirs, "I left without seeing him [offstage], yet in the days that followed, he was seldom out of my mind. My agitation grew and I did nothing about it—in much the same way as a man nurtures his sense of excited anticipation over a woman the sight of whom has deeply disturbed him and of whom he feels quite certain that there will one day be something between them." In 1964 Welles called Houseman "an old enemy of mine," and he always believed that Houseman spread malicious and untrue gossip about him, including helping Kael with her essay that claimed he tried to steal credit from Mankiewicz for *Kane.*

It's possible to see echoes of Welles's tortured relationship with Houseman, which Welles described as "a real Russian novel," throughout his film work. The central theme of a Welles film usually is betrayal, in nearly every case the betrayal of a male friendship. A book-length study could indeed be written about the barely repressed homoerotic overtones of the relationships between Welles's male characters, beginning with the deep friendship between Kane and Leland, who wind up betraying each other. Other examples include Macbeth and Macduff; the weird male triangle of Bannister, Grisby, and O'Hara in *Shanghai;* the supermasculine Othello and the feline Iago, who betrays him because of what Welles had MacLiammóir play as homosexual jealousy; Arkadin and Van Stratten; Quinlan and Menzies in *Touch of Evil;* the sadomasochistic tensions between Joseph K. and the Advocate in *The Trial;* the voyeuristic sexual dynamics between Mr. Clay and the young sailor Paul in *The Immortal Story;* and, supremely, Falstaff and Hal, whose relationship is echoed in Hannaford's tortured involvements with both John Dale and Otterlake. The exploration of complex male relationships is at the heart of Welles's work, which shows a relatively limited interest in heterosexuality.

❖ ❖ ❖

The theme of betrayal loomed large in his own life story, an obsession that can be traced back to his primal abandonment by his mother when she died and of his own abandonment of his loving but deeply flawed father. It seems clear in retrospect that Welles, in both his personal and professional dealings, often seemed to provoke the situation he most feared. Indeed, there was something in Welles that seemed to set up situations in which people's loyalty was tested under extreme duress and then (almost inevitably) found wanting. Always looking for his Judas, Welles found him in many different guises. Spending years struggling in Hollywood and encountering the hostility he faced from the beginning of his time there would be enough to give any filmmaker a degree of paranoia.

During the filming of *Other Wind,* even his devoted young crew were accused of betraying him, in an episode described by assistant director Lou Race as "the Friday Night Massacre." They were exhausted from shooting at Bogdanovich's Bel-Air home until 4:00 A.M., with two hours of cleaning up before they could go home, and Welles had scheduled the next call for noon. Graver asked him for a 2:00 P.M. call. The cameraman recalls, "The crew said collectively, we work late at night and can't get much sleep. We're tired. I went to Orson and said, I'm speaking on behalf of the crew, they need at least six or eight hours of sleep." Welles, dead tired himself, exploded, "I can't work in this atmosphere, with everybody against me." Firing the entire crew, he announced that he was canceling the shoot and leaving for France in the morning. Instead, after a few days' break, the shooting quietly resumed with all but a handful of the crew intact.

Explaining the dedication so many actors and crew people offered Welles, Jeanne Moreau put it best: "If he calls you and says, 'I need you,' then you say 'Orson needs me and it's something important.' His career is so strange because he's capable of such beautiful things and it's so hard for him now to make a film that you wouldn't be the little stone that would stop the machine from going, once he has the chance to make a film. I think that's why we all do react that way." Still, Moreau's unwillingness to complete her dubbing for *The Deep* shows that even she had her limits about how far she would go for Welles. She was angered when Welles gave her a role secondary to the younger and inexperienced Oja Kodar; according to Welles's daughter Christopher, Moreau felt insulted when Welles explained, "Please forgive me, Jeanne, but you are no longer twenty." But Moreau's less than perfectly selfless loyalty toward Welles does not negate her basic point; her participation in *The Trial* and *Chimes at Midnight* at the height of her international stardom helped him get those films produced at a time when he had been having trouble finding employment as a director even in Europe. Another actress who worked with Welles repeatedly, Mercedes McCambridge, told me early in the shooting of *Other Wind*, "I would do anything for Orson. If he told me to jump off the Empire State Building, I would do it and not ask why."

Lou Race put the matter of loyalty another way, wryly describing the overworked, underpaid cast and crew of *Other Wind* as members of an organization called "VISTOW," or "Volunteers in Service to Orson Welles." The final credits still have to be sorted out, but other key members of the loyal young crew, most recruited from previous work with Graver or Bogdanovich, were camera operators Michael Ferris and Rick Weaver; assistant cameramen R. Michael Stringer and Leslie Otis; production manager Frank Marshall; production associates Neil Canton, Richard Waltzer, Larry Jackson, and Sally Stringer; key grip Bob McVay; and property master Glenn Jacobson. Actor Peter Jason did double duty as an all-around crew member, as did Kodar. Paul Hunt recorded the production sound; Welles fired his original soundman when he interrupted a scene on the first day of shooting, announcing, "We have overlapping dialogue!" "We *always* have overlapping dialogue," grumbled Welles, who had been celebrated for that technique since his radio days. Another time, when his script supervisor questioned him about a shot, Welles told her to stop making notes and for the rest of the shooting kept the continuity entirely in his head.

Welles often gave Graver a hard time, yelling at him, ordering him around, and working him mercilessly, contributing to the collapse of Graver's first two marriages. One night over dinner, Gary and Oja took Welles to task for treating people so roughly, but to no avail. Gary considered him "a child who'd never grown up and always wanted his way." The unflagging loyalty of the crew was all the more remarkable for the constant abuse they had to endure, as Welles well knew. "A director is a lover," he once said. "He must constantly make love to the actors. I *don't* make love to the crew. I make the crew my enemy, so the actors constantly say, 'Look how mean he could be with us' [laughs]."

But on his TV pilot *The Orson Welles Show*, Welles also acknowledged the crew's immense importance to the director:

> directing being the one job in movies where you can scoot along for forty years with a little luck and no talent at all, without ever getting caught. . . . [W]e're all of us, good and bad, pretty talented in the fine art of conning ourselves. It's so easy to start thinking you're great when you see these marvelous things happening all around you and you remember that you did indeed say, last Wednesday, something like that. You asked your crew to figure out a way to give you some crazy and impossible camera shot. Today, when they've performed a miracle and somehow managed to give it to you on film, all you seem to remember is that you, godlike, gave the command, forgetting very conveniently that just asking for a miracle is no trick at all, and what's wonderful is the way your technicians accomplished it.

After the Friday Night Massacre on the set of *Other Wind*, Welles improvised a scene Race described as "Orson's tribute to the little people—sort of like kicking somebody in the mud for an hour and then offering them a flower." At the end of the drive-in screening of Jake's film, the Baron (Tonio Selwart) pays tribute to Hannaford's devoted crew people, telling Otterlake, "What's important for you now is to get soldiers—good soldiers. . . . They followed Napoleon, they followed Hannibal: They *really* crossed the Alps. They're the real heroes of any story."

❖ ❖ ❖

When I was summoned to Los Angeles for more shooting in May 1971, a production assistant picked me up at the airport and took me on a hair-raising nighttime drive at high speed through the canyons along Mulholland Drive. The company put me up in the sprawling white ranch house being used for the shooting; it had just been vacated by Hollywood's latest divorced couple, Cary Grant and Dyan Cannon. We shot party scenes there with dozens of extras, and other scenes on and around the school bus driving through Bel-Air, Hollywood, and the San Fernando Valley. Sporting a "Happy Birthday Jake" banner, the yellow school bus was filled with creepy-looking dummies of John Dale being used as props in Hannaford's movie, and several members of the "Hannaford mafia," Stewart, McCambridge, O'Brien, and Cameron Mitchell.

Though most famous as Raymond the butler in *Kane*, Stewart was Welles's right-hand man in the *Mercury Theatre on the Air* in the 1930s. Stewart would rehearse the company all week until Welles stepped in for the final run-throughs; Welles told me Stewart was largely responsible for the quality of *The War of the Worlds*, and he went on to a successful career as a Hollywood character actor and television director. I had trouble playing my entrance scene on the bus with Stewart's Matt Costello. I was supposed to climb inside, pause next to the driver, say a few words to Costello about why I had been thrown out of Hannaford's car, listen to his reply, then move on as I resumed talking. It may not sound very difficult, but for me it was as daunting as playing Hamlet. Despairing of getting me to understand my behavior, Welles said, "Paul, can *you* tell him how to do it?" With a succinct bit of advice from Stewart, I managed my scene in the first take, after which Welles began referring to me as "One-Take Pister." Stewart told Welles, "He'll probably become some funny new kind of star." That was my happiest moment during the filming.

Another day, the bus took off without me into the fathomless depths of the San Fernando Valley. Welles said they'd be back shortly and told me to wait with Lou Race outside a porno shop ("SWINGER'S [*sic*] ADULT BOOKS—NUDIST MAGAZINES—8 MM ART FILMS"), holding a parking spot for the bus so we could film a scene with the store visible through the bus windows. We waited for three hours. As they were off shooting, Graver recalls, "Finally Orson says, 'Wrap it.' I said, 'You left Joe there in front of the porno shop.' He said, 'Oh, my God, I feel bad, I forgot about them.' That was really funny." In the meantime we had turned away dozens of cars, including one driven by folksinger Pete Seeger, who cheerfully backed out when we said we were making a movie with Orson

Welles (Seeger wasn't headed for the 8 MM ART FILMS, by the way). For years afterward, Welles would fondly recall the time Joe and Lou stood guard outside the porno shop to save a space for Jake Hannaford's bus.

The shooting was a film buff's fantasy land, offering the constant opportunity to ask the older cast members about their classic films. I would pump Paul Stewart about *Citizen Kane*, Cameron Mitchell about *They Were Expendable*, Mercedes McCambridge about *Johnny Guitar*. McCambridge regaled us once with her horrific rendition of the demon's voice from *The Exorcist*. And Rich Little delighted both Welles and Huston by doing scenes from *The Maltese Falcon* in every character's voice.

Edmond O'Brien had been a member of Welles's Mercury Theatre, taking over Welles's own role of Brutus in the touring company of *Julius Caesar*. Although Eddie still had a powerful acting presence, he slurred his words, and his face looked bloated and battered. We thought he was suffering from advanced alcoholism, but, like Welles's ex-wife Rita Hayworth, who was prey to the same mistaken impressions, O'Brien, it turned out, was in the early stages of Alzheimer's disease. He was only fifty-five when he began work on *Other Wind*, but it was one of his final roles. One day in 1971 we were assembling in the parking lot of a Howard Johnson's Motel in Hollywood. Eddie was holding a bullhorn to round partygoers into the bus, and I asked him to say his lines as the grizzled old crook Sykes from Sam Peckinpah's 1969 Western *The Wild Bunch:* "They? Who's *they?* Who the hell is *theyyy?*" Eddie happily complied, broadcasting the lines throughout the parking lot as Bogdanovich pulled up in his convertible.

Peter barged over to Welles, who was huddled with his crew, looking over the script. Peter was making a documentary for the AFI, *Directed by John Ford*, and brashly reminded Welles that he still needed to record his narration. Welles gestured at the actors and crew gathered around the parking lot and said evenly, "Peter, I'm trying to make a movie here." Peter whined that Welles had been promising for weeks to do the narration, and now the deadline was fast upon them. Welles stared hard for a moment and said, biting off his words, "You know, Peter, sometimes you can be a *real shit.*" He grabbed the tape from Peter's hands, summoned soundman Peter Pilafian, and marched into a room in the motel. Twenty minutes later, Welles emerged and thrust the tape wordlessly at Bogdanovich, giving him a withering look. Peter just grinned a Cheshire-cat smile as he passed me with the precious audiotape. He locked it in the trunk of his car and sped off to finish his documentary. The irony is that Welles's delivery of the narration under those hectic conditions is so eloquent, his voice caressing each word, bringing out subtle tones of humor and loving respect while betraying no hint of preoccupation.

At 11:00 one night when several cast members were slumped wearily in the living room of some house waiting to shoot our scenes, Eddie O'Brien, who had been sitting quietly and seemingly comatose for an hour, suddenly exclaimed, "Ah, we used to make movies and fuck all night!" That funny and poignant remark captured the essence of the moment we were sharing in Hollywood history, a transition from the detritus of the golden age to the fool's gold of the *Easy Rider* era.

When I had trouble reading a speech on the bus—literally reading, from a transcript of a taped Hannaford diatribe about hippies and radicals—Welles took me aside to say he was giving the speech to O'Brien. Much to my relief, since I didn't understand what tone I should use for Hannaford's reactionary outburst or even what some of it meant, Welles said I would start reading from the sheet of paper but that Eddie would grab it from my hands. Welles took unusual pains not to blame me for fumbling the speech. He explained that he wanted O'Brien to read it because "Eddie is such a *magnificent ruin.*"

For scenes showing the ruination of Hollywood, Welles needed a rundown old studio lot. Graver was sent on scouting trips all around Arizona and Nevada, photographing ghost towns for possible use in the film. Eventually, Welles figured out a way to use the decrepit back lot of MGM in Culver City, once the film industry's crown jewel. Graver, claiming he was a student filmmaker, rented it for a weekend for only a few hundred dollars. Welles ducked out of sight as he was driven onto the lot, and the studio never realized what his crew was shooting. "We had every set imaginable out there," Graver says. They shot on the lot for several weekends, and Welles finally stayed up for forty-eight hours straight to finish shooting all the scenes on the back lot.

Whenever Welles needed a location cheaply, Graver "was always the beard." For the Century City scenes, the cameraman "got a permit for one weekend. No one was out there on Sundays, because it was all office buildings in those days, so we went in one Sunday. Every week after doing the cinematography, one of my jobs was to erase the date on the permit and retype it. By the end, the paper was all worn away." For the ending scenes at the Reseda Drive-In Theatre in Reseda, where Bogdanovich had shot much of *Targets,* Welles tried to conceal himself by turning away as his convertible entered the lot. "Pretty hard to ignore that it was Orson Welles sitting there. We didn't pay for the drive-in, we just

Peter Bogdanovich brought aspects of his own complex relationship with Welles into *The Other Side of the Wind.* The young director plays Brooks Otterlake, the protégé and patron of an older filmmaker desperately trying to keep working in the *Easy Rider* era. The tensions between Otterlake and Jake Hannaford (John Huston) are evident at the birthday party promoting Hannaford's return to Hollywood. *(SACI/Les Films de l'Astrophore)*

snuck in and did it." Welles told the crew that if anyone asked what he was doing, they were to say he was "Professor Welles, teaching a class," but no one ever questioned his presence.

Welles needed a shot of a car filled with partygoers pulling out of the famous old Paramount gate, the one prominently featured in Billy Wilder's *Sunset Boulevard.* Just after sunrise on a Sunday morning, Welles had his crew quietly "steal" the shot (i.e., take it without asking permission from the studio). The moment was resonant with other memories, since the sprawling Paramount facilities included the former RKO lot where Welles had worked in the 1940s. To celebrate after filming the scene, Welles took the cast and crew to lunch at Nickodell's, a longtime studio hangout on Melrose Avenue, next door to a former RKO soundstage. Welles was crammed into a booth with, among others, Rich Little.

A young waitress came to take our orders and immediately recognized the impressionist. Seeing Welles with him, she turned to Little and asked, "Who's your fat friend?"

❖ ❖ ❖

John Huston was a particularly apt choice for Jake Hannaford, not only because of his long personal and professional relationship with Welles but also because his public personality often seemed to echo Hemingway's. With his battered, bearded face, his emotional remoteness, and his charismatic aura of sadism, romance, and mystery, Huston brought a life's worth of devilishly colorful overtones to his portrayal of the legendary director. I was surprised to find in talking with Huston in 1975 that he was not aware (or disingenuously claimed ignorance) that Hemingway was Welles's principal model for Hannaford. Because his own affinities with Hemingway were so obvious, Huston may have found it superfluous to search for parallels while playing the role.

"The man's as fascinating and as various as his own films," Welles said in his magnificent speech at the 1983 AFI Life Achievement Award tribute to Huston. "He is the silken dazzle of a Renaissance prince—the cool panache of a Regency rake—and the gallant courtesy of a gentleman cardsharp on a Mississippi riverboat. . . . There's the irresistible caress of that hypnotic voice, and what serves him well as a director, that riveting and magisterial attentiveness. He's a great listener. And this carries with it a faint whiff of the confessional, a priestly touch of incense, with just that tang of sulfur which befits an outrageously seductive, unfrocked cardinal. You all know what I mean—that air of high benevolence amounting to a benediction."

Writer Peter Viertel, who counted both men among his friends, recalled, "Orson had always scoffed a little at Huston's personage, probably because he recognized a rival act when he saw one, but before they had finished the first week of working together [on *Other Wind*] he fell under the spell of John's charm and larger-than-life personality, feelings that were mutual. John told me that he had enjoyed the experience . . . because the movie was 'such a desperate venture.' . . . which made work the kind of perilous undertaking John enjoyed, an adventure shared by desperate men that finally came to nothing."

Perhaps the most vivid demonstration of Welles's diplomacy with actors was the tactful way he treated Huston, who, being a director himself, was always the most docile and obedient of actors. Since Huston was his peer in age and career stature, Welles obviously had to avoid any appearance of ordering him around, but it was marvelous to witness the finesse with which he molded the performance. Welles wasn't satisfied, for example, with the way Huston turned a lecherous eye on his blonde teenaged companion (Cathy Lucas) in one of the Arizona scenes. But rather than find fault with his performance in front of the company, Welles paused for a moment and said, "John, do you know who you remind me of in this scene? Your father." Huston beamed, as he did whenever his father, the great actor Walter Huston, was mentioned. "Oh, really, Orson? Why?" "Because he had that kindly, paternal air—but nobody ever had a higher score." Huston, delighted, picked up on the suggestion and played the scene with a sly, roguish charm that injected the note of irony Welles was seeking.

Susan Strasberg gives a splendidly assured performance as Juliette Riche, the sharp-witted film critic modeled after Pauline Kael (before Kael's attack on Welles, he thought of this character as a TV interviewer, "Candy Bergen with brains"). The script calls Riche "a rat of a woman," but the direction and acting are more nuanced. She comes to the party and spits out bitchy but accurate digs about Hannaford's masculinity and his relationship with Otterlake.* When I simplistically asked Strasberg how she felt about playing a "castrating woman," she astutely observed of Hannaford, "He's castrated *himself.*"

When Otterlake boasts that Riche's reviews can't do him much harm—"I mean, how much harm can you do to the third biggest grosser in movie history?"—Hannaford says facetiously, "Did it really make that much? How *marvelous.*"

> *Riche:* Yes, did you know that when his own production company goes public, that your friend there stands to walk away with forty million dollars?
>
> *Otterlake:* Yeah, and she's gonna say that I—she's gonna keep on writing that I—I—that I stole everything from you, Skipper. I'm never gonna walk away from that.

---

* The role was written for Jeanne Moreau, but Welles did not offer it to her, perhaps because of the lingering bad feelings over *The Deep* and because Oja also has such a prominent role in *Other Wind.* Bogdanovich's then wife, Polly Platt, *Other Wind*'s production designer, made a brief stab at playing Riche before McCambridge recommended Strasberg. Moreau had been considered for the Zarah Valeska role after Marlene Dietrich rejected it, not wanting to be photographed and certainly not in the cinema verité style. Lilli Palmer's scenes as Zarah were shot at her home in Spain, and Huston's matching shots in Arizona.

> *Hannaford:* Well, it's all right to borrow from each other. What we must never do is borrow from *ourselves.* Come on, Brooksie.*
>
> *Riche:* Of course you're close, you two—you *have* to be—you have no choice.
>
> *Hannaford:* Please, dear lady, don't tell us what you . . . mean by that.

The facade of Hannaford's omnipotence breaks down later as he confesses to "Brooksie" that he needs his help to keep his career alive. Huston's most demanding scene is a drunken, anguished rant in a bathroom as Hannaford washes his face, trying to sober up before the screening of his unfinished film. As he rails to Otterlake, Lear-like, about the movie business, Hannaford knows that his shattered career—even his life—is on the line, and the prospects for both are bleak. Hannaford's shame and desperation over his professional dependence on his young protégé underlie the cruelty he displays toward Otterlake. The echoes of Welles's sometimes fraught relationship with Bogdanovich are inescapable. The atmosphere in the Arizona house when the bathroom scene was shot in 1973 was as tense as anything I experienced on *The Other Side of the Wind.* Welles ordered the rest of us to stay out of the way, crammed into another little room during the long hours it took to film the scene.

Welles encouraged Huston to say the lines any way they came to him and to drink heavily as he worked, figuring that this would liberate deeper emotions than he usually revealed in his acting. Huston did his best work, Welles noted, at "the vodka hour." Every so often, Huston would ask, "Orson, what page are we on?"

"Well, John, what the hell difference does it make?'

"I want to know how *drunk* I'm supposed to be."

❖ ❖ ❖

What ever happened to *The Other Side of the Wind?* Why hasn't it been released? When I lunched with Huston in December 1975, on the eve of the premiere of *The Man Who Would Be King,* the masterpiece he had knocked off in a few short months on break from working with Welles, he expressed concern about the progress of Welles's film and his continued problems with raising money. "I'll have to find out where Orson is,"

---

* Welles said he borrowed Hannaford's warning against self-imitation from Pablo Picasso.

he said. "I'm going to call him up and say, 'Why the hell don't you finish it?'" Graver offered me the following explanation in 1976, near the end of the shooting: "It's really a handmade movie, frame by frame, and nobody makes a movie like that anymore; that's why it's taken so long." Unfortunately, the answer is not that simple. Nor is there an easy answer to the question of how much responsibility for its incompletion lies with Welles and how much with other people. Huston observed, "It's about as complicated a situation as a picture can get into."

The filming began with Welles's and Kodar's own money. Welles said they poured about $750,000 into the production. Because he was a notoriously bad businessman, the financial structure of his projects often seemed cloudy at best. His frequent dealings with dubious characters only exacerbated his problems, even if such dealings can partly be explained by the slippery nature of the film business and the reluctance of more conventional producers to work with him. When his use of a Swiss corporation as a production company came under the scrutiny of the IRS in the early seventies, he was unable to use the money CBS paid him for his only partly completed TV special *Orson's Bag* to help fund *Other Wind*. According to Leaming, that forced him to seek outside investors for *Other Wind*, which proved disastrous. Welles also was burdened by a change of tax laws in the early seventies for Americans living overseas, who had thought they were exempt from U.S. taxation on European earnings but then were forced to make retroactive payments. Welles blamed those latest tax problems for forcing him to interrupt the filming of *Other Wind* and return to Europe to act in more movies to raise money and find outside investors so he could finish his picture. Nevertheless, in those days, notes Graver, "He wasn't prevented from coming back and forth."

It's regrettable that Welles, the lifelong progressive, made what seems to have been a Faustian pact to help fund some of his late projects. Perhaps out of desperation, he became a flack for the shah of Iran, the U.S.-installed tyrant whose intelligence and security organization, SAVAK, was notorious for its reliance on torture. Welles narrated a laudatory hour-long Iranian documentary, *The Shah of Iran* (1972), and the following year received a Golden Winged Ibex award for career achievement from the International Film Festival of Tehran when *F for Fake*, also made with Iranian backing, received its premiere.

The deals for the Iranian government to help finance *Other Wind* and *F for Fake* were made in the early seventies with Mehdi Boushehri, the shah's brother-in-law and head of the Paris film company Les Films de l'Astrophore. According to Boushehri's French line producer, Dominique Antoine, who brokered the deal, Boushehri's investors in Iran had a twofold purpose, "to promote Iranian movies and make a big international coproduction" with a major name in world filmmaking. But this alliance led to bitter conflicts between Welles and the Iranians over finances and over the artistic control of *Other Wind.* Welles originally sold the Iranians 50 percent of the film but saw his share continually being whittled down as production expenses grew and his backers increased their investment. In a further complication, another person involved with the production was accused of absconding with part of the money the Iranians thought they were investing in the film, including money owed to Huston, whose estate is still due part of his $75,000 salary.

"*Again! It's happening again!*" Welles said, breaking down when told of the vanishing funds during the Arizona filming.

Soon after that, Huston recalled, "Orson ran out of cigars. I was a cigar-smoker, too, and though mine were not quite as big, full-bodied and rich as Orson's Havanas, he was reduced to smoking them. It crossed my mind that maybe Orson was also running out of money. The fleeting thought later proved to have substance."

The house in Carefree used for filming, balanced on huge rocks, had been rented by a crew member pretending to be looking for a vacation retreat. The windows were covered with black tarpaulins so that filming could take place at all hours. Not far away in that lunar-looking landscape was the house Antonioni had used (and blown up, using a miniature) for *Zabriskie Point.* "Orson's next-door neighbor turned out to be a drunk who didn't quite know what was going on but suspected some kind of orgy," Huston recalled. "He appeared periodically and threatened everyone, and even once brought the police in. They recognized Orson and me and were duly respectful, leading the gentleman from next door back to his own premises. After that he stood in his own driveway, shaking his fist and swearing at us. It added an appropriately bizarre note." Welles joked that Carefree was a place "for senior citizens who think Ronald Reagan is a Communist."

Welles's already troubled involvement with his Iranian backers—a situation he would come to regard as a "nightmare to end all nightmares"—finally blew up in his face after the shah was deposed by the Ayatollah Khomeini's fundamentalist revolution in January–February 1979. While in the process of confiscating foreign property of the shah's family, the ayatollah reportedly sent agents out looking for the negative of *The Other Side of the Wind.* Welles hid the negative in the wine cellar of a friend's restaurant outside Paris. Today the ten hours of negative, jointly owned by Boushehri's company and Oja Kodar, is stored in a Paris laboratory. Graver has inspected the negative and found it in good condition, unlike the battered work-print material edited by Welles that has been seen publicly in various venues.* Welles seized possession of the work print, Kodar recalled, when he "realized that Boushehri was planning to take the film away from him and to let [French documentary filmmaker] François Reichenbach finish it. So one Sunday, Orson and Gary Graver went to the editing room [in Paris] with a car and picked up the working print and the sound tapes—they literally stole the print and shipped it to L.A. At last Boushehri understood that he can get his invested money back only when we reach an agreement" (which they eventually did in 1998).

"It's hard to imagine a movie career more littered with sensational catastrophes than mine," Welles admitted in January 1979 when we held our AFI seminar program on *Other Wind.* Speaking shortly before the ayatollah's return to Iran to take over from the recently departed shah, Welles said with undue optimism, "The end of it all is that when the telephones work again and the banks open again, it may be possible to detach this film from the Iranians. You can imagine with what interest I watch the evening news. The chant 'Death to the Shah' does not come solely from the Iranians."

The earlier AFI tribute at the Century Plaza Hotel, on February 9, 1975, had come at a seemingly propitious time for Welles, even though the award was not universally popular in Hollywood. "Why Orson Welles?" asked director Henry Hathaway. "He's only made one movie." Veteran journalist Thomas M. Pryor, my hard-boiled editor at *Daily Variety*, stood with the rest of the crowd to applaud as Welles entered the ballroom, but muttered to me, "The son of a bitch doesn't deserve it." The festivities provided an opportunity for Welles to showcase scenes

---

* These venues include the AFI Life Achievement Award tribute, the "Working with Welles" seminar, Graver's 1993 documentary *Working with Orson Welles,* and *Orson Welles: The One-Man Band.* The Munich Film Museum in 2002 assembled and screened thirty minutes of footage at the Mannheim (Germany) Welles conference under the title *Scenes from "The Other Side of the Wind."* That footage also has been shown in other Welles retrospectives in Europe and the United States.

from *Other Wind* and to make a dignified yet self-consciously humorous plea on national television for "end money."

His situation with Boushehri had reached a stalemate, with both sides arguing over how much was required to finish the film and how much each side owned. Welles by then had found himself forced to surrender much of his remaining share to Boushehri in order to get enough funds to keep shooting. *Other Wind* was still filming nights at Bogdanovich's Bel-Air home at the time of the AFI tribute. Welles hoped a studio might step in, settle the remaining financial issues, and enable the film to be completed and distributed. But he had to argue with AFI chairman George Stevens Jr. to be permitted to use his acceptance speech to promote his unfinished picture, making that a condition of accepting the award. When Stevens chafed at Welles's demands, Welles said indignantly to Graver, "I think I know something about putting on a show."

Stevens's words in presenting the award, like much about the evening, carried unspoken ironies:

> Too often we measure a film only by its bank account. That is why in making this award, the [AFI] trustees emphasize the test of time. Tonight you have seen inspired films which have met that test. And remembering the stormy seas that Orson Welles has weathered in his long career, hear what the writer John Ruskin said one hundred years ago in noting that many of the most enduring works of art and literature are never paid for: "How much," he asked, "do you think Homer got for his *Iliad*, or Dante for his *Paradise?* Only bitter bread and salt and walking up and down other people's stairs." . . . So tonight we measure Orson Welles by his courage and the intensity of his vision. . . . He reminds us that it is better to live one day as a lion than a hundred years as a sheep.

Although Stevens added that Welles "has had many days as a lion," his way of offering praise had the unfortunate side effect of feeding into the common perception that Welles's career had climaxed with *Citizen Kane.*

What Welles had hoped for—a studio offer for his work in progress—actually materialized because of the award. But the Iranian company held out for a better offer. None came, and the offer went away. About that spectacular instance of bad judgment, producer Dominique Antoine admitted, "I am really sorry, because I think the picture would have been finished now and released." She said in 1998, "One of the biggest legends about Orson is his lavish spending and the cost of his films. It was ridiculous. What *The Other Side of the Wind* cost over five years [i.e., the years following the initial 1970 shooting] was exactly two million dollars. Now, it would be necessary to add to that the interest for the last twenty years." At the 2005 Locarno Welles conference, Antoine amplified on those observations: "Nobody in the world could say, 'I produced a picture of Orson Welles.' He was the producer. It was his own picture. He said to me, 'Producers don't exist, just bankers.' Orson did not know about money. But there is a big lie with Orson that he cost so much money. It is not true. What I gave to Orson is now the cost of one TV picture in France."

In 1977, Welles wrote Mehdi Boushehri to vent his frustrations about the production and to try to break the impasse with his backers:

> My own first priority, for much too long now, has been "THE OTHER SIDE OF THE WIND." Tragically, very little of that time has been spent on constructive work. Overwhelmingly, it has been time lost in simply waiting for the *chance* to work—time utterly wasted. Weather in the movie business is highly changeable. The market itself fluctuates quite wildly, and my "market value" both as a performer and filmmaker has slipped to the lowest point in all my career.
>
> The Film Institute "Tribute" dramatized the presumed advent of "THE OTHER SIDE OF THE WIND." That picture, so eagerly looked forward to, has failed to appear. And for me, professionally, that failure has been mortal. As a director, my reputation by now appears to have been blackened beyond reparation. In this industry—in this small town—two things are said of me today. "That picture isn't finished yet—the Crazy Welles . . ." and "No use offering him a part, he'll turn it down; he doesn't want to work."
>
> The "Tribute" should have been a turning point. It certainly created for me a notable renewal of interest on the part of the Hollywood Community. During the year that followed, and for several months after that, I received any number of film, theatre and TV offers—all of which I turned down. What I could have accepted (without any conflict in time) comes—according to [his attorney L. Arnold] Weissberger's documentation—to something more than two million dollars.
>
> I sacrificed all this, as you know, in order to keep myself free for the completion of our film. . . .
>
> I have been in the performing arts, working for my living, for some forty-seven years. I have never been rich. In this rather ridiculous business we learn to sustain ourselves on hope and enthusiasm. So I've never been really poor.
>
> But today I find myself not only without income, but without prospects. With my professional credit destroyed, it's not too easy—in the sixty-second year of my life—to make plans for a fresh start.

Despite it all, Welles was able to view his difficulties with some levity.

Once, when the fifteenth take of a complex shot for *Other Wind* went wrong, Welles rose from his chair and began walking away. Graver, finally solving the technical problems, called out, "I've got it!" But Welles wearily replied, "No, Gary. *God* does not want me to make this shot." And one night during shooting at Bogdanovich's house, when technical problems were keeping Welles from rolling the camera on another intricate setup, I heard his booming voice from the next room asking humorously, "As the old saying goes, Who do I have to fuck to get *out* of this picture?"

The Other Side of the Wind was also a terribly frustrating experience for the many actors who appeared in it, the veterans who needed visibility in an important film to revitalize their careers and the newcomers who counted on a role in a Welles film to help make their names. Several key players have died without seeing the film released. Ironically, because of its inaccessibility, the film also became a convenient vehicle for many Hollywood actors to pad their résumés, regardless of the size of their roles and whether they actually appeared in the film or not.

Welles's later years found him involved in a protracted court fight in France for control of the negative. Claiming precedence as the film's author, Welles sued for ownership. He marshaled high-level support in France from critics and fellow directors; the Académie des beaux arts, which made him a member; and President François Mitterand, who presented him with the Order of Commander of the Légion d'honneur in 1982. The court agreed that Welles was the auteur of *The Other Side of the Wind* and as such retained final cut but decreed that Boushehri's part ownership had to be settled before the film could be released. The stalemate between Welles and Boushehri over financial terms and artistic control would continue well beyond Welles's death. Antoine told me in 2005 that she considered the saga of *Other Wind* "a total disaster."

Joking bitterly about "all the psychiatrists among the *cinéastes* explaining my *latest* maneuver to keep from having to finish the picture," Welles told Leaming that he had a "very strong temptation through the last years of all this to just forget about movies. It just was one too many, you know."

❖ ❖ ❖

Will *The Other Side of the Wind* ever be released? Or will it remain a tantalizing, legendary "lost" work, perhaps the most famous of all unfinished films?

Over the years, I made many informal attempts to drum up interest in raising end money for *Other Wind.* While writing screenplays for the independent producer Roger Corman in the late seventies when he was still distributing "art" films theatrically, I asked if he'd be interested in picking up Welles's film. Corman said he would, but only if he could first be assured that all the ownership issues were settled. "Otherwise," he said, "I'd be served with three lawsuits at noon on the day it opened."

After Welles's death, Graver, Kodar, Bogdanovich, and Frank Marshall continued to put in long and dedicated efforts on the film's behalf, screening footage and showing rough cuts to many potential backers, who almost invariably reacted with incomprehension. Rough cuts are hard for "civilians" to understand, and even people in the film industry have trouble envisioning the final form a rough cut might assume. *Other Wind*'s unconventional style and structure makes it especially hard to show in unfinished form. Kodar showed it to Huston and asked him to complete the film, but *he* found the challenges too difficult. After watching the footage, Oliver Stone told Kodar and Graver, "It's too experimental." George Lucas, who could bankroll the completion by signing a check from petty cash, declined to do so. "I introduced Orson to Lucas at a big party at USC," Graver recalls. "I thought Orson could talk to Lucas and get some money. The three of us sat there. Orson was nice and smiling, he said some things, but Lucas was shy or something, didn't say a word. Then Lucas said, 'Nice to meet you,' and left. After Orson died, I showed Lucas *The Other Side of the Wind* in [Steven] Spielberg's projection room. Lucas just shrugged his shoulders and said he didn't know what to do with it, that it wasn't commercial."

Clint Eastwood, whose work as a director Welles admired, asked to see the rough cut after Welles's death. But it turned out that he was only interested in studying Huston's performance so he could imitate him in *White Hunter, Black Heart*, his 1990 film of Peter Viertel's roman à clef about the shooting of *The African Queen.* Eastwood also borrowed an exchange of dialogue in which Phoenix radio personality Pat McMahon, playing a pretentious interviewer, charges up to Hannaford as he arrives at the party. Calling Hannaford's name four times, McMahon's character finally announces, "I'm Marvin P. Fassbender!" After a pause, the gimlet-eyed old director replies, "Of course you are." Eastwood has been criticized by Kodar and others for ripping off Welles, but Welles told me he stole Hannaford's riposte from Noël Coward, who once said it to an especially bumptious admirer.

The theatrical success of the revised *Touch of Evil* in 1998 suddenly awakened genuine interest in the commercial prospects of *Other Wind.* Surely, with all the popularity of "restorations" and "directors' cuts" of classic and even not-so-classic movies, a *new film* by Orson Welles would find a sizable market. Rick Schmidlin, who produced the *Touch of Evil* revision, and I worked out a plan to serve as producers in shopping and completing *Other Wind*. We consulted extensively with Graver and Kodar before pitching the project to film companies. We estimated conservatively that *Other Wind* would gross $3 million theatrically in the United States and abroad and, with a long shelf life, would bring in at least a couple million more in the cable television and home-video markets. Graver and editor Frank Beacham put together a two-hour rough cut, the most elaborate yet assembled, but still missing some key scenes that hadn't been printed from the negative and a couple of shots that still remained to be filmed, including the ending of Hannaford's film vanishing from the screen of the drive-in theater (a location that will now have to be doubled since it has been demolished). After all the party guests who were watching the screen have gone, the apocalyptic wind of the title blows through the drive-in and topples the studio sets in Hannaford's film, and the screen-within-the-screen goes white.

"That's an optical," Graver says, "and the only other shot we need to make is the explosion of the Porsche. We're going to just do black smoke going up behind the drive-in screen, like [the smoke from the final explosions] in *The Trial*. The drive-in is empty, and Huston drives his car off the road, it blows up, and you hear his voice on the little drive-in speakers, reverberating, 'Cut! Cut! Cut!,' echoing . . ."

❖ ❖ ❖

We showed the rough cut to Universal,* where Frank Marshall had considerable clout; October Films, a Universal art-house subsidiary; and Sony Pictures Entertainment, where it was championed by executive Michael

---

* Universal asked me in 1998 to write and direct a documentary on the making and revision of *Touch of Evil*, to be released with it for the home-video market. But the studio later decided to hire Laurent Bouzereau, a specialist in such documentaries. I was paid Writers Guild of America minimum for an outline I had written at the studio's request. The documentary, *Restoring "Evil,"* which used a few of my ideas (uncredited at my request), was shown on cable television but was not included on the DVD edition of the revised *Touch of Evil*. Beatrice Welles sued to block Universal's release of the revised feature theatrically and on home video, claiming that the studio was "trading on" her father's name by reediting the film based on his fifty-eight-page memorandum, which she asserted was "only intended to make less objectionable the violence the studio had done to his artistic creation." The studio eventually paid her a settlement.

Schlesinger, who shepherded the *It's All True* documentary to completion at Paramount in 1993. I wrote and rewrote for each company a lengthy memo with suggestions about how the film could be completed.

And I proposed that another entire film could be fashioned from the outtakes and added to the DVD: ninety minutes of black-and-white footage of Welles (off-camera, sitting in for Hannaford) discussing the then contemporary cinema scene with three young directors at the party, Paul Mazursky, Dennis Hopper, and Henry Jaglom. "Orson had them all up to Lawlen Way and got them drinking and smoking pot, got them stoned," Graver recalls. "I lined up nine cartridges, loaded with film, so you don't have to thread the camera, you just slap it on and go. They had totally different views of Hollywood, and Orson was just egging them on." Since the lights were supposed to have failed at Jake's party, Welles had the scene lit entirely with kerosene lamps. When Hopper arrived, he exclaimed, "Man—is *this* the lighting?" "Yeah," said Welles. "That's cool, man," replied Hopper. Welles filmed the young filmmakers' ad-lib interchange with the intention of cutting it down to a few minutes for *Other Wind*, but he never shot Huston's side of the conversation. Mazursky said of the experience, "I'm excited by Welles's improvisatory methods, which have influenced my own." The footage could stand apart as a fascinating document of the period.

Nothing concrete resulted from my pitches, however, until 1998, when I managed, with Schmidlin and Graver, to get Showtime Networks interested. Graver had earlier pitched the film to that cable television company without success, but through a friend who worked as an interviewer for Showtime, Susan Bullington Katz, I made a written pitch to Matthew Duda, Showtime's executive vice president of acquisitions and planning, that finally brought results. Graver's delicate shuttle diplomacy, conducted over several months, brought the co-owners, Kodar and Boushehri, into agreement for the first time on how the proceeds should be divided. Welles had asked Bogdanovich to finish the film if he died without managing to do so, and Peter agreed to supervise the complex editing and sound work that remained. With all these elements in place, Showtime agreed to put up $3 million to buy and complete the film.

Finally, it seemed a "go" project. At that point, Kodar and Bogdanovich froze me out of the project. Oja pronounced it "ridiculous" that I wanted to be a producer of *The Other Side of the Wind*, even though she had sat next to me, raising no objection, when Schmidlin and I pitched the project on that basis to Sony's Schlesinger before we took it to Showtime. Bogdanovich accused me of being "greedy" for planning to draw a salary of $50,000 over the year and a half Schmidlin and I estimated would be required for postproduction. Peter added that, of course, *he* would have to be paid back the approximately $200,000 of his own money that he said he had put into the production. Not wanting to do anything to disrupt the film's chances for completion, I washed my hands of it after almost thirty years of involvement.

Then everything fell through again with *The Other Side of the Wind.*

Beatrice Welles learned of the deal and caused Showtime to back away from the project. As Tim Carroll reported in London's *Sunday Times Magazine* in 2005 on the "byzantine legal wrangle" surrounding the film, "Kodar wanted to complete the editing of *The Other Side of the Wind;* Beatrice insisted it should remain unseen." According to Graver, Beatrice objected to him, Bogdanovich, Kodar, et al., completing *Other Wind* because she said she didn't want people to "tamper with Daddy's film." In a 2004 article for the *Los Angeles Times*, Beatrice wrote, "For the last 19 years, I have dedicated most of my life to protecting and preserving the work of my father, Orson Welles." That contention rings hollow because of the changes she made in *Othello* and her attempt to prevent Universal from releasing its version of *Touch of Evil* revised according to her father's own wishes. Beatrice's claim to have any control over *Other Wind* seems dubious. Even under the California law giving an heir rights of ownership to a dead celebrity's image, it would be outside Beatrice's reach since her father does not appear in it. The legal disposition of the footage in his estate also seems clear.

Welles's 1982 will left his house at 1717 North Stanley Avenue in Hollywood and its contents to Oja, and his other properties, including his house at 3189 Montecito Drive in Las Vegas, to his wife, Paola. (For tax reasons, Welles was a legal resident of Nevada, where he had a corporation.) Each of his three daughters (Christopher, Rebecca, and Beatrice) was left $10,000. Perhaps because no specific provisions were made in the will about the ownership of his unfinished film and television projects, and because Paola was left his "pictures, paintings, works of art and other personal effects" other than those in the Hollywood house, Welles signed a separate agreement on June 19, 1985, clarifying possible ambiguity about the ownership of the films and TV shows.

The "Confirmation of Ownership Rights" states that Welles and Kodar had no prior written agreement about the projects on which they worked together, but he confirmed that they "have at all times been associating together on various projects pursuant to an oral agreement that Miss Kodar would have any and all available rights of any kind whatsoever in such projects and that Welles would never obtain or receive any interest in and to such rights." Projects specified in the agreement include *The Other Side of the Wind*, *The Dreamers* (and film rights to the two Isak Dinesen stories used as source material), *The Deep* (and film rights to Charles Williams's source novel, *Dead Calm*), *Don Quixote*, *The Orson Welles Show*, *Orson Welles: The One-Man Band*, and *Orson Welles Solo;* written material including *The Big Brass Ring*, *House Party*, and "Crazy Weather" (see chapter 6); and rights to the BBC TV documentary *The Orson Welles Story* and the French documentary *Orson Welles à la Cinémathèque française*. The document adds, "It is the intent of Welles that this Confirmation may be used by Miss Kodar for purposes of documenting the lack of any ownership interest of any kind in the above projects by Welles, including the registration of any copyright or the registration of any story treatment or screenplay with any guild." (Kodar in 1986 copyrighted the *Other Wind* screenplay in her name as an unpublished work.)

In a 2002 article in Britain's *Sunday Telegraph* entitled "Daughter and Lover Fight over Unreleased Orson Welles Film," dealing with the dispute over the ownership of *Other Wind*, Chris Hastings reported that Beatrice "insists that she is responsible for the director's estate" (her mother having died in 1986 after being hit by a car near her home in Las Vegas) and that as such Beatrice claims "she is the rightful owner of the film under United States copyright laws which were introduced to protect the moral rights of the author." Kodar responded that Welles "left me the rights to all of his unseen films in his will" and that Beatrice "knows that and she did not contest the will at the time. I think it is unfair that she is trying to block the film. It is heartbreaking for me. I have worked for years to get this film onto cinema screens. I know in my heart it is what Orson wanted." Beatrice's representative Thomas White, described by Hastings as "an artistic rights enforcement consultant," told the newspaper, "Miss Kodar may think that she has optioned the film to Showtime but the simple fact is that without my client's consent the company cannot go ahead with the release of this film. As yet my client has not given that consent. . . . Oja Kodar has nothing to do with the estate of Orson Welles. I don't accept she is the partner of Orson Welles in any sense of the word. Partnership is a relationship based on equality. How can she be equal to one of the world's greatest film talents?"

But, as if Welles had foreseen the kind of objections Beatrice would later raise to Oja's inheritance, his will states, "If any beneficiary under this Will in any manner directly or indirectly contests or attacks this Will or any of its provisions, including paragraph B of Article FOURTH hereof giving the entire house [in Hollywood] to Olga Palinkas [Kodar's real name], any share or interest in my Estate given to such beneficiary under this Will is revoked and shall be disposed of in the same manner provided herein as if such beneficiary had predeceased me leaving no living lawful descendants." A court would probably have to decide whether the "Confirmation of Ownership Rights" should be considered part of Welles's will and whether disputing her father's "Confirmation" document could subject Beatrice to a revocation of her inheritance.

Nothing could have been more frustrating for those of us who had worked on *The Other Side of the Wind* for so many years than to see the Showtime deal collapse because of objections from the director's youngest daughter. But film and television companies often run away when threatened with a legal fight that could bring about unwanted public controversy, particularly one involving a filmmaker's heir. Nevertheless, Carroll's 2005 article in the *Sunday Times Magazine* offered some hope that *The Other Side of the Wind* might yet see completion: "According to Bogdanovich, Beatrice is no longer blocking the film's release, and the myriad people who have spent nearly 30 years quibbling over fees and shares of profit are also on the verge of reconciliation: 'The cable company [Showtime] is talking to everybody involved.'" However, that verge had still not been crossed by mid-2006; like so much else about the film's history, such optimism could prove chimerical. After thirty-six years, I have learned to be skeptical and resigned about the fate of *The Other Side of the Wind.* With her legal challenges to companies attempting to complete and release her father's unfinished work, Beatrice became the nemesis of his afterlife, the new William Randolph Hearst. What a tragic irony, with echoes of *King Lear*, that his own daughter would wind up being, in effect, his greatest enemy.

Certainly one can sympathize with the fact that being an heir to Orson Welles ensures frustratingly little financial reward. But one has to speculate whether some subconscious animosity toward her father is at work with Beatrice as well. "I remember childhood as being this big adventure," Beatrice has recalled, "and I was absolutely spoiled with love and attention. But Daddy was not an easy person to live with." His public displays of temper made her want to "crawl under the table," and she complained that he responded in a "very selfish" fashion when she left home in 1978 to work for an Arizona radio station, telling her, "You're not going to get any financial help from me. But if you ever get into trouble, you can always come back home."

Beatrice's conflicts about her father may stem in large part from his relationship with Oja, who evidently was bitterly resented by Paola. According to Beatrice, her parents "sort of separated toward the end because he had a girlfriend. My mother found out about it, and he denied it. She told him he could come back home as soon as he stopped lying to her. He didn't come home during that last year of his life, but he and my mother talked on the phone every day."

Beatrice has argued that Kodar has a bad track record of presenting versions of Welles's unfinished work in *Don Quixote* and *One-Man Band.* While there's some validity in the charge as it applies to the botch Kodar enabled Jesús Franco to make of *Don Quixote*, the fact remains that Oja was left the rights to Welles's unfinished films and that she intends to complete *Other Wind* with such experienced filmmakers as Bogdanovich and Frank Marshall, both of whom Welles trusted to work on the film while it was in production. Welles's two older daughters, Christopher Welles Feder and Rebecca Welles Manning (who died in 2004 at the age of sixty, the mother of Welles's only grandchild, Marc Welles), never raised obstacles to their father's legacy being shared with the public. Rebecca, for example, sold the illustrated manuscript of a small book about a festival in St.-Tropez that he had crafted as a present for her in 1956, *Les Bravades*, for $30,000, enabling it to be published forty years later. Christopher broke her long public silence about her father in 2005 at the Locarno Welles conference to criticize Beatrice, saying she was "appalled" that her sister was interfering with the release of their father's work: "I believe my father's work should be shown at every opportunity, even his unfinished work. Everything should be shown because everything is valuable."

Graver jokingly suggested that *Other Wind* be released without a directing credit, just saying "Directed by a Guy Whose Daughter Doesn't Want His Name On It." Graver thinks the real reason Beatrice has blocked the film is that "Beatrice hates me and Oja." I told him I could understand her enmity toward her father's mistress, but why, I asked Graver, would she hate *him*, the man whose loyalty and dedication made Welles's later work possible? He replied simply, "Because Oja and I were his family."

❖ ❖ ❖

When I finally saw the two-hour rough assemblage of *Other Wind* in 1998, I found that while the languid visual style of the film-within-the-film interludes would give the audience ample time to recover from the frenetic pacing of the party scenes, a more serious obstacle to the film's playability is the largely undramatic nature of much of the material putatively shot by Hannaford.

Little or nothing happens in these sequences except for Oja mysteriously wandering seminude around picturesque locales and Bob Random doggedly roaring his motorcycle through expressionistically lit landscapes. The footage is beautifully shot, and there is some stunning photographic magic, such as a sequence filmed among the skyscrapers of Century City with the two characters' images vanishing into ten mirrors arranged invisibly among the stone steps and glass columns of the coldly geometrical modern office buildings. "Orson did all the opticals on camera," Graver notes. "No trick photography. The light had to be right. We did a shot of Random running across a bridge with a piece of glass reflecting Century City behind him so it looked like an overlap of the city. I would never have thought of that stuff, but he did." However, in the rough cut assembled by Graver to show to potential investors, the film-within-the-film sequences not only interrupt the narrative but also go on at such length that they lose their satirical point, becoming exasperating examples of what Welles was trying to spoof.

I didn't realize for many years that most of *Other Wind*'s problems can be traced back (as problems with films usually can) to its screenplay. I should have trusted my first reaction to the script Welles distributed in 1971, when shooting began in earnest. The basic storyline was rich with multilayered allusiveness and a quasi-Dickensian array of bizarre yet lifelike characters and incidents. Many scenes were invested with knowing and pointed satire of Hollywood's absurdities, and there were dramatic epiphanies that promised to be powerfully moving. But I found the dialogue too arch, elliptical, and wisecracky. Being able to work with Welles in rewriting my own scenes helped allay my concerns. Still, the presentation of characters, even the major ones, was on the shallow side. The structure sometimes seemed arbitrary, chaotic, or simply un-thought-through, with many story issues and transitions left to be resolved in the editing process.

I convinced myself that Welles, in shooting and postproduction, would manage to make this offbeat mélange of ideas and imagery come together as a satisfying whole. I reacted much the way the loyal Hannaford retainer Billy Boyle does while screening the baffling film-within-the-film footage for the studio executive Max David. When Max asks, "Jake is just making it up as he goes along, isn't he?" Billy says with an anxious shrug, "He's done it before." One always has to be careful not to judge any Welles film project by its script. While this one was especially malleable, with constant revisions and improvising encouraged by the loose format, the scripts of such Welles classics as *Kane* and *Ambersons* similarly give little indication of the films' visual style or the complex texture of their soundtracks. Nevertheless, the stories and characters are clearly laid out in those scripts in a three-dimensional way that the *Other Wind* script lacks. Perhaps the script was handicapped by the hybrid nature of the project, combining as it does elements of Welles's *Sacred Beasts* concept with Kodar's satirical embellishments on the story's masculine sexual intrigue and her rather vague concepts for Hannaford's comeback film.

The uneven quality of the script buttresses arguments advanced by various writers that Welles needed a professional screenwriting collaborator such as Herman Mankiewicz to do his best work, or a literary "collaborator" like Shakespeare, Booth Tarkington, or Isak Dinesen. This doesn't mean that Kael was right to claim that Mankiewicz was the primary creative force on *Kane* or that Welles's stature is seriously diminished if it's admitted he was a better director than writer. Kenneth Tynan once described him, with considerable accuracy, as "a superb bravura director, a fair bravura actor, and a limited bravura writer; but an incomparable bravura personality."

The script problems of *Other Wind* finally became clear to me when I wrote my memoranda for prospective backers in 1998, outlining my ideas on how the film should be completed in Welles's absence. Though not insuperable, these problems would require some creative solutions to transform the footage in ways Welles might or might not have worked out himself. Making such arguments put me in the ironic position of trying to reedit and "improve" his work, a job I didn't relish but felt was necessary if the film were ever to be seen in its entirety outside of film archives. And I realized that the final result probably would still show some serious inherent flaws that would prevent the film from reaching the artistic heights of Welles's greatest work. Bogdanovich's declaration in 1974 that "I think this is Orson's most exciting film since *Citizen Kane*" seems too hopeful in retrospect.

In my September 10, 1998, memo to Showtime's Matthew Duda, I offered my tentative suggestions on how to deal with the problems posed by the film-within-the-film and with other challenges involved in the material:

> What remains to be done with the film is expressed by my favorite quote about the editing process, Michelangelo's explanation of how he went about making a statue: "I take a block of marble and cut away everything that isn't the statue." . . . What is now required is not undue reverence or trepidation in finishing the chiseling process, but taking the imaginative leap of finish-

ing it in a way Welles would have approved. I am certain that if Orson were here to finish the postproduction himself, he would approach the material with a vigorous hand and a fresh perspective, reshaping it wherever needed, discarding whatever "isn't the statue," and adding further dimensions in the editing, sound, and music. . . .

The film-within-the-film presents the most complex creative questions involved in completing *The Other Side of the Wind*. . . . In talking with Orson about his narrative strategy, I knew that in one sense he regarded the film-within-the-film as an elaborate joke. . . . But it is also clear from the rough cut that Welles was attempting something radically new with his intercutting of the film-within-the-film sequences and the central narrative about Hannaford's attempt to make a comeback in Hollywood. He intended his dual narrative structure to reveal simultaneously Hannaford's inner life (via his unfinished film) along with his public persona (the party sequences). Much that we learn about Hannaford's sexual obsessions, for instance, is shown by means of his film footage, which serves as a kind of Rorschach blot of his disintegrating psyche. If Hannaford's footage seems incoherent, that is not only because Welles is spoofing artsy filmmaking, but also because he is giving us visual evidence of the breakdown of Hannaford's artistic personality . . . a visual metaphor not only for his dissolution but also for the collapse of the Hollywood studio system.

. . . The danger in letting this footage run too long (as it does in this assembly) is twofold: (1) It runs the risk of disrupting, rather than serving as an ironic counterpoint to, the narrative of Hannaford's birthday party and his dramatic/comedic interactions with colleagues, cronies, adulators, and skeptics; and (2) letting the sequences from Hannaford's film play too long risks turning *The Other Side of the Wind* itself into an arty, pretentious film, rather than a satire of such a film. As much as Welles enjoyed shooting and editing these scenes, and as beautiful as Gary's lighting is, I am convinced that Orson would not have let these scenes play as long as they do in the rough cut. . . .

Ironically, to be true to Welles's vision we will have to take many liberties with the material he has left us, as he himself would do. This was not done with the *Four Men and a Raft* segment in the restoration of *It's All True*, which allowed Welles's beautiful shots to play longer than he would have played them. "What separates the men from the boys among directors," Welles once said, "is the ability to throw out your most beautiful shots." Or, I would add, to cut them to the bone, to astonish the audience not by dwelling on them but almost by tossing them off, as we can see him doing in *Othello*, with shots of breathtaking beauty that run only three or four seconds on the screen.

When I pointed out these problems with the film-within-the-film to Oja Kodar in 1999, she bristled, insisting that the sequences had to be allowed to run in their entirety. I argued that if that were the case, *Other Wind* would risk losing the audience's attention, which would be fatal to its chances of being shown in theaters. Oja held firm, and it eventually became clear why: these sequences were as much her work as Welles's. Indeed, Welles sometimes let Oja direct parts of that material herself, including a bizarre sequence of a huge black phallic object toppling over in the wind as she parades haughtily past it in the foreground, flaunting her ripe figure as if to magically demonstrate her witchlike sexual powers. Most of the sets for the film-within-the-film were miniatures designed by Polly Platt and shot by Graver in forced perspective, with the lens stopped down. "That's one reason he chose Arizona," the cameraman explains, "it was always hot and bright, so everything would be in focus from close-up to infinity with a wide-angle lens."

Oja's shocked expression when I suggested cutting the film-within-the-film down to brief fragments made me realize that she seemed to actually take the "Hannaford" material seriously as some kind of poetic meditation on sexuality, while Welles "was making fun of that style of film," Graver confirms. "He was anti that kind of filmmaking. He liked fast-paced stories, rich characters, lots of dialogue." Unfortunately, we see here in stark form the dangers involved in a filmmaker allowing his inamorata to run naked (literally) through his work. When I discussed the problem with Bogdanovich, he said he always believed Welles intended the film-within-the-film to be seen only in brief snippets, sometimes full-screen but more often on movie or TV screens in the background of the party, reflected on glass doors, and so forth. Welles, he was sure, never intended the footage to stop the narrative dead cold on a regular basis, as it does in the rough cut.

However, Welles told *Los Angeles Times* film critic Charles Champlin in a 1973 interview that Hannaford's footage would comprise "about 50% of the whole movie." And Graver confirms that Welles intended to show the film-within-the-film in sequences of about ten minutes each interspersed throughout the framing story, advancing the development of Hannaford's sketchy cinematic narrative in parallel with the drama of the old director trying to raise money to complete his picture. But would Welles have stuck to that plan so schematically in postproduction? Jonathan Rosenbaum told me he tended to agree with Kodar about letting the sequences run at length, and argued that Welles once again is playing with the conventions of screen narrative in a way that provocatively challenges the audience's conventional expectations. Welles's juxtaposition of Hannaford's macho, reactionary personality with directorial work more characteristic of a European postmodern aesthete is, in Rosenbaum's view, a deliberate incongruity. This rhetorical clash of styles, Rosenbaum believes, expresses Welles's radical assertion of the unsolvable mysteries of human personality, a thematic pattern established at the beginning of his filmmaking career by the reporter's declaration in *Citizen Kane*, "I don't think any word can explain a man's life."

Given the crucial importance Welles placed on the editing stage of filmmaking, I believe that the conundrum of how to deal with the film-within-the-film in *Other Wind* remains an open question. Welles probably figured on making sense of it all in the editing room. "I don't know of any more fun than making a movie, and the most fun of all comes in the cutting room when the shooting is over," he told Bogdanovich. Welles declared on another occasion, "In the editing room, there is always a better way."* His belief that a film only fully comes to life in postproduction helps explain why it's been so hard for other people to put together parts of *The Other Side of the Wind*. A suspicion lingers: could Welles deliberately have made the footage next to impossible for anyone else to edit and deliberately chosen not to record the opening narration, thus ensuring his continued involvement on the project? It wouldn't have been the first time a director tried such a stratagem; John Ford made a practice of "cutting in the camera," shooting only the footage needed to make the scene play and not giving his editors or producers any options except to cut off the slates.

It's been suggested, as an alternative to fully editing *Other Wind*, that the forty-two minutes of scenes edited by Welles be used as the centerpieces for a documentary about the film. Welles himself considered that as a fallback plan. After making his 1978 documentary *Filming "Othello,"* he had the intriguing idea of transforming the *Other Wind* footage into what would later be called a mockumentary. Welles envisioned a sort of serious parody of the "making-of" genre. "If I ever get it again, I'm going to do it as an entirely different film," he explained to Bill Krohn in 1982. "I'm going to stand outside of it and talk about it, as myself. . . . [and turn it into] a movie within a movie within a movie. It's one of those endless plots. Not so much the making of it, the unmaking of it. . . . [T]he only way to make sense of it now, because too many of the actors are dead, is for me to be showing it to something like the UCLA audience and talking about

---

* He said this to Welles scholar Ciro Giorgini, who, with Gianfranco Giagni, directed the insightful 1993 documentary *Rosabella: La storia italiana di Orson Welles (Rosebud: The Italian Story of Orson Welles).*

it." Graver adds that Welles wanted to foreground the process of incompletion by starting and ending *Other Wind* with shots of cans of unfinished film piled up in storage, like the detritus of a famous man's life piled willy-nilly in the great hall of Xanadu during the final scene of *Kane*.

But without Welles around, it would be harder to do the kind of mockumentary he envisioned. So I argued for finishing *Other Wind* in the closest possible approximation of Welles's original plan, as did Graver and Kodar. Virtually all of it was shot, and Graver, Bogdanovich, and Kodar know what Welles wanted from every scene. I suggested that unedited rushes and outtakes be presented as extras on the DVD edition, so that people could see what we had to work with. There was even talk of releasing Graver's two-hour rough cut, including the work prints of the scenes edited by Welles, as a supplement on the DVD. Bogdanovich seemed somewhat ambivalent about how to proceed but was willing to try putting it all together as a theatrical feature in the Wellesian style. Schmidlin pushed the documentary route, partly because it would have caused fewer legal and aesthetic problems. After the Showtime deal collapsed, Beatrice Welles made it known that she might not object to a documentary but did not want other hands to edit the footage her father left unedited.

Dominique Antoine has also taken that position, declaring in a 1998 interview that she wants the film "to come out just as it is. In other words, to present it as an unfinished work by Orson Welles. But that has been questioned by all the vultures who would like to make a finished film out of it. But finished by whom? Who can you substitute for Orson Welles? In the beginning, I hoped to see it come out in my lifetime, with this one absurd obsession that its first public screening would take place at the Paris Opera House. Now, I don't think that will ever happen." Antoine claims that Welles once showed her a work print of the film running two hours and forty minutes, telling her he planned to cut it by twenty minutes. It is that version she wishes could be released, "just spruced up and with music." But Kodar and Graver insist that such a work print never existed. This remains a *Rashomon*-like point of dispute, typical of the many perplexing questions Welles bequeathed us as part of his artistic legacy. At the 2005 Welles conference in Locarno, Antoine declared, "It's a pure scandal that the picture will never be finished. . . . I think it's obscene to hide this masterpiece from the public."

Like Graver and Kodar, I remain convinced that Welles would have wanted his collaborators to do their best to finish *Other Wind* and present it to the public even as an imperfect approximation of his vision, rather than letting most of what could stand as his artistic testament remain disassembled in cans moldering in a film laboratory. As I write the present chapter in the improbable, exasperating saga of *The Other Side of the Wind*, these and other issues remain unresolved and perhaps intractable, thirty-six years after we began shooting.

A portrait of the artist as an old man: Welles in the 1980s. *(Gary Graver)*

Chapter Six

"NO WINE BEFORE ITS TIME"

I think, at the end of the day, Orson Welles just plain loved making movies. He didn't care who paid for it, how it happened, or even if he had a crew. He just wanted to get up every day and make movies. And in the last years of his life, that's exactly what he did.

—Peter Jason, cast and crew member of *The Other Side of the Wind*

Welles would became impatient in later years when people tried to take him on what he called a "stroll down memory lane," with its implication that his past was far more glorious than his present. When the respectful young director Rob Reiner tried to quiz him about *Citizen Kane* on *The Merv Griffin Show*, Welles brusquely changed the subject. Even when Gary Graver would ask how he did certain shots in *Kane*, Welles resisted, changing the subject to their current project: "We're doing *this one* now." So when the AFI began planning the "Working with Welles" seminar in 1978, I suggested we end our series of panel discussions and screenings with a program on Welles's future. When Welles heard about the program, he joked, "What a witches' sabbath that will be!"

But he kept creating literally right up to the end of his life, defying the prophecy Tanya makes to Hank Quinlan in *Touch of Evil*, "Your future is all used up." When Welles died of a heart attack in the upstairs bedroom of his Hollywood home in October 1985, he had been working into the early-morning hours on notes for a new project he was planning to start shooting with Graver later that morning at UCLA. Welles had been invited to speak to a film class and with characteristic ingenuity agreed to do so if given a soundstage and a student crew for a couple of days' shooting on a one-man film of *Julius Caesar*, as well as some more magic tricks for his longtime work in progress *Orson Welles' Magic Show*.

Welles turned out an astonishing amount of film and video material in the nine and a half years that followed the last shooting on *The Other Side of the Wind.* "Orson always liked to have irons in the fire, four or five things going on at once," recalls Graver. Welles's problems raising funds and completing projects caused him terrible frustration, never more so than in his final months of life. Nevertheless, his last years saw a continually new Welles, indefatigably industrious and fecund with imagination. The seemingly willful ignorance of much of the press toward his work, and his own secretiveness, meant that he operated largely invisibly, and what was reported about his creative activities tended to be distorted.

"Whenever I get interested in a movie I'm going to make, I often do a scene or two of it, which gives rise to the legend of my not finishing movies," Welles told Bill Krohn in 1982. "What I'm really doing is trying to find out how I want to make the movie. You know, I should call them tests or something" (as he did with the first scenes shot for *Kane* and *Other Wind).* When pressed for details by Krohn about unfinished projects, Welles pointed out,

> I've wasted an awful lot of my life trying to finish them, rather than just letting them go, which is what I should have done, and to hell with everybody. I deeply regret this steadfast and stubborn loyalty that I've expended on them, now that I look back on it. If people see it the other way, I can understand it, because on the face of it there are these unfinished films, you know. But, God, what I've been through trying to get 'em done. What I've never done was to leave a film because I was tired of it or angry at somebody or fed up. . . . I've only left a film when there wasn't any way to shoot it, no money.

❖ ❖ ❖

At the beginning of his 1974 film *F for Fake,* Welles tells the audience, "For my next experiment, ladies and gentleman, I would appreciate the loan of any small personal object from your pocket." The self-reflexive nature of that allusion to his habitually precarious financial state is obvious in his wry expression. Welles's experimentation in his later years with a grand disregard for commercial prospects can be seen as frustrating and foolish, or brave and adventurous, or, indeed, all of these at once. Even though, as Graver put it, "Orson really wanted to be a Hollywood player," he had more or less resigned himself to working on the margins of the industry, making his bounteous art from the slenderest of means. Graver says Welles told him

> that being Orson Welles was pretty tough, because each time out he was

> expected to make an Orson Welles movie. And he told me, "Somebody always has to be ahead of everybody else. I have to be steps ahead of everybody. I have to be more inventive and do things that nobody else has done."
>
> Orson was not a big fan of making movies inexpensively, but he was a big fan of being independent. One morning he said, "We're two talented fellows in Hollywood and we're working in the suburbs of the cinema." He had to find ways to be creative, because he just didn't have the money. He was one of the first people to use car mounts [for moving-camera shots], in *Touch of Evil.* And on *F for Fake* we were doing cuts that were less than a foot long! There weren't even edge numbers for the negative cutters to work from. Keep in mind that Welles did this ten years before MTV and the whole rapid-cutting thing.

Welles was not lacking for money in his later years. In fact, says Graver, "Orson was making a lot of money, he had two houses, one in Nevada and Oja's house in Hollywood. He said he was proud that for the first time in his life he had Visa and MasterCards." Welles once told actress Geraldine Fitzgerald, "Don't worry about money on your way up. No one makes money on their way up. All the money is made coming down." And a few months before his death, he reflected, "I suppose I'm paying for years of nobody offering me a job by having many too many things to do in the time that's left."

For three years, Welles's contract for Paul Masson wine commercials alone earned him $500,000 a year plus residuals. That, notes Graver, "gave him a lot of independence." But Welles sometimes had a prickly relationship with the winery. "He would argue with the people. He'd get a text and look at me and say, 'They're not gonna have me say this, that this wine is finer than a Stradivarius!' So he didn't." Paul Masson eventually dropped him for mischievously disparaging their product on a TV talk show, saying he no longer drank wine because he was dieting. A new light wine was being pushed by Paul Masson, so the company turned to John Gielgud, who had the requisite lean and hungry look.

Besides his many national and foreign commercials—for Eastern Airlines, Texaco, Post's Shredded Wheat, Vivitar cameras, Perrier, Jim Beam, Pedro Domecq sherry, and Japan's Nikka whiskey (one of the latter commercials, directed by Welles, is seen in the 1995 German documentary *Orson Welles: The One-Man Band)*—Welles even made TV and radio commercials for American regional markets. From commercials and voice-overs, Welles earned thousands of dollars for a few hours' work reading lines in a studio or at home, enabling him to spend more of his remaining days on his own projects. In the final weeks of his life, he recorded condensed versions of short stories, novels, and other literary works on audiotape for the Japanese market, a job he treated with his usual care and seriousness.*

Even in making commercials, Kodar pointed out, Welles "was not cynical—he rewrote his text, tried to do his best." Welles's sideline in commercials, which he had been doing since the 1930s, did not become an issue until late in his career, when his detractors seized on it as an excuse to gloat over his supposed "downfall." If the Paul Masson commercials are exhibit A for the anti-Welles crowd, exhibit B is a bootleg audio recording that has been circulating for years, first hand to hand and latterly on the Internet, of Welles rehearsing a peas commercial for British television. Undeniably hilarious, the audiotape has been cited as evidence of the depths to which Welles supposedly sank and as proof of his "difficult" nature. No doubt that's partly true, but his arguing with the producers over the tongue-twisting, absurdly written copy can also be read as evidence of his refusal to be pushed beyond certain limits of commercial shilling.

> *Welles* [reading copy]: "We know a remote farm in Lincolnshire where Mrs. Buckley lives. Every July, peas grow there." Do you *really* mean that?
>
> *Producer:* Uh, yeah. . . .
>
> *Welles:* Don't you think you really want to say "July" over [images of] snow? Isn't that the fun of it? . . . I think it's so nice that you see a snow-covered field and say, "Every July, peas grow there." . . .
>
> *Producer:* Can you emphasize a bit "in"—"*in* July"?
>
> *Welles:* Why? That doesn't make any sense. Sorry. There's no *known* way of saying an English sentence in which you begin a sentence with "in" and emphasize it. Get me a jury and show me how you can say "in July," and I'll go down on you. That's just idiotic, if you'll forgive me saying so. That's just stupid. . . . Impossible. *Meaningless.* He isn't thinking. . . . There's too much

* Welles adapted the works himself, drawing from such favorite authors as Isak Dinesen ("The Old Chevalier" and "The Heroine"), Oscar Wilde ("The Happy Prince"), Joseph Conrad ("The Secret Sharer"), and Ernest Hemingway ("Ten Indians" and "In Another Country"). In August and September 1970, shortly after the start of shooting on *Other Wind*, Welles and Graver made six half-hour films for Sears, Roebuck, intended for release on videocassette, of "The Happy Prince," "The Golden Honeymoon," and other stories and speeches.

directing around here. [Reading copy for another spot]: "We know a certain fjörd in Norway near where the cod gather in great shoals. There, Yonster Stengelind . . ." *Shit.*

Producer: A fraction more on that "shoals" thing, 'cause you rolled it around very nicely.

Welles: Yeah, roll it 'round. And I have no more time. You don't know what I'm up against. Because it's full of things that are only correct because they're grammatical, but they're tough on the ear. You see, this is a very *wearying* one; it's unpleasant to read. Unrewarding. . . . [Reading another spot] Here, under protest, is "Beef Burgers": "We know a little place in the American Far West where Charlie Briggs chops up the finest prairie-fed beef and tastes . . ." This is a lot of *shit,* you know that? You want one more? More on what—"beef"?

Producer: You missed the first "beef," actually, completely.

Welles: What do you mean, missed it?

Producer: You were emphasizing "prairie-fed."

Welles: But you can't emphasize "beef." That's like his wanting me to emphasize "in" before "July." Come on, fellas, you're losing your heads! I wouldn't direct any living actor like this in Shakespeare, the way you do this. It's *impossible.*

Producer: Orson, you did six [of these spots] last year, and [they were] by far and away the best . . .

Welles: The right reading for this is the one I'm giving it. I've spent *twenty times* more for you people than [for] any other commercial I've ever made. You are such *pests.* Now what is it you want? In your *depths* of your ignorance, what is it you want? Whatever it is you want, I can't deliver, because I just don't see it.

Producer: That was absolutely fine. It really was.

Welles: No *money* is worth what you . . . [He walks out of the studio.]

❖ ❖ ❖

Welles also continued to subsidize his filmmaking by acting in other people's movies. "Nobody in the world has acted in worse films than I," he admitted. "They hire me when they have a really bad movie and they want a cameo that will give it a little class." Indeed, the motley list of Welles's later acting roles includes mostly trifles, such as spoofing the film and TV mogul Lord Lew Grade as "Lew Lord" in *The Muppet Movie* or playing an old hack magician who teaches his craft to Tom Smothers in Brian De Palma's *Get to Know Your Rabbit.* Perhaps the most ignominious moment of Welles's screen-acting career—and that's saying a lot—comes when he and Smothers roll around the floor inside a gold-colored bag. It's a truly embarrassing experience to hear his voice coming out of that bag, even if, as it seems, he may not have been physically present in it. The only role Welles badly wanted in later years was one he couldn't get: Don Corleone in *The Godfather.* Director Francis Ford Coppola sensibly decided that he couldn't see Welles as the aging Mafia boss and gave the part to Marlon Brando, whose offbeat casting helped make the movie a classic. "I would have sold my soul to have been in *The Godfather,*" Welles lamented.

Welles amiably provided narration for a wide range of films, including Robert Amram's tongue-in-cheek documentary based on Hal Lindsey's absurd best-selling book of apocalyptic prophecy, *The Late Great Planet Earth* (I wrote the film's equally facetious press kit); another ludicrous turn as the portentous host of a pseudodocumentary on Nostradamus, *The Man Who Saw Tomorrow;* and, at the other end of the scale, the story of Yiddish filmmaking in the delightful *Almonds and Raisins.* Welles sometimes balked at the voicing demands for movies as well as for commercials. His line readings as Long John Silver in the 1972 Spanish film *Treasure Island* are "mumbled through his beard in a strange pseudo-Cockney accent that sounds like Falstaff with a terrible hangover" (as I wrote in my 1977 book on Welles's acting career); that's because, as I subsequently discovered, he dubbed the entire part in a Rome studio one night while guzzling from a bottle of white wine. Embarrassed, Welles claimed in 1979 that the role had been dubbed by another actor: "He may be a good actor, but it's certain that as Long John Silver he gives a definitively lousy performance." Welles cowrote that dreadful movie but took credit under the W. C. Fields–like pseudonym of O. W. Jeeves. He supposedly was to have directed *Treasure Island* as part of the deal to finance *Chimes at Midnight*, but though he shot shipboard scenes for a couple of days in 1965, he never seriously intended to remain as director, and his footage was not used in the film.

Shortly before his death, Welles recorded perhaps his most bizarre screen role, as the voice of the Planet Unicron in a Japanese animated film, *The Transformers.* It was difficult to understand why he was hired, since his voice was so distorted in postproduction that the thunderously growling, rampaging planet can hardly be identified as Orson Welles. Barbara Leaming relates that Welles spoke of this job in a "voice dripping with contempt": "I played the voice of a toy. Some terrible robot toys from Japan that change from one thing to another . . . all bad outer-space stuff. I play a planet. I menace somebody called Something-or-other. Then I'm destroyed. . . . I tear myself apart on the screen." But if there seemed no low to which Welles would not sink as a movie star for rent, that was not quite the case, for he turned down the role he was offered in *Caligula* and also rejected, Graver recalls, "a Pasolini film where he had to pee on a kid, or a kid peed on him. I think it was *Salò*."*

Nevertheless, some of Welles's later roles contain more sophisticated glosses on his own screen image. The French director Claude Chabrol, like Bogdanovich a critic before turning filmmaker, cast Welles in a fascinatingly bizarre homage, *La décade prodigieuse (Ten Days' Wonder)* (1971). Chabrol was as steeped in Welles's work as he was in Alfred Hitchcock's, and he designed the film as both a compendium of the Welles oeuvre and a commentary on it. Ostensibly a mystery story adapted from an Ellery Queen novel, *Ten Days' Wonder* casts Welles as Theo Van Horn, a wealthy man who wills himself out of the common rut of the modern world, living a perfectly artificial and anachronistic 1920s lifestyle. From *The Trial*, Chabrol drew Anthony Perkins to play Van Horn's drug-addicted son; from *Kane*, he took the Xanadu-like mansion with its statues and baroque bric-à-brac; from *Othello*, the jealousy toward a beautiful young wife, played by Marlène Jobert; from *Arkadin*, the evasive mythmaking; and from *The Immortal Story*, the final decrepitude and dissolution.

As the most generous homage of all, Chabrol let Welles wear the most outrageously phony nose of his entire career, a ghastly gray-green creation that changes color from shot to shot. One of the film's detractors said the only suspense was in waiting to see if Welles's nose would fall off on camera. Admitting that the nose was rather weird, Chabrol told me that there wasn't much he could do about it: "I asked Orson to change the nose one day, because it was too green, and he said, 'My dear Claude, I am a changing character—at the end of the film my whole face will be green.' What can you say?"

---

* The controversial *Salò o le 120 Giornate di Sodoma (Salo, or The 120 Days of Sodom)*, 1975. Rosenbaum, however, reports that Welles turned down the role of a German pig in Pasolini's 1969 film *Porcile (Pigsty)*. Welles plays the decadent director making a Bible movie in Pasolini's 1962 segment of *RoGoPag, La Ricotta (Cream Cheese)*, which brought Pasolini a four-month suspended prison sentence for blasphemy.

❖ ❖ ❖

The two most important things for him, Welles said, were "a good pair of shoes and a good typewriter." In *One-Man Band*, Oja Kodar adds that he "had two more things—one is this 16mm editing table that went all over the world with us, and something more precious than that, at least for me, is this suitcase. Often people took Orson's cigar as his trademark, but to me it was this [large, brown, battered] suitcase. It contained, as he used to say, the tools of his profession. During these years we were on the road most of the time, and Orson wanted to be able to shoot at any moment, in any place. We traveled for months with very unusual objects which he used to tie up different scenes, different locations, projects. Seeing our luggage, people must have thought that we were completely crazy. . . . He was always doing different projects at the same time. Occasionally I would leave him for a day or two, and when [I came] back, he would present me with something new."

Welles's nearly total freedom from commercial strictures allowed him more flexibility, in one sense, than he had ever enjoyed, but it also brought more frustrations and false starts. Even with his bohemian approach, he was often stymied by the harsh realities of the cumbersome and expensive "paintbox" he was using, as he described the film medium. This real-life catch-22 was, as Welles told the audience at his AFI Life Achievement Award tribute while quoting Dr. Samuel Johnson, his own particular "contrariety," the lonely path he chose to follow.

"To show people that Orson was working the last twenty years of his life," Kodar authorized *One-Man Band*, the feature-length documentary she and Vassili Silovic directed about Welles's uncompleted films. The title comes from Welles's comment to Kodar, "I myself have always been a one-man band." She adds, "He was planning to do his autobiographical film, and this was going to be its title." (For a while the title was also used for the unfinished TV special that started filming as *Orson's Bag.*) *One-Man Band* includes scenes at their home in Orvilliers, France, outside Paris, describing it as "a mini film studio where he could work on his projects in peace." The film draws liberally from the footage Welles left with Kodar in storage in Los Angeles. Anyone who still tries to claim that Welles was inactive in his last two decades would have to explain away this mountain of film, now housed in Munich.*

* Some of Welles's memorabilia were destroyed in the fire at his Madrid home in 1970. But a fine collection of his papers, stills, recordings, and other materials

Kodar says in *One-Man Band* that when people

> see this material, you will see what a youth he had in him, and what an energy! And what fun he had. You know, all these things that he was trying to do and couldn't do didn't turn him into a bitter old man. . . . He came back to Hollywood with a lot of energy, new ideas, projects. He didn't dislike being in Hollywood again, far from it. . . . He kept saying, "Sour grapes is not my dish." . . . What I want to show is that he was an unbeatable man, that he had an enormous courage, that nothing was going to stop him [from] making movies. Sometimes in my heart I hoped that he *would* stop making movies, because just to look for money, it takes half of your life. And that's what happened.

While Welles carried too much personal, professional, and political baggage to be considered "bankable" in the Hollywood of the 1970s and 1980s, younger American filmmakers were given the freedom he should have had to continue breaking taboos of both style and theme. Coppola showed the most Wellesian boldness with his *Godfather* films and *Apocalypse Now*, loosely based on Conrad's *Heart of Darkness*, which Welles had wanted to film as his first Hollywood project; even the collapse of the bearded young Coppola's Zoetrope Studios carried Wellesian overtones, duly noted in the press. As Coppola and other young filmmakers commanded ever more extravagant budgets, Welles went to the opposite extreme. His isolation from mainstream Hollywood, from both necessity and desire, and his increasing physical infirmity, which often caused him to use a wheelchair, gradually made his filmmaking more concentrated in physical scope, more solipsistic, often with a cast of one (himself) performing all the parts. He described himself as "the cheapest movie star I know," so it was natural for him to create projects that did not require much more than his own brain and body, a free location or a rudimentary set, and Graver's endlessly resourceful lighting. Indeed, Welles toyed with the title *Orson Welles Solo* for a loosely structured documentary series

---

dealing with the Mercury stage, radio, and film productions from 1936 through 1948 is open to scholars at the Lilly Library of Indiana University at Bloomington. Without the foresight and dedication of Richard Wilson, the collection would have been lost, like Kane's sled, in unclaimed storage. Wilson paid the storage bills for many years and eventually housed the collection in the garage of his Santa Monica beachfront home. In the 1970s, he sold it to the Lilly for $250,000, splitting the money with Welles, who put most of his share into *Other Wind*. Another cache of Welles papers has been obtained by Welles scholar Catherine Benamou for the University of Michigan.

that would have served as a kind of cinematic notebook. The interview Welles filmed in 1978 with his elderly schoolmaster Roger Hill as a possible part of that series contains a searching discussion of death. Hill's ruminations on what Welles teasingly calls "a subject you've faced with gallant loquacity for over thirty years" recall the final monologue of Major Amberson; Hill bears an uncanny resemblance to Richard Bennett's Major. No one knew what final shape *Orson Welles Solo* would take. Most of his late projects had that malleable, mercurial nature.

Welles wanted to film *Moby-Dick—Rehearsed*, his 1955 flamboyant stage adaptation of Herman Melville's novel, but he abandoned his first attempt that July, dissatisfied with seventy-five minutes of footage he shot in two London theaters with a cast that also included Gordon Jackson, Joan Plowright, and Patrick McGoohan. Welles had hoped to sell the film to the CBS-TV *Omnibus* series, for which he had starred in the live broadcast of *King Lear* two years earlier. The *Moby-Dick—Rehearsed* footage is currently missing.* The uncompleted *Moby-Dick* Welles began filming in Strasbourg, France, while acting in *Ten Days' Wonder* in 1971, and continued shooting at his house in Orvilliers was intended as a one-hour adaptation of his play. The Munich Film Museum has assembled twenty-two minutes of Welles's expressionistically lit 16mm color footage of himself looking diabolical in a Melvillian beard, holding a book as he reads the roles of Ahab, Ishmael, and other characters in stentorian, florid, and sometimes genuinely moving tones.

Rather than shooting at sea as John Huston did in the 1956 *Moby-Dick* in which Welles gives a rousing sermon as Father Mapple, Welles incorporated the sea's reflection rippling and flashing on his face and body before Graver's blue or orange backdrops. "He had me get a two-thousand-foot film can from Chabrol's production company," Graver relates. "He had me buy a mirror and hammer, smash the mirror to pieces, and put the mirror in the film can, then pour water in that. Then he'd read off the cue cards for *Moby-Dick*, and with both hands he'd wash the water back and forth over the broken mirrors, which gave the im-

---

* Jim People, who worked for Britain's Associated Rediffusion TV in 1955 as a film editor and director, recalled that many cans of *Moby-Dick—Rehearsed* footage were delivered to the company at its Television House in Kingsway in the late 1960s with a customs demand for duty. He believed that the cans were returned to customs because the company wouldn't pay the duty. Welles's 1955 British TV series *Around the World with Orson Welles* was made for Associated Rediffusion.

pression of him being at sea." Assembled by the Munich Film Museum for public showing at its Welles conference in that city in October 1999, the footage plays engrossingly as a chamber piece, aflame with the intensity of Welles's readings of a text for which he felt a strong affinity.

Welles gave himself an unexpected, larkish outing as "a low comedian, a baggy-pants comic" in parts of his abortive TV special *Orson's Bag*, filmed in Europe from 1967 through 1971. Welles said he was "almost finished with the picture" when CBS canceled it in 1969 because of his tax problems. But he continued to work on it anyway. Several segments poke broad fun at the British. "Stately Homes" is a fey sketch about mincing, down-at-the-heels aristocrats forced to sell tours of their family estate. "Tailors" is a short, painful routine with two sniggering tailors mocking Welles's weight as they measure him for clothes. In "Four Clubmen," a skit about stuffy old fossils in overstuffed chairs, Welles plays every part, disguised with ingenious variations (unfortunately, the sound is missing for this segment). Welles introduces another virtuoso piece, the "Swinging London" segment, by claiming, "I'm a quiet country boy who hasn't seen a bright light worth mentioning in years." He then appears as a variety of street Londoners, including a mustachioed bobby, a blowsy housewife, a decrepit old flower lady ("Dirty postcards?"), a leering Chinese doorman at a Soho strip club, and a street busker playing his one-man band of drum, tambourines, and harmonica.

Buffoonish in the extreme, those skits agreeably display a playful side of Welles that peeked out only in his more absurd film roles, such as his Porky Pig–like British ferryboat captain, Cecil Hart, in *Ferry to Hong Kong* and his fey London advertising man, Jonathan Lute, in *I'll Never Forget What'sisname.* The Munich Film Museum's 1999 assemblage of comedy material from *Orson's Bag* intercuts Welles's impersonations of street Londoners with linking footage, making the gag play more effectively than in the rapidly condensed montage of characters seen in *One-Man Band,* which comes off as merely bizarre. *Orson's Bag* also contains a "Churchill" skit, filmed largely in silhouette, with Welles delivering some of the British statesman's most famous quips to reporters and photographers; he speaks other Churchill lines in front of large blowups of other public figures who inspired the quips. Kodar appears in silhouette as Bessie Braddock, MP, the woman who chastised Churchill for being drunk, only to be told, "And you, my dear, are ugly—but tomorrow I'll be sober." In another segment partly restored by the museum, "Orson Welles' Vienna," Welles's recollections of *The Third Man* prompt a view of the Prater and a spy spoof involving the "most beautiful woman in Vienna"

Among the major unfinished works by Welles is his condensed version of Shakespeare's tragedy *The Merchant of Venice*, in which he plays Shylock with righteous anger (frame enlargement). Shot in Europe in the late 1960s and partly lost, Welles's *Merchant* was intended as part of his uncompleted television special *Orson's Bag*. *(Orson Welles: The One-Man Band; Medias Res/The Criterion Collection)*

(Senta Berger) and her kidnapper (Mickey Rooney). The director puckishly doubles Vienna with scenes shot in Zagreb and in a Los Angeles studio with Peter Bogdanovich disguised in trench coat and dark glasses as a magician's assistant, helping Welles perform what he disarmingly describes as a "stupid" trick. The segment includes a tour of faux "Viennese" pastry shops, zooming in voyeuristically to close-ups of rich desserts as Welles recites their names with almost pornographic relish, remarking, "When the world was young, I used to run riot in there. How sweet it was!"

Fragments from Welles's abortive film of *The Merchant of Venice* can be seen in partial work-print form in *One-Man Band.* This condensed version of Shakespeare's tragedy was to have been a forty-minute section of *Orson's Bag*. Welles plays Shylock, with Charles Gray as Antonio and Irina Maleva as Jessica. Shooting (in color) was completed around 1970, and the film was scored and mixed, but the finished negative was stolen from Welles's Rome production office, making this one of his most tantalizingly incomplete projects. Almost certainly his *Merchant of Venice* would have ranked among his major films. Hauntingly stylized, the available footage blends Italian and Yugoslavian locations with the kind of creative geography the director had been employing from *Othello* onward; after filming establishing shots in Venice, Welles moved the production to the Dalmatian coast so he could shoot more inexpensively. The ornate architecture and elegantly patterned stone promenades through which Shylock passes contrast starkly with the raw emotions loosed by the play's themes of anti-Semitism and revenge. Welles intercuts documentary footage he and Graver shot of gondolas and costumed Venetian festival participants gliding through the canals. Welles's equally baroque compositions of masked revelers (some of them full-size wooden puppets) serve as visual counterpoint to his somberly attired Shylock, who walks among them as if invisible, or in silent reproof (the scenes look like precursors of Stanley Kubrick's masked orgy in his 1999 valedictory, *Eyes Wide Shut*).

Welles's playing of Shylock is all the more powerful for its understatement, such as when he delivers part of his speech to Antonio from the "pound of flesh" scene with matter-of-fact disgust and indignation: "You call me misbeliever, cut-throat dog / And spit upon my Jewish gaberdine, / And all for use of that which is mine own. / Well then, it now appears you need my help." Responding to the modern debate over whether Shakespeare's play is anti-Semitic, Welles insisted, "It's a marvelous portrait of a Jew. In fact, word for word, it's neither anti-Semitic nor pro-Semitic. . . . I think if it's done absolutely purely, you can do it even after the Holocaust because the cruelty and shallowness of the Christians is such that Shylock does not have to be made *good* for us to see who's *bad*. . . . It's just everybody behaving badly, I think, except Portia." (Welles's condensed version, however, takes the radical step of eliminating Portia from the play, a decision he made after Kodar told him she was not up to playing the role.)

Shylock's "Hath not a Jew eyes?" speech is among the parts missing from the film. But *One-Man Band* and the Munich Film Museum's half-hour compilation *Orson Welles' Shylock* contain footage of Welles, wearing a modern trench coat, delivering that speech against a brilliant sunrise with tears in his eyes. He filmed it in Malaga, Spain, while there to shoot Lilli Palmer's scenes in *Other Wind*. The night before, Welles and Graver stayed up late eating dinner and drinking wine. "I went to bed about 3

A.M.," the cameraman remembers. "At 5 A.M. he called me and said, 'Get up and get over here with the camera and the soundmen—it's going to be a fabulous sunrise.' He could handle the two hours' sleep; I couldn't. And then we went on to Lilli Palmer's after that." Welles said he didn't like the take of Shylock's speech because of his tears, which, according to the cameraman, may have resulted from wind blowing in Welles's face rather than from the emotion he was experiencing. But I wonder. Perhaps Welles was simply embarrassed at this unaccustomed show of raw feeling. He seldom allowed himself such a naked display on-screen; his room-smashing scene in *Kane* and his tearful close-ups as Falstaff in the banishment scene of *Chimes at Midnight* are notable exceptions. Or perhaps Welles preferred the tone of cold fury with which he delivered Shylock's soliloquy on *The Dean Martin Show* in 1967, a majestic single-take performance also included in *Orson Welles' Shylock;* that interpretation would be consistent with his rewriting of Kafka to make *The Trial*'s post-Holocaust version of Joseph K. defiant at the end rather than acquiescent in his own execution.

Buster Keaton is hailed for his surreal brilliance for playing all the parts in the vaudeville segment of his 1921 tour-de-force short *The Playhouse.* But the sight of Welles holding up a clapper board in front of his own face in his 1971 *Moby-Dick* fragments is a litmus test for one's attitude toward the filmmaker's later career. Depending on one's point of view, it can be seen as sad or valiant that Welles was reduced to the ultimate solipsism of becoming a one-man film, playing all the roles as he does in *Moby-Dick* and parts of *Orson's Bag* and was planning to do in his *Julius Caesar.*

❖ ❖ ❖

Henry Jaglom suggested that Welles set up a pre-positioned video camera in his house in Hollywood to record himself whenever he felt the urge to reminisce. Ultimately, the footage would have been released under Welles's umbrella title *Orson Welles Solo.* Graver recalls that Welles "had me light a studio in a little side room, kind of a library—front light, back light, rim light. I got these little inky midget lights and I put them up on the ceiling. He could throw a switch, one switch, so he could light himself. He bought a video camera, which was hooked up so he could have remote control, and he was going to sit and videotape his life. Anytime he wanted, when he couldn't sleep, he could go in there, turn the lights on, it was already lit, and turn on the [audio] recorder—he had a microphone hanging down. To my knowledge, he never used them."

Glory or indignity?: A litmus test for one's attitude toward Welles's later career is the sight of the filmmaker playing all the parts and even holding his own clapperboard in the fragmentary footage of his *Moby-Dick*, which he began filming in 1971 (frame enlargement). This uncompleted one-man show was adapted from *Moby-Dick—Rehearsed*, his 1955 stage version of the Herman Melville novel. *(Orson Welles: The One-Man Band; Medias Res/The Criterion Collection)*

Welles was deeply ambivalent about reminiscing, perhaps because he would have had to address issues he usually found too painful or delicate to discuss, such as his sexuality, his family life, and some of his more traumatic experiences in Hollywood. He returned advances from two publishers for autobiographies, eventually producing only the two haunting sketches on his parents that appeared in *Paris Vogue*. Although coaxed to reminisce at length on audiotape by Bogdanovich for what would become *This Is Orson Welles*, Welles frequently jousted with his Boswell when prodded to make personal disclosures and kept making excuses, delaying the book's publication beyond his lifetime.

❖ ❖ ❖

Welles's *Don Quixote*, begun in France in 1955 and filmed intermittently for many years in Mexico, Spain, and Italy, mostly with the director's own funds, is the ne plus ultra of his unfinished work. After the Mexican producer Oscar Dancigers pulled out of the project in 1957, Welles no longer worried unduly about problems with financiers, weather, or actors (even after his two principal actors died). The delays in bringing it to the screen in his later years were all his own: "I keep changing my approach, the subject takes hold of me and I grow dissatisfied with the old footage. I once had a finished version where the Don and Sancho go to the Moon, but then [the United States] went to the Moon, which ruined it, so I scrapped ten reels. Now I am going to make it a film essay about the pollution of the old Spain. But it's personal to me."

After he replaced his first Quixote, Mischa Auer, with Francisco Reiguera, the shooting continued to drag on for many years, and Reiguera began sending telegrams to Welles imploring him to hurry up and finish the film so that he could have the leisure to die. Such a mundane concern did not faze Welles, who had enough footage of Reiguera in the can to finish the film, even though the actor never fully dubbed his role before his death in 1969. As late as 1972, Welles sent Gary Graver out to shoot color footage of windmills in Seville.

Most of that footage, intended as part of new wraparound segments for the black-and-white film, "disappeared in Spain somewhere," Graver said, but one of the shots, of a windmill viewed through a wooden door frame, can be seen in *One-Man Band.* Graver found it bizarre doing second-unit work on a film whose shooting he had read about in his boyhood. He thinks *Don Quixote* was never completed because Welles "moved around too much, stuff got lost." Not long before his death, Welles retrieved a partial work print from Europe. Since the splices had deteriorated, he sent it to a film "rejuvenation" company to be put back in showable form. Then he started reediting the film once again in a cutting room set up in his garage. He was still working happily on *Don Quixote* when he died and talking about doing more shooting. Welles left behind about a thousand pages of script for *Quixote.*

After Welles's death, forty minutes of *Quixote* was assembled for the Cinémathèque française by the director Costa-Gavras and screened at the 1986 Cannes Film Festival. Despite the fragmentary nature of the footage, the print quality was excellent, demonstrating the film's compositional beauty (Jack Draper was the principal cinematographer). Bogdanovich told me in 1970 that *Don Quixote* (which he had watched privately in Rome) is "Welles's most Fordian film," and some of the long shots I have seen of Quixote and Sancho Panza riding their donkeys through spectacularly clouded landscapes are indeed evocative of Ford's elegiac imagery; Rosenbaum similarly describes *Quixote* as "Welles's only Western." Much of the footage from the project eventually was sold by Kodar to the Filmoteca española in Madrid; some, including Welles's work print, is held by the Cinémathèque française. Parts of the film, including the key sequence of Quixote's attack on a movie screen (Welles's version of the attack on the windmills), have remained in Italy with one of the editors, Mauro Bonnani, who had worked on *Quixote* with Welles in Rome in 1969.

Bonnani refused to provide his holdings for *Don Quijote de Orson Welles (Don Quixote by Orson Welles)*, the botched 1992 feature-length version assembled by Spanish filmmaker Jesús (Jess) Franco, who worked as an assistant to Welles on *Chimes* but is best known for directing lurid sex and horror movies. Among its many other sins, Franco's version interweaves material from Welles's TV documentary series *In the Land of Don Quixote*. So as we watch the blinkered Knight of the Sad Countenance and his squire having their mad adventures, we catch incongruous glimpses of Welles wandering around Spain holding a movie camera or roaring through the film in his sleek black Mercedes limo.

Kodar unwisely authorized Franco's version, but after being blocked from participating in the final editing, she denounced him for "throwing it together." However, according to Rosenbaum, Kodar, who is billed as "general supervisor," imposed some questionable conditions on the project. One was that Franco not use the footage Welles shot in Mexico in 1957 with Patty McCormack, the child actress best known for her Oscar-nominated title role in the 1956 film *The Bad Seed*. Welles cast her as a twelve-year-old American girl named Dulcie, after Cervantes' Dulcinea. The director, smoking a cigar, tells her the story of *Don Quixote* on a hotel patio and in a horse-drawn carriage; she also appears in the movie-theater sequence. Welles told Kodar he was going to reshoot the McCormack material with his daughter Beatrice, "but Welles never shot it, and that was the main structuring device of the movie!" Rosenbaum pointed out. "It's almost as if Welles never wanted the film to be shown unless he was able to finish it himself. As a result, they took out all this footage that was essential to the film. Then, to replace it, they used material from a hack documentary that Welles had done in Spain called *In the Land of Don Quixote*."

Not only are important scenes missing in the Franco fiasco, but the editing (only partly by Welles) is often ragged and indulgent, and the soundtrack of the English-language version is an off-putting mélange of dubbed voices. Reiguera and Akim Tamiroff (who died in 1972) were dubbed by Welles himself and by other actors brought in by Franco. The most disgraceful aspect of Franco's assemblage is that the print quality is so poor. Franco did not have access to the original negative, only work-print material, and the images are fuzzy and indistinct dupes, making the film all but unwatchable and utterly misrepresenting the crystalline quality of Welles's imagery. Stefan Drössler understates in calling the result "disappointing. In an effort to bring a narrative thread into the film, many sequences of the work print were rearranged, arbitrarily shortened, or modified by intercutting; finally even newly filmed scenes and digitally manipulated images were added."

Franco's version was offered to Roger Corman's Concorde–New Horizons for theatrical release in the United States, but Corman and his head of production, Jonathan Fernandez, were understandably baffled by its poor quality. They asked my opinion, and I urged them not to release it, for a bastardized version of Welles's dream project would only have damaged his reputation in America. Even if Welles had finished the film, his sometimes inspired, sometimes slapdash *Quixote* might not have been the masterwork we've hoped it would be in light of his extraordinarily long attachment to the project. But any final, or even tentative, judgment must be reserved until a version emerges that more closely represents Welles's intentions.

Tamiroff's bountiful embodiment of the earthy Sancho is, as Welles believed, the performance of his life, and the cadaverous Reiguera looks like a Gustave Doré illustration of Quixote sprung magically to life. Welles's adventurous visual style mixes formal compositions reminiscent of Ford and El Greco with playful nouvelle-vague-ish scenes of the Don and Sancho wandering bemusedly through the alien landscape of Franco's Spain. Welles displays his penchant for playing with narrative formats (as, indeed, Cervantes did throughout the novel); at one point Sancho even meets up with Welles and becomes an extra in the film we are watching, but Quixote rails against the tools of filmmaking as "demonic instruments" and rides off disgustedly for the moon, the last frontier where "there may still be room for knight errantry." Welles's *Quixote* is his wry, melancholic valentine to Cervantes' blinkered visionary, whom the filmmaker loves for fighting wrongs with "so much heart and so few means," a phrase clearly connecting the character to Welles himself. Thanks to Tamiroff's performance, the film is equally a valentine to Sancho, the Don's profoundly human squire, "a personality marvelous even in his stupidity."

Thematically, the film represents Welles's seriocomic reflection on the clash between the medieval ideals he revered in Spain, where he maintained a home for many years, and the lamentable crudity of the modern world with its noisy cars and motor scooters, tacky architecture, and junkyards (a memorably bizarre sequence takes place in a huge landscape of junked cars, appliances, and other rusted machinery). Don Quixote takes a bath in a barrel with a large, garish beer advertisement in the background, a sign touting Don Quixote Cerveza. Such absurdist, Beckett-like vaudevillian skits collide stylistically with the lavishly beautiful cinematography. Whether a Quixote can survive in such a debased world is at issue, and, by extension, the survival of traditional Spanish values in the post-civil-war era, and even the question of human survival itself.

Rosenbaum, who has seen much of the existing *Don Quixote* material, considers it "the major unfinished Welles project." I share his view that the Don's attack on the movie screen, filmed without sound in Mexico, is "the single most powerful scene" yet shown publicly from Welles's *Quixote* (in such venues as the Locarno Welles conference and on Italian television). Since the Spanish public within the film follows the adventures of Quixote and his squire (as it did in the novel), Sancho has become a popular favorite, and he draws applause from the theater audience as he enters. On the screen is what appears to be an Italian spectacle from the 1950s, of the kind known as "peplum" or a "sword-and-sandal" saga. Confused by his surroundings, Sancho sits next to Dulcie, who is still holding her copy of the Cervantes novel (earlier she had told Welles, "There was quite a rumpus about [Quixote] tearing up the movie screen"). She offers Sancho a lollipop but has to show him how to eat it without chewing the wrapper. Quixote, seated nearby, is mesmerized by the sight of a battle with charging horses. Not understanding the difference between representation and reality, he advances with his sword and starts slashing holes in the screen. He becomes enraged at the lurid sight of a woman being crucified and cuts the screen to pieces while attempting to rescue the buxom damsel in distress.

"Up to this point, the scene has been gently and genuinely comic," Rosenbaum notes, "but now it turns cruel and harsh in a manner that seems peculiar to Cervantes," as the on-screen audience turns riotous. Some members mockingly cheer Quixote on, young boys in the balcony react with glee and throw their hats, but most of the adult spectators are angry at him for disrupting the movie. Oblivious, Quixote continues grimly shredding the screen, deranged in his chivalric obsession, as Dulcie watches in astonishment. Welles transforms Cervantes' celebrated attack on the windmills into a darkly comical commentary on the crassness of modern mass entertainment and, by extension, of modern life in general. With Welles's characteristic moral irony and an advanced sense of postmodernism in playing with the nature of the medium and spectatorship, the scene criticizes twentieth-century culture through the eyes of a man whose anachronistic romantic idealism has driven him to madness and despair. As Rosenbaum puts it, the scene "carries a raw, primordial force in its present state that is paralleled by only a few moments in the rest of Welles's work."

❖ ❖ ❖

The cinematographer who shot the first footage for Welles's unfinished feature *The Deep* in 1963, Willy Kurant, subsequently photographed *The Immortal Story.* But it was not until many years later that Kurant learned that another cameraman, Ivica Rajkovic, had filmed additional material for *The Deep* (estimated by Kurant as about half the picture) in the late 1960s. Much of the funding for the second phase of the shooting came from Welles's payment for his acting role in the lavish Yugoslavian World War II film *Bitka na Neretvi (The Battle of Neretva)* (released in 1969). The production scale for *The Deep* was minimal, with only five people in the cast, but shooting on two yachts in the Adriatic was not easy. Welles later told Graver that one of the oldest caveats in filmmaking was well founded: "Don't ever make a movie out on a boat." In 1970–71, Welles enlisted Roger (Skipper) Hill, who was running a charter-boat business in Florida, to do some second-unit shooting from his boat in the Bahamas involving Oja Kodar's Rae and a double for the director's character, a wealthy buffoon named Russ Brewer ("the funniest part I've ever played").*

Welles spent several months in Munich working on the editing in

---

* Another film in which Welles was involved with Hill was *Rip Van Winkle Renascent,* directed in 1948 at the Todd School by Hill and his son-in-law Hascy Tarbox. This stylized political allegory, mostly written by Hill and cast with Todd students, portrays Rip as the archetypal American Everyman, sleeping through much of history but forced to wake up to his responsibilities when the dropping of the atomic bombs threatens the world's existence. As a favor to Hill in the 1980s, Welles did some uncredited postproduction tinkering on the thirty-eight-minute musical so it could be marketed on home video. According to Welles's daughter Christopher Welles Feder, "Contrary to Hill's claims after Welles's death, Welles had very little to do with either the script or the movie, which is corny and amateurish, to put it mildly."

1970 but gave various excuses for why *The Deep* was not released, such as Laurence Harvey's death and Jeanne Moreau's not finishing dubbing her role. However, Harvey died in 1973, long after it had finished shooting. Some of his and Michael Bryant's lines in the work print are dubbed by Welles, and some of Welles's own lines were never dubbed or have been lost; Bryant too has since died. In 2005 the Munich Film Museum showed a 115-minute version of its restoration in progress at Locarno, drawn from twenty reels of film in two different work prints (though not from Welles's 1970 edit, which was destroyed). Some scenes are missing from the latest version, and some variant scenes are included, as well as footage printed in monochrome and day-for-night scenes printed for daylight (a 90-minute version had been premiered at the Mannheim Welles symposium in October 2002). The negative is lost, two hundred reels having been seized by French customs officials and presumably discarded; eight reels of silent dupe negative material survive in a French laboratory but are legally inaccessible at present. So it is unlikely that *The Deep* can ever be assembled as anything more than an approximation of what it might have been if Welles had not given up on the editing in 1975. "Additional work has so far been thwarted by lack of approval from Oja Kodar," reports the Munich Film Museum's Stefan Drössler, who eventually hopes to release both the rough cut and a more polished version on DVD.

Welles hoped for a commercial success with *The Deep*, but when *Other Wind* was delayed, he didn't want to be represented on theater screens with a minor effort. "It shows its poverty, and it looks like a TV movie, I think, but it's terribly well acted," he told Bill Krohn in 1982. Welles added, "I'm tired of it now. I would hate to go back on the ocean and make it a more important movie." Welles subsequently sold options on the source novel to various people, and Phillip Noyce directed another version in 1989, *Dead Calm*, with Nicole Kidman, Sam Neill, and Billy Zane. The rights have since reverted to Kodar.

In promotional trailers assembled by Welles for *The Deep* (one of which is excerpted in *One-Man Band*), the film seems ragged and ridiculous, veering jarringly from melodrama to broad comedy. But in the rough assemblage, the outlines of a potentially compelling psychological study of sexuality, jealousy, and murder can be glimpsed. Although bearing some similarities to the intricately perverse yacht scenes of *The Lady from Shanghai*, *The Deep* most closely resembles Roman Polanski's 1963 thriller, *Knife in the Water*; Welles said half-jokingly, "It was very much that sort of thing, except it wasn't that exquisitely framed." The handheld photography of *The Deep* is often intricately composed, and the staging feels both spontaneous and precise, giving the film an intimacy rare in Welles's work. But at least in its current state, *The Deep* lacks the cohesion and clarity of Polanski's expert thriller. Polanski acknowledges his profound indebtedness to Welles (saying in 1969, "He'll always be my master"), so it is ironic that the master fell short of the pupil's standard with what, for Welles, was not particularly congenial material.

One indication that Welles may have been uncertain about how to tell the story is the existence of a dream sequence that casts doubt on the reality of the rest of the plot, suggesting that the complex power struggles among the various characters might be a projection of psychosexual problems between Kodar's Rae and her new husband, John Ingram (Bryant). Stefan Drössler's assemblage has taken the liberty of framing *The Deep* with the dream, an anomaly in the work of a director who usually scorned such devices; Drössler speculates that Welles may have shot it under the influence of Luis Buñuel's 1967 *Belle de Jour*, which freely intermingles the mundane and dream life of a pristinely beautiful prostitute (Catherine Deneuve).

The youthful Kodar's minimal acting experience and range are serious drawbacks in *The Deep*, which revolves around Rae's sexual cat-and-mouse game on the boat with the suave but disturbed Hughie Warriner, who may or may not be a murderer. Harvey's playing of Hughie's oscillation between sexual attraction to Rae and menace is riveting. Welles's mockery of Brewer, whose hobby is big-game hunting—"He loves to kill animals," Moreau's Ruth Warriner says contemptuously—resembles his farcical playing for other directors of such Hemingwayesque blowhards as Cy Sedgewick in *The Roots of Heaven* and Plankett in *The Southern Star* and prefigures his satirical treatment of Jake Hannaford in *The Other Side of the Wind*. It transpires that Brewer is the true villain of the piece, but the violent denouement, his underwater battle with Hughie and their death by shark, was never completed; the footage shot by Hill was spoiled by the use of fake blood that turned green in the water, and was later destroyed. In any case, it is hard to imagine the scene playing convincingly, and Welles's decision to farm it out to Hill seemed an admission of his own unsuitability to direct it.

Like every other Welles film, *The Deep* found him adventuring into unexpected waters and exploring previously uncharted areas of his artistic personality. Representing the early stages of Welles's "Oja period," the film reflects the director's somewhat tentative and only intermittently successful foray into the sexual themes that would become increasingly prominent in his work.

❖ ❖ ❖

The critic Stuart Byron aptly described Welles's 1970s documentaries *F for Fake* and *Filming "Othello"* as "grace-note metafilms." Welles called them "essay films" and thought he had found the perfect format for his favored blend of loosely structured reflections and entertainments unified by his own presence and ideas. He told Krohn, "I do very well know where I got my style: the inspiration for my essay style is Sacha Guitry."* Welles offered a "maybe more technically ingenious extension" of the Guitry style of a filmmaker "shamelessly" foregrounding himself and commenting on his stories. Welles was interested in the format partly because it avoided "the greatest handicap of the motion picture form. . . . By the process of making a movie, which takes so long, it is, by necessity, a year out of date. . . . The essay does not date, because it represents the author's contribution, however modest, to the moment at which it was made. And we never get tired of Hazlitt or Montaigne or anybody good like that."

Welles also was attracted to the essay-film format because he believed he was "a better actor than I'm a director, and I've never had a chance to prove it. I'm very serious. I know that the thing I do best in the world is talk to audiences. And that's really what confuses me and makes me think I should have been in politics, which is nonsense. . . . My favorite mask is myself. And I feel much more at ease on the stage talking to the audience than I do pretending to be somebody else. With most actors it's exactly the opposite."

F for Fake is a particularly brilliant display of what can be achieved with the essay-film format. Drawing from Welles's *First Person Singular* radio style and some of his previous experiments with narrative in film and television is not only a clever way of surmounting the financial and physical limitations of his later years but also a spur to creatively forging new meanings drawn from montage juxtapositions and intercutting. "He loved the editing process," Graver says. "Ever since he lost control on *Ambersons*, he was trying to protect everything. He said, 'I'm not going to let anyone else cut my pictures anymore.' We had one big room at the LGC Lab [in France] for cutting *The Other Side of the Wind*. He had six cutters, all with their own machines. He called the shots, he said exactly

* The Russian-French playwright, screenwriter, actor, and director directed Welles in two 1955 films, *Si Versailles m'était conté (Royal Affairs in Versailles)* and *Napoléon*.

what to cut where. He wouldn't sit down. He'd start someone on a scene, he'd mark it, and he'd cut that. He'd go see the next person, mark the film, cut it. Before that, I was told, he went from room to room. He'd have six rooms at once."

Filmed in Madrid, at the Spanish resort of Puerto Rey, and at Welles's home in Orvilliers and edited at Paris's Studio Antegor, *F for Fake* was made relatively quickly, within a nine-month period in 1972–73. It deals with the relationship between the Hungarian art forger Elmyr de Hory and his biographer, Clifford Irving, who, in a delicious irony, became infamous as the author of a fake biography of the reclusive tycoon Howard Hughes. As Elmyr and Irving circle around each other with wary fascination, they form another of Welles's Falstaff-Hal pairings compounded of equal parts friendship, exploitation, and betrayal.

The germ of the idea came to Welles when he watched a BBC documentary on Elmyr by François Reichenbach, *Elmyr: The True Picture?* Welles had been the subject of a Reichenbach documentary himself and appeared as a party guest in some of the footage on Elmyr.* After getting Reichenbach's consent to reuse his material, Welles "found all the stuff he'd thrown out, and all of what I did not shoot, myself, was from the dustbin. But then these extraordinary series of events took place. We used Clifford Irving as our authority on the psychology of a man who could perpetrate a fake, and it is really true that in the afternoon, just at that time, he was writing his biography of Howard Hughes. . . . and the story kept changing. We had to keep changing the movie. That looks like a contrivance of mine. It is not a contrivance. In fact, it's exactly as it happened."

Welles throws his own history of trickery and artifice into the mix, describing himself as a "charlatan" and discussing his *War of the Worlds* hoax in a faux confessional tone. Befitting his multilayered magic-box approach, the version of the Martian broadcast we hear in the film is faked, as is a newsreel about Hughes that parodies the newsreel in *Kane* and is narrated, like the original "News on the March," by William Alland. When Welles found that the stock footage he had bought of Hughes mistakenly included a shot of the actor Don Ameche, he used it anyway, in his general spirit of prankishness, telling Graver, "I can't believe I picked this clip of Don Ameche. Don't say anything to anybody."

* *Portrait: Orson Welles* (1968), a haphazardly assembled cinema verité short codirected by Reichenbach and Frédéric Rossif for French television, was written by Maurice Bessy, author of a critical study of Welles. It was shown as a companion piece to *The Immortal Story* in some European theaters.

Welles later explained that in *F for Fake* he "said I was a charlatan and didn't mean it . . . because I didn't want to sound superior to Elmyr, so I emphasized that I was a magician and called it a charlatan, which isn't the same thing. And so I was faking even then. Everything was a lie. There wasn't anything that wasn't." Novelist Robert Anton Wilson has described *F for Fake* as "a documentary about the impossibility of making a documentary. It's a documentary in which everybody is lying, including Welles himself. You never can figure out who's the worst liar and how much you can believe. Some of it is true, but you can never be sure which part. Other documentaries are terribly dishonest compared to that one, which admits it's lying. A documentary that admits it's lying is honest, a documentary that pretends to be honest is lying."

As *F for Fake* progresses, its playfully expressed concerns assume increasing gravitas. Welles's dazzlingly edited blend of found footage and newly shot material becomes a meditation on the art of the cinema and the meaning of authorship. When I showed *F for Fake* to Jean Renoir, he said, "*F for Fake* is a very important film because it asks the question every artist has to face at some time in his career: What is art?" Welles's answer is that art is a form of magic. Whether it's a trick, a fake, doesn't really matter. In a sequence filmed in an apocalyptic dusk outside Chartres Cathedral (beautifully shot by Graver from the director's sketches), Welles delivers a magnificent soliloquy on the cathedral, "the premier work of man, perhaps, in the whole Western world—and it's without a signature." With unabashed emotion in his voice, he concludes, "Maybe a man's name doesn't matter all that much."

The man who so often boasted "My name is Orson Welles" was the least anonymous of filmmakers. Not for him the self-effacing craftsmanship of the builders of Chartres. But Chartres, that medieval hymn to the glory of God, that awesome reminder of man's secondary role in the universe, is the one place Welles would choose, if all else were destroyed, "to mark where we have been—to test what we had it in us to accomplish." His answer to despair and death is simply, "Go on singing."

François Truffaut told me he was convinced that Welles made *F for Fake* for only one reason: to refute Pauline Kael's charges that he tried to steal credit for the *Citizen Kane* script from Herman Mankiewicz. All of Welles's ruminations about the fallibility of art experts and the ultimate unimportance of credit to the value of a work of art are, in Truffaut's view, "an attack on Pauline Kael." Truffaut's observation is perhaps the key to understanding this kaleidoscopically dense film, which, to avoid what Welles once called "that odious thing, 'a reply to the critic,'" hides its central concern behind a surface of smoke and mirrors, much as Welles hid his other replies to Kael behind the subterfuge of Bogdanovich's authorship of "The *Kane* Mutiny" article in *Esquire* and by fictionalizing Kael as Juliette Riche in *The Other Side of the Wind.*

Welles had an offer from independent art-house distributor Joseph E. Levine to release *F for Fake* in the United States, even though Levine had fallen asleep while watching the film, but Welles rejected the offer, expecting a better one that didn't come. So it took four years for *F for Fake* to appear in the United States after its 1973 premiere in Tehran. The trailer Welles made for the American release blames the delay on the fact that Howard Hughes was still living until 1976. As Graver admits in the trailer, "the following commercial message . . . is fairly brief and completely dishonest." Bearing out Welles's concerns about films being out of date by the time they appear, Elmyr allegedly committed suicide on December 11, 1976, to escape a probable jail sentence (although some believe Elmyr even faked his own death). Welles identified closely with Elmyr's precarious financial state, with his ingenious ways of putting off the inevitable disaster, and he was thrown into a severe depression by the report of Elmyr's suicide. Rather than seeming "dated," the film gains in fascination because of its eerie prescience.

Many references are made to the old forger's fear of imprisonment and death, and Irving makes a comment that could be applied to all of Welles's other screen heroes: "He has developed a fiction about his life, and to destroy that fiction would be to tear down that castle he has built—his illusion." Ironically, that is just what Irving does by exposing Elmyr. The relationship between the two men on-screen is closely akin to all the other Wellesian male friendships. Welles makes the Falstaff-Hal comparison explicit by describing Elmyr as "the old emperor of the hoax" and Irving as "the pretender."

Hughes was living at Las Vegas's Desert Inn when Welles made the film, and no one on the outside knew then that Hughes was, like the elderly Kane, a virtual prisoner in his own private kingdom. Yet Welles, looking up at Hughes's hideaway, muses, "What was he doing up there? What were *they* doing to him? If he broke his silence, would it be—a cry for help?" Although Oja said that Welles "had a lot of friends" in Hollywood and "loved to be around young people," Welles seemed to identify with Hughes's isolation, complaining that he lived a "gloomy and hermit-like life" in the midst of the largely hostile film colony. And like Hughes, who had also been an eccentric filmmaker with a tendency to go over schedule ("I only wish I were still in the movie business," the elderly

Hughes is heard to say in *F for Fake*), Welles found Las Vegas a convenient hideout in old age.

The elaborate and unconventional trailer Welles shot for the U.S. release of *F for Fake* was not used by the distributor and almost became a lost film. According to Graver, Specialty Films did not want to go to the expense of making copies of the nine-minute short. Like the tongue-in-cheek trailer Welles shot for *Kane*, which contains no footage from the actual film but only prankish shots introducing the cast and a montage of characters talking about Kane, the *F for Fake* trailer is a zany parody of the coming-attractions genre. Graver stars as the gee-whiz host breathlessly spewing out praise for *F for Fake*, egged on by Welles's voice, as figure studies of Kodar are intercut with snatches of cryptic footage from *F for Fake* of Elmyr and Irving.

Facetious in the extreme but entertaining in its mockery of conventional expectations,* the trailer no doubt also flummoxed the distributor with its unusual length and its plethora of nudity. The original double-system, color work print of the trailer was lost, but a black-and-white dupe survived. The reason it exists only in that form is that in the late 1970s, I borrowed the color print from Graver to show at the AFI seminar and became concerned that it might never be seen again. So, before returning it, I had three black-and-white 35mm dupes made by a friend who was editing a feature for a Hollywood studio. Eventually I gave my dupe to Graver, who used it in his documentary *Working with Orson Welles*. Graver passed the copy to Kodar, and it wound up in the Munich Film Museum, which undertook a "restoration" of the trailer by using color outtakes and tinting some black-and-white footage, a sleight-of-hand feat that closely resembles the original, a "forgery" of which Elmyr himself might be proud.

Unfortunately, but not surprisingly, *F for Fake* failed to find much of an audience in the United States. Even if it had been handled better, it's unlikely that such an audaciously original and uncategorizable film would have found a sizable niche in a marketplace increasingly indifferent to both personal filmmaking and the documentary genre. Most American reviewers simply didn't get it. Stanley Kauffmann derided the film in the *New Republic* as "a piece of gimcrack japery, an *ad hoc* pastiche that Welles

---

* At one point the trailer shows a still picture of a bearded young man holding a camera as Graver asks, "And who is this man? See *F for Fake*—the movie that dares to ask that question." The mystery figure is R. Michael Stringer, one of Welles's faithful crew on *Other Wind* and *F for Fake*.

is trying to pass off as a planned work of charlatanry. . . . It simply tries the eyes and suggests very early that we're getting all this editing glitter because there's so little film underneath." It wasn't until many years later that Michael Moore demonstrated with such films as *Roger and Me* and *Bowling for Columbine* that a profitable market exists for his populist version of the essay-film format.

"When I finished *F for Fake*," Welles said in 1982, "I thought I had discovered a new kind of movie, and it was the kind of movie I wanted to spend the rest of my life doing. And it was the failure of *F for Fake* . . . in America and also in England, [that] was one of the big shocks of my life. Because I really thought I was onto something." The fact is, however, that he stubbornly kept doing essay films despite the failure of his best one.

❖ ❖ ❖

Filming "Othello" was the last film Welles managed to release before his death. Filmed in Los Angeles for West German television between 1974 and 1978 for producers Jürgen and Klaus Hellwig, this eighty-four-minute documentary feature was shown briefly in the United States in 1979 but has seldom been seen here in its entirety since then. Parts of the 16mm film were included in the 1995 Criterion Collection laserdisc of the 1955 American release version of *Othello*, which was licensed by Kodar but subsequently pulled from release because of objections by Beatrice Welles. Welles subsequently shot, but did not edit, a similar documentary, *Filming "The Trial."* He told Graver he was planning to do a documentary on each of his films. His most ambitious plans along those lines were to reframe *Don Quixote* and *The Other Side of the Wind* as works in the "making-of" essay genre. But a documentary on *The Lady from Shanghai* was next on his list, because there were such interesting stories to tell about that experience, Welles told an audience member at the Cinémathèque française in 1982.

"This is a Moviola" is the opening line of *Filming "Othello."* Welles is speaking to the audience from his editing table. His choice of the principal setting for this documentary emphasizes the critical importance he places on editing in the filmmaking process, especially in light of his career-long struggle to retain control of the final shape of his work. "When we say that we're editing or cutting a film, we aren't really saying enough. Movies aren't just made on the set—a lot of the actual *making* happens right here. So a Moviola like this is very much as important as a camera. Here films are salvaged, saved from disaster, or—savaged out of existence. This is the last stop on the long road between the dream in a filmmaker's head and the public to whom that dream is addressed."

Truffaut commented on Welles's approach to editing: "They often speak of Orson Welles as a poet; I see him rather as a musician. . . . Orson Welles's work is prose which becomes music on the cutting bench. His films are shot by an exhibitionist and edited by a censor." Echoing that insight, Welles tells the audience in *Filming "Othello"*: "Carlyle said that almost everything, examined deeply enough, will turn out to be musical. Of course, this is profoundly true of motion pictures. The pictures have movement, the movies move, and then there's the movement from one picture to another. There's a rhythmic structuring to that, there's counterpoint, harmony, and dissonance. A film is never *right* until it's right musically. And this Moviola, this filmmaker's tool, is a kind of musical instrument. . . . So if you find me winding up our conversation here, you understand that as a filmmaker I'm speaking to you from my home."

While telling the story of *Othello*'s production with his marvelous skills as a raconteur—"There were moments of sheer desperation, and there was much delight"—Welles points out that the film's style was largely dictated by its circumstances. A film intended as a lavishly designed production to be shot mostly in an Italian or French studio became a catch-as-catch-can independent production whose dizzying leaps of continuity, sometimes jumping from country to country within a single scene, were all carried in the filmmaker's head. Given one more go at *Othello*, Welles offers newly reedited and condensed versions of scenes from his 1952 film, which he had further recut for the 1955 version. Welles's continual revising of his own work, perhaps in part a reaction to the trauma of others' forcible remaking of his films, has made life more complicated for Welles scholars and admirers, but it was part of the engine that drove him to keep creating incessantly in later years and added fresh layers of style and meaning to his work. *Filming "Othello"* can be seen as Welles's dignified plea for understanding of the often bizarre circumstances and idiosyncratic methodology of his post-Hollywood work, not as an alibi for its ragged aspects, but as a justification of his independence and a defense of the artistic virtues of what Graver has called Welles's "handmade" films.

Welles relies on Jack J. Jorgens, the author of *Shakespeare on Film* (1977), to provide most of the thematic and visual analysis in *Filming "Othello,"* which also includes critiques borrowed from André Bazin. Jorgens's vivid descriptions are filled with insight into Welles's visual strategies and how they express the themes of Shakespeare's tragedy. On first viewing, I found it surprising and disappointing that Welles's commentary on his own film leans so heavily on other people's, but I came to accept the wisdom of what he says on-screen: "Don't imagine for a moment that I'm pretending to be modest. It's just my fixed conviction that critical opinions about one's own work should be left to others." Welles's reticence recalls Robert Frost's customary response when people asked him to explain his poetry: "I have written my poem as well as I possibly could, and now you want me to restate it, using inferior language?"

But Welles admits at the end of *Filming "Othello"* that he has borrowed "critical interpretations corresponding fairly closely to my own ideas." "Quoting or misquoting" from those critics, Welles concedes that his film is more memorable for its direction than for its acting, unlike Laurence Olivier's 1965 filmed *Othello*, which he describes with admirably restrained condescension as "a cinematic record of a stage production" focusing on Othello's personal psychology. "My film, by contrast, tried to depict a whole *world* in collapse, a world that is a metaphor not just for Othello's mind but for an epic, pre-modern age. . . . The visual style of the film mirrors the marriage at the center of the play, which is not that of Othello and Desdemona, but the perverse marriage of Othello and Iago." The film's "romantic and heroic" imagery is Othello's, but "the dizzying camera movements, the tortured compositions, the grotesque shadows, and insane distortions, they're Iago. For he is the agent of chaos. . . . And the intent of our camera was to create that sense of vertigo, a feeling of tottering instability." Welles does not mention that the style also reflects his own sense of disorientation as a political and artistic exile from his native country and his heightened sense in those years that the world was out of control.

Perhaps the highlight of *Filming "Othello"* is Welles's reunion in Dublin with his old friends and colleagues Micheál MacLiammóir and Hilton Edwards. Their spirited, erudite conversation about Shakespeare and the play is so fascinating that one wishes it could have served as the basis for an entire film. The footage of MacLiammóir and Edwards was shot separately from Welles's questions and reaction shots. Graver tried to get Welles to shoot his side of the conversation at the same time, but Welles insisted on doing it later. By that time, the film stock used for the earlier scenes was unavailable. The difference is obvious, and Welles's visual manipulations seem jarring. But his disregard for the conventions of matching could be read as an insistence on the artificiality of documentaries, which are always stitched together, condensed, and rearranged, a point similarly kept in the foreground of the viewer's mind throughout *F for Fake*. Filming his side of the conversation separately for *Filming "Othello"* gives Welles the last word, enabling him to rethink and carefully phrase his views and ostentatiously allowing him, as director, the utmost control over what was otherwise a spontaneous event.

Welles loved exploring such paradoxes with mischievous wit in his essay films, as indeed he always did in his narrative films, beginning with his bold juxtapositions in *Kane* of conversational exchanges seemingly taking place over many years. During the making of *Filming "Othello,"* MacLiammóir told Graver how disconcerting he found it to watch his performance as Iago and see how Welles had stitched it together: "My God, I say something, some remark to Othello, and they cut away to Orson, they cut back, and it's months later and my face is all fat and puffy." "Well, you *don't* notice it," adds Graver. "It was Micheál's vanity."

Filming "Othello" has been seen as a veiled pitch from Welles for more financial support, but it is a melancholy form of self-advertisement. He tells the audience, "I leave you with a confession. This hasn't been as easy as I could have wished. There are too many regrets, too many things I wish I could have done over again. If it wasn't a memory, if it was a project for the future, talking about *Othello* would have been nothing but delight. Promises *are* more fun than explanations. With all my heart, I wish that I wasn't looking back on *Othello* but looking forward to it. *That Othello* would be one hell of a picture." Lighting a cigar as the camera zooms slowly back and the screen dims around him, he says "Good night," rises from the editing machine, gives a small, sad wave, and exits.

With a student audience at the University of Southern California's Norris Theater on the night of November 14, 1981, Welles and Graver shot about an hour and a half of 16mm footage, with a single camera, for *Filming "The Trial."* The impetus was Welles's discovery of a pristine 35mm print of his 1962 feature, which had gone into the public domain in the United States. Welles planned to intercut footage from *The Trial* with the audience discussion, but he never did any more work on the documentary.

Welles had filmed a discussion in the same theater for *The Other Side of the Wind* in 1971, taking the place of Jake Hannaford to field questions from film students. On the way to the theater that night, I passed a classroom where a professor was about to begin lecturing. Surprised, I asked, no doubt undiplomatically, why he wasn't letting his students go talk with Orson Welles and appear in his film. The professor replied huffily, "Once he learns to walk on water, I might consider it." Such disdain for Welles in academia was reciprocated. When asked how he would teach filmmaking, Welles said that he wouldn't show or talk about movies. Instead, he said, "I'd teach the history of the world."

Filming "The Trial" premiered at the Munich Welles conference in October 1999, with minimal tightening for public presentation by the museum. A European cable-TV network that was offered the documentary rejected it because of the "unstable" nature of the handheld camerawork in the first ten minutes before Graver switched to a tripod. That was a transparently feeble excuse, for Graver, stationed in front of the stage doing whip-pans from the audience to tight, low-angled shots of Welles, effectively varies the image sizes, keeping the discussion lively to watch as well as to hear.

The question I ask of Welles on camera—why he dubbed other characters' voices in *The Trial*—produces a perfunctory response: he claims it was solely for reasons of economy. But *Filming "The Trial"* mostly finds Welles in expansive form and plays satisfyingly as a record of his good-natured jousting with his enthusiastic and well-informed young audience. Asked how he created the effect of dizziness in the trial sequence, Welles waves his arm grandly, exclaiming, "The mastery of the cinema!" *Variety* critic Todd McCarthy provocatively asks Welles whether he was still as politically engaged as he had been in earlier years. He replies, "I'm much more interested in politics than I am in movies. . . . The truth is every work of art *is* a political statement." But he reminds the audience that he has always tried to avoid falling into rhetoric: "God deliver us from the people who tell us what is right and what is wrong."

Another audience member asks, "Talking about money, do you think if you'd had a great deal of it, it would have made your films better, or did your poverty help your creativity?" "Did my poverty help my creativity?" Welles muses. Then, after a long, Jack Benny–ish pause, he replies, "No." When the laughter subsides, he adds, "I think, however, that it is possible to spoil a young director by giving him too much money, so that he does not learn one of the main arts of directing, which is the ability to walk away from something."

Henry Jaglom recalled what Welles told him on that subject: "I was complaining on a particular movie to Orson Welles that I didn't have enough money—that I didn't have enough time—and Orson said to me that 'the enemy of art is the absence of limitations'—that if you had all the time and money in the world to make a movie, then in fact you wouldn't be forced to find creative solutions to problems. If you have money and time, you just throw those things at the problems."

Joseph McBride with Welles in 1978 during a break in the taping of *The Orson Welles Show* in a Hollywood TV studio. Welles shot the pilot for his own talk show series "movie-style" but couldn't find a buyer. McBride appeared as a member of the studio audience. *(Gary Graver)*

❖ ❖ ❖

To a questioner in *Filming "The Trial"* who asked how much obligation he felt to a mass audience, Welles declared, "I would *love* to have a mass audience. You're looking at a man who's been searching for a mass audience—and if I had one, I'd be obliged." He never gave up hope of making more mainstream projects. But all his attempts at being "commercial" in later years were unsuccessful, proving that when he tried his hardest to become a "popular artist," his efforts tended to fall flat and were, if anything, harder to market than his more personal, ostensibly more esoteric work. "The artists I personally have always enjoyed the *most* are popular artists," he told Bogdanovich. "I *wish* I were one—but I'm not. I'm more like Céline—writing away at books no one ever reads."

Supported by his old friend and *Dean Martin Show* producer Greg Garrison, Welles made his futile foray into the TV talk-show format with *The Orson Welles Show* in 1978–79. Welles ruminates about television, the acting profession, and his own career in show business; performs magic tricks with Angie Dickinson, his friend and favorite restaurateur Patrick Terrail, and Roger Hill (footage borrowed from another project, *Orson Welles' Magic Show*); clowns with the Muppets ("The Muppets, for my money, are the most original thing that ever happened on the box") and chats with Muppet creator Jim Henson and puppeteer Frank Oz; and has a thoughtful discussion about stardom with Burt Reynolds.

Welles took directing credit as "G. O. Spelvin," which presumably stands for "George Orson Spelvin" (George Orson Welles was his full name, and George Spelvin is a traditional show business pseudonym for someone who doesn't want his name used). Shot at a Los Angeles TV station with Graver as director of photography on both video and film, the pilot was completed in 1979 but remained unsold. "No network would touch it," Welles admitted to the studio audience. "Or if they would, I wouldn't touch *them*—too many committees. Syndication is the nearest thing to freedom on TV." But even syndication wouldn't touch it. The seventy-four-minute program's first public showing came in 1999 at the Munich Welles conference.

In his opening monologue, delivered from a chair surrounded by audience members seated on platforms, Welles declares, "As entertainment, anyway, radio and movies never came near to what that little box has come to mean to us now." His monologue and comments between segments are less successful than the other parts of the show because they seem so obviously scripted and overenhanced with stage reaction shots and embarrassingly "sweetened" laughter from the studio audience (of which I am a member). Directing with one eye on a video monitor, enabling him to give quick and precise instructions to Graver and the camera operator, Welles used feature-film shooting methods: one camera, many retakes, carefully directed "spontaneous" audience reaction shots, and a blend of elaborate tracking shots with more conventional television setups. He told the studio audience, "You'll get a little tired of this—there's going to be two or three takes, movie-style."

At one point, while doing a close-up of himself to insert later into a conversation with Reynolds (who wasn't there, having been taped some weeks earlier), Welles peered into the monitor and told the operator, "When you're tight, cut into my head and leave the beard free, rather than the other way around." He improvised camera movements and lighting effects ("There's no spotlight on me, sorry, start again"), and while doing reverse angles on audience members asked the operator to give the appearance of roughness and spontaneity: "Can you fish more? It's too neat." People selected to ask questions of Welles and Reynolds were rehearsed, cajoled, and even given line readings, while being warned by the director not to change the dialogue. "Do we have any bodies, Gary, that are wasted?" Welles asked at one point. "I don't mean in the profoundest sense." Among those asking questions on camera are director Joe Dante, Welles crew member and producer-director Frank Marshall, and Mark Goldblatt, a film editor best known for the first two *Terminator* movies.

When he taped the sign-off, Welles used the line he had been using for forty years—"I remain, as always, obediently yours"—but after reciting it, he asked Graver, "Did that sound phony?" Assured that it did not, Welles pondered a moment and decided to redo it anyway. This time his voice was less resonant, and there was a small, but significant, change in the wording: "As for me, I *hope* to remain, as always, obediently yours." He finally opted not to use that admission of insecurity, settling for a simple "Good night."

The overall effect of *The Orson Welles Show* is of a curiously stilted hybrid, intriguing mostly because Welles continually reflects on and/or parodies the format. He took weeks to shoot the show and edit it (with Stanley J. Sheff), which probably gave potential backers pause. Graver insisted that Welles only intended to use such elaborate methods for the pilot, and that for the regular weekly series he would have departed from customary TV practice only by shooting considerably more material than he needed and quickly cutting the conversations down to their highlights. Welles admitted in retrospect, "It was frankly an attempt to enter the commercial field and earn my living as a talk show host. It was just a flop, that's all, nobody wanted it."

In any case, would it have been worth Welles's time to do his own American talk show? As an occasional guest host on *The Tonight Show*, he tended to talk too much for an interviewer, monopolizing the attention from his interviewees, and often seemed impatient (understandably so) with the banal chitchat required by the format. He would have been better suited to the more thoughtful, discursive, and reflective British talk-show format, as was demonstrated by his memorable conversations with such highly literate hosts as Michael Parkinson, Huw Wheldon, and Melvyn Bragg.

Even more dispiriting than *The Orson Welles Show* was a six-minute video pitch by Welles for a multimedia project called *The Good Life*. Sitting in a white chair, wearing a would-be-jaunty-looking maroon sport-coat and wide-collared black shirt but looking tired and sickly, Welles describes his plans for a series of TV specials, videocassettes, and audiocassettes offering pointers about world travel, fine dining, sightseeing, and other diversions. Welles promises to take "a very personal approach," but his unabashedly consumerist approach, addressing the show "to that new leisured class," makes it seem as if he were auditioning to be just another seedy infomercial huckster. Perhaps *The Good Life* could have been transformed into something like his *Around the World with Orson Welles* series of quirky TV travelogues, but the proposal did not encourage optimism, and Welles was clearly getting too old to keep gallivanting around the world.

Graver remembered the sudden onset of another Welles notion:

> We were doing *F for Fake* and had a set in the house at Orvilliers. I came down, and there was a bunch of pots and pans on the set. He looked at me like I should have known and said, "The cooking show!" He wanted to do a gourmet cooking show on TV. He would be the chef. We never did it, but he wanted to do a series, he wanted me to build the sets for that, and he acted like I was a mind reader. When Orson cooked, he looked like a bull in a china shop. Oja would say, "Don't let him in the kitchen." There'd be flour all over, a big mess, but he'd come out with something good.

Graver insisted that Welles in his later years, contrary to his public image, "didn't overeat. He just gained weight. I ate nearly every meal with him in Europe. We ate the same things. He had insomnia, and maybe he ate during the night, which I didn't see. But I never saw him overeat or overdrink."

❖ ❖ ❖

Far more personal than *The Orson Welles Show* is Welles's piece of hocus-pocus vaudeville, *Orson Welles' Magic Show*. Filmed in 35mm and 16mm in Los Angeles and Atlanta from 1976 intermittently until his death in 1985, it was intended as a television special but was really more of a hobby. Graver admits, "I knew it was always going to be a work in progress." German television eventually showed an assemblage of the incomplete *Magic Show*, restored by the Munich Film Museum. The museum's 2000 reconstruction, twenty-seven minutes long, includes a prologue, "The Duck Trick," separately filmed in 1970, as well as episodes entitled "The Light Box," "Abu Khan's Levitation Trick," "The Magic Mummy," "Chung Ling Soo," and "The Thread Trick." In the cast besides Dickinson and Hill is magician Abb Dickson, whom Welles described as "a very talented young fellow from Atlanta who plays the head of a sort of group of Keystone Kops" (in a sequence harkening back to the slapstick comedy in Welles's 1930s silent films *The Hearts of Age* and *Too Much Johnson).*

"Magic—it has an innocence that appeals to me," Welles explained on another occasion. "It's a return to childhood. It renews the sense of wonder on a certain level. It's like playing with toys. It's pure play, and sometimes it can have a little more than that—it can have a kind of second-rate poetry that I find attractive. Great magic, you know, there's a moment when you suspend disbelief and it becomes a very *good* kind of theater."

His *Magic Show*—tongue-in-cheek, corny, and (literally) flashy—was a cinematic plaything he would turn to whenever he craved that childlike pleasure. It's a color equivalent of the brilliant black-and-white magic act he directed in the 1944 troop-entertaining movie *Follow the Boys.* Welles and Graver and another cameraman, Tim Suhrstedt, who shot parts of the *Magic Show,* have fun with dazzling lighting effects and bold primary colors arranged in cubist patterns. Welles sports a cape and a turban and wields his cigar like a scepter. Costuming his assistants (including Graver) as astronauts, he makes a slinky, silver-clad young woman disappear and reappear inside a transparent box using smoke, mirrors, and cinematic sleight of hand, all the while keeping up a line of patter that comments obliquely on his art and the art of the cinema itself.

"Do you believe in magic?" he asks the audience. "Well, you do believe your *eyes,* don't you? And our cameras do not lie. Really. They're seeing what you see without the slightest hint of technological trickery, sidearm snookery, hanky-panky, or ranny-gazoo." And he invites us to share his mischievous love of illusionism, assuring us in his most earnestly deadpan manner, "I wouldn't fool you . . . for the world."

❖ ❖ ❖

Welles expressed regret about his absence from the United States during most of the 1960s, when the country was going through political upheavals. He told Bill Krohn, "I was *forced* by my stubborn insistence that I was a movie director to stay where I hoped I could get work, and that really cut me off from becoming the male Jane Fonda." But Welles and Fonda could have teamed on a political project in 1982 if only she had been willing.

The project was an unusual, indeed somewhat bizarre, television event for which I was the principal writer: the United States International Communication Agency's worldwide TV special about the Solidarity movement, *Let Poland Be Poland*, broadcast live on January 31, 1982. Conceived by agency director Charles Z. Wick, a former Hollywood producer and close friend of President Ronald Reagan, the show was a potpourri of footage from pro-Solidarity rallies around the world with taped testimonials about Polish freedom by world leaders and personalities from the arts. Although the show was obviously propaganda (I cherish the review from the Warsaw army newspaper claiming that the script was written by "that degenerate cowboy Ronald Reagan"), I considered it propaganda for a worthy cause that transcended Reaganism. The show was properly derided for the use of such Hollywood personalities as Bob Hope and Frank Sinatra, but I did my best to keep the tone as serious as possible.

Inspired by Welles's recordings of poetry and historical speeches, I had the idea of pairing him with Jane Fonda at lecterns alternating readings from famous texts about liberty. Welles enthusiastically agreed to appear with her and we made her an offer, but the agency became anxious about having her on the program. Her reputation as a protester of the Vietnam War did not endear her to the Reagan administration. I suggested to the show's producer, Eric Lieber, that we resign in protest if Fonda were banned from appearing. He agreed. But while the agency was still considering the matter, it became moot when Fonda turned down our invitation, declaring that talk was no substitute for action. Welles came in a wheelchair to a small Hollywood studio to tape his contribution, a recitation of John Donne's meditation "No man is an island," as well as two speeches that, unlike the Donne reading, unfortunately didn't make it into the final cut. Welles concluded with the show's best delivery of the title phrase: "Let Poland . . . be . . . *Poland.*"

Welles made a more memorable appearance on *The American Film Institute Salute to John Huston*, which I cowrote with producer George Stevens Jr. for CBS-TV in 1983. I arranged Welles's appearance through Graver, but when I called Welles to suggest we get together to talk about what he was going to say, he replied brusquely, "There's nothing to talk about, because *I'm* going to write it. But I'd like to see *you.*" Welles didn't understand that I didn't want to tell him what to write; no one could have improved on his speech, which turned out to be a classic of its kind. But I needed to know roughly what he planned to say in order to avoid repetition in other speeches I was writing and to give his speech the optimum placement on the show. His remark made me realize that he simply didn't take me seriously as a collaborator. So, under the circumstances, I had no desire to accept his invitation to pay a social call.

That was my last conversation with Welles, and it came as the climax of what I saw as his bullying condescension. I realized later that by not wanting to see him, I was guilty of a form of betrayal, like the betrayals of friendship in so many of his films. But Welles put up formidable barriers to close friendship. Geraldine Fitzgerald, the Irish actress who worked with Welles in the Mercury Theatre production of *Heartbreak House* in 1938 and in his 1956 stage production of *King Lear*, considered Welles adept with quick intimacy but unable to sustain it. She compared him to a lighthouse beam shining on you briefly but then moving on, plunging you into darkness. David Thomson for once had it right: "Time and again, he avoided acolytes, cut them short in praise, was downright rude and surly. It was a peculiar but revealing trait, a dread of the thing most desired that involved vanity and its opposite, a need for glory and friendship and an insistence on isolation."

Nevertheless, turning my back on Welles had as much to do with my unhappiness over my own Hollywood career as it did with our relationship. Although I was having a degree of success writing TV specials, the screenplays I'd been writing since *Rock 'n' Roll High School* in 1979 weren't selling. With the film industry's increasingly mindless and juvenile turn during the Reagan years, the kinds of stories I wanted to tell were not what Hollywood wanted to make.

For *Daily Variety* in 1977, I interviewed George Coulouris, the Mercury Theater actor who plays Walter Parks Thatcher in *Kane*, when he returned to Hollywood in his venerable old age to play King Lear in the Globe Theater on Santa Monica Avenue. Coulouris urged me to write a Welles biography, but I found myself replying, "I want to write my own stuff." Preoccupied with writing screenplays and a novel, I foolishly thought of nonfiction as a less creative form than fiction. Coulouris insisted that a Welles biography *would* be "your own stuff," and how right he was. Seven years later, in May 1984, I decided to abandon the screenwriting profession to write books full-time. The Writers Guild of America award I won later that year for the Huston tribute ironically crowned my desire to quit the business. I didn't even bother to show up to accept it, but I figured that the award from my peers, along with being vested for a pension after ten years as a working screenwriter, enabled me to go out on a high note.

Deciding to write "my own stuff" rather than following the advice Mister Pister received from Jake Hannaford to "eat a little shit" in Hollywood was the second hardest decision I ever made, second only to leaving the Catholic Church. Both were literally lifesaving decisions.

❖ ❖ ❖

After *The Other Side of the Wind*, the most deeply personal of Welles's late projects was *The Dreamers*. Filmed at the house Welles and Kodar shared in Hollywood, *The Dreamers* was shot with their own money between 1978 and 1985. They worked in "secrecy," Kodar recalled, "because we knew that under these circumstances shooting could maybe go on for years, and he was afraid to be blamed for not finishing the film in time." This haunting, fragmentary, mysterious fable, set in nineteenth-century Europe, contains some of Graver's most beautiful color photography, delicately fantastic in tone. Based on two stories by Isak Dinesen, the title piece and "Echoes," *The Dreamers* is a hypnotically lyrical pas de deux expressing the deep friendship between a former opera singer, Pellegrina Leoni, and her shadowy patron, Marcus, an elderly Jewish merchant. "The greatest singer in the world," Pellegrina has lost her singing voice after being injured in an opera-house fire. As a result, she continually restarts her life, restlessly pursuing different identities, watched over discreetly and kindly by Marcus.

Describing Pellegrina as a "light-footed ferocious wench," Dinesen has her explain her wanderings in words Kodar might have addressed to Welles himself: "I have come from far away, and I have got far to go. I am nothing but a messenger sent out on a long journey, to tell people that there is hope in the world." The elusive Pellegrina is simultaneously artist, mother, temptress, angel, and witch; the elderly Marcus, her worshipful protector, is unable to hold on to this mercurial woman who gives him hope and keeps his spirit alive. Like so many Welles characters, Pellegrina shows godlike presumption: she attempts to control the process of resurrection. The heroic yet melancholy nature of her odyssey, and her affinity with another figure much beloved by Welles, is suggested by Marcus in Dinesen's "Dreamers" when he calls her "a Donna Quixotta de la Mancha."

In a recording made by Welles for one of the stories he audiotaped for the Japanese market, used by the Munich Film Museum to help introduce its restoration of *The Dreamers*, he calls Dinesen "a writer I love as Ben Jonson did Shakespeare, 'this side idolatry.'" Truffaut pointed out that long before Welles began filming Dinesen's work, he created a character resembling Dinesen (Baroness Karen Blixen) in Katina Paxinou's Baroness Sophie in *Mr. Arkadin*. The wizened grande dame, who pages through a scrapbook revealing Arkadin's past, refuses to condemn her former lover for constructing an elaborate myth about himself. In that

Oja Kodar, a Yugoslavian actress-sculptor-writer, was Welles's companion from 1962 through the end of his life in 1985, collaborating with him on many film and television projects. With them in this picture taken in Welles's final months is his poodle, Kiki. *(Gary Graver)*

film's most moving moment, Sophie says with weary grace, "If that's the way he remembers it . . ." Dinesen's mystical tales appealed to Welles in his later years because they offer an intensely poetic vision that captures the simultaneously tragic and absurd nature of life, its riotous emotions and their ultimate evanescence. Her preoccupation with mortality in a godless yet richly spiritual world echoed Welles's own lifelong obsession with death, showing him a new approach to his ambivalent feelings about his own impending extinction. The writer's serious play with narrative form, her way of using artifice within artifice to bring meaning to the chaos of life, struck a receptive chord with Welles, who had been conducting similar experiments since his early days as a radio storyteller.

Krohn aptly describes *The Dreamers* as "an attempt at a summing-up . . . of [Welles's] period of wandering and independence." As in so much of Welles's late work, *The Dreamers* contains many echoes of his relationship with Kodar herself: his ambiguous status as her lover and patron, their poignant discrepancy in age, their nomadic lives, her artistic pursuits, his kaleidoscopic genius, even the "unfinished" nature of their careers, searching for meaning in lives filled with chaos. Kodar has pointed out that in light of the various careers she has pursued, she identifies with Pellegrina's need to be "many persons."

Welles intended the 35mm footage he shot for *The Dreamers* as promotional material for a feature; until the end of his life, he vainly sought outside investors to fund its completion. Graver and Kodar think the "test" footage would have wound up being used in the film if it had been fully financed.

While transforming the Spaulding house in Hollywood into a nineteenth-century villa in Milan, Welles kept augmenting the backyard for use as a set, building a walkway and a circular dolly track, erecting a piece of metal fence, and hanging lights around the garden. "When we shot in the garden," Graver recalls, "we had very little light. He said, 'Darker, Gary.' I said, 'We don't even have the exposure.' He said, 'Well, just barely get it.' Those night exteriors were the toughest challenge I had with Orson." The most beautiful image is a magical long shot of Pellegrina sitting before a fountain in the garden, shimmering lights playing all around her; Welles had Graver position little lights and mirrors on the trees and bushes.

For another scene in the garden, the small crew produced huge clouds of smoke, which brought out the local fire department. As Oja and the crew hurried to conceal the props and themselves in the shed housing the pool equipment, Welles sat "serenely" in a chair under a tree smoking his cigar, Kodar recalled. When the fire chief arrived, Welles said disingenuously, "I am enjoying this evening!" The chief replied, "Mr. Welles, I know you are a great magician, but please don't make me believe that all the smoke is coming out of your cigar!" The media's knee-jerk obsession with Welles's weight colored the reporting of that event in the *National Enquirer:* "Orson Welles had a backyard barbecue that got out of hand. His hamburgers sent up so much smoke that neighbors called the fire department." This silly item is a striking example of how the media discourse on Welles in his later life substituted a derisory passion for food for his true passion, independent filmmaking, which was considered unnewsworthy and thus deemed nonexistent.

Usually Welles was able to work with ease within his low-budget limitations, finding ingenious solutions that didn't cost much if anything. Occasionally, though, he chafed at his limitations, and his eyes became too big for his wallet. For one of the last shots filmed on *The Dreamers*, Graver lit a room, and "Orson said he wanted some depth, so we lit the room beyond that. We lit the yard, then we lit the backyard. I said, 'This'll be expensive.' He said, 'Get the lights.' I said, 'OK, I'll do whatever you want.' And then he wanted to light the bushes, the trees, he kept adding on. We needed more crew, a generator. The lighting bill for one night's shoot was a thousand dollars. He got mad at me for letting him go on and on: 'Why do you let me do this? Toland would never let me do this. We only used one light for a lot of the shots in *Kane.*'"

According to Graver, "We were going to shoot it in Europe and he was going to use [mostly] English actors, because they were close and they were better than Hollywood actors." The casting Welles had in mind included Timothy Dalton as Lincoln Forsner, Peter Ustinov as Baron Clootz, Oliver Reed as Guildenstern, the American actor Bud Cort as Pilot, Jeanne Moreau as an old woman in a nightclub, and perhaps an unknown Mexican boy as Emmanuele, whose singing voice eerily resembles Pellegrina's. Filmmaker Hal Ashby's Northstar Productions paid Welles to write *The Dreamers* but dropped the project after receiving his draft. According to *One-Man Band*, the script was rejected as "too poetic" and "too romantic." After Welles's death, Kodar made attempts to complete the shooting with other filmmakers, approaching Bogdanovich and Bernard Rose. (Jonathan Rosenbaum also suggested Raul Ruiz, but Kodar did not pursue that idea.) Since Marcus was to appear mostly as a shadowy presence following Pellegrina, Kodar felt *The Dreamers* could be completed without Welles, using another actor's voice to dub some of his lines.

"Then I understood—I understood the meaning of heaven and earth, and the stars and life and death and eternity": Welles delivers a monologue in a monastery in *The Dreamers* (1980–82), his unfinished adaptation of two Isak Dinesen tales filmed at his home in Hollywood. The merchant Marcus Kleek tells how he first heard the voice of the opera singer Pellegrina Leoni (Oja Kodar), who "took you out into a rose garden filled with nightingales and then lifted you up with her, higher than the moon" (frame enlargement). *(Orson Welles: The One-Man Band; Medias Res/The Criterion Collection)*

But when Rose and producer Denise DiNovi pitched the project to Columbia Pictures executive Amy Pascal in the 1990s, the response they received spoke volumes about modern Hollywood's true feelings toward Welles. Rose recalled, "We walked into her office and she said, 'Well, what's your idea?' And I said, 'Well, it's this old Orson Welles script . . .' And I think I got about that far into the pitch and then Amy Pascal went, 'Oh, no, I'm not doing that!'" In Woody Allen's 2002 film *Hollywood Ending*, the studio executive played by Treat Williams speaks for his fellow moguls when he declares, "I didn't get to run a studio by kowtowing to the temperamental demands of every director who thinks he's Orson Welles."

The last scene Welles ever directed was his monologue in a monastery, telling the story of Pellegrina to the offscreen "young gentleman" Lincoln Forsner. Graver remembers: "He had me pick up some black-

and-white film and come over one afternoon. We just shot it with true light, one through the window and one on his face. He was leaving it, almost like he knew something might happen to him." Marcus sits in a wooden chair, light streaming softly through the window in the background to the right of the frame. He wears a pointed white beard, square glasses, top hat, and a dark coat with winged shirt collar protruding. He relates that when he first heard the voice of Pellegrina Leoni from a Venice theater stage, "Then I understood—I understood the meaning of heaven and earth, and the stars and life and death and eternity. She took you out into a rose garden filled with nightingales and then lifted you up with her, higher than the moon." When twenty-four minutes of *Dreamers* footage was assembled by the Munich Film Museum in 2002 for public showings in Europe and elsewhere (including the 2004 Welles retrospectives at the American Cinematheque in Hollywood and the Film Forum in New York), Welles's monologue was effectively intercut with other scenes. This condensed version works surprisingly well as a self-contained short film with the heightened intensity of a lyric poem.

The farewell between Marcus and Pellegrina is among the most moving scenes in Welles's later work. An earlier version was shot inside the house, but the scene was moved outside, allowing deeper shadows (both versions are included in the Munich assemblage). The exterior scene is shot entirely over Marcus's back, his presence shadowing Pellegrina as she moves restlessly back and forth. Their melancholy, hypnotic voices in this beautiful exchange are played against the low hum of traffic noises from the unseen Hollywood street, making the nineteenth-century scene seem eerily outside real time:

> *Marcus:* I do not ask where you are bound for.
>
> *Pellegrina:* Many places . . .
>
> *Marcus:* Little lioness, you will need money.
>
> *Pellegrina:* I will earn my money, whoever I will be. [Fiercely] Marcus, I will be many persons.
>
> *Marcus* [giving her a ring]: Let this go with you, little lioness. I should like it to be easy. This ring will carry you left or right, in all of your directions.
>
> *Pellegrina:* Left or right, Marcus, but never home again.
>
> *Marcus:* Not—ever? Let me at least follow you. If you need a friend to help, then you could send for me.

Pellegrina [pacing the garden fence as the camera tracks with her]: Oh, Marcus, I would like it to be easy, and your heart to be light again. Try being someone else. Give up this game of being Marcus Cocozza. And then what possible difference does it make to the world if one person, one old man, stands here in this garden for a night or two, mourning a singer he has buried in her grave. All the people in the world ought to be, each of them, many persons. Then they'd be easy at heart. . . . What do you think, Marcus, of this paradise they talk about? Is it anywhere really?

The screenplay for *The Dreamers* was originally titled *Da Capo*, Italian for "from the beginning." That cue for opera singers can be heard in *Citizen Kane* when the exasperated Signor Matisti, giving a lesson to the hapless Susan Alexander, says wearily, "Da capo, eh?" For Welles, though, *The Dreamers* proved to be not a new beginning but a valedictory.

❖ ❖ ❖

"I limp along through the years writing hundreds of scripts and selling them from door to door. Usually they're slammed in my face," Welles said in 1978 while accepting his career achievement award from the Los Angeles Film Critics Association. The scripts he tried to sell in those years have a fascinatingly wide range of subject matter, reminding us how differently we would view the Welles canon if he had been able to make more of the projects he intended. He pointed out, "One makes generalizations about film directors, forgetting how hard it is to get a movie made. And if it just happens that you do three stories about detectives, then you're 'obsessed with detectives.' You know, directors have lots of obsessions, but they only get to show some of them." Among the scripts are *Assassin* (aka *The Safe House)*, about Sirhan Sirhan and a man who brainwashes him to serve as the patsy in the Robert Kennedy assassination; adaptations of Joseph Conrad's 1915 novel *Victory: An Island Tale* and Graham Greene's 1973 novel *The Honorary Consul;* Welles's cheerily autobiographical account of his early days in the theater, *The Cradle Will Rock;* and his and Kodar's dark, expressionistic fable about politics and homosexuality, *The Big Brass Ring.*

Only *The Big Brass Ring* has been filmed, though extensively rewritten by Welles scholar F. X. Feeney and the film's director, George Hickenlooper. Writing unmade screenplays channeled some of Welles's prodigious creative energies but ultimately proved even more frustrating than directing uncompleted films. What's hard about writing, Welles joked, is "that terrible silence when you wind up a chapter and the typewriter doesn't burst into applause."

Welles adapted *Assassin*, alternately titled *The Safe House*, in the late 1970s from a script by the playwright and screenwriter Donald Freed. Freed had collaborated with Mark Lane on the story of the 1973 film *Executive Action*, a prototype for Oliver Stone's 1991 *JFK*. Welles's adaptation of Freed's Sirhan script put his own distinctive inflections on the Nietzschean character of Sirhan's controller, Dr. William A. Must, a "behavior modification" specialist who voyeuristically observes the subject of his psychological experiment from behind a one-way mirror. Must appears to have been based on Dr. William Joseph Bryan Jr., a portly specialist in hypnosis whom William Turner and Jonn Christian, in their 1978 book *The Assassination of Robert Kennedy: The Conspiracy and Coverup*, suggest was Sirhan's CIA-connected "programmer." In Welles's screenplay, the wheelchair-bound Dr. Must, who would feel at home in a Dostoyevsky novel, is given intellectually sophisticated arguments, such as his contention that assassination is the most humane form of warfare because it does not kill en masse. Sirhan is portrayed sympathetically, as a weak, lonely young immigrant easily manipulated by a female agent, a refugee from torture by the Greek military junta, who uses sex and other ego-building maneuvers to lure him to the safe house (another part obviously designed for Oja Kodar).

The programming of Sirhan to serve as a patsy in the RFK assassination is portrayed as a red herring designed to distract attention from the actual instigators and perpetrators of the plot. The script identifies the FBI as the agency behind the plot, which is delegated to a paramilitary group, some of whose members evoke real-life characters who later surfaced in the Watergate scandal; the handling of Sirhan by Dr. Must echoes the CIA's infamous mind-control experiments that led to Richard Condon's brilliant 1959 novel about the "brainwashing" of a programmed assassin, *The Manchurian Candidate*. Welles's *Assassin* would have been a more dramatically concentrated, less surreal companion piece to the 1962 John Frankenheimer film of Condon's novel, and as such could have been filmed inexpensively. Relentlessly intercutting its taut storyline with newsreel footage leading to the assassination at Los Angeles's Ambassador Hotel on June 5, 1968, *Assassin* would have raised provocative questions about an event whose many unsolved questions have drawn far less attention than the killing of Robert Kennedy's older brother.

In his commentary accompanying the 2001 DVD edition of *JFK*,

Oliver Stone says that Welles "should have really made this movie. . . . [H]e had that jigsaw mind; I wonder what he thought." Stone evidently did not know about Welles's plans to make *Assassin.* Welles had a lifelong affinity with the kind of radical filmmaking Stone has sporadically succeeded in pushing through the commercial system; New Orleans district attorney Jim Garrison, the protagonist of *JFK,* appears briefly as a character in *Assassin.* One of the principal characters is a former Secret Service agent who was fired after trying to tell the Warren Commission the truth about what happened to JFK in Dallas; he joins the RFK campaign and tries vainly to prevent the hit on his candidate. The Welles-Freed script powerfully combines a suspense plot with complex reflections on American history but found no takers because its political viewpoint was too provocative.

Surinam, written in the early 1970s, is Welles's loose, streamlined adaptation of Joseph Conrad's oft-filmed *Victory.* Welles's last work for a major studio, the screenplay was written for Paramount and its subsidiary the Directors Company, the short-lived collaboration of Bogdanovich, Francis Ford Coppola, and William Friedkin. Conrad's Swedish loner, Axel Heyst, is changed by Welles to James Luce, an ex-priest whose retreat from society was caused by his loss of faith (Welles wanted to cast Ryan O'Neal, who was then close to Bogdanovich, his director on *Paper Moon, What's Up, Doc?* and *Nickelodeon).* The world comes to Luce in the grotesquely comical form of a trio of thugs seeking the fortune they are convinced Luce must have secreted on the island.

Unfortunately, *Surinam* is one of Welles's least dynamic screenplays, with an uncharacteristically forced happy ending and an only thinly developed treatment of Luce's redemption through a newfound faith in humanity. There are only intermittent suggestions of how Welles might have enlivened the drama by orchestrating the island atmospherics and bringing out the story's resemblances to Shakespeare's *Tempest* (which he quotes in *The Other Side of the Wind* by having Bogdanovich's Otterlake say mournfully at the end, "Our revels now are ended"). Bogdanovich claimed that *Surinam* was not made because "the rights to the novel fell apart," but no doubt the real cause was the collapse of the Directors Company in 1974 due to differences with Paramount over its penchant for projects the studio considered uncommercial. Welles's longtime interest in Conrad, whose *Heart of Darkness* he had chosen for his first Hollywood project, also led him to write an adaptation of *Lord Jim* in the early 1960s, but he had to drop it when Richard Brooks filmed the book in 1965 with Peter O'Toole. Welles told Bogdanovich, "If I were police commissioner of the world, I would put Richard Brooks in *jail* for what he did to *Lord Jim*!"

In the late 1970s, Welles became excited by the idea of filming *The Honorary Consul,* a novel rivaled for richness and complexity in Graham Greene's body of work only, perhaps, by *The Power and the Glory* and *The End of the Affair.* Welles made preliminary inquiries about the price of an option on the 1973 book (a relatively small sum) and then began writing the screenplay with Kodar. Welles's interest in the story stemmed from its complex pattern of betrayals among a small group of Latin American revolutionaries and the minor British functionary they hold hostage. The betrayals reflect the larger treachery of the police state and the former British colonialists, giving Welles ample room for interweaving the political and the personal. Welles and Kodar somewhat confusingly retitled the story *The Other Man*, which foregrounds its tragicomedy of machismo by pointing to the cuckoldry of the aging central character, Charley Fineman, by his amoral young wife and a revolutionist doctor (in the novel, Charley's surname is Fortnum, but the screenplay heightens his outsider status by making him Jewish).

Welles was to have played Charley, an overweight alcoholic treated by virtually everyone as pathetic and ridiculous until his experience with his kidnappers enables him to behave with unexpected nobility. Not surprisingly for a Welles screenplay, his character achieves equal dramatic status with Greene's tormented protagonist, Dr. Eduardo Plarr, whom the script renames Dr. Farrel. The essentially claustrophobic nature of the narrative makes *The Honorary Consul* problematic film material, but the Welles-Kodar screenplay maintains a taut suspense throughout while allowing the characters full dramatic latitude to explore their philosophical and political battleground. It's an effective adaptation of a novel whose density would have defeated most screenwriters. But Welles's hopes of making the film collapsed when he neglected to send in the check for the option, and a film company bought the rights while he and Kodar were still finishing the script. Welles went to the company, offering to sell them his services as writer, director, and star, but the company, fearing legal consequences, refused to read the script. "I wish I could buy it back," Welles said, "because I believe in it very much." (The book was filmed in 1983 by director John Mackenzie; in the United States the title was changed to *Beyond the Limit.*)

At one point when they were trying to market their script, Kodar recalled, Welles told her, "It should say, 'By Oja Kodar and Orson Welles.' I said, 'Don't be stupid, Orson. Who's going to buy a script written by

Oja Kodar?' With some little things I wrote, he said, 'Add my name—it's much easier to place something of Orson Welles than of Oja Kodar. Nobody knows about you. And later we'll take it off.' Then one day, he came from some meeting, very disappointed, and said, 'Baby, I was wrong. Take my name off everything. Your name might go through, but my name won't!'"

She wondered why Welles kept having such difficulties finding backers for his work.

> I asked him, because it puzzled me. I knew how he worked, how responsible he was, his love for the work. I said, "Baby, what is this thing?" And he said to me, "Once you get branded . . . " And I didn't understand: it seems to me too hard, too crazy to be true. . . . [T]hen once while we were shooting *The Other Side of the Wind* in Arizona, I went to see a rodeo, and I saw the branding of a calf. I came back home and I said, "Orson, I think I understand. It's a piece of hot iron, and you can never take it off. " He said it started basically with *It's All True*. And it *wasn't* all true. It started with that, and it continued.

Autobiographical overtones abound in a screenplay Welles wrote in the last year of his life, *House Party*, based on a story Kodar wrote in the 1970s, "Crazy Weather" (that and *Blind Window* were alternate titles for the script). Suffused with poetic imagery and narrative ambiguities, *House Party* deals with a theme that would assume increasing importance to Welles in his old age (and beyond): inheritance. Set in a decadent, labyrinthine old house in the rainy countryside of northern Spain over a three-day period in 1931, this seriocomic story details the power struggles of a grotesque set of greedy, desperate characters squabbling over the estate of the recently deceased Don Eduardo. Some of the characters seem explicitly modeled on people in Welles's life, including Francine, the "Princessa" Tremonte, Eduardo's ex-wife and claimant, who resembles Welles's wife Paola Mori, the Italian Countess di Girfalco; and Daddo, a greedy and effete interior decorator and antique dealer "vaguely Russian, on his mother's side" and named after Welles's own "Daddo," his Russian-born guardian Dr. Maurice Bernstein, whom he blamed for stealing part of his estate. Welles probably would have played Prince Willi, Francine's second husband, who, though Sicilian and Polish, is described as "so perfectly an Edwardian figure of a man that he actually resembles the King for whom the age was named." Like Daddo, Willi is portrayed as homosexual.

The house is said to be haunted, but the supernatural elements of the script are rendered more playfully than insistently. Mercedes, a young maid gradually revealed to be Eduardo's illegitimate daughter, "haunts" the estate through her moral claims upon it. Her insistence on her right to inherit Eduardo's property, though it is blocked by his crooked lawyer, mysteriously causes the death of the Princessa; Mercedes is regarded as a "witch" because of the strange power she exerts, a function of the other characters' unacknowledged guilt. The mortal struggle of wills between Mercedes and Francine (who might have been played by Kodar) eerily prefigures the battle that later ensued over Welles's estate between Kodar and the Paola/Beatrice side of his unconventional ménage. Even though Mercedes is portrayed as ruthless and vindictive, the script's sympathies largely go to her, because she has been so unjustly slighted.

Written in novelistic narrative form but in the present tense of a screenplay, *House Party* is among the most fully fleshed-out of Welles's scripts, vividly conjuring up rich visual imagery and eerie sound patterns; it reads so much like a film directed on paper that the reader can't help wondering if Welles realized he would never get to film it. Welles started a rewrite with a new title, *Mercy*, keeping the European background of some of the characters but relocating the story in 1931 Kentucky. Less poetic in tone, *Mercy* might have failed to replace *House Party*'s fascinating tension between modern characters and the quasi-medieval milieu of pre-Franco Spain, but the later draft's fragmentary nature leaves that an open question. (The name of the central character in both versions seems a nod to Welles's old friend and colleague Mercedes McCambridge, known to her friends as "Mercy.") Welles shares credit with Kodar for his unfinished *Mercy*, his last work as a writer.

❖ ❖ ❖

Welles also tried to help Gary Graver with his directing career. During the 1970s, Graver planned to direct Welles in a low-budget film, *A Hell of a Woman*, which they adapted from Jim Thompson's novel about a door-to-door vacuum cleaner salesman who becomes involved in a string of murders. Bud Cort and Kodar were to play the leads, with Welles as the salesman's boss; the Welles and Kodar characters were to be Mexicans. Graver found the down-and-out, formerly blacklisted Thompson

> living in an apartment right behind the Chinese Theater [in Hollywood]. He gave me all his pocket books without even knowing me. I Xeroxed them

and gave half to Orson. Orson said the best one to do would be *Pop 1280*, but that it would be too expensive because we would have to burn down a black shantytown [it was filmed in 1981 by Bertrand Tavernier as *Coup de Torchon*], so he said, "Let's do *A Hell of a Woman.*" Orson gave me two thousand dollars, twice, to option it.

Orson sent me to the meat market for a roll of butcher paper and told me to buy Magic Markers and thumbtacks. He said, "Tape the butcher paper around three walls. Draw square boxes on the paper. Write what happened in each chapter. Put a chapter here and the notes there. Rewrite." We wrote it together—he would sit there and say, "Let's move that. Cut a square out and move it here." I couldn't raise the money, and lost the option. Thompson's wife and family sold the rights to a French producer [after the writer's death in 1977], and it was made [by director Alain Corneau in 1979] as *Serie Noire.*

Welles also did some writing on a clunky horror movie Graver directed in 1982, *Trick or Treats*, but was credited only as "magical consultant." Graver's adolescent son Chris stars as a demented practical joker in this tongue-in-cheek *Halloween* ripoff, filmed for only $50,000. Traces of Welles's satanic young alter ego Eldred Brand from his 1933 play *Bright Lucifer* can be faintly discerned in the character of young Christopher in *Trick or Treats*, who plays with black magic.*

Gary Graver's absorption in his work with Welles undoubtedly hampered his career in mainstream movies. He occasionally has been called upon to do second-unit shooting for major films, such as on Steven Spielberg's *Raiders of the Lost Ark*, *The Color Purple*, and *Always;* Walter Hill's *The Driver* and *The Warriors;* and the Bruce Lee martial arts film *Enter the Dragon.* But the films Graver has directed and/or photographed have tended to be marginal, low-budget programmers, and his major work for Welles has gone largely unseen in the United States. Graver was even excluded from credit on *Orson Welles: The One-Man Band*, de-

---

* *Bright Lucifer*, set in an isolated cabin near an Indian reservation in Wisconsin, had its first production in 1997, when a Madison theater company staged it under the direction of Jay Rath. Ariel Molvig played the "bitch boy" Eldred, an orphan who falls under the care of a vaguely Hearstian newspaper editor, W. B. (Bill) Flynn, and his brother Jack, a John Barrymore–like horror-movie actor. The play's largely incoherent ruminations on evil and its confused homosexual undertones baffled me when I first read this half-baked roman à clef in the 1960s, without the benefit of later research into its autobiographical aspects. (The manuscript survives at the State Historical Society of Wisconsin in Madison, to which it was donated in 1962 by Welles's longtime attorney, L. Arnold Weissberger.)

spite the fact that he shot most of the footage in that compendium. Bogdanovich gave Graver his rightful credit on the reedited American version, which debuted on Showtime in 2003.

Undaunted, Graver has found enterprising ways of making his contributions more visible. He produced the documentary *Working with Orson Welles* for the home-video market in 1993, and with his third wife, former actress Jillian Kesner, established the Orson Welles Archive. They travel the world showing their collection of Welles films (finished and unfinished) to enthusiastic audiences at film festivals and museums. While not as satisfying as it would be to have *The Other Side of the Wind* playing in theaters, Graver's talks and screenings provide the kind of guerrilla-filmmaker, alternative-cinema distribution that Welles would have appreciated.

Welles paid a heartfelt tribute to his indispensable cameraman in 1979:

> Gary is an absolutely first-class cinematographer. He has a strong visual sense and the taste to go with it. He commands the highest degree of technical expertise, and I know of nobody who can lead a crew with more authority. His people always like him, and he knows how to get that extra degree of effort, and to maintain an atmosphere of enthusiasm on the set. As a director-producer, I especially prize him for being such an exceptionally fast worker. You are always ahead of schedule with Gary Graver. . . . Above all, he knows how to get it all up on the screen, to make every dollar count. This degree of efficiency and this combination of talent is rare indeed.

❖ ❖ ❖

Welles had many unproductive lunches with potential investors at the West Hollywood bistro Ma Maison, whose proprietor, Patrick Terrail, welcomed him as a regular guest along with his tiny, mischievous poodle, Kiki. Once in a great while, however, Welles received an actual offer to make a film.

He told me in 1970 that he had been asked to direct a film for Warner Bros. in the late 1960s. The offer came from the studio's production chief, John Calley, an unusually sophisticated Hollywood executive who supervised Stanley Kubrick's films for the studio and was one of the producers of *Catch-22*. But Welles said he declined because "I can't get up at six o'clock every morning." "That's not true," Graver insists. "He used to love to get up at six in the morning. Every set I was with him anywhere in the world he was acting, he was the first person there, waiting for everybody else to come in. He didn't sleep straight through the night, he had insomnia. He slept strange hours, took naps." Graver thinks Welles's excuse was one of his ways to "put people off." By this stage of his career, he was understandably skittish about dealing with major studios. He also told me that he was resisting suggestions to take a regular role in a television series. The grueling work schedule on a series "would kill me," he said. "It would literally kill me."

Welles was offered an unlikely big-budget project by Paramount and Disney, the 1980 live-action film version of E. C. Segar's comic strip *Popeye.* Maybe they thought of Welles because the title character is so identified with a food that gives him superhuman strength (spinach). Even though Welles was a comic-book fan in his youth and showed the influence of *Batman* in the boldly angled expressionist style of *Citizen Kane*, he "didn't want to do [*Popeye*] because it was a cartoon," Graver reports. The lucrative job went to Robert Altman, who made the poorly received film with Robin Williams in the title role.

An even more bizarre mismatch was the courtship of Welles by the Utah-based independent company Sunn Classics, which successfully produced wilderness-adventure movies such as *The Life and Times of Grizzly Adams* and *Adventures of Frontier Fremont* and pseudodocumentaries on subjects including Bigfoot, UFOs, and Noah's Ark. Relying to what was then an unusual degree on market-testing techniques, Sunn four-walled (that is, rented theaters to exhibit) its low-budget films to rural and small-town audiences. "Orson and I went to Sunn Classics; they wanted him to do an animal picture," relates Graver. "At the office, we saw trailers for their movies. Orson asked them how they knew what the audience wanted. They said, 'We go to this place'—which is now the Harmony Gold Theater on Sunset—'and we wire people's wrists when they're watching animal footage. We check the seismograph, and if they get excited, we make a picture about that.' Orson just shook his head in disbelief."

Welles told Graver that "for the rest of his life, he didn't want to do any films unless he wrote them himself. He said he wasn't a director for hire anymore, he didn't want to do anyone else's material: 'I'm only doing my own stuff.'" But shortly before Welles's death, producer Jimmy Hawkins asked Graver to sound him out about writing and directing a TV miniseries called *The Robber Barons.* Evidently the project was to have been based on leftist historian Matthew Josephson's 1934 book of that title about J. P. Morgan, John D. Rockefeller, Andrew Carnegie, E. H. Harriman, and other titans of nineteenth-century American capitalism. For Welles, the subject matter would have harked back to the progressive concerns of the Popular Front and *Citizen Kane*, whose industrialist Walter P. Thatcher is partly based on Morgan; Welles plays Morgan in the 1980 Yugoslavian film *Tajna Nikole Tesle (Tesla)*. Welles said he was interested in *The Robber Barons*, but the project died with him.

❖ ❖ ❖

Peter Bogdanovich sought to help Welles professionally in his later years, but their relationship became increasingly "poisonous" (Bogdanovich's word) during the 1970s, partly because of Welles's jealousy over the brief flourishing of his protégé's directing career. Their interview book was stalled because Welles instead made deals with book and magazine publishers to write his memoirs. In the summer of 1985, Welles accused Bogdanovich of holding on to the interview transcripts, which had been misplaced, to "just publish" after his death, and Bogdanovich returned the material to him, eventually recovering it to publish a 1992 volume edited by Jonathan Rosenbaum (the book became part of Welles's legacy to Oja). Bogdanovich let Welles stay at his Bel-Air home for about two years during the 1970s and shoot party scenes there for *The Other Side of the Wind*. Once when Bogdanovich poked his head into a room where Welles was editing some footage, Welles barked at him to get out. Another time, while Welles was busy with *Other Wind* and Peter was in Europe making *Daisy Miller*, Welles sat in Peter's posh living room and remarked to anyone within earshot, "If *I* had lived here when I was young, I would have had parties every night. Peter just sits around like an old man who can't get it up anymore."

Peter tried to get Welles work as a director on *Surinam* and other projects, but Welles felt that Peter didn't do enough for him. They had improbable plans to costar in a film Welles was to direct on Dumas père and fils, a project of Welles's since the 1950s and an outgrowth of his unsold 1956 TV pilot *Camille, the Naked Lady, and the Musketeers*. Some of Welles's suggestions to Bogdanovich may have contained an element of malice, such as endorsing his notion of shooting *At Long Last Love* in black-and-white or urging him to film Henry James's novella *Daisy Miller* with Cybill Shepherd. Bogdanovich talked about playing Winterbourne in *Daisy Miller* with Welles directing; fortunately, Barry Brown was cast in that part, but Shepherd, although physically right for the title role, proved unable to handle its dramatic demands. Those two resounding flops sank Bogdanovich's career, prompting an orgy of schadenfreude from the Hollywood community, which resented both his success and his arrogance.

The Welles-Bogdanovich relationship fell apart over a project Welles was planning to direct with Bogdanovich producing, the film version of Paul Theroux's novel about a Singapore pimp with a heart of gold, *Saint Jack.* Shepherd had been granted the film rights as the result of a legal dispute with *Playboy* over its unauthorized use of frame enlargements from her nude scene in *The Last Picture Show.* Bogdanovich, in need of work himself, took over the project from Welles, claiming he felt obligated to Shepherd. "Welles said he understood, but in effect this ended our work together," Bogdanovich recalled.

> What had been a kind of specter behind our friendship—that I was in some way playing Prince Hal to his King Henry IV or Falstaff—had finally become a reality neither of us had wanted. . . . He was very demanding, he was difficult. He gave a lot in return. There came a point in a lot of people's lives with Orson when they had to decide whether they were going to pursue their own life, or just take care of Orson. Or at least help Orson take care of himself. There came a point in my life where I just had to move on.

Bogdanovich had hoped to cast Welles in his 1976 film about early Hollywood, *Nickelodeon,* but Columbia balked at Bogdanovich's insistence on shooting in black-and-white, as Welles had urged. Bogdanovich recalled, "The project *(Nickelodeon)* was abruptly canceled (though later reestablished at far worse terms [in color and without Welles, whose role as a film company boss went to Brian Keith]) and when I told him, Orson made what I thought at the time was a strange remark, 'Well, that's the end of my career in Hollywood.'"

Not quite.

❖ ❖ ❖

In 1985, Welles almost directed a film about his youthful experiences staging Marc Blitzstein's controversial labor opera, *The Cradle Will Rock.* Welles wrote the script for producer Michael Fitzgerald, taking off from an earlier script by the formerly blacklisted screenwriter Ring Lardner Jr., a member of the Hollywood Ten. Offered the project in 1983, Welles told Fitzgerald he would rewrite the Lardner script and instead completed an original screenplay that was published in 1993 by Santa Teresa Press. The nostalgic, gently self-mocking film Welles envisioned, with Rupert Everett playing his younger self, came close to fruition before the funding collapsed a few months before Welles's death.

Welles's *Cradle* film was planned as a relatively low-budget ($5 million) production to be photographed by Graver on color film stock for release in black-and-white. Shooting was planned for Los Angeles, New York, New Jersey, and Rome's Cinecittà, where shooting of interiors was set to begin in January 1985. But in December the major investor, Washington, D.C., exhibitor Ted Pedas, pulled out because Fitzgerald and executive producers John Landis and George Folsey Jr. could not find a distribution deal.* When his *Cradle* film fell apart, Welles sarcastically told Leaming, "Another splendid example of my obsessive need not to finish a picture. . . . Every studio and every major distributor has had the script and turned it down. If I were a young man today and I had a script for *Citizen Kane*, I wouldn't get a distribution deal! It's crazy. . . . It's the most ungrateful medium in the world. . . . I don't know how to write one more marketable. It just shows me that I really shouldn't have stayed in this business, because it's too ridiculous."

Cradle is an unmade Welles project of unusual interest because it would have been the most openly autobiographical of his dramatic films, a portrait of the artist as a twenty-two-year-old wunderkind. His *Cradle* film would have served as an opportunity for Welles to reflect on the theater and on youthful idealism, making it the obverse of his darkly satirical reflection on the cinema and disillusioned old age in *Other Wind*. Rather than showing an elderly director at the end of his tether, in the *Cradle* screenplay Welles offers a portrait of himself at a perilous moment of youthful glory when the world was still his to conquer. But that portrait remains somewhat indistinct because of the way Welles sanitizes both his politics and his sexuality.

Amy Irving was to have played Welles's first wife, Virginia Nicolson, whose marriage to him already was shaky at the time he staged Blitzstein's *Cradle*. When the funding for his *Cradle* film became uncertain, Welles made a failed pitch for help to Irving's then husband Steven Spielberg at a lunch that has passed into Hollywood legend. One Welles scholar, Richard France, even wrote a play about that lunch portraying Spielberg as a villainous symbol of New Hollywood selfishness and greed. The lunch occurred not long after Spielberg, an admirer of Welles's work, paid $60,500 for a sled said to have been one of those used as Rosebud in *Kane*. Welles mischievously told the press that "the sled he bought was a

---

* The manslaughter charges originally filed in 1983 against Landis and Folsey for their involvement in the deaths of actor Vic Morrow and two illegally hired children, Renee Shin-Yi Chen and My-ca Dinh Le, during the 1982 filming of *Twilight Zone—the Movie* could not have helped their efforts to find a distributor for the Welles project. Landis, director of that *Twilight Zone* segment, and Folsey, its associate producer, were not acquitted until 1987.

fake," a comment that could not have pleased Spielberg. Around the same time, Welles was fretting over the fact that Spielberg had never offered him a job directing for his television series *Amazing Stories.* "Why can't I direct an *Amazing Stories*?" Welles wondered to Graver. "Everybody else is doing *Amazing Stories.*" Welles hoped Spielberg's deep pockets would open up to make his *Cradle* film a reality and had cast Irving partly for that reason.

Although it's a shame that Spielberg failed to make the project happen, he may have resented Welles's transparent maneuvering. During their lunch at Ma Maison, the younger director pointedly ignored the subject of *Cradle* and spent most of his time asking Welles about *Citizen Kane.* Welles later complained that Spielberg didn't even pick up the check, although Emily Post probably would observe that it was Welles who invited Spielberg to lunch, not the other way around. Welles perhaps was not aware of Spielberg's Oedipal feelings toward David Lean and other legendary old directors, whom he has tended to view not only as father figures but also as rivals.* Nor did Welles factor in Spielberg's conflicted feelings about his wife's career and his reluctance to mix his personal and professional lives, a habit that also caused Irving great frustration and may have contributed to the failure of their marriage. Spielberg, however, insisted to Graver in 2005 that he had sent Welles's *Cradle* script around Hollywood and offered to put his name on the film as presenter, but that he could raise no interest in it.

So it was left to Tim Robbins to become the cinematic chronicler of the saga of *The Cradle Will Rock,* a task he faced with what seems a similarly Oedipal ambivalence toward the larger-than-life figure of Orson Welles. Writer-director Robbins's 1999 film *Cradle Will Rock,*† which deals in part with the Welles-Houseman stage production, gives Blitzstein screen credit for his contribution but none to Welles himself. Rob-

---

* During the shooting of *Other Wind,* Welles was riding in an open convertible eastward on Sunset Boulevard near the Bel-Air gate. As his car pulled up for a red light next to a bus stop, he came face-to-face with a young woman sitting on a bench. She was reading a book on David Lean and was startled to see Orson Welles staring at her from a few feet away. Welles said simply, "Wrong director, my dear." Then his car sped away, probably leaving her wondering if she had been hallucinating.

† Omitting the definite article in the film's title is a clumsy affectation perhaps meant to suggest that *Cradle Will Rock* is not strictly an adaptation of the work of either Welles or Blitzstein.

bins splendidly re-stages parts of the historic 1937 New York opening night, but the events surrounding it are only part of a sweeping, boldly illuminated cinematic mural about the artistic and political ferment of the Popular Front period. Also depicting such flamboyant historical characters as the Mexican painter Diego Rivera (Rubén Blades), William Randolph Hearst (John Carpenter), and Nelson Rockefeller in his youthful days as an art patron (John Cusack), Robbins sets them and the production of *Cradle* against a backdrop of American labor unrest, the rise of European fascism, and the start of the anti-Communist crusade led by Rep. Martin Dies and HUAC.

Robbins's dominant theme is the seductive power of money on artists in America. In one way or another, the various artists portrayed on-screen are tempted to compromise their idealistic visions by selling out to the system, represented by corrupt patrons such as Hearst, Rockefeller, and the federal government. "Artists are whores, like the rest of us," gloats Hearst. This echoes Blitzstein's Brechtian depiction of the social contract as a pervasive form of prostitution. His Steeltown boss, Mister Mister, proclaims, "Every man has his price." Blitzstein (played by Hank Azaria) counters this cynicism with a fervent plea for mass solidarity. Robbins faithfully renders the composer's touchingly naive hopefulness while also suggesting that because of the stubborn durability of the American system, revolution can succeed in the United States only in the form of theater.

Although Welles might have admired the way Robbins widens the social context of the *Cradle* controversy, the more intimate treatment of the subject in the Welles script, partly dictated by budget considerations, allows greater opportunity to explore his own character. But despite having Houseman observe that Welles is "Mephistophilis [Christopher Marlowe's spelling] to his own Faust," Welles's script never fully confronts the implications of that provocative phrase, which Welles also used to describe John Huston in his speech at the 1983 Huston AFI award tribute. The most we get in Welles's *Cradle* script is his self-critical rumination:

> I might find some way to get the show on in spite of everything—and that could help to make the actors' careers—it would certainly save Marc's artistic life. Mr. Sheldon* says yes—I'm on to a great project. But like every great project, he says, there's something wrong with it, and somebody will have to pay. The "somebody" this time would be our theater—the people left in it, who could be punished. It might even turn out that I'm the one

---

* Edward Sheldon, a paralyzed playwright who served as a dramaturge to Welles and many others in the New York theater.

> who has the most to gain. I could look braver than I am, and be more famous than I deserve to be.

The *Cradle* script leaves most of these themes tantalizingly unresolved. Welles seemed to admit as much when speaking to Leaming about his character in the story: "I really don't know this man," he conceded. Perhaps Welles would have come to a clearer understanding of the character in the filming process, as he did with his protagonist in *Kane*. But Charles Foster Kane was a fictional character Welles could examine from a detached perspective; it is less certain he could have done so with a character directly representing himself.

The depiction of Welles is even more glaringly unrecognizable in Robbins's *Cradle*. As played by the Scottish actor Angus MacFadyen, Welles is little more than a bemused spectator to the rush of events around him, rather than a guiding force in an innovative theatrical event. Drunken, pretentious, and overbearing, this director is a shambling, self-destructive buffoon who cares little for the radical message of Blitzstein's opera, regarding it largely as a vehicle for reckless self-promotion. MacFadyen utterly lacks Welles's youthful charm and charisma; the role should have been played by Robbins himself, whose tall, baby-faced, commanding presence is remarkably Wellesian. But such close identification with Welles does not fit Robbins's agenda.

Both Welles's script and Robbins's film introduce the young Orson as he rehearses *Faustus*, his Federal Theatre production of Marlowe's *Doctor Faustus*. The *Faustus* rehearsals are shown at greater length in Welles's script, with loving attention to the technical wizardry employed. His film would have been as much about the theatrical black magic of *Faustus* as about the stark simplicity of his staging of *Cradle*. Robbins shows little interest in Welles's brilliance as a stage director, using *Faustus* merely as a backdrop for depicting Welles as a screaming bully. In emphasizing that tyrannical side of Welles's directorial personality, Robbins misses the side that inspired fierce loyalty in almost everyone he worked with in theater and film. Robbins disregards Houseman's insightful tribute to Welles's "surprising capacity for collaboration" and extraordinary ability "to apprehend other people's weakness and strength and to make creative use of them: he had a shrewd instinctive sense of when to bully or charm, when to be kind or savage—and he was seldom mistaken."

Why Robbins chose to denigrate Welles while ostensibly celebrating a major achievement of his youth is hard to comprehend, although unfortunately symptomatic of the wider pathology of American hostility toward Welles. Perhaps Robbins's attempt to belittle Welles also stemmed from the competitive impulse between directors, an envious need to tear a giant down to ordinary proportions. But to give Robbins the benefit of the doubt, he may have been trying to demystify the role of the director, to focus attention on theatrical group effort. He goes too far, however, in making the final shape of the *Cradle* production seem merely accidental. One of Welles's great strengths as a director of both theater and film was his ability to improvise, his boldness in coming up with unexpected solutions that would turn defeat into advantage (hence his definition of a film director as "a man who presides over accidents").

Though Welles's essential radicalism was somewhat muted in later years due to the traumatic effects of the blacklist period, he never lost his intense interest in politics. When I asked Graver what he and Welles talked about in their many casual discussions over meals, he said they tended to discuss two subjects: filmmaking and Richard Nixon. The dark figure of Nixon occasionally haunts Welles's work. A Welles caricature of Nixon is displayed by Kodar in *One-Man Band:* two beady white eyes shining desperately, and scarily, out of a dark blue-gray background. One of the characters in Welles's *Surinam* screenplay is explicitly modeled on Nixon. And in his *Big Brass Ring* script, Welles has the old political hand Kim Menaker refer, not unsympathetically, to "poor Dick Nixon—mincing about inside his fortress in the Oval Room, all bristling with bugs—hoping a playback would eventually inform him who he was. . . . He told us often what he *wasn't*, but he never really got it figured out."*

Welles continued to develop projects on controversial contemporary political issues. He announced in 1977 that he planned to make a film about Patty Hearst, the kidnapped granddaughter of William Randolph Hearst. Describing her as "the central victim of our time," Welles contended that public opinion went against Hearst because of her family's riches; her story, he felt, was "the best human story in the last thirty years; better than *Kane.*" But the project went nowhere.†

---

* This description of Nixon anticipates the surreal portrait of the tormented ex-president offered by Donald Freed (coauthor with Welles of *Assassin)* and Arnold M. Stone in their 1983 play *Secret Honor*, filmed in 1984 by Robert Altman, with Philip Baker Hall playing Nixon.

† In 1988 director Paul Schrader made the film *Patty Hearst* from a screenplay by Nicholas Kazan, based on the book *Every Secret Thing* by Hearst and Alvin Moscow.

❖ ❖ ❖

After his relationship with Bogdanovich soured, Welles developed a close friendship with the independently wealthy filmmaker Henry Jaglom, who finances his own idiosyncratic low-budget movies. In equal parts maddening and enthralling, Jaglom's films play like extended improv sessions, usually about the filmmaker's relationships with his female friends and companions. His self-indulgence extends to his fellow actors and, for both good and ill, allows them a degree of freedom they seldom have in more mainstream films. When Jaglom pitched Welles the role of a magician in *A Safe Place*, the young director's first feature, Welles listened with an apparent lack of interest until he suddenly asked, "Can I wear a cape?" An image of Welles from that film has been used ever since by Jaglom as the logo for his International Rainbow Pictures: Welles as the archetypal cinematic magician, taking a rainbow out of a box.

Welles enjoyed the spontaneity of working with Jaglom, and his delightfully relaxed and witty performance as himself in *Someone to Love* is the closest he ever came on-screen to the way he usually behaved offscreen. A Jaglom talkfest filled with single Los Angeles women (including Kodar) trying to explain why they don't have mates, *Someone to Love* was filmed in the summer of 1985 at a small theater in Santa Monica and was released two years after Welles's death, providing a fitting valedictory to his screen career. He sits in the back of the theater ("I'm speaking from the cheap seats, not from Mt. Sinai") expounding eloquently, and never pretentiously, to Jaglom on the changing roles of the sexes in American life.

Welles's most memorable moments in *Someone to Love* come, fittingly, under the end credits: "Endings are a great American preoccupation," he says. "And happy endings, which is really what you are looking for, because you're a sentimentalist—happy endings depend on stopping the story before it's over. . . . For—what is it?—twenty thousand years, all the generations that have passed through all the civilizations of the world have been totally alone. We come into the world alone, we die alone, we live alone. Love and friendship is the nearest thing that we can find to create the illusion that we are not totally alone."

Reluctant to let him go, Jaglom keeps the cameras rolling, but Welles mischievously points out, "By this time, the credits are rolling down, and the audience, such as it may be, is on its way up the aisles. As far as this movie is concerned, it seems to me you've got your ending." "Why?" asks Jaglom. "Because we have come to the *end*," Welles says with a laugh, adding, "We really can't go on recording this. It's got too sweet."

Jaglom allows Welles the opportunity to end his acting career by calling "Cut!" repeatedly. "I'll say 'Cut'—*I'm* a director," Welles bellows. "'Cut!' . . . You want me to say 'Cut' *again?* He's a *born* director—he wants to improvise and do it twice. *'Cut!'*"

Welles is last seen without sound, as if already an image in memory, laughing his uproarious, volcanic laugh.

Jaglom was frustrated over Welles's difficulties trying to launch film projects: "I spent a lot of time trying to get *The Dreamers* made [as a $5 million production]. Going to everyone I knew in this town [Hollywood], and London, and Paris, and Hamburg, and Amsterdam. Endless meetings with people. And the consensus was they were all too scared of this with Orson Welles because they all had this mythology about him, all of which was untrue. . . . They had the excuse in this case to say, 'It's much too poetic, it's not commercial.' And maybe they were right, in their terms." Jaglom then volunteered, in 1981, to help Welles set up a different production. He urged Welles to write an original screenplay, and Welles responded with a contemporary political allegory, *The Big Brass Ring*, which he wrote with Kodar.

Described by Welles as "a terrible love story between two men," it deals with a rising American politician, Senator Blake Pellarin, and his mentor, Kimball Menaker, a former Roosevelt aide and Harvard professor whose political career was destroyed by a homosexual scandal (as was the career of Sumner Welles, Roosevelt's undersecretary of state, no relation to Orson). On a trip to Spain after losing a presidential election, Pellarin is reunited with the bitterly jealous and cynical Menaker, who has become the adviser to an Idi Amin–like African dictator.

To Krohn, Welles described Pellarin as "kind of a Hamlet. A self-destructive man who should be president or shouldn't, we're not sure." As the name Pellarin (cf. *pèlerin*, French for pilgrim) suggests, the script follows his quest to understand his own nature, a tragic coming to terms with his true desires, ambitions, and shame. In a climactic scene that Welles admitted was overtly symbolic, the reckless and guilt-ridden American politician gratuitously murders a beggar, demonstrating how low his surrender to his baser impulses has brought him and, by extension, how ambition and imperialism have fatally tarnished even the best in American political life. In the ironic denouement, Welles shows Pellarin getting away with his crime and taking off on a train with Menaker. The last line of the script is: "(If you want a happy ending, that depends, of course, on where you stop your story.)"

Welles's admission of his own brief ambition for the presidency in the 1940s helps make this character's conflicts seem personal to the filmmaker. Welles told Jaglom that Pellarin "is a great man—like all great men he is never satisfied that he has chosen the right path in life. Even being President, he feels, may somehow not be right. He is a man who has within him the devil of self-destruction that lives in every genius. . . . It is not self-doubt, it is *cosmic* doubt! What am I going to do—I am the best, I know that, now what do I do with it? . . . [T]his thing that always stops conquerors at the moment of victory[:] *That* is what *The Big Brass Ring* is about."

Jaglom was enthusiastic about this dark political allegory, which both men felt had some strong commercial elements, and he brought the Israeli financier and producer Arnon Milchan to the project. The budget was set at $8 million. Milchan set Welles only one condition: he had to convince a major star to play Pellarin in order to make the film commercially viable. The not ungenerous sum of $2 million was allocated for the salary offer, and a list of six stars was agreed upon by Welles and Milchan. The script went out in 1982 to Jack Nicholson and Warren Beatty (Welles's first and second choices), Clint Eastwood, Paul Newman, Robert Redford, and Burt Reynolds. They all passed.

"They hurt him very badly," said Jaglom. "In the fifteen years I knew him, that hurt him more than anything. . . . Orson always understood why the studios never wanted to finance his movies. He knew his name didn't guarantee them a profit. But he never understood how people who had wanted to be his friend, who talked publicly about how great he was, wouldn't help him when they had the chance."

Their reasons for rejecting it were varied: According to Jaglom, Nicholson wanted more money, Beatty wanted final cut as well as the right to rewrite and produce the film, Eastwood said his own political plans could be clouded by identification with the character, another said he didn't understand the script, and one of the stars (whose name was not disclosed by Jaglom) admitted that he was anxious about the homosexual theme. One star who, in Jaglom's words, "posed as one of Orson's closest friends, appearing on talk shows with him and having lots of lunches with him" (Reynolds, evidently) turned down the project through his agent, who said, "Our client is busy for the next five years, making *real* movies." Perhaps some of these men had valid artistic reservations about the project as well. Still, this sad chronicle is complicated by the fact that, as Jaglom revealed, "To Orson's discredit, the one person who he could've gotten to do it, he rejected. Bobby De Niro was willing to do it, but Orson felt he was too ethnic and urban for the part of the senator."

Nevertheless, the Welles-Kodar script suffers from an excess of what critic Manny Farber, referring to an Ingmar Bergman film, described as "undigested clinical material." Too many elements of Welles's personal psychodrama are touched upon yet not fully realized dramatically. Part of the problem was that some key elements of Pellarin's romantic life were drawn from Welles's relationship with Kodar, such as the story of the love letter Pellarin writes to his French-Cambodian mistress but Menaker doesn't deliver. Kodar's influence is also seen in the depiction of the character she was to have played, Cela Brandini, the inquiring TV reporter who serves as Pellarin's conscience; the role recalls Kodar's creative prodding of Welles and her beginnings in TV news. But the imperious Brandini outwardly resembles the Italian journalist Oriana Fallaci, grand inquisitor of dictators and other political criminals, who so fascinated and amused Welles that he also used her as a partial model for Susan Strasberg's character in *The Other Side of the Wind*. Borrowing aspects of Kodar for *two* characters in *The Big Brass Ring* somewhat muddies the already murky psychological waters, as does the general Welles-Kodar tendency to treat love stories as a poetic mélange of romanticism, cynicism, and impenetrable, almost private mystery.

Pellarin's deeply ambivalent relationship with Menaker, on the other hand, is more fully dramatized. It draws both from Welles's lifelong platonic friendship with his surrogate father, Roger Hill ("I'm the boy you could have had"), and from Welles's more conflicted, sexually charged relationships with various gay or sexually ambiguous friends and colleagues. The harsher side of Menaker's jealously vindictive behavior toward Pellarin is a reversal of Jake Hannaford's sadism toward the gay schoolmaster played by Dan Tobin in *Other Wind*. Pellarin, for his part, is halfheartedly accepting of Menaker's erotic attraction to him, perhaps out of guilt for the harm their friendship has caused the older man. Although Pellarin evidently did not reciprocate Menaker's advances while his student at Harvard, Menaker had to leave the university as a result, and the scandal has shadowed Pellarin ever since.

It's hard to believe that the continuing innuendos wouldn't already have fatally damaged Pellarin's career in politics or made him more cautious than he appears in the script. But the script should not be analyzed in strictly realistic terms: it has a fantastic, dreamlike aura. As was his practice, Welles barely indicates how he wants the story to look onscreen. A striking exception is the most bravura sequence, that of Pellarin and his mysterious female lover having a strange sexual encounter in a room overlooking an amusement park while Menaker watches from his perch on a Ferris wheel. Welles indicates that color flashes from offscreen fireworks should illuminate the room, interrupting the film's black-and-white cinematography, a potentially dazzling coup de théâtre.

Even more than most people's screenplays, Welles's scripts can be judged only tentatively as blueprints for filming, but overall this one seems sketchier than most. Jaglom was engaging in somewhat wishful thinking when he described it as "the bookend to *Citizen Kane*. It was about America at the end of the century—socially and politically and morally—as *Kane* and *Ambersons* are about America at the beginning of the century." In the end, Welles's *Big Brass Ring* seems a tantalizing disappointment. No doubt if he had been able to film it, that tentative judgment would have to be revised; comparing the script to *Touch of Evil* and *The Trial*, Rosenbaum observed that they "are all like the volcanic eruptions of a caged beast kept too long in confinement—excessive at times to the point of losing control over their own meanings, yet richer and more thrilling for all the headlong risks they take."

In 1997 writer-director George Hickenlooper filmed an imaginative six-minute teaser for *The Big Brass Ring*, accompanying his comments on the story with fragmentary scenes he and Matt Greenberg adapted from the Welles-Kodar script, starring Malcolm McDowell as Kim Menaker and Ivana Milcevic as Cela Brandini. That led to Hickenlooper's 1999 feature-length version for the Showtime cable TV channel, from the new adaptation he wrote with F. X. Feeney that stars William Hurt as Pellarin, Nigel Hawthorne as Mennaker (the film's spelling), and Irène Jacob as Cela Brandini. The screenwriters took considerable liberties with the original material, causing a backlash in some Wellesian quarters, but one has to grant them the same freedom Welles always took with *his* source material, including Shakespeare, whose plays he radically rearranged.

The Big Brass Ring film abounds in self-conscious allusions to other Welles works, including *Kane*, *Touch of Evil*, and *Chimes at Midnight*. There are even arcane allusions to his unmade film *Heart of Darkness* and his play *Bright Lucifer*. The title of that play is borrowed for Brandini's biography of Mennaker, whose book jacket carries a blurb from Knowles Noel Shane, a pseudonym Welles used as a young tabloid columnist in Dublin to praise his own theater performances. The film's broadest change, transferring the story from Spain to Hickenlooper's hometown of St. Louis, jettisons some of the original's cosmopolitan sensibility but has compensatory virtues in anchoring the moral problems bedeviling the American politician squarely in the heartland of darkness. A more drastic change is in the nature of Pellarin's confrontation with a shadowy figure from his past, transforming that figure from his former French-Cambodian mistress to his long-lost brother (Gregg Henry); that idea is already alluded to in Hickenlooper's short version.

Feeney wrote that the reasons for this

> one radical liberty we have taken . . . were partly practical—a mistress is no longer the kind of secret that can destroy a presidential hopeful, in America post-Clinton—but a more profound consideration applies, too, which is that Blake's anguish, his capacities as a leader, a lover, an amateur thief and possible killer, all register more tellingly if his guilt and shame are directed at a betrayed blood-relative. In writing free of the script, we sought inspiration from the life: Welles himself had a ghostly relationship with his schizophrenic older brother, Richard—a derelict to whom he provided lifelong income but whose path he crossed no more than once or twice after becoming famous.* This is a topic Welles never touched on [directly] in any of his films, doubtless because the pain was too deep. We broached it in his honor, not to "improve" Welles or invade his privacy, but to enter those uncharted spaces his death left unexplored, where his deepest sorrows may break bread with all of ours.

Though the subplot about the errant brother is intriguing, it makes *The Big Brass Ring* a much different picture from the one Welles intended. Jettisoning Pellarin's relationship with his ex-mistress dilutes his conflicts over his sexuality. And even if the Feeney-Hickenlooper script is looked at solely in its own terms, the intensity of the brothers' relationship unfortunately detracts from the centrality of the Pellarin-Mennaker relationship (Feeney is surely mistaken when he describes the mistress in the Welles-Kodar script as "the central figure from [Pellarin's] past"). A further problem with the film is that in the flashbacks showing Pellarin and his brother in their youth, the actors, Thomas Patrick Kelly and Carmine Giovinazzo, tear their passion to tatters so wildly that it's hard for the audience to relate to the largely unexamined conflicts these scenes are supposed to express. On the other hand, the rich love-hate tensions between Pellarin and Mennaker are brought splendidly to life. Hawthorne's performance, all silky malice and melancholic corruption, couldn't have been bettered by Welles himself, and Hurt, whose work usually seems

---

* Perhaps more often than that. In a January 1942 report from the set of *The Magnificent Ambersons*, *Los Angeles Times* film critic Philip K. Scheuer wrote, "When a carpenter somewhere offstage got in an extra blow with the hammer after the bell, Welles himself bellowed, 'Quiet!' He grinned. 'That's my brother,' he explained largely. 'Nice enough chap—but can't do a thing with him.'"

too constricted, rises to the challenge by tapping into unexpected emotional reserves. Hurt movingly conveys Pellarin's deepening sense of guilt for damaging, in his pursuit of political power, the people closest to him and his own elusive sense of personality.

Not all of Welles's friends and admirers were unequivocally pleased with Jaglom's efforts on Welles's behalf for *The Big Brass Ring* and other projects. Graver maintains that for all Jaglom did to try to find financing for *The Big Brass Ring*, he could have personally financed a Welles film but somehow never got around to doing so. Jaglom also stirred controversy by taping his luncheon conversations with Welles at Ma Maison. Jaglom claimed that Welles was aware of the taping and planned to use the material for his autobiography. Others have claimed that Welles didn't know about the taping until shortly before his death and felt betrayed by it. Welles's relationship with Jaglom, like his relationship with Bogdanovich, gave him vital encouragement he needed to keep going during the final difficult period of his life, but it was not the panacea he perhaps hoped it would be for the hurdles he continued to face in getting his films finished and released.

During the shooting of *A Safe Place*, Welles gave Jaglom some advice about filmmaking: "Make them as good as you can, so that you are satisfied, never compromising, because they are going to show up to haunt you for the rest of your life. Don't let anybody tell you what to do. And never make a movie for anyone else, or on some idea of what other people will like. Make it *yours*, and hope that there will be others who will understand. But never compromise to *make* them understand." Welles also told him, "Never give them control of your tools. Make the movies you want to make. On your own. And be free."

❖ ❖ ❖

Today, with the digital video revolution, it's become possible to shoot a feature for next to nothing. Graver says he could now make a movie for less than $1,000. What Welles could do with just a video camera and a small group of actors! But the biggest problem still is getting a film shown. Most theaters still require film prints, and the most insurmountable problem independent filmmakers have always faced is not raising the money to make a film but finding a distributor to get behind it. Today filmmakers have begun exploring promising new paths of distribution on the Internet and by releasing their films directly to the audience on DVDs. Welles could have used such networks to reach a substantial niche audience. When I met him in 1970, he spoke eagerly of the day when he could work for pay TV, explaining that it would enable him to work cheaply and for a specialized audience, bypassing the mass-market dictates that always bedeviled his career as a film director. That was not to happen, although he spent more and more time working in various forms of television during his later years.

Always pushing the bounds of cinematic technique, Welles said in his 1982 appearance at the Cinémathèque française, "I'm very interested in making films with video—we've been experimenting with it just now." As far back as the shooting of *Citizen Kane*, he had wondered aloud why it was necessary for film to go through a camera, and his great cinematographer Gregg Toland, just as much a visionary, predicted that some day the image would be transmitted electronically, bypassing film entirely. Welles declared at the Cinémathèque that it would be only a few years, or even a few months, before "we will be using tape with greater facility than we use film today *et avec la même définition* [and with the same definition]. . . . I like the look of video very much and I like video sound even though it's bad—probably that's *why*—and I love the control that I have over color and many other things." But he cautioned that whether or not video became a "new form" would be up to the new generation of filmmakers: "There is a great temptation to use the electronic world as a cheap form of movies. It's in your hands."

Unfortunately, Welles's hope for video proved too optimistic for the little time he had left. He wanted to shoot his last major project, *King Lear*, partly on video—for the intimate, interior scenes—with the crowd and exterior scenes to be shot on film. Welles told Krohn his *Lear* would be "the anti-spectacle. . . . Much, *much* more severe than anything I've ever done before. It will just be the actors, and that's all, absolutely all" (his description sounds not unlike the Peter Brook staging of *Lear* in which he starred on live television in 1953). Welles said he would approach the play as an "intimate, domestic tragedy, rather than an epic. The epic quality has to be in its poetry and in the minds of the audience. I think it's the only way to reach people today with that play. I don't think people have the ear or the *taste* for the operatic approach to it."

When Welles went to France in early 1982 to be inducted as commandeur of the Légion d'honneur and to try to win control of *The Other Side of the Wind*, he also used his cachet with the French to seek financing for his long-cherished film of *Lear*. If it had been made in America, the interiors would have been shot in the desert around Palm Springs; Kodar was to play Cordelia, and Welles was considering Mickey Rooney, Bud

Cort, or Abb Dickson as the Fool. Welles told Graver they would shoot *Lear* in black-and-white, but Welles eventually did some rethinking. His cinematographer on *The Trial* and *Chimes at Midnight*, Edmond Richard, recalled that Welles asked him in France in 1985 if he would be interested in shooting *Lear*. "It would have been very stylized," Richard reported. "He could not make it in black-and-white without being unable to find distribution in America, but he had a holy horror of color, and he said to me, 'I would make it in color without colors.'"

Meanwhile, Graver shot a four-minute test with Welles on color video, which was to have been transferred to black-and-white: "Just his head, moving around. Just like the still I have in *Working with Orson Welles*, same lighting. Damn good. It's disappeared—we never took it out of the lab." Welles also made a six-minute pitch for funding—on video—in March 1985, somberly dressed in gray and black, seated in front of two abstract paintings. That tape was shown publicly at the Rotterdam Film Festival in January 1986 and surfaced again in a third- or fourth-generation dupe at the 2005 Locarno retrospective. The extent of Welles's personal identification with Lear and all the play represents is impossible to miss in his comments on this unrealized project:

> *King Lear* is Shakespeare's masterpiece and, stripped of its classical or stage trappings, it's as strong now and as simple and as timeless as any story ever told. And what is simple for the story of *King Lear*—what is truly important—is not that the tragic hero is an old king, but that he's an old man. Just such an amiable, egocentric family tyrant as holds sway in the domestic scene even nowadays. Of course, we've been so famously liberated from the spice of the forbidden that nothing can be counted as truly obscene. But there is one exception: death.
>
> "Death" is our only dirty word. And *King Lear* is about death and the approach of death, and about power and the loss of power; and about love. In our consumer society, we are encouraged to forget that we will ever die, and old age can be postponed by the right face cream. And when it finally does come, we're encouraged to look forward to a long and lovely sunset.
>
> "Old age," said Charles de Gaulle, "old age is a shipwreck"—and he knew whereof he spoke. The elderly are even more self-regarding than the young. To their dependents the elderly call out for love, for more love than they can possibly receive, and for more than they are likely—or capable—of giving back. When old age tempts or forces a man to give away the very source of his ascendancy over the young, his power, it's they, the young, who are the tyrants, and he, who was all-powerful, becomes a pensioner.
>
> Of all the aches of the elderly, the loss of power is the most terrible to bear. The strong old man, the leader of the tribe—the city, the church, the

state, the political party, or corporation—demands love as a tyrant demands tribute; and, bereft of power, he must, like Lear, plead for it like a beggar. When, by self-abdication or forced retirement, such a one is suddenly deprived of his own life-sustaining tyranny, he can only flounder to the grave, struggling vainly to exact from those who have been the subjects of his whim some portion of that suffocating pity he now feels for himself. Impotent, from side to side he swings like the clapper in a bell, ringing soundlessly. He is then a castaway, banished to the desert island of his loneliness, cast out indeed from his own personal identity. "Who is it?" cries the old King Lear. "Who is it that can tell me who I am?" He has given up not only his crown; he has given up himself.

Well, you must forgive me if I've been telling you what our film will be about. To tell you what it'll be like won't be so easy. I can't really describe something which just at the moment is only in my mind. Even with a movie already on the screen, words don't get us very far. What I *can* tell you, though, is what this movie will *not* be. In any sense of the word, it will not be what is called a "costume movie." That doesn't mean that the characters are going to wear blue jeans; it does mean that a story so sharply modern in its relevancy, so universal in its simple, rock-bottom humanity, will not be burdened with the timeworn baggage of theatrical tradition. It will be just as free from the various forms of cinematic rhetoric—my own as well as the others—which have already accumulated in the history of these translations of Shakespeare into film. What we'll be giving you, then, is something new: Shakespeare addressed directly and uniquely to the sensibility of our own particular day.

The camera language will be intimate, extremely intimate, rather than grandiose. The tone will be at once epic in its stark simplicity and almost ferociously down-to-earth. In a word, not only a new kind of Shakespeare, but a new kind of film. I intend to keep the promise, and there's some basis for some optimism in the fact that I've invested so much time and energy and love in its preparation. Most importantly, the material from which this project will be realized is quite simply the greatest drama ever written.

Please forgive my outrageous lack of modesty, and thank you for giving me so much of your kind attention.

In February 1985, after another visit by Welles to France, Hervé Bourge, president of the television network TF-1, announced that it would coproduce *King Lear. Variety* reported that *Lear* was to be shot in French studios, in English, as early as that summer. But an alert reader of the trade paper could sense a certain porousness in the project's funding structure: French minister of culture Jack Lang had "promised an unspecified amount of coin from state coffers, pending more advanced production arrangements. The minister a couple of years back had shown willingness to invest in another Welles project, *The Dreamers*, provided essential backing could be ensured. Nothing came of it." As for the "more advanced production arrangements," *Variety* mentioned only "some talk of Canadian and American participation."

When the French funding fell through, for reasons not explained publicly until after his death, Welles felt deeply, even mortally, betrayed. "He died of *King Lear*," Dominique Antoine believed. "It killed him."

❖ ❖ ❖

To mark Welles's seventieth birthday on May 6, 1985, BBC TV showed a series of his films. Nothing comparable to that tribute appeared in America. On the contrary, the reviews of Barbara Leaming's biography in the weeks just before Welles's death that fall, sometimes in conjunction with reviews of Charles Higham's venomous *Orson Welles: The Rise and Fall of an American Genius*, read like premature obituaries. Most of the notices were depressingly and disgracefully similar in their ill-informed condescension, reflecting the reviewers' blithely unapologetic ignorance of Welles's body of work.

For Alden Whitman in the Hearst organization's *Los Angeles Herald-Examiner*, "[E]ver so often *Citizen Kane* appears on TV to illustrate what might have happened many times if its maker had been less self-indulgent. . . . But the stubborn fact is that Welles, for all the awe and affection he inspires, has not made a Hollywood film since *Touch of Evil* in 1957 [Whitman evidently never heard of *The Other Side of the Wind* or perhaps is too narrowly defining "Hollywood film"]. There have been European movies, to be sure, but these are seldom seen here." Julie Salamon in the *Wall Street Journal* lamented "a life that peaked 45 years ago . . . the best reminder this century has that the only thing worse than never achieving one's potential is to achieve it too early." Otto Friedrich in *Time* felt that Welles's is "one of the saddest stories of success and failure in American life. Sad because such enormous promise has remained so unfulfilled for so long. . . . Ever since *[Kane]*, for nearly half a century, it has been all downhill, all the way down to that obese figure holding up a wineglass in a TV commercial." If Welles read those reviews, they must have seemed a bitter premonition.

Toward the end, Welles was having trouble working for more than a few hours at a time and needed help from his driver and manservant, Freddie Gillette, to get out of bed. Suffering from diabetes, he went on a crash diet that enabled him to lose more than a hundred pounds in his final months, but the weight loss made him look unnaturally gaunt and sallow. While the diet may have been a necessity, it may also have been what killed him. A few months before he died, Welles had color portraits taken for that July's serialization of Leaming's book in the *New York Times Magazine.* "He kept saying to me, 'Time is precious,'" Graver reports. "He was so damn mad that he sat all day for this still photographer. He goes, 'It's the same shot, same width, the same angle, over and over. They said they had to get it right.' He said it was a waste of his day." The words chosen for the title of the cover story made it even more painful: "Orson Welles: The Unfulfilled Promise."

On October 9, the day before his death, Welles lunched with Burt Reynolds at Ma Maison. Although Reynolds had turned down *The Big Brass Ring,* he had made an amiable appearance on Welles's talk-show pilot *The Orson Welles Show* and, at that last meeting, was still professing eagerness to act for Welles. Reynolds said he wanted to star for Welles in a segment of Spielberg's TV series *Amazing Stories.* When Reynolds remarked that Welles looked drawn, Welles admitted he wasn't feeling good. He told Reynolds with dismay that he had just seen pictures taken of him by Michael O'Neill for a *People* magazine feature: "I look like I'm about to be laid out in a coffin." (One of those photos later appeared on the cover of *This Is Orson Welles,* and Welles's pained, sallow look bears out his observation.)

In the early evening of October 9, Welles went to the Celebrity Theater at Sunset and Vine in Hollywood to tape an appearance with Leaming on *The Merv Griffin Show* to help promote her biography. Seeing Welles arrive, Griffin thought he looked "haggard," and, indeed, his complexion on the show looked deathly pale and heavily age-spotted. His blue jacket hung limp around his hollowed-out frame, and his polka-dotted cravat sagged around his neck. But Welles told Griffin before the show, "Tonight, I feel like talking. . . . I feel expansive tonight. You know all those silly, gossipy little questions you've been trying to ask me for years about Rita and Marlene? Well, go ahead and ask me. Ask me anything you want." Griffin, "taken aback," wondered if he could ask about what he considered "the most taboo subject of all" in a Welles interview, the making of *Kane.* "Ask me!" commanded Welles. And so Griffin did, gaining no fresh revelations about Welles's work but what Griffin nevertheless considered "far and away the most candid discussion we ever had" in their almost fifty shows together. Though Griffin brought up a title seldom discussed during Welles's talk show appearances, *Chimes at Midnight,* none of his film work for the last nineteen years of his life was mentioned.

Leaning on a cane as he shuffled about the stage, Welles seemed briefly energized while doing some last card tricks and making patter about cardsharps, enjoying the interaction with audience members and basking in their genuine appreciation. In the conversation with Griffin and Leaming that followed, Welles paid warm tribute to his ex-wife Rita Hayworth, then suffering from Alzheimer's disease ("one of the dearest and sweetest women that ever lived"),* but feigned indignation while kidding Griffin and the giggly, gushing Leaming for their fascination with his reported love affairs, insisting, "So you see, it's all a tissue of lies from a lot of people who are safely gone to their reward." When Griffin asked if there had been periods of great joy in his life, Welles turned more serious, responding, "There are certain periods of every *day* that are joyous. I'm not essentially a happy person, but I have all kinds of joy." And Welles was at his most reflective when Griffin brought up his recent seventieth birthday, eliciting applause. Griffin expressed surprise that the milestone hadn't been celebrated more publicly (i.e., in America).

"I didn't *celebrate* it," Welles replied. "I just *had* it. . . . Believe me, it's nothing to applaud about. . . . Oh, no, I hate birthdays, you know, really. Because you always think, Wouldn't it be nice if it was a lot less candles on the cake. As it is now, when they bring out a cake with my right number of candles, it looks like the Chicago fire."

As he had in his videotaped proposal for *King Lear*, Welles quoted de Gaulle about old age being "a shipwreck," which Welles told Griffin was "the truth about it." Asked by the indefatigably upbeat host, "But you feel wonderful, don't you?" Welles replied, "Oh, sure," rolling his eyes to the heavens, to audience laughter. "All these old people who walk around saying they feel just the way they did when they were kids—*liars!* Every one of them!"

Prince Alessandro Tasca di Cuto, Welles's European production man and good friend, was the last person who saw him alive. They had dinner with Leaming at Ma Maison, and Tasca drove him home. It was, recalled Tasca, a happy night of talk that never got around to the next day's shoot-

---

* I encountered Hayworth at a Hollywood fundraising party when it was generally assumed that she was suffering from alcoholism rather than from the disease that finally killed her. When I started talking to her about Welles, all she could do was wave her hand, roll her eyes, and exclaim, "*Oooh*, Orson!" A few years earlier, she told an interviewer that she still had something he had left behind: his magic (in a box).

ing plans, but Welles was anxious to be reassured that his appearance on the Griffin show had gone well.

And what was Welles's "Rosebud"? The last words anyone reported hearing from him were on Henry Jaglom's answering-machine tape. At Welles's memorial service, Jaglom recalled, "On Wednesday night [October 9] I went to bed about three o'clock and I checked my messages—there were a few, none from Orson, and I went to sleep. When I woke up in the morning at ten o'clock on Thursday there was a number '1' on the answering machine and I turned it on and it said, 'This is your friend. Don't forget to tell me how your mother is . . . ' Which means sometime that night he had left that message. And I called my mother and found out what I found out"—that Welles had died. Since the loss of his mother in childhood had haunted Welles all his life, it was fitting that among his last thoughts was the importance of devotion to one's mother.*

❖ ❖ ❖

Welles's body was discovered on the floor of his second-story bedroom at about 10:00 A.M. on October 10, 1985, when Freddie arrived for work. There was a typewriter on Welles's bed table; after returning home, he had been writing up notes for the morning's shooting at UCLA. The first of Welles's friends to arrive at the house was one of his colleagues of the longest duration, Paul Stewart, the Mercury Theatre veteran who had played Raymond the butler in *Citizen Kane.* Stewart was at the Directors Guild of America headquarters a few blocks away when he heard the news. Graver points out the irony: "He found Charlie Kane. Weird, isn't it?"

Graver learned of Welles's death while getting ready for that day's shooting: "It was mid-morning, and I was in Hollywood at an equipment rental place, checking out some cameras and stuff. Somebody just casually said to me, 'Oh, it was on the radio, Orson Welles died.' I couldn't believe it. I got in the car, I was five minutes away, I went over to the house. A whole bunch of TV reporters were there with cameras, people were wandering around. I didn't even go in the house. I guess they'd taken his body away. There was nothing to go in there for. I was stunned."

---

* Welles's autobiographical fragments in *Paris Vogue* include a chilling account of his last visit with his dying mother, a scene he powerfully evokes in Isabel's deathbed farewell to George in *The Magnificent Ambersons.* Welles's reminiscence was filmed more literally for the heavy-handed prologue of the 1999 cable-TV movie *RKO 281*, to "explain" why Welles had trouble expressing love.

I was in an isolated cabin in the San Bernardino Mountains a hundred miles from Los Angeles, writing my biography of Frank Capra. The news came in a phone call that afternoon from my hometown paper, the *Milwaukee Journal*, asking me to write a memorial piece on deadline. I couldn't gather my thoughts and feelings about Welles that quickly, so I had to decline.

"When his body was taken down to the morgue," Graver relates, "they waited for Oja to fly in from Croatia the next day to view him. About a week later, they had the funeral." Before the funeral, Paola and Welles's three daughters, Christopher, Rebecca, and Beatrice, but not Oja, joined Graver for a reception at the home of actor Roddy McDowall, the actor who had played Malcolm in Welles's film of *Macbeth* and was friendly with both Orson and his wife.

The brief private ceremony was held at the Cunningham and O'Connor mortuary in Hollywood, where John Ford's body had been taken for visitation twelve years earlier. A man from the mortuary joined the immediate family members, Roger Hill, Greg Garrison, and Graver in the small room. It was the first time all three of Welles's daughters had been together.

"Just as I went in to close the doors," Graver recalls, "there was Barney the cue-card guy with a handful of flowers." Welles relied for years on Barney McNulty, appreciating both his loyalty and his uncanny sense of timing, which enabled Welles to speak in natural rhythms for long stretches in his films as well as his TV appearances. "I know I'm not invited," McNulty told Graver at the mortuary, "but I had to be here. Please take [the flowers] in the room and give my condolences to the family."

Welles's surrogate father, Roger Hill, said a few words over his pupil's coffin. But Welles's oldest daughter, Chris, recalled the event as a horrible experience, a bare-bones affair in a stark setting that looked "like the motel in *Psycho*." "We sat in a little room," Graver relates, "and they presented Beatrice with a simple pine box of ashes. Orson didn't want to be cremated, and they cremated him. I was emotionally upset."

Beatrice stayed in town for a few days, and while Graver drove her around on errands, Welles's ashes went along for the ride: "We kept them in the trunk of the car, and at night she'd take them into her bedroom, where she was staying with friends. Very strange. Also ironic." Beatrice kept the box under her desk at her home in Las Vegas until 1987. On what would have been her father's seventy-second birthday, May 6, she interred his ashes, along with her mother's, in a flower-covered well on the ranch of bullfighter Antonio Ordóñez near Ronda, in the Andalusian province of Málaga. Welles's odd resting place, in an orchard near a busy highway, is marked by a simple metal scroll. The well is not open to tourists but can be glimpsed in Kristian Petri's 2005 Swedish documentary on Welles in Spain, *Brunnen (The Well)*.

❖ ❖ ❖

The November 2, 1985, public memorial tribute at the Directors Guild of America Theater on Sunset Boulevard was, gratifyingly for a life spent in show business, SRO. People were lined up around the block when I arrived at 9:00 in the morning to go over the script and staging for the 2:00 event with Richard Wilson and our host, Peter Bogdanovich. A couple hundred people had to be turned away. Since Welles had come to prominence as a disembodied voice over the radio, we began with his voice on audiotape giving his definition of a director, words he had spoken in November 1981 at a tribute from the Hollywood Foreign Press Association:

> You know, there's been some talk here tonight about directors, as though they were a separate breed. And I'm afraid I have to take exception to that. I believe that directors are, all of them, actors. . . . You can't think of a role that a director doesn't have to play.
>
> But none of them are really important compared to his real role, which is to be what is absent in the making of a movie—the audience. The director is simply the audience. So the terrible burden of the director is to take the place of that yawning vacuum—to *be* the audience—and to select from what happens during the day which moment shall be a disaster and which a gala night.
>
> And the trouble with movies today, *I* think—and nobody asked me—is that all of us are too much in love with them. And there is no damn cure for it.

There were speeches by such old and younger Wellesians as Roger Hill, Norman Lloyd, Geraldine Fitzgerald, Dan O'Herlihy, Robert Wise, Charlton Heston, Janet Leigh, Greg Garrison, Henry Jaglom, and Ma Maison's Patrick Terrail. And there were messages from absent friends. The ailing Joseph Cotten asked us to read Shakespeare's thirtieth sonnet in his behalf, just as Welles had done earlier that year in an audiotaped message for Cotten's eightieth birthday: "But if the while I think on thee, dear friend, / All losses are restored and sorrows end." We ended with the last of several film clips from throughout Welles's career, the finale of Jaglom's as-yet-unreleased *Someone to Love*. So the memorial came to a close recalling Welles the way his collaborators knew him in his happiest moments of creation, calling "*Cut!*" and blowing kisses, and applauding the audience, laughing his Falstaffian laugh.

The memorial was Dick Wilson's idea and did not meet with the blessing of Paola and Beatrice (Chris later said she was hurt not to have been invited). But in addition to giving colleagues the opportunity for a few words of gratitude, it offered a platform for Oja Kodar to make a fiery speech condemning those who had let Welles down. Dressed in black, Kodar gave her eulogy in ferocious words that stunned the audience:

> Orson said to me once, "Death is the coronation of life." It would please him seeing you here confirming his words by not mourning but by celebrating. . . . Being immensely generous, Orson, I'm sure, would have liked to forgive some who kept restlessly plucking at his wings for a feather or two, and quite often, not only to advance and adorn their own little dreary selves but to stop *him* [from] defying the law of gravity. This constant *déplumage* made, of course, everything much more difficult for him. But knowing Orson, I promise you it never affected the height of his flight.
>
> He was blessed by God, because in spite of many hardships he did not know bitterness or lamentation. But I did see him cry a couple of times. One evening while on the location of *The Other Side of the Wind*, I heard some strange noise coming from his room. I peeked through the crack of the door. There he was sitting in front of [a] TV set, his eyes streaming with tears. I did not enter for fear of embarrassing him. Behind his back on the dark glass panel of his window, I saw the reflection from the screen. They were playing a film that, he said, "They cut and recut and destroyed for me." They were playing *The Magnificent Ambersons*.
>
> Just a few weeks ago Orson was on the verge of finally getting money for almost all of his projects. . . . Before anything else, I must strongly emphasize how much the French public loved Orson, and what a deep and sincere respect he had for them. The French president, François Mitterand, sent a telegram of condolences, which he also released to the French press. . . . I'll translate: "With Orson Welles, a genius of cinema has gone forever. We have followed his itinerary from film to film and we have seen this actor transform himself while maintaining all the strength and the power of his youth. His last film, *King Lear*, was to be made in France. [Kodar's voice dripped with angry sarcasm as she read Mitterand's next sentences:] He may not have been able or have not wanted to follow to an end this film testament on power and solitude. He leaves us with sorrow of a great project unachieved. Orson Welles had many friends and admirers in our country. I address to his family and to those near him all my sympathy. François Mitterand."
>
> I am sorry that Monsieur Mitterand, even at this sad hour, had to still play politics and defend his establishment. I must explain that after long negotiations, Orson started to suspect that [the] French government and their gov-

ernment-owned television never sincerely intended to make the film. This was just a political move. Who would be the best person to help French minister of culture Jack Lang to take his foot out of his mouth for openly declaring his dislike and disdain for "[the] existing imperialism of nonexistent American culture." Who else? Welles. The conditions with which they presented him, favorable as they seemed to be at first, when he came to Paris started slowly to lose their luster and shrink into something which Orson describes [as], I quote, "an outright diktat." To mention only one item, the budget had been so inflated that Orson decided to reduce it by taking off $300,000 of his own salary and one more time in his life make a donation to the screen.* Finally, with a broken heart, he was forced to forget the whole project. The message he sent to Paris [by telegram to Hervé Bourge] in [the] month of May ended this way:

"In the fifty-five years of my professional career, I have never, not even in the worst days in the old Hollywood, encountered such a humiliating inflexibility. Need I say that this is a bitter disappointment to one who has until now received so much heartwarming and generous cooperation in France. To my profound regret, therefore, I must accept that your own last Telex is the last word about *Lear*, and that there is no longer any hope that in this affair a constructive relationship is possible."

And now with your permission I would like to read for you a few words from the end of *The Dreamers*, the last of Orson's dreams.

"There are only two things it is ever seemly for an intelligent person to be thinking. Yes—one is: What did God mean by creating the world? And the other: What do I do next?"

"Who is that woman dressed in black?" a stunned-looking Robert Wise, who cut *The Magnificent Ambersons*, asked afterward as he wandered backstage.

---

* Welles submitted a budget of $1,787,500 to make the film on locations in Spain and in a UK studio. It noted, "No charges are given for SCRIPT, PRODUCER & DIRECTOR. It is hoped that something will be left for this from the contingency fund." He felt that the $5 million budget he was offered for *Lear* was excessive and that he would be blamed for overspending. He also objected to what he considered inadequate studio facilities he was offered in France and to a stipulation that he would not be paid until after the film was completed, with the editing to be done in France. That stipulation, he concluded, meant that the producers thought he wouldn't finish the film. According to Kodar, Welles offered to do a preliminary edit of the film on videotape in France and leave it with the producers while doing his final editing on tape in the United States, so they could release the film if he were incapacitated or otherwise unable to finish it. But, on principle, he wouldn't agree to the "outright diktat" that he defer his payment until after the film was completed.

As powerful as Kodar's words were, the more I thought about the Welles memorial, the more I came to realize that the most moving tribute of all was given by Gary Graver. In his characteristically generous and unassuming manner, Graver thanked the crew members of *The Other Side of the Wind*, who "must fill half this place," and expressed his love for Welles with images drawn from a literary fable that holds personal resonance for both of them:

> The thing that's sad to me, really, is that I want to *talk* to Orson. I wish I could talk to him and tell him a lot of things right now. . . . The thing that I really remember about Orson, I don't know why—when I was a child in kindergarten, they put us down on a blanket and gave us chocolate milk, and we had to go to sleep. They would play us, from time to time, a recording of Oscar Wilde's "The Happy Prince" narrated by Orson and with Bing Crosby and Lurene Tuttle. And for some reason I never ever forgot that story or his telling of it.

As Graver recounted the story, it could be seen a parable of Welles's career. Like the Happy Prince, Welles was a regal figure whose lavish gifts were freely bestowed on the public, making him seem bereft in the eyes of those who value only the outward show of success. The statue of the Happy Prince is covered with gold leaf and has sapphires for eyes. But at Christmas, the prince tells a swallow to peel off his gold leaves and drop them to poor people so they can eat. When all the gold is gone, the bird plucks out the prince's eyes. Finally the prince is cast on a junk heap along with the body of the dead bird. Graver continued:

> As Orson said it in the recording—this is Oscar Wilde [somewhat revised]—"'Bring me the two most precious things in the city,' said God to one of His Angels; and the Angel brought Him the dead bird and the leaden heart of the Happy Prince. 'Of what use are these?' said the Angel. And God said, 'In my kingdom of Paradise the swallow shall sing forever more, and in my city of gold the Happy Prince shall praise me.'"
>
> Well, I shall always think of Orson as the Happy Prince, and I think he really now is in his own city of gold.

❖ ❖ ❖

"You don't imagine that posterity's judgment, do you? Posterity is a whim. A shapeless litter of old bones: the midden of a vulgar beast: the most capricious and immense mass-public of them all—the dead"—thus speaks Kim Menaker, Welles's aging alter ego in his screenplay *The Big Brass Ring*. To place hope for vindication in posterity, Welles must have felt, would be to care less for the moment of creation than for how it is received. That would be an uncertain prospect at best, as he came to know and accept, despite his largely unrequited desire for popular success as an artist. But those who admire his work care passionately about how posterity regards him.

Beatrice Welles's attempts to control her father's legacy raise the question of who "owns" a dead artist's work. Is it his family? His financiers? The public? And *which* public, today's or tomorrow's? Far too often, families and friends of dead artists have been responsible for censoring, withholding, or even destroying their works. Companies that own movies in the business sense of the word have felt free to disregard, alter, or even destroy them with an abandon that would be considered scandalous if such liberties were taken with paintings. Ted Turner offered a notorious justification for his colorization of classic films. As the Associated Press reported in 1986, Turner declared, "The last time I checked, I owned those films. I can do whatever I want with them." That's the extreme capitalistic view of art; a more democratic view would be that we *all* share in the ownership of these movies and should be free to see them. Shortly before his death, Welles told Jaglom, "Make me one promise. Keep Ted Turner and his goddamned Crayolas away from my movie." Fortunately for Welles, his extraordinary contract for *Citizen Kane* made it impossible for Turner to colorize that film, which would have been the ultimate sacrilege, although Turner *did* manage to colorize *The Magnificent Ambersons*, of which Welles's contract, disastrously, was less protective. Turner claimed to have been baiting his critics when he announced plans to colorize *Kane:* "I was doing it mainly just to rub their noses in it."

Beatrice Welles, who has contributed little of her own to the world of films, has asserted control over significant parts of her father's artistic legacy and has tried to extend that control over parts she does not own. In 2003 she even tried to stop the British Film Institute from showing *Kane* in a London retrospective of her father's work because of a lawsuit she had filed against RKO, claiming rights to the film that her father had signed away in 1943 (as well as rights to *Ambersons*, which he also gave up in his futile attempt to finish *It's All True*). Showing more fortitude than most organizations she has gone after, the BFI successfully defied her. Reporting on that incident in the British newspaper the *Guardian*, Geoffrey Macnab wrote, "It occasionally seems that Beatrice is on a one-woman crusade to stop her father's movies [from] being shown. . . . Ironically, in her actions suppressing her father's work, she is behaving just like the production companies and distributors who treated Welles so shabbily." The irony is almost too much for an admirer of Orson Welles to bear.

Beatrice was born when Welles was preparing his New York stage production of *King Lear* in 1956. Her role in her father's posthumous career calls to mind Lear's furious lamentation: "How sharper than a serpent's tooth it is / To have a thankless child!" But Welles was often an indifferent father, and his oldest daughter, Chris Welles Feder, draws a different kind of analogy to *King Lear* in her partly fictionalized memoir of her father, *The Movie Director* (2002). Fittingly written in blank verse to help convey his Shakespearean complexity, it is a work of extraordinary understanding and compassion, simultaneously conveying love and respect for her father and anguish over his human limitations. She describes him as "a dazzling creature seen from afar / who dropped in on my life every now and again." This "man on safari from another world," she writes, could see himself and all three of his daughters reflected in Shakespeare's starkest tragedy: "In place of yourself, you had offered an act of magic: / first we all become Cordelia. Then we all disappear."

Welles's guilt over his treatment of Beatrice and his other two daughters may be reflected in a scene from his screenplay *House Party*, depicting the illegitimate, dispossessed Mercedes "at the mirror. . . . She has come here to this house to establish what her father had always chosen to deny—the simple reality of her existence. But what she finds now in the mirror is only hatred." In light of the script's depiction of Mercedes as a kind of "witch" taking revenge against her father and his other claimants, it's intriguing that when Welles tells a fanciful story about Beatrice in *Orson Welles' Magic Show*, he describes her as "no mean sorceress herself." The reverberations of this vagabond director's unconventional and often troubled family life continue to haunt his cinematic legacy.

❖ ❖ ❖

Perhaps Welles would indeed have been better off if he had yielded to the temptation of quitting the movie business long before he died. He would have avoided so many years of struggling, hoping, and creating in solitude. But once seduced by the art form of which he became the consummate master, he was unable to escape its embrace. And if he had managed to do so before his final years, we would have been deprived of many more hours of Welles films, unfinished though most of them are. A man who created so many enduring and influential works of art in a commercial medium and kept working right up to the end was no failure but a roaring success. Like Charles Foster Kane when asked in old age how he evaluated his achievements, Welles could say with a wry smile, "I think I did pretty well under the circumstances."

I've never forgotten what my film teacher at the University of Wisconsin, Russell Merritt, told us on the first day of class: to have good films, we need not only good filmmakers, we also need good audiences. The real fault with what happened to Orson Welles lies with us, his audience, who have failed to support his art as conscientiously as we should. It is not too late to rectify at least part of the injustice done to one of America's greatest artists.

In the meantime, I'm still keeping my Mister Pister costume in a box in the attic.

Near the end of his life, Welles tried valiantly to mount an innovative film version of Shakespeare's play *King Lear*. His identification with the old king desperately struggling to hold on to his fragmenting kingdom was intense. Before the project collapsed, Welles had this test shot taken of himself in costume as Lear. In a pitch for funding he shot on video a few months before his own death in 1985, Welles said, "*King Lear* is about death and the approach of death, and about power and the loss of power; and about love." *(Gary Graver)*

ACKNOWLEDGMENTS

My foremost thanks are due to Gary Graver, Welles's cinematographer and right-hand man for the last fifteen years of the director's life, a good friend of mine these many years and a bounteous supporter of my research into his and Welles's work together. Gary's wife and partner in the Orson Welles Archive, Jillian Kesner, also provided unstinting help with this project. Bill Krohn, Welles scholar, Hollywood correspondent for *Cahiers du Cinéma*, and codirector of the documentary *It's All True: Based on an Unfinished Film by Orson Welles*, generously supplied me with voluminous research materials and shared his brilliant ideas about Welles, as well as commenting insightfully on the manuscript itself. My partner, Ann Weiser Cornell, was a fountain of encouragement, companionship, and advice on this project; she also helped edit the manuscript with a keen and knowledgeable eye. Ruth O'Hara urged me to write this book and once again offered a wealth of valuable insights and editorial suggestions. My son, John, is a great source of joy and inspiration in every aspect of my life.

Stefan Drössler of the Filmmuseum München (the Munich Film Museum) went beyond the call of duty in showing me Welles films from the museum's collection, discussing his restoration work, inviting me to participate in the 2005 "Magnificent Welles" conference at Locarno, and sharing research materials. Welles scholar Jonathan Rosenbaum offered his insights and information over the years and gave valuable suggestions after reading the manuscript. Kohlim Jaeger ably transcribed interview tapes and copied photographs. Maurice L. Muehle, my indispensable counsel, provided expert legal advice and encouragement for this book and for our mutual attempt to help find end money for *The Other Side of the Wind*. My agent Richard Parks, who is always a loyal supporter of my writing career, went beyond the call of duty with his multifaceted and vigorous work in my behalf during the five years this book was in the works, assisted by Barbara Levy of the Barbara Levy Literary Agency, London. My old friend and fellow Hollywood historian Patrick McGilligan graciously recommended this book to the University Press of Kentucky. Leila Salisbury, who edited the book; her associate John P. Hussey; editing supervisor David Cobb; and copy editor Cheryl Hoffman gave it the caring support I needed to bring it to fruition.

George Coulouris, who plays Charles Foster Kane's guardian, Walter Parks Thatcher, helped plant the idea for this book when we met in Hollywood in 1977 while he was playing King Lear onstage. Orson Welles made this book possible by encouraging my dual role in his life as chronicler and character. Peter Bogdanovich introduced me to Orson and graciously shared research information. I am grateful for the friendship of Welles's oldest daughter, Christopher Welles Feder, and her husband, Irwin Feder.

For additional help with my Welles research over the years and for other support during the writing, I thank Alan Andres, Frederic Baker, Catherine Benamou, Rudy Brueggemann, Lawrence Chadbourne, Charles Champlin, Virginia Clark, William Donnelly, Jim Emerson, Barbara Epstein, F. X. Feeney, Lawrence French, Nadine Goff, Lee Gordon, Ray Greene, Curtis Harrington, Patricia Harty, Andrew Holmes, Henry Jaglom, Susan Bullington Katz, Joe Kaufman, Oja Kodar, Jonathan Kuntz and Maria Elena de las Carreras-Kuntz, Milton Luboviski, Marian McBride, Russell Merritt, James Naremore, Noel and Hetty O'Hara, James Pepper, Lou and Judy Race, Daniel Rafaelic, Leon Rizmaul, Roger Ryan, Jeff Schwager, Bob Thomas, Peter Tonguette, Helena Walsh, Tony Williams, Michael Wilmington, Jeff Wilson, and Richard Wilson. I found research material at the Wisconsin Center for Film and Theatre Research of the State Historical Society of Wisconsin; the University of Wisconsin Memorial Library; the Margaret Herrick Library of the Academy of Motion Picture Arts and Sciences; the Lilly Library at Indiana University, Bloomington; and the Federal Bureau of Investigation.

The audiences for Welles programs I hosted at the Directors Guild of America, the University of Southern California, and the Wisconsin Film Society also contributed to my understanding of his work. I am grateful to Michael Webb and Jean Firstenberg for asking me to cohost the 1978–79 American Film Institute seminar "Working with Welles" at the DGA Theater and to Richard Wilson for letting me collaborate with him in presenting Welles's memorial tribute there in 1985. My colleagues at San Francisco State University—especially Stephen Ujlaki, Steven Kovacs, Larry Clark, Jim Goldner, Jim Kitses, Keith Morrison, and Wan-

Lee Cheng—have provided me a fruitful base of support; thanks as well to my students in the course I taught on Welles at SFSU in 2003.

The people who have discussed Welles with me over the years have greatly increased my understanding of his life and work. They include Dominique Antoine, Frank Beacham, Joseph Biroc, Claude Chabrol, Charles Champlin, Stanley Cortez, Linwood G. Dunn, Michael Ferris, Robert Fischer, Richard Fleischer, Norman Foster, Ljuba Gamulin, John Gielgud, Claudio Guzman, Curtis Harrington, Henry Hathaway, Howard Hawks, Jürgen Hellwig, Roger Hill, Felipe Herba, Charlton Heston, John Houseman, John Huston, Larry Jackson, Henry Jaglom, Peter Jason, Aleksandra Jovicevic, Pauline Kael, Harry Keller, Willy Kurant, Janet Leigh, Eric Lieber, Norman Lloyd, Fletcher Markle, Mercedes McCambridge, Patty McCormack, Pat McMahon, Myron Meisel, Burgess Meredith, Cameron Mitchell, Jeanne Moreau, Walter Murch, Terry Nelson, Edmond O'Brien, Peter O'Toole, Carl Peppercorn, Anthony Perkins, Dido Renoir, Jean Renoir, Esteve Riambau, Martin Ritt, Rick Schmidlin, Bert Schneider, Maurice Seiderman, Tonio Selwart, Eric Sherman, Georgina Spelvin, George Stevens Jr., James G. Stewart, Paul Stewart, Susan Strasberg, Michael Stringer, François Thomas, François Truffaut, Kenneth Tynan, Dennis Weaver, Robert Wise, and Elizabeth Wilson.

For photographs, thanks to Graver, Krohn, the State Historical Society of Wisconsin, Felipe Herba, Collectors Bookstore (Hollywood), the Larry Edmunds Bookshop (Hollywood), and Jim Davidson and Dave Weingarten of Second Sight Video & Multimedia (Walnut Creek, California). Some material in the book is drawn from my article "The Greatest Movies Never Made: Robbing the Cradle" in *Reel*, March/April 2000, about the various versions of *The Cradle Will Rock;* my 2000 reel.com review of the DVD edition of *Around the World with Orson Welles;* and my observations of the taping of *The Orson Welles Show* in "All's Welles," *Film Comment*, November/December 1978. I wrote about the filming of *The Other Side of the Wind* in "The Other Side of Orson Welles," *American Film*, July–August 1976, and in my two previous books on Welles.

My research would have been far more difficult if it had not been for the diligent work of the many other Welles biographers, critics, and scholars who have studied him over the years. Welles is such a large subject that it takes a whole community of scholars around the world to help us understand his legacy.

Joseph McBride
Berkeley, California
June 6, 2006

SOURCES

Abbreviations used in these sections include OW for Orson Welles; AFI: American Film Institute; AMPAS: Academy of Motion Picture Arts and Sciences; BFI: British Film Institute; BK/OW: Bill Krohn, 1982 OW interview, first published in French translation as "Troisième Entretien," *Cahiers du Cinéma* OW issue, 1982, and in the original English as "'My Favorite Mask Is Myself'—Interview with Orson Welles" in *The Unknown Orson Welles,* ed. Stefan Drössler (Munich: Filmmuseum München [Das Filmmuseum im Münchner Stadtmuseum / Munich Film Museum] & belleville Verlag, 2004); Brady: Frank Brady, *Citizen Welles: A Biography of Orson Welles* (New York: Scribners, 1989); Callow: Simon Callow, *Orson Welles: The Road to Xanadu* (London: Jonathan Cape, 1995); Drössler: Stefan Drössler, ed., *The Unknown Orson Welles*; *DV: Daily Variety;* Estrin: Mark W. Estrin, ed., *Orson Welles: Interviews* (Jackson: University Press of Mississippi, 2002); FT: François Truffaut; GG: Gary Graver; GG/JM: Graver interview with author; *HCN, Hollywood Citizen-News; HR: Hollywood Reporter;* JH: John Houseman; JM: Joseph McBride; JR: Jonathan Rosenbaum; *LAHE: Los Angeles Herald-Examiner; LAT: Los Angeles Times;* Leaming: Barbara Leaming, *Orson Welles: A Biography* (New York: Viking, 1985); MacLiammóir: Micheál MacLiammóir, *Put Money in Thy Purse: The Making of "Othello,"* preface by OW (London: Methuen, 1952); *NYT: New York Times;* OK: Oja Kodar; *Other Wind:* OW's film *The Other Side of the Wind;* PB: Peter Bogdanovich; PB/OW: Orson Welles with Peter Bogdanovich, *This Is Orson Welles,* ed. Jonathan Rosenbaum (New York: HarperCollins, 1992; rev. ed., New York: Da Capo, 1998); RW: Richard Wilson.

References to other books and articles are listed fully the first time; subsequent references include only the author's last name (and, where there is more than one book or article by a single author, the title).

Epigraphs

OW's "railroad train" quote: Alva Johnston and Fred Smith, "How to Raise a Child: The Education of Orson Welles, Who Didn't Need It," *Saturday Evening Post*, February 3, 1940, reprinted in Estrin, the final installment of a three-part series (the other parts of "How to Raise a Child" ran January 20 and 27). Jean-Luc Godard comment: *The Orson Welles Story*, BBC TV documentary produced by Leslie Megahey and Alan Yentob, 1982.

Introduction: "The high priest of the cinema"

Books

F. Scott Fitzgerald, *The Last Tycoon*, ed. Edmund Wilson (New York: Scribners, 1941); JM, ed., *Persistence of Vision: A Collection of Film Criticism* (Madison: Wisconsin Film Society Press, 1968) (includes essays by JM on *Citizen Kane, The Magnificent Ambersons,* and *Chimes at Midnight);* JM, *Orson Welles,* BFI Cinema One (London: Secker & Warburg; New York: Viking, 1972), in French translation by Christiane Stoll and Bernard Turle (Paris: Rivages, 1985); rev. ed. (New York: Da Capo, 1996) (includes accounts of meeting OW and working in *Other Wind);* JM and Michael Wilmington, *John Ford,* BFI Cinema Two (London: Secker & Warburg, 1974; New York: Da Capo, 1975); JM, *Orson Welles: Actor and Director* (New York: Harcourt Brace Jovanovich, Pyramid Books, 1977); OW, with OK, *The Big Brass Ring* (screenplay), preface by James Pepper, afterword by JR (Santa Barbara, CA: Santa Teresa Press, 1987) ("the devil of self-destruction"); PB, *John Ford* (London: Movie Magazine, 1967; Berkeley: University of California Press, 1968; 2nd ed., 1978); PB/OW.

Articles and Essays

Capital Times (Madison, WI), "Cartoonist, Actor, Poet and Only 10," including OW's poem "The Passing of a Lord," on the newspaper's School Page, February 19, 1926 (the source of this first published article on OW is sometimes incorrectly given as the *Madison Journal* or the *Wisconsin State Journal);* Donald Davies, "Film Fervor Leads to Book on Welles" (interview with JM), *Wisconsin State Journal* (Madison), October 15, 1970; FT, *"Citizen Kane," L'Express* (Paris), November 26, 1959, trans. Mark Bernheim and Ronald Gottesman, in *Focus on "Citizen Kane,"* ed. Ronald Gottesman (Englewood Cliffs, NJ: Prentice-Hall, 1971); JM,

"Le Grand Cinéaste: Welles at 52," *Daily Cardinal* (University of Wisconsin, Madison), July 7, 1967; JM, "Orson Welles Returns from Obscurity," *Wisconsin State Journal* (Madison), September 14, 1970; JM, "Welles' *Immortal Story*," *Sight and Sound*, Autumn 1970; JM, "County Mayo Gu [*sic*] Bragh . . ." (interviews with John Ford and Jean Renoir), *Sight and Sound*, Winter 1970/71; JM, "First Person Singular" (on *The Fountain of Youth*), *Sight and Sound*, Winter 1971/72; JM, "Joseph McBride on The Prologue" (on OW's life up to his arrival in Hollywood), in AFI Life Achievement Award program booklet, 1975, ed. David Lunney; JM, "The Other Side of Orson Welles," *American Film*, July–August 1976; JM, "All's Welles," *Film Comment*, November/December 1978; JM, "The Lost Kingdom of Orson Welles," *New York Review of Books*, May 13, 1993; Margy Rochlin, "Peter Bogdanovich Doesn't Live Here Anymore," *L.A. Weekly*, February 19, 2002; Pete Trotter, "Local *Citizen Kane* Fan Writes Book on Orson Welles' Films" (interview with JM), *Catholic Herald Citizen* (Milwaukee, WI), October 17, 1970; John Updike, "Hub Fans Bid Kid Adieu," *New Yorker*, October 22, 1960.

Films

Citizen of America: Orson Welles and the Ballad of Isaac Woodard, 2005 (Norman Corwin on OW).

Other Source

F. X. Feeney to JM, January 10, 2006.

1. "God, how they'll love me when I'm dead!"

Chapter title: OW quoted in PB's "My Orson," introduction to the 1998 edition of PB/OW; the epigraph is from the audiotape edition of PB/OW, ed. JR, Caedmon, Harper Audio, 1992.

Books

David A. Cook, *Lost Illusions: American Cinema in the Shadow of Watergate and Vietnam, 1970–1979*, History of the American Cinema 9 (New York: Scribners, 2000); Charles Higham, *The Films of Orson Welles* (Berkeley and Los Angeles: University of California Press, 1970); JM, *Orson Welles: Actor and Director*; JR, *Movie Wars: How Hollywood and the Media Conspire to Limit What Films We Can See* (including the chapter "Orson Welles as Ideological Challenge") (Chicago: Chicago Review Press, 2000); Leaming; MacLiammóir; David Thomson, *Rosebud: The Story of Orson Welles*

(New York: Knopf; London: Little, Brown, 1996); OW and OK, *The Other Side of the Wind* (1971 screenplay) in *The Other Side of the Wind*, ed. Giorgio Gosetti (Paris and Locarno: *Cahiers du Cinéma* and Festival International du Film de Locarno, 2005).

Articles and Essays

Australian Broadcasting Corporation, "Orson Welles's Multimedia Talent on Show" (Stefan Drössler interview), www.abc.net.au, August 12, 2005; Vincent Canby, "Welles: Touch of Genius," *NYT*, October 11, 1985; Canby column, "Orson Welles Began an Ongoing Revolution," *NYT*, October 20, 1985; Ian Christie, "The Rules of the Game," *Sight and Sound*, September 2002 (on *Sight and Sound* Top Ten Polls, 1952–2002); Peter S. Greenberg, "Saints and Stinkers: The *Rolling Stone* Interview [with John Huston]," *Rolling Stone*, February 19, 1981, reprinted in *John Huston: Interviews*, ed. Robert Emmet Long (Jackson: University Press of Mississippi, 2001); Charles Higham, "And Now—The War of the Welles," *NYT*, September 13, 1970, with letters from PB and Raymond A. Sokolov; Charles Higham, "Orson's Back and Marlene's Got Him," *NYT*, January 31, 1971; Higham, "The Film That Orson Welles Has Been Finishing for Six Years," *NYT*, April 18, 1976; JM, "AFI Presents Orson Welles Its Third Life Achievement Award," *DV*, February 11, 1975; JM, "The Other Side of Orson Welles"; JM, "Commentary: McBride on the Battle over Orson Welles," www.CreativePlanet.com, December 14, 1999; JM, "The Greatest Movies Never Made: Robbing the Cradle," *Reel*, March/April 2000 (on OW's project *The Cradle Will Rock* and the 1999 Tim Robbins film *Cradle Will Rock);* JR, "The Invisible Welles: A First Inventory," *Sight and Sound*, Summer 1986; Pauline Kael, "Orson Welles: There Ain't No Way" (review of *Chimes at Midnight*, aka *Falstaff*), *New Republic*, June 24, 1967, reprinted in Kael's collections *Kiss Kiss Bang Bang* (Boston: Little, Brown, 1968), and *For Keeps* (New York: Dutton, 1994); Stanley Kauffmann, "Notes by a Contemporary," *New Republic*, November 11, 1985; *NYT*, "Orson Welles Is Dead at 70: Innovator of Film and Stage," October 11, 1985; OW, "But Where Are We Going?" *Look*, November 3, 1970; PB, "Is It True What They Say about Orson?" *NYT*, August 30, 1970; Mordechai Richler, "'There, but for the Grace of God, Goes God'" (review of Leaming), *GQ*, October 1985; Peter Tonguette, "You Look Pretty Splendid Yourself, Orson: A Conversation with Curtis Harrington," *Bright Lights Film Journal*, May 2004; Kenneth Tynan, "*Playboy* Interview: Orson Welles," *Playboy*, March 1967, reprinted in Estrin.

Films/TV Shows

The American Film Institute Salutes Orson Welles, CBS-TV, February 17, 1975 (the text of OW's acceptance speech was published in *AFI News*, March 1975, and *American Cinematographer*, April 1975); *The Dean Martin Show*, NBC-TV, September 14, 1967; *Filming "The Trial"* (1981; first public screening, 1999); *The Merv Griffin Show*, October 9, 1985 (OW's final TV appearance, aired October 15); *Orson Welles à la Cinémathèque française*, 1982 documentary by Pierre-André Boutang; *Orson Welles: What Went Wrong?* 1992 documentary by Robert Guenette; *The Other Side of Welles*, 2005 documentary by Daniel Rafaelic and Leon Rizmaul (OW describing himself as an "amateur director"); OW BBC TV interview by Michael Parkinson, 1974, repeated in 1985 as *Parkinson: The Orson Welles Interview;* Paul Masson wine commercials with OW for the Doyle Dane Bernbach advertising agency, including *"Gone With the Wind,"* May 4, 1979.

Other Sources

Samuel Taylor Coleridge's unfinished poem "Kubla Khan: Or, a Vision in a Dream. A Fragment," 1797 or 1798, first published in his collection *Christabel* (London: William Bulmer, 1816); Greg Garrison speech at OW's memorial service, Directors Guild of America Theater, Hollywood, November 2, 1985, videotaped as *Remembering Orson . . .* , produced by Frank Beacham; Walter Murch, lecture at San Francisco State University, March 9, 2006; George Orson Welles, Certificate of Death, State of California, filed October 11, 1985, County of Los Angeles, Department of Health Services; *Orson Welles: The One-Man Band*, press kit, 1995; OW's CBS Radio series *This Is My Best* (for Cresta Blanca wine), 1945–46.

2. "Committing masterpieces"

Chapter title: OW in *F for Fake*. Epigraph: JM, *Orson Welles;* Betty Lasky, *RKO: The Biggest Little Major of Them All* (Englewood Cliffs, NJ: Prentice-Hall, 1984).

Books

Samantha Barbas, *The First Lady of Hollywood: A Biography of Louella Parsons* (Berkeley and Los Angeles: University of California Press, 2005); Joanne Bentley, *Hallie Flanagan: A Life in the American Theatre* (New York: Knopf, 1988); Brady; Robert L. Carringer, *The Making of "Citizen Kane"* (Berkeley and Los Angeles: University of California Press, 1985);

Carringer, *The Magnificent Ambersons: A Reconstruction* (Berkeley and Los Angeles: University of California Press, 1993) (includes cutting continuity and dialogue of uncut 132-minute version); Larry Ceplair and Steven Englund, *The Inquisition in Hollywood: Politics in the Film Community, 1930–1960* (Berkeley and Los Angeles: University of California Press, 1979); Marion Davies, *The Times We Had: Life with William Randolph Hearst*, ed. Pamela Pfan and Kenneth S. Marx, foreword by OW (Indianapolis: Bobbs-Merrill, 1975); Hallie Flanagan, *Arena* (New York: Duell, Sloan & Pearce, 1940); Paul Green and Richard Wright, *Native Son (the Biography of a Young American)* (New York: Harper & Brothers, 1941), play adapted from Wright's 1940 novel, *Native Son* (New York: Harper & Brothers); Fred Jerome, *The Einstein File: J. Edgar Hoover's Secret War against the World's Most Famous Scientist* (New York: St. Martin's, 2002); Richard B. Jewell with Vernon Harbin, *The RKO Story* (New York: Arlington House, 1982); JH, *Run-Through* (New York: Simon & Schuster, 1972); JM, *Persistence of Vision: A Collection of Film Criticism* (the *Ambersons* essay includes a verbal reconstruction of the film, amplified in JM, *Orson Welles*, 1972 and 1996 editions); JM, *OW: Actor and Director*; Laurence Klavan, *The Cutting Room* (novel) (New York: Ballantine, 2004); Leaming; Sinclair Lewis, *Main Street* (New York: Harcourt Brace & Howe, 1920); Richard Meryman, *Mank: The Wit, World, and Life of Herman Mankiewicz* (New York: Morrow, 1978); Laura Mulvey, *Citizen Kane* (London: BFI, 1992); PB/OW; Louis Pizzitola, *Hearst over Hollywood: Power, Passion, and Propaganda in the Movies* (New York: Columbia University Press, 2002); Victor S. Navasky, *Naming Names* (New York: Viking, 1980); OW foreword to pamphlet, *The Sleepy Lagoon Murder Case* (Los Angeles: Mercury Press, 1943); OW, *The Cradle Will Rock: An Original Screenplay*, ed. and introduction by James Pepper, afterword by JR (Santa Barbara, CA: Santa Teresa Press, 1994); PB/OW (includes partial visual and verbal reconstruction of *Ambersons*) and PB's "My Orson" in 1998 edition; V. F. Perkins, *The Magnificent Ambersons* (London: BFI, 1999); Hazel Rowley, *Richard Wright: The Life and Times* (New York: Henry Holt, 2001); Dalton Trumbo, *The Time of the Toad: A Study of Inquisition in America and Two Related Pamphlets* (New York: Perennial Library, 1972).

Articles and Essays

Action! "*Citizen Kane* Remembered," May–June 1969; James Bacon, item on Marion Davies and "Rosebud," *Beverly Hills (213)*, August 7, 1996; Catherine Benamou, "*It's All True* as Document/Event: Notes Towards an Historiographical and Textual Analysis," special issue on OW, *Persistence of Vision*, no. 7, 1989; Thomas F. Brady, "Welles versus Hollywood Again," *NYT*, July 26, 1942; Robert L. Carringer, "The Scripts of *Citizen Kane*," *Critical Inquiry* 5, no. 2 (Winter 1978), and "Rosebud, Dead or Alive: Narrative and Symbolic Structure in *Citizen Kane*," *PMLA* 91, no. 2 (March 1976); *Diário da Noite* (São Paulo), "They Should Have Stayed Far Away, in the Land of Itacema," May 20, 1942; *DV*, "Welles Buys That Million $ Brazil Picture from RKO," January 10, 1945; F. X. Feeney, "Dark Hearts and Worldly Power," *Written By*, June/July 2003 (on OW's *Heart of Darkness* film project); F. Scott Fitzgerald's short story "Pat Hobby and Orson Welles" appeared in *Esquire*, May 1940, and in his collection *The Pat Hobby Stories*, introduction by Arnold Gingrich (New York: Scribners, 1962); Lawrence French, "An Interview with Jonathan Rosenbaum," www.wellesnet.com, 2003; FT, "*Citizen Kane*," in Gottesman, *Focus on "Citizen Kane"*; FT, "The Welles Look" in Lunney, AFI Life Achievement Award program booklet; Douglas Gomery, "Orson Welles and the Hollywood Industry," special issue on OW, *Persistence of Vision*, no. 7, 1989; Greenberg, "Saints and Stinkers"; Charles Higham, "*It's All True*," *Sight and Sound*, Spring 1970; JH, "*Native Son*," *New Letters*, Winter 1971, reprinted in his collection *Entertainers and the Entertained: Essays on Theater, Film, and Television* (New York: Simon & Schuster, 1986); JM, "*Citizen Kane*," *Film Heritage*, Fall 1968; JM, "Rough Sledding with Pauline Kael," *Film Heritage*, Fall 1971; JM, "Wise Move Raises *Kane* for Viewers," *DV*, May 1, 1991; JM column, "Welles' *Ambersons:* Mutilated Yet Magnificent," *DV*, July 23, 1992; JM, "Robert Wise at 85: Retiring in Style," www.creativeplanet.com, March 29 and 31, 2000; JM, "The Greatest Movies Never Made: Robbing the Cradle"; *HCN*, "Wellesian Feet to Be Eyed," May 16, 1941; *HCN*, "Welles Classified as 1-B," May 27, 1941; *HCN*, "Brazil Hero, in Welles' Film, Drowns" (on death of Jacaré), May 19, 1942; Johnston and Smith, "How to Raise a Child"; JR, "The Voice and the Eye: A Commentary on the *Heart of Darkness* Script," *Film Comment*, November 1972; David Kamp, "Magnificent Obsession" (on search for missing *Ambersons* footage), *Vanity Fair*, January 2002; Pauline Kael, "Raising Kane," *New Yorker*, February 20 and 27, 1971, reprinted in *The "Citizen Kane" Book*, by Pauline Kael with Mankiewicz and OW (Boston: Little, Brown, 1971) (includes Mankiewicz-Welles screenplay of *Citizen Kane* and dialogue transcription of film), and in *For Keeps;* Stuart Klawans, "Orson Welles Hollowed Out," *Nation*, January 8/15, 1996; James Gordon Meek, "Orson Welles Betrayed to FBI by Mystery Woman," www.APBnews.com, October 13, 2000;

Life, "*Life* Goes to Rio Party: Orson Welles frolics at famous Mardi Gras," May 18, 1942; *Los Angeles Herald*, "Orson Welles Put in 1-B Selective Service," May 27, 1941; *Los Angeles Herald*, "Welles Ousted by R-K-O," July 2, 1942; James Gordon Meek, "Orson Welles Betrayed to FBI by Mystery Woman," www.APBnews.com, October 13, 2000; James Naremore, "The Trial: The FBI vs. Orson Welles," *Film Comment*, January–February 1991; *NYT*, "Hearst Objects to Welles Film," January 14, 1941; John O'Hara, *Kane* review, *Newsweek*, March 17, 1941; Frederick C. Othman, United Press, "Orson Welles' Staff Tossed Out by RKO," *HCN*, July 2, 1942; OW letter to *Times* (London), "The Creation of *Citizen Kane*," November 17, 1971; PB (and OW, uncredited), "The *Kane* Mutiny," *Esquire*, October 1972, reprinted in Gottesman, *Focus on Orson Welles;* RW, "It's Not *Quite* All True," *Sight and Sound*, Autumn 1970; Andrew Sarris, "Citizen Kael vs. Citizen Kane," *Village Voice*, April 15, May 27, and June 3, 1971, and "The Great *Kane* Controversy," *World*, January 16, 1973; Jack Sher and John Keating, "The Secret Life of Orson Welles," *Pageant*, August 1946; Raymond Sokolov, "Orsonology" (review of Higham, *The Films of Orson Welles*), *Newsweek*, August 3, 1970; Robert Stam, "Orson Welles, Brazil, and the Power of Blackness," special issue on OW, *Persistence of Vision*, no. 7, 1989; Fred Stanley, "Off the Hollywood Wire," *NYT*, January 21, 1945; *Time*, "Marvelous Boy: Shadow to Shakespeare, *Shoemaker* to Shaw" (cover story on OW), May 9, 1938; Michael Tunison, "Model *Citizen*" (*Kane* restoration), *Cinescape*, November 15, 2001; Kenneth Tynan, "Genius without Portfolio: Orson Welles," *Show*, November 1961 (the first part of this profile, "Orson Welles: My Signature against the World," appeared that October; both are reprinted in Gottesman, *Focus on Orson Welles*); Tynan, "*Playboy* Interview: Orson Welles."

Films/TV Shows

The Battle over "Citizen Kane" (1996 documentary); *It's All True* outtakes provided by BK; *It's All True: Four Men on a Raft* (1986 short film directed by RW, produced by Fred Chandler); *It's All True: Based on an Unfinished Film by Orson Welles* (1993 documentary); *The Orson Welles Story*, transcript in Estrin; Parkinson; *Hollywood, The Golden Years: The RKO Story*, part 4, on OW (1987 BBC TV documentary).

Other Sources

Reginald Armour interview by RW and June 11, 1987, interview with RW used as research for *It's All True: Based on an Unfinished Film by Orson*

Welles; Catherine L. Benamou, "*It's All True* Preservation Project (IATPP) Synopsis," and "New Footage from the *It's All True* Preservation Project, Based at the UCLA Film and Television Archive in Los Angeles," notes prepared for Locarno (Switzerland) International Film Festival Welles conference, 2005; FBI files: "Subject: Orson Welles," file no. 100–23438 (195 pages), FBI, Freedom of Information/Privacy Acts Section, and FBI New York field office file on OW (27 pages); "Handbook of Production Information" on *It's All True*, Paramount, 1993; Marian Dunne McBride to JM: Bryan Foy's father, Eddie Foy Sr., had a sister named Bridget who married Jimmy Dunne, the great-grandfather of JM's mother, making Bryan JM's great-uncle;

N. F., "Brief of Part Production Agreement," RKO, on contract with Coordinator of Inter-American Affairs and RKO Radio Pictures Inc., April 1, 1942, for *It's All True;* OW radio play *His Honor, the Mayor,* Free Company, CBS Radio, April 6, 1941, text published in *The Free Company Presents . . .* (New York: Dodd, Mead, 1941); OW, *Mexican Melodrama* screenplay (aka *The Way to Santiago),* 1941, State Historical Society of Wisconsin, L. Arnold Weissberger collection; Herman J. Mankiewicz and OW, *Citizen Kane* screenplay (final), RKO, June 18, 1940; OW, *The Magnificent Ambersons* screenplay (final), based on the novel by Booth Tarkington, RKO, October 7, 1941; OW on his relationship with Franklin D. Roosevelt, *The Tonight Show,* NBC-TV, 1976;

Phil Reisman cablegram to George J. Schaefer, May 20, 1942; Reisman to Schaefer, May 25, 1942; RKO, affidavits of eyewitnesses to Jacaré's death, 1942; RKO "Daily Picture Cost" sheet, June 22, 1942, with *It's All True* production costs as of that date; RKO transcript, "Conversation between Mr. Schaefer (in N.Y.) and Mr. [Reg] Armour—12:20 A.M.—April 24, 1942"; RKO transcript, "Conversation between Phil Reisman (in N.Y.) and Mr. Armour—April 27, 1942—12:30 A.M."; Schaefer to OW, April 29, 1942; Schaefer telegram to OW in Rio, date illegible; RKO, "Addenda to List of Persons Going to Brazil," February 27, 1942 (includes Robert Wise as *It's All True* editor); Lynn Shores (*It's All True* production manager in Rio) to Walter Daniels, RKO Hollywood office, March 9, 1942; Shores letters (1942) quoted in Stam: to Dr. Alfredo Pessoa, Brazilian Department of Press and Propaganda, April 11 ("continued exploitation"); to Daniels, April 14 ("some very dirty"); and to Daniels, April 30 ("carnival nigger"); Shores cablegram to Daniels on Jacaré's death, RKO, May 19, 1942;

The Tenney committee's 1948 report to the California legislature, *Fourth Report of the Senate Fact-Finding Committee on Un-American Activi-*

ties 1948: Communist Front Organizations, Senate of California, 1948; John Hay Whitney telegram to OW, December 20, 1941; Wise to OW, March 31, 1942; RW Rio notes, 1942.

3. Orson Welles at large

The chapter title is that of OW's proposed series for ABC-TV in 1958 (the pilot was *Viva Italia! / Portrait of Gina*). Epigraph: Herbert Drake, marginal notes by OW, "Orson Welles—Still a Four-Ply Genius," *Look*, August 19, 1947.

Books

Michael Anderegg, *Orson Welles, Shakespeare, and Popular Culture* (New York: Columbia University Press, 1999); Lucille Ball and Betty Hannah Hoffman, *Love, Lucy* (New York: Putnam, 1996); Eric Bentley, ed., *Thirty Years of Treason: Excerpts from Hearings before the House Committee on Un-American Activities, 1938–1968* (New York: Viking, 1971) (includes "Statement of Elia Kazan before the House Committee on Un-American Activities" and his other testimony on April 10, 1952); Brady; Carringer, *The Making of "Citizen Kane"*; Carringer, *The Magnificent Ambersons: A Reconstruction;* Ceplair and Englund; Max Allan Collins, *Angel in Black* (novel) (New York: NAL, 2001); Terry Comito, ed., *Touch of Evil* (New Brunswick, NJ: Rutgers University Press, 1985) (includes transcription of film); Drössler; Davide Ferrario, *Dissolvenza al nero* (novel) (Milan: Longanesi, 1994), French translation by Sophie Bajard as *Black Magic* (Paris: Rivages, 2002); Leonard H. Goldenson, with Marvin J. Wolf, *Beating the Odds: Behind the Rise of ABC* (New York: Scribners, 1991); JH, *Run-Through*;

JM, *Orson Welles;* JM, *Orson Welles: Actor and Director;* Leaming; James K. Lyon, *Bertolt Brecht in America* (Princeton, NJ: Princeton University Press, 1980); MacLiammóir; Adrienne L. McLean, *Being Rita Hayworth: Labor, Identity, and Hollywood Stardom* (Piscataway, NJ: Rutgers University Press, 2004); Paul Mazursky, *Show Me the Magic* (New York: Simon & Schuster, 1999); James Naremore, *The Magic World of Orson Welles* (New York: Oxford University Press, 1978; rev. ed., Dallas: Southern Methodist University Press, 1989); Navasky, *Naming Names;* Michael O'Brien, *McCarthy and McCarthyism in Wisconsin* (Columbia: University of Missouri Press, 1980); OW, *Il piccolo principe*, screenplay of Antoine de Saint-Exupéry's novel *Le petit prince (The Little Prince)*, Italian translation by Fabricio Ascari, afterword by Enrico Ghezzi (Milan: Bompiani, 1995); Joseph E. Persico, *Edward R. Murrow: An American Original* (New York:

McGraw-Hill, 1988); Victoria Price, *Vincent Price: A Daughter's Biography* (New York: St. Martin's, 1999); Mary Pacios, *Childhood Shadows: The Hidden Story of the Black Dahlia Murder* (Bloomington, IN: 1st Books Library, 1999; rev. ed., 2000); Pizzitola; *Red Channels: The Report of Communist Influence in Radio and Television*, American Business Consultants, *Counterattack*, New York, 1950; PB/OW; Esteve Riambau, *Orson Welles: Una España inmortal* (Valencia: Filmoteca Española, 1993); Thomson, *Rosebud.*

Articles and Essays

Val Adams, "Random Notes on a Shakespearean Rehearsal," *NYT*, October 18, 1953; Anderegg, "Orson Welles as Performer," special issue on OW, *Persistence of Vision*, no. 7, 1989; Albert Bolduc, "Télévision, Patisserie, Espoirs" (on *Around the World with Orson Welles*, including *The Third Man in Vienna), Positif*, no. 80, December 1966; Michel Boujut, "Five Days in the Life of Commander Welles," OW issue of *L'Avant-Scène Cinema*, July 1982, reprinted in Estrin, trans. by Alisa Hartz; Charles Champlin, "Paying Tribute to Citizen Welles," *LAT*, April 21, 1978; Juan Cobos, Miguel Rubio, and J. A. Pruneda, "A Trip to Don Quixoteland: Conversations with Orson Welles" (1964 interview), *Cahiers du Cinéma in English*, no. 5, 1966, trans. Rose Kaplin, reprinted in Estrin and in Gottesman, *Focus on "Citizen Kane"*; Bernard Drew, "John Huston: At 74 No Formulas," *American Film*, September 1980; *DV*, "Orson Welles Appeals Gov't's 24G Tax Claim," September 19, 1952;

French, "An Interview with Jonathan Rosenbaum"; Douglas Gomery, "Orson Welles and the Hollywood Industry," special issue on OW, *Persistence of Vision*, no. 7, 1989; Lawrence Grobel, "*Playboy* Interview: John Huston," September 1985, reprinted in Long, *John Huston: Interviews;* John Harlow, "Writer Accuses Welles of 'Black Dahlia' Murder" (on Pacios book), *Sunday Times* (London), August 20, 2000; *HCN*, "Orson Welles Sued by U.S. for Old Tax Claim," January 23, 1953; *HR*, "Continue Service of Tax Summons vs. Welles," July 27, 1953; Hedda Hopper syndicated column, "Orson Reveals Life Goal: Wants to Be a Teacher," *LAT*, October 28, 1945; Hopper column, "Orson's Always Doing Something Different," *Chicago Tribune*, July 27, 1947; Hopper column, "The Return of Orson," *Chicago Tribune Sunday Magazine*, September 16, 1956;

David Impastato, "Orson Welles' *Othello* and the Welles-Smith Restoration: Definitive Version?" *Shakespeare Bulletin* 10, no. 4 (Fall 1992); Johann F. Janka, "Davide Ferrario," www.Buchkritik.at, n.d.; JM, "First

Person Singular"; JM, "All's Welles," *Film Comment*, November/December 1978; JM, "The Lost Kingdom of Orson Welles," *New York Review of Books*, May 13, 1993; JR, "The Seven *Arkadins*," *Film Comment*, January–February 1992; JR, "*Othello* Goes Hollywood," *Chicago Reader*, April 10, 1992; Kael, "Orson Welles: There Ain't No Way"; John Kobler, "Citizen Welles Rides Again," *Saturday Evening Post*, December 8, 1962; Francis Koval, "Interview with Welles," *Sight and Sound*, December 1950, reprinted in Estrin;

Los Angeles Examiner, "Rita Hayworth Wins Divorce," November 11, 1947; *LAT*, "Rita Hayworth Files Suit to Divorce Orson Welles," October 2, 1947; *Life*, "MURDER! Orson Welles Doth Foully Slaughter Shakespeare in Dialect Version of His *Tragedy of Macbeth*," October 11, 1948; Tim Lucas, "Will the Real *Mr. Arkadin* Please Stand Up?" *Video Watchdog*, March/April 1992, and "*Mr. Arkadin:* The Research Continues," July/August 1992; Todd McCarthy, "UCLA Reconstructs Original Version of Welles' *Macbeth*," *DV*, April 18, 1980; Walter Murch, "Restoring a Touch of Genius to a Classic Film" (on *Touch of Evil*), *NYT*, September 8, 1998; Andrew Myers, "Resonant Ripples in a Global Pond: The Blinding of Isaac Woodard," 2002, www.faculty.uscs.edu/amyers (includes Walter White, executive secretary, NAACP, to OW, July 24, 1946); James Naremore, "The Trial: The FBI vs. Orson Welles," *Film Comment*, January–February 1991; *New York World-Telegram*, "Hollywood Drive on Reds Brings Another Libel Suit" and "Woll Retracts Charge against Miss Loy," October 22, 1946; OW, "The Third Audience," *Sight and Sound*, January–March 1954; OW, "Twilight in the Smog," *Esquire*, March 1959; OW, "But Where Are We Going?"; OW, "Memo to Universal," introduced by JR (a lengthy excerpt from OW's 1957 memo to Universal's Edward Muhl on *Touch of Evil*), *Film Quarterly*, Fall 1992 (excerpts also appear in PB/OW, 1998);

PM, "Why Marlene Is on the Side of the Angels," October 22, 1944; Esteve Riambau, "*Don Quixote:* The Adventures and Misadventures of an Essay on Spain," in Drössler; Edwin Schallert, "Welles Remains a Mystery Man," *LAT*, October 9, 1955; Lloyd Shearer, "Orson Welles: The Most Fearless Man in Show Business," *Parade*, 1959 (AMPAS); Tynan, "*Playboy* Interview: Orson Welles"; *Variety*, "Welles' Tax Appeal," September 24, 1952; Earl Wilson syndicated column, "Orson Back after 5 Long Years," *L.A. Daily News*, October 12, 1953; Bret Wood, "Recognizing *The Stranger*" and "Kiss Hollywood Goodbye: Orson Welles and *The Lady from Shanghai*," *Video Watchdog*, May–July 1994.

Films/TV Shows

Around the World with Orson Welles (five parts of OW's 1955 documentary series), Image Entertainment DVD, 2000; *The Dominici Affair* (2000 documentary), about "The Tragedy of Lurs" (OW's unfinished 1955 documentary for his *Around the World with Orson Welles* series, restored in 2000 by Christophe Cognet), both released in the United States in 2001 by Image Entertainment; *The Battle over "Citizen Kane"* (1997 documentary); *Orson Welles en el país de Don Quijote / Orson Welles in the Land of Don Quixote* (2000 documentary); *The Orson Welles Story; Orson Welles à la Cinémathèque française?; Orson Welles' Sketch Book*, third segment, May 7, 1955, BBC TV; Parkinson; *We Work Again* (1937 documentary with clip from OW's "Negro *Macbeth*"): *Treasures from American Film Archives*, National Film Preservation Foundation DVD set, 2000.

Other Sources

The Begatting of the President recording, Mediarts Records, 1969; FBI files on OW; press kit for restored *Touch of Evil*, Universal, 1998; presentations on *Mr. Arkadin* by Stefan Drössler and Claude Berteme at Locarno conference, 2005; Murch lecture at San Francisco State University, 2006.

4. "Twilight in the Smog"

Chapter title: OW's 1959 *Esquire* article of that title, which he told GG inspired *Other Wind* (GG/JM). Epigraph: BK, "Interview with Oja Kodar."

Books

Tom Bates, *Rads: The 1970 Bombing of the Army Math Research Center at the University of Wisconsin and Its Aftermath* (New York: HarperCollins, 1992); Brady; Drössler (including "Oja as a Gift: An interview with Oja Kodar by Stefan Drössler"); Gosetti, *The Other Side of the Wind;* JM, *Orson Welles*, 1972 and 1996 editions; JM, *Orson Welles: Actor and Director;* Leaming; Kate Millett, *The Basement: Meditations on a Human Sacrifice* (New York: Simon & Schuster, 1979); PB/OW and Caedmon audiotape edition; Andrew Yule, *Picture Shows: The Life and Films of Peter Bogdanovich* (New York: Proscenium, 1992).

Articles and Essays

Army Archerd column, Just for Variety, *DV*, July 2, 1970; Cobos, Rubio, and Pruneda; Bosley Crowther reviews (1967) of *Chimes at Midnight* (aka *Falstaff*): "Screen: Orson Welles Is Falstaff in Uneven Film," *NYT*, March 20, and "The Mighty?" *NYT*, March 26; *DV*, "Bob Shaw Loses Screenplay in Fire" (at OW's villa in Spain), August 24, 1970; Sean Graver, "Biography for Gary Graver," Internet Movie Database, www.imbd.com; JM, "*Citizen Kane*"; JM, "Welles's *Chimes at Midnight*," *Film Quarterly*, Fall 1969; JM, "Welles before *Kane*," *Film Quarterly*, Spring 1970; JM, "Welles' *Immortal Story*," *Sight and Sound*, Autumn 1970; JM, "The Other Side of Orson Welles"; David Konow, "The Kaleidoscopic Cinema of Gary Graver," *Filmfax*, January–March 2004; Enrique Martinez, "The Trial of Orson Welles," *Films and Filming*, October 1962; OW, "But Where Are We Going?"; Kevin Thomas, "An Eye Trained on Welles" (GG interview), *LAT*, February 8, 2004; Michael Tunison, "The Other Side of Orson Welles" (interview with PB), *MovieMaker*, Winter 2002; Tynan, "*Playboy* Interview: Orson Welles"; *Variety* item on *The Deep* (then titled *Deadly Calm*), January 31, 1964; *Variety*, "Crowther, Please Stay Home," December 21, 1966.

Films/TV Shows

Mike Nichols's DVD commentary on his 1970 film *Catch-22*, with Steven Soderbergh, Paramount Home Video, 2001; Huw Wheldon, "The BBC *Monitor* Interview," March 13, 1960, transcript in Estrin; *The Other Side of Welles*, Croatian documentary directed by Daniel Rafaelic and Leon Rizmaul, 2005 (Jeanne Moreau on OW's laugh).

Other Sources

Emily Dickinson to Thomas Wentworth Higginson, June 8, 1862, first published in Higginson, "Emily Dickinson's Letters," *Atlantic Monthly*, October 1891; GG at Locarno Welles conference, 2005; Lawrence French, "Oja Kodar and Gary Graver on *The Other Side of the Wind*," *Other Wind* press kit; Murch lecture at San Francisco State University, 2006; OW, *Dead Reckoning* screenplay (aka *Deadly Calm*, *The Deep*), 1960s, from the novel *Dead Calm* by Charles Williams (New York: Viking, 1963) ("Dialogue Script" with script supervisor's notes); OW and OK, *The Masque of the Red Death*, screenplay based on the story by Edgar Allan Poe and Poe's "The Cask of Amontillado," c. 1967; OW and OK, *Other Wind* screenplay, 1971; *Chimes/Falstaff* advertisement, Town Underground Theatre, Chicago, January–February 1967.

5. "Your friendly neighborhood grocery store"

Chapter title: OW acceptance speech, AFI Life Achievement Award, *The American Film Institute Salute to Orson Welles*, CBS-TV, 1975. Epigraph: JM, "The Other Side of Orson Welles."

Books

Brady; Callow; Joseph Cotten, *Vanity Will Get You Somewhere* (San Francisco: Mercury House, 1987); Drössler; Gosetti, *The Other Side of the Wind;* Ernest Hemingway, *The Dangerous Summer*, introduction by James A. Michener (New York: Scribners, 1985); Higham, *The Films of Orson Welles;* John Huston, *An Open Book* (New York: Knopf, 1980); JH, *Run-Through;* JM, *Orson Welles*, 1972 and 1996 editions (quotes Jeanne Moreau interview, *Cinema* [U.S.]); JM, *Orson Welles: Actor and Director;* Leaming; Bridget Gellert Lyons, ed., *Chimes at Midnight: Orson Welles, Director* (New Brunswick, NJ: Rutgers University Press, 1988) (Keith Baxter interview); MacLiammóir; Mazursky, *Show Me the Magic;* Ronald Martinetti, *The James Dean Story: A Myth-Shattering Biography of an Icon* (New York: Birch Lane Press, 1995); OW, *The Unthinking Lobster*, 1950 play, published as *Miracle à Hollywood*, with OW's play *Fair Warning* (as *À bon entendeur)*, trans. Serge Greffet (Paris: La Table Ronde, 1952); OW, *The Cradle Will Rock* (James Pepper's introduction quotes OW's 1977 letter to Mehdi Boushehri); OW, afterword by Simon Callow, *Les Bravades: A Portfolio of Pictures Made for Rebecca Welles by Her Father, Christmas 1956* (New York: Workman, 1996); PB, *Who the Devil Made It: Conversations with Legendary Film Directors* (New York: Knopf, 1997); PB/OW and audiotape edition; Riambau, *Orson Welles: Una España inmortal;* Peter Viertel, *Dangerous Friends: Hemingway, Huston and Others* (London: Viking; New York: Doubleday, 1992).

Articles and Essays

Robert Aiken, "Citizen Welles," *North Shore News* (North Vancouver, B.C.), February 8, 1999; André Bazin, "De la politique des auteurs" (On the auteur policy*)*, *Cahiers du Cinéma*, April 1957, trans. Peter Graham, in *Cahiers du Cinéma, The 1950s: Neo-Realism, Hollywood, New Wave*, ed. Jim Hillier (Cambridge, MA: Harvard University Press, 1985); Jean-Pierre Berthomé, Dominique Antoine interview, *Positif*, July 1998; PB, "Is It True What They Say about Orson?"; BK/OW; Tim Carroll, "Awesome Welles," *Sunday Times Magazine* (London), February 13, 2005 (on the "byzantine legal wrangle" over *Other Wind*); Charles Champlin, "Falstaff in King Hollywood's Court," *LAT*, May 12, 1974, reprinted in Gottesman, *Focus on Orson Welles* (where it's incorrectly dated 1973); Cobos, Rubio, and Pruneda; Bill Desowitz, "Orson Welles Gets Final Cut—at Last" (on *Touch of Evil* restoration), *LAT*, January 31, 1998; Joyce Haber column, *LAT*, 1974, reprinted in *Arizona Republic*, March 21, 1974; Chris Hastings, "Daughter and Lover Fight over Unreleased Orson Welles Film," *Sunday Telegraph* (UK), August 18, 2002 (on *Other Wind*); *HR*, Legal Briefs (on Beatrice Welles suing Universal over *Touch of Evil*), January 22, 1999;

JM, "Orson Welles Returns from Obscurity"; JM, "*Touch of Evil*" (letter on different versions), *Sight and Sound*, Spring 1976; JM, "The Other Side of Orson Welles"; JM, "O'Toole Ascending" (Peter O'Toole interview), *Film Comment*, March–April 1981; JM, "John Huston Finds that the Slow Generation of *King* Has Made It a Richer Film" (on *The Man Who Would Be King*), *DV*, December 16, 1975, reprinted in Long, *John Huston: Interviews;* JM, "The Lost Kingdom of Orson Welles";

Leonard Lyons column, "Orson Welles Plans Series of Projects," *HCN*, August 9, 1961; Geoffrey Macnab, "Orson Welles: Cinema's Lost Genius," *Independent* (UK), September 22, 2005 (Chris Welles Feder quote, "I believe"); Eleanor Mannikka, review of *The Shah of Iran* (1972 documentary), *All Movie Guide*, quoted on www.blockbuster.com; Myron Meisel, "The Night Orson Welles Told the Truth—Maybe," *L.A. Reader*, November 24, 1978; *NYT*, "Antonio Ordóñez Dies at 66; Matador in Hemingway Book," December 21, 1998 (OW's ashes interred at Ordóñez ranch); Ann W. O'Neill, "Court Files: A Touch of Litigation," *LAT*, January 24, 1999 (on Beatrice Welles suing Universal over *Touch of Evil*); Robert Osborne, "Orson Welles," *Now Playing*, May 2005 (Henry Hathaway quoted on OW); Dorothy Parker, "The Artist's Reward" (Hemingway profile), *New Yorker*, November 30, 1929;

OW, "My Father Wore Black Spats" and "A Brief Career as a Musical Prodigy," *Paris Vogue*, December 1982–January 1983 (OW was the issue's guest editor); PB (and OW), "The *Kane* Mutiny"; PB, "The Cowboy Hero and the American West . . . as Directed by John Ford," *Esquire*, December 1983; *People*, "Once Moor with Feeling: Orson Welles's Daughter Beatrice Restores His Lost Masterpiece, *Othello*," April 27, 1992; Dale Pollock, "Welles Says 'A' Budget Pic Not in Future," *DV*, January 30, 1979; Rex Reed, "Holden Caulfield at 27" (Peter Fonda profile with his comment on Roger Vadim), *Esquire*, February 1968 (and

Tunison for PB claim about saying "phallus" line in *Other Wind);* Philip K. Scheuer column, "Town Called Hollywood," *LAT,* January 18, 1942; Lloyd Shearer, "Welles Goes Porno," *Parade,* July 1, 1973; *Tacoma (WA) News Tribune,* "Rebecca [Welles] Manning" (obituary), October 21–22, 2004; Tim Tully, "The Sounds of *Evil,*" *Videography Magazine,* January 1999; Tynan, "Genius without Portfolio: Orson Welles"; Gore Vidal, "Remembering Orson Welles," *New York Review of Books,* June 1, 1989, reprinted in Estrin; Beatrice Welles, "And the Oscar Goes to . . . the Man in the Back Row for $1 Million," *LAT,* March 17, 2004 (on being dedicated to "protecting and preserving" her father's work).

Films/TV Shows

The American Film Institute Salute to John Huston, CBS-TV, 1983; *The American Film Institute Salutes Orson Welles; It's All True: Based on an Unfinished Film by Orson Welles; Orson Welles Madrid Juin 1966; The Orson Welles Story; The Other Side of Welles* (OW on making love to actors); Parkinson; *The Spanish Earth* (1937 documentary): OW's narration (on separate track from Hemingway's) on 2000 Slingshot Entertainment DVD edition, from print discovered in director Joris Ivens's archives; *Working with Orson Welles.*

Other Sources

BBC Radio report on Beatrice Welles and *Other Wind,* August 19, 2002; Ciro Giorgini presentation at Locarno conference, 2005; GG diary, August 23, 1970; JM, 1998 *Other Wind* memoranda, including June 17 to Bingham Ray (October Films) and Paul Hardart (Universal), June 18 to Walter Murch, June 30 to Jay Roewe (HBO Pictures), September 10 to Matthew Duda (Showtime), September 17 and October 15 to Michael Schlesinger (Sony Pictures), and September 30 to GG, and JM memos (2000) to Jeff Schwager (www.Reel.com), January 10, and PB, February 15 (and PB response to JM, February 24); Mankiewicz and OW, *Citizen Kane* screenplay; *Other Wind* press kit; OW, *The Magnificent Ambersons* screenplay; OW and OK, *Other Wind* screenplay (and OK copyright of screenplay, September 2, 1986, U.S. Copyright Office, Library of Congress, No. PAU 889–550); OW, "Last Will of Orson Welles," January 15, 1982, and "Petition for Probate of Will and Issuance of Letters," filed by Greg Garrison (OW's executor), Eighth Judicial District Court, Nevada, November 7, 1985 (OW legal resident of Nevada for tax reasons: GG to JM); OW, "Confirmation of Ownership Rights," June 19, 1985; Universal

Studios Home Video Inc. and JM, settlement agreement, July 31, 1998, on JM proposal (to Hardart, March 26, 1998) for a documentary about *Touch of Evil* and its restoration; Robin Wood to JM, November 29, 1969.

6. "No wine before its time"

Chapter title: OW's catchphrase on Paul Masson wine commercials. Epigraph: David Geffner, "A Tribute to Orson Welles," program booklet, Hollywood Film Festival, October 1997.

Books

Brady; Drössler (includes OW's budget for *King Lear* film project); Isak Dinesen, "The Dreamers," in her collection *Seven Gothic Tales*, introduction by Dorothy Canfield (New York: Random House, Modern Library, 1934), and "Echoes," in Dinesen's collection *Last Tales* (New York: Random House, 1957); Chris Welles Feder, *The Movie Director: Dramatic Monologues and Poems*, self-published, 2002; Gosetti, *The Other Side of the Wind* (including Drössler essay, "(Re-)Constructions: Dealing with Unfinished Films"); Jack J. Jorgens, *Shakespeare on Film* (Bloomington: Indiana University Press, 1977) (a shortened version of Jorgens's *Othello* chapter, "Welles's *Othello:* A Baroque Translation," appeared earlier in Gottesman, *Focus on Orson Welles*, where OW may have first seen it); JM, *Orson Welles;* JM, *Orson Welles: Actor and Director;* Leaming, including epilogue to 1995 edition (and July 14, 1985, *NYT Magazine* serialization, "Orson Welles: The Unfulfilled Promise"); JR, "Orson Welles's Essay Films and Documentary Fictions," in *Placing Movies: The Practice of Film Criticism* (Berkeley and Los Angeles: University of California Press, 1995); OW, with OK, *The Big Brass Ring* (JR afterword quotes OW in Henry Jaglom memo to Jack Nicholson, May 20, 1982); PB/OW; Cary Reich, *The Life of Nelson A. Rockefeller: Worlds to Conquer, 1908–1958* (New York: Doubleday, 1996); Tim Robbins, *Cradle Will Rock: The Movie and The Moment* (New York: Newmarket, 2000); Claudia Thieme, *"F for Fake" and the Growth in Complexity of Orson Welles' Documentary Form* (Frankfurt: Peter Lang, 1997); William Turner and Jonn Christian, *The Assassination of Robert Kennedy: The Conspiracy and Coverup* (New York: Random House, 1978; rev. ed., New York: Thunder's Mouth Press, 1993); Yule, *Picture Shows.*

Articles and Essays

Robert M. Andrews, Associated Press, "A Growing Challenge to Film Coloring," *Philadelphia Inquirer*, November 5, 1986, quoted in Stuart Klawans, "Colorization: Rose-Tinted Spectacles," in *Seeing through Movies*, ed. Mark Crispin Miller (New York: Pantheon Books, 1990) (Ted Turner quote "The last time I checked"); Connie Benesch, "As Welles Put It: 'Just Wait Till I Die,'" *LAT*, May 27, 1997; Jean-Pierre Berthomé and François Thomas, "Sept années en noir et blanc" (Seven years in black-and-white) (Edmond Richard interview), *Positif*, July–August 1992; BK/OW; Gregory Bishop, "Interview with Robert Anton Wilson," 1992, www.elfis.net; Mary Blume, OW interview, *International Herald Tribune*, December 9, 1983; Lawrence Christon, "An Outing with Orson Welles," *LAT*, November 24, 1978; Michel Delahaye and Jean Narboni, "Interview with Roman Polanski," *Cahiers du Cinéma*, January 1969, trans. Paul Cronin and Remi Guillochon, in *Roman Polanski: Interviews*, ed. Paul Cronin (Jackson: University Press of Mississippi, 2005); *DV*, "Welles to Act in, Direct French-Funded *King Lear*," February 8, 1985; *Express* (UK), "Orson Welles Daughter Doesn't Want His Uncompleted Final Film Shown," August 31, 2002 (on Beatrice Welles and *Other Wind*); Stephen Farber, "The Man Hollywood Loves to Hate," *LAT Magazine*, April 30, 1989 (Ted Turner on his attempt to colorize *Kane*); F. X. Feeney, "Reaching for *The Big Brass Ring*," *Written By*, December 1998 / January 1999;

Otto Friedrich, "The Mystery of Citizen Welles," *Time*, October 7, 1985 (review of Leaming; Carringer, *The Making of "Citizen Kane"*; and Charles Higham, *Orson Welles: The Rise and Fall of an American Genius* [New York: St. Martin's, 1985]); Nadine Goff, "Welles' Play Brought to Vivid Life, but Hype Blurs Facts" (on production of *Bright Lucifer*), *Wisconsin State Journal* (Madison), October 9, 1997; Kiku Iwata, "A *Don Quixote* Crusade: Orson Welles' Mythic Film Finally Pieced Together" (on Jesús Franco version), and "An Obsession for Restoring Welles' Works," *LAT*, June 30, 1992; JM, "All's Welles"; *Johns Hopkins Gazette* (Johns Hopkins University, Baltimore), "In Brief" (PB interview), June 2, 1997; JR, "The Voice and the Eye"; JR, "The Invisible Orson Welles"; JR, "Orson Welles' Essay Films and Documentary Fictions: A Two-Part Speculation," *Cinematograph*, no. 4, 1991; JR and BK, "Orson Welles in the U.S.: An Exchange," *Persistence of Vision*, no. 11, 1995;

LAHE, "Welles Inducted into the Legion of Honor," February 23, 1982; *LAHE*, "Family of Welles Gathers for a Private Memorial," October 14, 1985; *LAT*, "Private Memorial Rites Held for Orson Welles,"

October 14, 1985; *Life*, item on publication of OW's book *Les Bravades*, November 1996; Kevin Lynch, "New Look at Orson Welles" (on production of OW's play *Bright Lucifer), Capital Times* (Madison, WI), September 17, 1997; Geoffrey Macnab, "One of Our Classics Is Missing" (on Beatrice Welles trying to stop London's National Film Theatre from showing *Kane), Guardian* (UK), August 29, 2003; Todd McCarthy, *DV* articles: "Orson Welles *Dreamers* Pic for Northstar," June 13, 1980, "Orson Welles to Direct *Cradle*," August 30, 1984, "Orson Welles Dies at L.A. Home, Yul Brynner in N.Y.," October 11, 1985, "Tribute to Orson Welles Draws Overflow Audience," November 4, 1985, "*Othello* Restoration: A Celebration with Reservations," April 24, 1992, and *Variety* review of *Don Quijote de Orson Welles*, May 25, 1992; *National Enquirer* item on smoke at OW's home, October 14, 1980;

NYT, "Life of Orson Welles and His Work Cited as 500 Mourn Loss," November 3, 1985 (on OW memorial tribute at DGA in Hollywood); OW letter to *New Statesmen* (London) on *Touch of Evil* ("that odious thing, 'a reply to the critic'"); OW statement on *Treasure Island* (in what appears to be a paid ad), *HR*, July 26, 1979; Dale Pollock, "Welles Says 'A' Budget Pic Not in Future," *DV*, January 30, 1979; Riambau, "Don Quixote: The Adventures and Misadventures of an Essay on Spain"; Howard A. Rodman, "The Last Days of Orson Welles," *American Film*, June 1987; Brent Roske, "Henry Jaglom Interview," May 21, 2001, www.Hollywood-Register.com; Julie Salamon, "Citizen Welles: The Curse of Genius," *Wall Street Journal* (review of Leaming), September 20, 1985; Scheuer, "Town Called Hollywood"; Audrey Stainton, "*Don Quixote:* Orson Welles' Secret," *Sight and Sound*, Autumn 1988; Peter Tonguette, "From the Beginning: Notes on Orson Welles' Most Personal Late Film," *Senses of Cinema*, July 2003, reprinted (revised) in Drössler; *Variety*, "International Sound Track," June 2, 1982; Alden Whitman, "Orson Welles, a Man with a Great Past," *LAHE*, September 8, 1985 (review of the Leaming and Higham biographies); Oscar Wilde, *The Happy Prince and Other Tales* (London: David Nutt, 1888).

Films/TV Shows

Orson Welles à la Cinémathèque française; Orson Welles en el país de Don Quijote / Orson Welles in the Land of Don Quixote; Orson Welles: The One-Man Band; Remembering Orson . . . ; The Orson Welles Show; The Good Life (video pitch).

Other Sources

BK, "Interview with Oja Kodar"; Lilly Library, Indiana University, Bloomington, *Guide to the Orson Welles Materials in the Lilly Library*, 1980, rev. 1997; documents on OW's *King Lear* film project from BK: "Telegram from Welles to Hervé Bourge," "Letter from Welles to Dussart," "The last 'diktat' from Dussart," and transcript of OW's 1985 video pitch for the film (*This Is Orson Welles* also offers a transcription); Chris Welles Feder, November 20, 2005, post on the Wellesnet Internet site, www.wellesnet.com, on *Rip Van Winkle Renascent;* Geffner, "A Tribute to Orson Welles"; GG and OK on filming *The Dreamers*, Locarno conference; Millennium Theater, Madison, WI, program for production of OW's play *Bright Lucifer*, produced and directed by Jay Rath, September–October 1997; Henry Jaglom, "Lessons from Orson," press kit for Jaglom's 1988 film *Someone to Love;* Jim People to JR, 1986; Oliver Stone on "Additional Special Features," 2001 DVD edition of *JFK*, Warner Home Video; press kit for *Orson Welles: The One-Man Band;*

OW, *Bright Lucifer* (play), 1933, State Historical Society of Wisconsin, Weissberger collection; OW's commercials outtake tape: Jay Rose's Digital Playroom Web site, www.dplay.com/audio/Orsonplay.htm; OW letter "To Whom It May Concern" (about GG), November 12, 1979, and OW screenplays: *Dead Reckoning* (aka *Deadly Calm*, *The Deep);* OW and Donald Freed, *Assassin* (aka *The Safe House)*, late 1970s; OW and OK, *The Other Man* (based on Graham Greene's novel *The Honorary Consul)*, late 1970s; *Surinam* (based on Joseph Conrad's novel *Victory: An Island Tale)*, 1970s; *The Dreamers*, based on Dinesen's "The Dreamers" and "Echoes" (9th rev. [final]), April 1985; OW, *House Party*, 1985, based on OK's story "Crazy Weather" (aka *Crazy Weather*, *Blind Window*), and revised version, *Mercy*, 1985, unfinished ("A Film by Orson Welles, Story and Screenplay by Oja Kodar").

INDEX

Note: For listings of Welles films; film projects; films as actor; films as narrator; radio, stage, and television appearances and productions; writings; other works, activities, and projects; and films and videos about Welles, see the entries for (George) Orson Welles. Dates are given here for non-Welles films, but since many of Welles's films were made over extended periods of time, dates are not given for his own films or for his television productions, and the reader is referred to the text for information about their production periods and (where applicable) release dates. Books are identified here by authors' names; further information can be found in the sources section. Numbers of pages that include photographs or other illustrations are in italics.